Liberated
SPIRITS

Liberated

TWO WOMEN WHO BATTLED OVER PROHIBITION

SPIRITS

HUGH AMBROSE

WITH JOHN SCHUTTLER

BERKLEY
New York

BERKLEY
An imprint of Penguin Random House LLC
375 Hudson Street, New York, New York 10014

Copyright © 2018 by Ambrose, Inc.

BERKLEY is a registered trademark and the B colophon is a trademark
of Penguin Random House LLC.

Library of Congress Cataloging-in-Publication Data

Names: Ambrose, Hugh, author. | Schuttler, John, author.
Title: Liberated spirits: two women who battled over Prohibition/
Hugh Ambrose, with John Schuttler.
Description: First edition. | New York: Berkley, [2018]
Identifiers: LCCN 2017052487 | ISBN 9780451414649 | ISBN 9780698183636 (ebook)
Subjects: LCSH: Willebrandt, Mabel Walker, 1889–1963. | Davis, Dwight, Mrs., 1887–1955. |
Prohibition—United States. | Women—Political activity—United States—History—20th century. |
United States—History—1919–1933.
Classification: LCC HV5089.A576 2018 | DDC 344.7305/41—dc23
LC record available at https://lccn.loc.gov/2017052487

First Edition: October 2018

Printed in the United States of America
1   3   5   7   9   10   8   6   4   2

Jacket photos: image of women courtesy of Old Visuals/Alamy Stock Photo;
background image of demonstrators courtesy of Sueddeutsche Zeitung Photo/Alamy Stock Photo
Jacket design by Emily Osborne and Colleen Reinhart
Book design by Laura K. Corless

For Ande, Elsie, and Brody
For ever

Liberated
SPIRITS

Introduction

The rumrunner* got word on Sunday evening that his ship would soon come in. Roy Olmstead†; his business partner, Tom Clark; and nine others drove north out of Seattle as the evening darkness settled, their convoy of eight cars driving fifteen miles on the Edmonds-Seattle paved highway to the rendezvous point, a dock jutting fifty feet into Browns Bay of Puget Sound near a small, little-used station on the Great Northern Railway called Meadowdale. Roy and Tom had both learned the art of bootlegging while working their "day jobs." In 1914, the citizens of Washington State

---

* The terms "rumrunner" and "bootlegger" are slang terms often used interchangeably. Americans in the 1920s commonly used the word "rum" when referring to any type of distilled alcohol. For the purposes of clarity, in this book the term "rumrunner" denotes someone who smuggles alcoholic beverages across the U.S. border and moves large lots of it around the country, selling it wholesale; while "bootlegger" specifies someone who, on either a wholesale or retail level, sells alcoholic beverages.

† Some newspaper reporters misspelled Roy Olmstead's last name, writing "Olmsted," for years. The correct spelling has been used throughout this text to avoid confusion.

had voted to outlaw the manufacture and sale, but not the consumption, of alcohol, and put the onus of enforcing the statute on their state and local police departments, such as the Seattle Police Department, which employed both Roy Olmstead and Thomas Clark. By the time national Prohibition went into effect, Seattle's cops had watched the inhabitants adapt for almost six years, finding ways to enjoy alcohol on a regular basis, their desires translating into handsome profits for the moonshiners who distilled alcohol and the rumrunners who imported it. While Olmstead never revealed when he got into liquor smuggling, his ability to secure probation rather than jail time for many criminals drew the gratitude of those willing to pay for his influence, his naked ambition following the quickest path to wealth. His ethics already compromised, Olmstead "saw no crime in buying and selling booze," and was unable to reconcile the law's allowance for consumption while forbidding a supply.[1] He had watched two rival gangs devoted to "rum-running" slowly destroy each other through years of warfare, leaving an open playing field even as the federal government began to enforce the ban on liquor.[2] The demand for good liquor, Lieutenant Olmstead knew, would continue to seek new sources; the way to profit from it was to import the best brands from Canada, a little more than a hundred miles to the north: a country where Scotch, gin, vodka, champagne, wine, beer, and so much more were still legally sold, purchased, exported, and consumed. Any boat could take on a load of good Canadian whiskey and steam away, so long as the export duties to Canadian customs had been paid. Islands great and small littered Puget Sound, the grand waterway connecting Seattle with two of Canada's bustling cities, Victoria and Vancouver, offering smugglers a more-than-sporting chance to evade the mere two U.S. Coast Guard ships patrolling the waters. Back in Seattle, bottles bearing brand names commanded almost double the price that Roy Olmstead paid for them, creating the opportunity for extraordinary profits, a river of income that made his new career irresistible. The intelligence, initiative, and competence cited by his superiors as reasons for his rise in the police department served him equally well in his new profession.[3] Roy Olmstead had the key assets to succeed: a talent for inspiring confidence in business partners for a venture in which no contract or agreement carried the force of law; the ability to manage an organization, a skill cultivated in his years rising through the ranks of the police force; and all the pluck and entrepreneurship of a born capitalist. This March evening found Olmstead and his associates exercising all their talents to bring in a large shipment of choice liquors and wines.

Just after one o'clock on Monday morning, the bootleggers turned left, off the paved road, and drove down the steep hill to the water. Their cars—rear seats removed to make room for the bottles, the cargo space supported by heavy-duty springs, the cars' engines tuned for maximum power—could not fit into the narrow roadway near the dock, so they stopped in a line and waited. Olmstead had one of his men begin flashing a light periodically, facing westward out into Puget Sound. In less than an hour, the engines of the *Jervis Island* could be heard approaching. With enough cargo space to convey nearly eleven hundred cases from Victoria, Canada, across the Strait of Juan de Fuca, and down Puget Sound, Roy's wooden-hulled boat had not been crafted for speed—it couldn't even make ten knots—but her stout frame handled the job in workmanlike fashion. As soon as she was tied to the pier, the unloading began.

Roy and Tom watched as their foreman, waving an electric flashlight and hollering profusely, directed the process of toting the cases from the boat and up to the waiting cars, sending each loaded automobile on its way and waving in the next. Satisfied with the arrangements, his own car loaded, Roy drove away up the hill, only to find a barricade of logs at the apex. Men brandishing guns—thieves or cops, he did not know—ordered him to stop. As they neared his car, Roy spotted a way around and gunned the engine. Shots from their pistols did the men no good as he swerved back onto the dirt road, eventually picking up the pavement and heading south at full speed, surely wondering whether the gunmen were stealing his liquor or arresting his men, who had been instructed simply to turn over the goods if waylaid by hijackers. If the ambushers proved to be revenuers (agents of the federal Internal Revenue Bureau*), or former revenuers recruited to be members of the brand-new Prohibition Unit, he had a different set of problems. In more than a century of chasing down moonshiners and others not in compliance with government liquor-tax policy, revenuers had built a reputation for unpredictability, some being virulent Prohibitionists smashing stills and bottles, others willing to take a bribe to turn a blind eye. It was unclear how they would handle their new job, enforcing the federal Prohibition law, any change in their tactics imperceptible since the law had gone into effect two months earlier. What exactly would happen to those arrested and what would be the long-term effects of this new force on his operation were serious questions for Olmstead.

Roy had been at home a few hours when the phone rang just after six a.m., his captain announcing that he knew all about the bust, as did the sheriff's office in Snohomish County, where the raid had taken place. The revenuers had recognized Lieutenant Roy Olmstead, a well-known rising star in the Seattle Police Department, and had arrested Sergeant Tom Clark and seven others at the scene. The police car arrived at Olmstead's house minutes later, one of Olmstead's own patrolmen at the wheel, to take him down to the station. Olmstead told the officer the same thing he would later tell the police chief: he had been excused from his regular shift to care

---

* The Internal Revenue Bureau was the precursor to today's Internal Revenue Service (IRS).

for his sick wife and daughter, knew nothing of the "liquor deal," and stood ready to face his accusers.[4]

The chief did not believe Roy, or Tom Clark, who claimed he had gone to the dock to arrest the bootleggers. Chief Warren fired them both summarily, sending Roy to the county jail to await further questioning and a statement of charges, while Clark, who had been arrested by federal agents, was jailed at the federal immigration detention station, no federal lockup being available.

The newspapers' evening editions spread the news across Seattle. In recent weeks, several landings of liquor had taken place at the Meadowdale dock, alarming the station agent for the railroad, a concerned citizen who had gotten in touch with Donald A. MacDonald, State Director of the new Prohibition Unit. MacDonald had been pleased to get the tip, eager to shift focus from arrests of peddlers of a few bottles to the rumrunner of several hundred.[5] Olmstead may have counted on the inexperience of the Prohibition Unit, but not on its luck. MacDonald's agents had almost missed the bust, three of them stumbling in the darkness, nearly shooting one another. "As fast as the cars were loaded with liquor and came up the hill we'd stop them, line the men up alongside the road and drive the car out of sight and gather in the next one," exclaimed the son of the railroad station agent. After they secured the cars, they went down the hill and tried to take the delivery boat. The boat captain could be heard trying to start its motors. The railroad agent fired repeatedly into its wooden hull before the engines caught and the hulking shape pulled away. Though the dark had prevented a good look at the boat, the agents thought the Coast Guard or U.S. Customs authorities would be able to identify it by all the bullet holes in its side.

The spectacle of police officers as rumrunners raised the public's interest and the importance attached to the case. The next morning, Olmstead, Clark, and their accomplices were charged with conspiracy to violate the Prohibition laws. Olmstead and Clark had their bail fixed at five thousand dollars, more than most men earned for two years' honest work. Their case allowed Donald MacDonald to crow that the big bust marked only the start of Uncle Sam's campaign to make Washington "Dry."[6] MacDonald told reporters those arrested were members of a major liquor ring operating throughout the Northwest.

Five days after the arrest, a grand jury indicted the members of the "police ring" on charges of conspiring to have and possess liquor; of conspiring to transport it by automobile; and of conspiring to transport, sell, deliver, and furnish it to unknown persons. The grand jury, and by extension the district attorney, did not ask for charges of smuggling, which would have required evidence of the ownership of the liquor.[7] The conspirators' attorney, Jack Sullivan, filed several objections, notably one claiming that the Eighteenth Amendment was unconstitutional, reminding the judge of a case pending before the Supreme Court, challenging the legality of the amendment.[8]

Just a few days before the next court date, Prohibition officers found the boat, the *Jervis Island*, that had brought the shipment to Olmstead and Clark.[9] The capture of the boat emboldened Mac-Donald to repeat his earlier prediction that other surprising arrests would follow as the tentacles of the "alleged far-reaching Northwest booze-ring" were traced.[10] In the meantime, Judge Neterer quickly dismissed Sullivan's earlier objections, showing he would not treat bootleggers with a wink and a smile, a charge leveled at state and local courts, which seemed to prefer levying fines over trials and jail time.[11] Clark and Olmstead would face the charges of conspiracy, which carried a two-year prison term and a fine not to exceed five thousand dollars, their coconspirators facing lesser charges because they had been employed. The trial was set for May.

Chapter 1

As the first weeks of the new decade passed in January 1920, Americans believed they understood the consequences as Prohibition descended upon the land, closing breweries, distilleries, and saloons. Even as bootleggers, rumrunners, and moonshiners—men like Roy Olmstead—stepped up to seize the opportunity, organizing themselves into conspiracies to obtain, manufacture, and sell liquor to willing buyers, few Americans imagined that the Eighteenth Amendment would not be a permanent fixture in their lives. Women activists, the foot soldiers who had won the battle to ratify the Eighteenth Amendment, were turning their attention to the impending ratification of the Nineteenth Amendment, giving women the vote nationwide. These twin amendments seemed to offer redemption, two chances to perfect the American soul, correcting the sins of the past and opening a new chapter for those women willing and able to face the challenges.

Pauline Sabin, a New York socialite, and Mabel Walker Willebrandt, the U.S. assistant attorney general, would not have charac-

terized themselves as redeemers, but they understood the importance of the moment and the public perception that forever defined
Prohibition as a women's issue. Prohibition's success or failure would
be measured in the public's consciousness, often, by the success or
failure of these two women, whose paths would cross only a few
times, but whose impacts must be weighed together. The political
education they received during the Prohibition era represented
American women's struggle to capitalize on their newfound power,
as voters and as standard-bearers for Prohibition, and defined the
means by which other women could exert their influence. In the
process, Sabin and Willebrandt absorbed lessons from the men they
encountered, some of whom assisted their efforts, others resisting,
and still others serving as touchstones for measuring advancement. One man, Roy Olmstead, the cop turned rumrunner, never
met either woman, but his experience would help them define their
beliefs about Prohibition, the limits of constitutional authority,
and the rightness of their paths, reaching two very different conclusions.

Mrs. Charles Sabin stepped lightly through the gilded reception
hall of the Hotel Astor, greeting national political figures, renowned business leaders, and members of New York's highest society, each a prospect to be cultivated in a few brief moments, a
daunting task as the rush of top hats and fur coats swept in. She was
too polished not to look composed, at home, despite being required
to balance different constituencies as on a knife's sharp edge. The
guests, including Mr. and Mrs. Cornelius Vanderbilt III and Mr.
and Mrs. Theodore Roosevelt Jr., recognized Mrs. Sabin as one of
their own by virtue of the political and business successes of her
grandfather, father, uncle, and husband. Along with her fellow
members of the recently created Republican Women of New York

State, Mrs. Sabin welcomed as many guests as she could, directing them to the bar or the cloakroom, or helping them find their seats. The women's club had produced the event, in early December 1919, to raise money for the party's campaign war chest and to inaugurate their organization with a grand splash at the hottest spot in Manhattan, in the French Renaissance Beaux Arts–style hotel built just for them: the wealthy, the powerful, and the famous.

The absence of the senior U.S. senator from New York, the powerful Republican James W. Wadsworth Jr., generated talk. Senator Wadsworth had sent a telegram, to be read from the podium, explaining why he could not attend, a cover story fooling no one. The antagonism between Wadsworth and club women was years old and well-known. The leaders of the Republican Women of New York State had declared war on Senator Wadsworth because of his opposition to women's suffrage, even as the proposed Nineteenth Amendment neared full authorization by the requisite thirty-six states.[1] Wadsworth further damaged his appeal by his opposition to the Eighteenth Amendment, weeks away from implementation, which had been carried to fruition by many of the same women supporting passage of the Nineteenth Amendment. Passage of the two amendments inspired "club" women to envision the next set of changes needed in government to improve society. Ousting Senator James Wadsworth seemed to many a logical step.

Like any apprentice activist at a key event, Pauline swung her head on a graceful swivel, offering a smile and a quick wave to Republican leaders, while keeping an eye out for members of the Women's Christian Temperance Union (WCTU) and League of Women Voters (LWV),* people the hostess needed to greet and

---

* The League did not adopt this name until 1920, existing as the National American Women's Suffrage Association, but I have chosen to use LWV throughout for consistency.

steer away from condemnations of Senator Wadsworth.* Criticism of New York's senior Republican senator at a Republican fundraiser, even one organized by a women's group, would be vulgar, to Pauline's way of thinking, and reflect poorly upon the group, endangering women's relationship to the party. She intended to become a Republican Party insider, someone who sat in on the councils where policy was formulated. Like her mentor, Mrs. Arthur L. (Henrietta) Livermore, Pauline refused to be relegated to the shaky, hastily constructed "women's divisions" being grafted onto the party apparatus.[2] Her goal placed Pauline Sabin in a precarious position between the "club" women seeking to maintain a unified front and the male party leaders seeking loyalty to Republican candidates.

The gala ended successfully for Pauline, with a request from Will Hays, chairman of the Republican National Committee, to join the party's Ways and Means Committee for New York City, raising money for the 1920 campaign.[3] Her work would focus on bringing other wealthy women onto the committee, using their endorsements to woo women voters. Pauline hoped exposure from her new position would impress the Republicans in and around Southampton, the community near the tip of Long Island, New York, where the Sabins' summer estate was located, and where she planned to convince the Suffolk County Republican Party to select her as one of its delegates to the party's state committee meeting in February 1920. For the first time, women would be permitted to vote in the party primaries, allowing them to help choose party leaders and frame party platforms, opening up new avenues of advancement within the party structure.

---

* Reading the dozens of notable books about the Eighteenth Amendment, as well as those histories concerning the Nineteenth Amendment to the Constitution, a reader might be convinced the two had nothing to do with each other.

———

She was introduced formally as Mrs. Arthur F. Willebrandt at the many political clubs and civic organizations she joined, although she would push past the necessary formalities as quickly as politeness would admit and establish herself as Mabel Walker Willebrandt. The day she walked into the Hotel Stowell, headquarters of the Republican Party in Los Angeles, and announced her intention to volunteer, the party hacks sat behind their desks, smoke rising from the ashtrays, typewriters clacking, and sized her up. Ignoring her credentials as a lawyer, they noted her dark suit, white blouse opened at the collar, and short hair, sure signs of a politically active woman. They calculated their response not by her dress, however, but by the fact that her husband was a political unknown and therefore she could be ignored. Mrs. Willebrandt knew how to acknowledge their hostility, delivering every word with a charming insouciance, while any man who addressed her received a leveled stare, her mind intently drinking in the words as if committing them to memory, an unnerving and ultimately unforgettable quality.

The indifference of the party men to female activists, however, ran deep.[4] Since women had won the vote in California in 1911, they had joined with progressives to push the City of Los Angeles to crack down on brothels and prostitution and outlaw saloons, and, at the state legislature, they had overcome two failed attempts at passing statewide prohibition. Yet their political demands had only grown, a trend many men found irksome.[5] Worse, Mrs. Mabel Walker Willebrandt's request to get involved in the party's organization, especially at the start of a presidential-election year, took a level of self-assertion most Americans of both genders found offensive. A lady was not supposed to work in offices alongside strange men, although exceptions were made for young women employed as teachers or stenographers. Political campaigns inhabited the rough-

and-tumble world of men: cutting deals, attacking opponents, sac-
rificing principles for political or personal gain; in politics, immorality abounded. The Republican Party headquarters, housed in
the twelve-story Hotel Stowell, in Los Angeles' downtown, was
no place for a lady.* The rebuff expected, Willebrandt could afford
them a gracious smile, one carrying a silent message: *if you think my
attempt to volunteer here is audacious, you haven't seen anything
yet.*

In 1920 her law practice, her pride and joy, was four years old,
situated just a few blocks from the Stowell, in an office she shared
with a friend from law school, Fred Horowitz. While Los Angeles
was bursting with waves of new inhabitants, new businesses opening, and real estate being developed for miles in all directions, the
idea of a female attorney had yet to take hold there. The census of
1920 identified 1,738 women, nationally, in the category of "lawyers,
judges and justices," representing .0002 percent of the more than 8.2
million women in the workforce.[6] Yet Willebrandt had managed to
build a practice successful enough to allow her to quit her part-time
teaching job at a local high school and to eschew divorce cases, the
primary source of work for female attorneys. Having a male col-
league certainly had helped land cases in the early days, but a growing list of victories in court, including securing one client an award
of ten thousand dollars in damages, boosted her reputation.[7]

For years she had served as an assistant in the Los Angeles Public Defender's Office, created in 1912 by progressives of the Republican Party to ensure effective legal representation for those who
could not afford to purchase it. While the U.S. Constitution mandated a defendant's access to representation, it had become a farce in

---

* In 1920, the area known as Los Angeles' downtown, a center of commerce, government,
culture, and public transportation, was already being pulled apart as the city sprawled in all
directions.

practice.[8] The public defender received compensation; the assistant public defender did not. But it was a demonstration of Willebrandt's merit, and brought her into contact with the District Attorney's office, judges, and her peers at the bar—although she was relegated to a special Woman's Court, advocating for, she later explained, "beaten wives and fallen women."[9]

One afternoon, as Assistant Public Defender Willebrandt looked upon an assembly of women arrested for prostitution, she learned that no effort had been made to arrest their clients. It lit a fuse inside her. The next day she dynamited the case against the prostitutes by proclaiming "the impossibility of bringing to justice but one person for an act which constituted a crime only when it implicated two."[10] The judge sustained her motion to dismiss, and the "originality" of the victory reportedly "won her recognition among many of the legal profession who hitherto had probably thought of her only as a woman aspiring to law."* Neither the first to name the "double standard" nor the last, Willebrandt hated what it represented: biased and unfair characterization of each gender, which led to the rigid roles society defined for males and females.[11] Her victory changed little, though. Around the Los Angeles courthouse, as across the land, men were "just being men" when they paid for sex, but society had no compassion for the women whom various circumstances had forced into prostitution. Women who violated the moral code would not be tolerated.

As a spokesperson for the women she represented, Willebrandt was not fighting to restore the status quo ante, which consigned

---

* Dorothy Brown, in her fine biography of Mabel Walker Willebrandt, stated that Willebrandt found a legal mechanism by which male patrons of brothels were compelled to stand trial, resulting in a marked decrease in customers. Brown based this claim on an interview she conducted in 1978 with one of her subject's dear friends. No record of the interview exists, according to Ms. Brown, and no independent evidence for this claim was uncovered.

women to the kitchen and the nursery, as espoused by the WCTU; she was trying to tear down the barriers to women's equality, an aim some women political activists shared. Of course, she never stated her goal in quite those terms, especially at this phase in her career and at a time when leaders and spokeswomen for national organizations were commonly disparaged publicly for allowing their club activities to divert "[their] attention from their domestic responsibilities," but her actions clearly set her apart.[12]

A year earlier, she had transitioned from volunteering in the public defender's office to the role of legal advisor for several women's clubs, most notably the Women's Legislative Council, an organization claiming to represent 187,000 female California voters through its affiliation with state branches of the WCTU, LWV, and many other groups.[13] Focused on issues in California, the Women's Legislative Council fought to put women on an equal footing with men beyond voting rights, most notably with the Community Property Law, which the legislature passed in the spring of 1919.[14] The version signed into law by the governor was a pale imitation of initial proposals, which would have granted wives rights equal to their husbands' in all decisions affecting a couple's community property. Hostile legislators winnowed it down, though one still complained, "These bills originated among foolish and ignorant persons who thought they would please women by passing them. Subservient males listened to the call."[15] As passed, the Community Property Law provided a woman with testamentary rights, including the right to bequeath her half of the community property to whomever she designated, so long as her husband approved, though she was permitted to bequeath her share to her children without permission.[16] The same rule applied to the husband, preventing him from willing *his* half of the community property to anyone other than his wife without her consent.[17]

The new law had generated a violent backlash from the business community, thoroughly upsetting merchants, bankers, the *Los Angeles Times*, and the state bar association, these groups uniting to "Avert <u>Dire</u> Peril," as one spokesman defined it. Angry men spent the summer and fall of 1919 securing the signatures necessary to force the legislature to prevent enactment of the new law until a ballot initiative was held.[18] They succeeded; in late 1919, at almost the same time as the state legislature ratified the Nineteenth Amendment, the Community Property Law was suspended, its fate placed on the ballot for the November 1920 election.

The Community Property Law represented one action of many advanced by the Women's Legislative Council and their legal counsel, Mabel Willebrandt, toward overturning laws denying a wife's right to make financial decisions about the money she earned, to build a career, or to protect her valuables, challenging the male's position as the head of the household in all respects.[19] A husband's domination kept wives in submission, if not in outright jeopardy. Willebrandt had suffered such indignities at the hand of her own husband and had witnessed them in the cases she handled as an assistant public defender. Establishing a woman's ownership of half of a couple's assets was a baby step, but a step nonetheless, toward revolutionizing the relationship between husband and wife.

Mabel Willebrandt's career success and her political beliefs represented a violation of the unspoken code, of the expectations imposed upon her gender, as did the passage of the Nineteenth Amendment. Although Prohibition, the suffrage movement's parallel achievement, was one of the main goals of the women's movement, Willebrandt ignored it, advocating instead for changes she believed would do more good for women. She saw nothing in the destruction of the saloon or the outlawing of liquor that would strike at the foundations of the problem of abusive men and fallen women.[20]

Little did she know her advocacy for protecting women would bring a spotlight upon her, requiring that she make her position on Prohibition known.

Pauline Sabin's decision to seek office as a Republican Party delegate would have been a controversial choice within the women's movement, whose members debated the merits of remaining non-partisan versus the benefits of joining a party.[21] The choice came freighted with concerns over women's role in society, feminine identity, and the perceived evils of partisanship. Driven to become involved in the issues of the day and having abandoned meaningless social engagements, which she derisively referred to as the "pink tea parties" of her youth, Pauline made the obvious choice.[22] The leadership of the most important women's organizations had solidified long ago, allowing little upward mobility, nor could she stand before the public in an election, having effectively disqualified herself years earlier by virtue of her divorce.

In 1907, at the age of twenty, Pauline had married an appropriate match, a graduate of Harvard University named J. Hopkins Smith, in a ceremony in the stunning grandeur of Saint Thomas Church in Manhattan; it was a massive affair attended by all the right people. In the following years, she gave birth to two sons, but, by 1914, being the heart of the Smith household was no longer enough for her. Unlike most women in this situation, Pauline had options. She had inherited millions of dollars from her father.* Fabulous wealth gave her the ability to support herself and her sons and, therefore, the

---

* Historians often attribute Pauline Sabin's wealth to her uncle, Joy Morton, founder of the Morton Salt Company, without offering any documentation or an explanation as to why her father's brother had been so generous. If he left the gift in his will, Mr. Morton passed away in 1934, long after his niece needed it.

ability to divorce Mr. Smith. Had she chosen to devote her time to the women's movement, she might have begun to ascend the ladder of club leadership. Instead, she had opened an interior design business.

Of this period in her life, as a single mother and businesswoman, Sabin never wrote, and for good reason. Most Americans considered her divorce shameful, an unforgivable disgrace, a sin casting her forever from the Episcopal Church to which she belonged. In wrecking her home, living alone in the big city, and running a business—in defiance of tradition, propriety, and decency—the former Mrs. Smith encapsulated all that was wrong with the moral direction of twentieth-century America. Even in New York, with its high tolerance for deviancy from social norms, a divorcée—actually, *any* single woman going out to dinner with friends—was subjected to rumors of immoral activities and to labels such as "floozy," "chippie," or worse.

Then came Charles H. Sabin, her darling "Charlie." Twenty years her senior, Charlie gave her the connection of equals for which she had been looking. Their commitment may have been strengthened by the improbable road he himself had traveled. The president of the Guaranty Bank, the nation's second largest, Charles, a man of astonishing wealth and towering influence, had started his career not in college, but as a clerk, then a teller, then a cashier, and on and on—climbing every rung.[23]

Married outside of their faiths in December 1916, at the Reformed Church in Bedminster, New Jersey, in front of a few dozen friends and relatives, the power couple then proceeded to take on World War I. Mr. Sabin worked with his fellow titans of Wall Street to raise a billion dollars and more in war bonds. Mrs. Sabin rolled up her sleeves and worked on many committees, with many different women's groups, sponsoring street fairs and special events to raise money for hospitals and disabled veterans at home, for war refugees

and reconstruction abroad. Their personal donations to causes, usually to the Red Cross but also in war bond purchases, were also
impressive. While others won the right for women to vote in New
York State during the same period, Pauline Sabin's involvement in
the suffrage movement remains unknown; perhaps it was as vigorous
as she later claimed.[24] Newspaper accounts chronicled her war efforts, but the knowledge gained in how groups of women formed,
found leaders, crafted plans and priorities, and created positive out-
comes went unreported.

Pauline enrolled herself in the Republican Party in 1918, one
year after New York enfranchised its female citizens. The following
year she won her first attempt at becoming a member of the Suffolk
County Republican Committee. The locals knew Mr. and Mrs. Sabin resided in Manhattan, but their summer estate, recently built,
was the county's largest and most expensive, set into the Shinnecock
Hills and featuring an expansive view of the island's inland waterway, Great Peconic Bay.[25] The residents of Southampton had heard
of the Sabins' patriotism during the Great War, some of Pauline's
volunteerism having occurred in the village, but of her declaration
of independence from tradition, likely nothing. If her rebellion had
not engendered enough press to remain in public memory six years
later, if even her peers thought twice of talking indiscreetly about
the wife of one of the giants of high finance, if her remarriage had
returned her to respectability, the effects seemed clear: Pauline
Morton had reinvented herself as Mrs. Charles Sabin.[26]

Winning her place in the local party's leadership had required
her to gain the support of her neighbors, and specifically those who
were enrolled party members, not the general public. Working with
small groups played to her strengths; having been raised to be ladylike in all circumstances, to be a thoughtful hostess, she knew how
to move gracefully, chat appropriately, and listen carefully as she
showed off the elaborate gardens of Bayberry Land—the name she

had chosen for her country estate—all while taking mental notes about her guests' politics.

Making female allies took tact and a readiness to acknowledge the insurgency expressed by so many club women. They intended to make their votes count, a sentiment she could agree with. When the other great female victory, Prohibition, became the topic of conversation, Pauline found common ground in her social stratum's hope that the Eighteenth Amendment would destroy the saloons clogging the streets of Manhattan; for without saloons, the infamous party hacks of Tammany Hall, the headquarters of the Democratic Party's corrupt political machine, would be shorn of their preferred venues for soliciting, organizing, and directing the hordes of immigrants' votes. Club women agreed on the attractiveness of this outcome, either because of an inherent bigotry or because countering the immigrant vote, a vote sold cheaply in saloons, was an important argument used by the women's movement to convince men to vote for suffrage.

Winning friends among the men required a different approach. In a conversation involving economics, politics, or other subjects regarded as in the male domain, a smart woman knew better than to call into question a man's reason or judgment, lest he feel antagonized. Men were commonly believed to be the rational gender, contrasted against irrational or emotional women. Subtle questions and suggestions disguised with deference, charm, or sociability prevented the confrontations provoked by some leaders of the women's movement; such subterfuge was an art designed to establish rapport with male politicians.

A few weeks after the successful fund-raiser at the Hotel Astor, in mid-January 1920, the storm Mrs. Sabin wished to avoid for as long as possible flung itself at Senator James Wadsworth. The League of Women Voters' New York chapter followed through on its earlier threats. "I don't like a fight," said its chairwoman, Mrs.

Frank Vanderlip, "but my office leads me to direct the women of this organization against Senator Wadsworth's re-election. Did he represent the state when he voted 'No' on the Federal Prohibition amendment and did he represent them by his votes on the League of Nations and the Peace Treaty?" Vanderlip, a woman Sabin knew because their husbands had worked together, called Wadsworth "obsolete, a thing of the past." The WCTU joined this anti-Wadsworth campaign, with the statement that the state chapter's fifty thousand women were "absolutely opposed to his re-election."[27] The Anti-Saloon League (ASL), a male-dominated organization aligned with many of the same church groups as the WCTU, was delighted to back the LWV's insurrection against "a wet United States Senator" in a state where political commentators believed that a majority of the people agreed with Wadsworth's opposition to Prohibition, a judgment all the more important because accurate polling data did not exist.[28]

Pauline's mentor, Mrs. Henrietta Livermore, also chose mid-January to reiterate the demand for equality with the Republican Party, a powerful statement from the chairwoman of the Women's State Executive Committee, but not nearly so radical as the other demands. Livermore reminded party leaders that a half million women in New York still had not enrolled in either party, and these women would join the GOP if given the proper incentive. She intended to hold the party to Chairman Will Hays' admonition not to relegate women to "auxiliary, supplemental or ancillary" membership.[29] Pauline Sabin's party had contorted itself in the past few years, offering women a place alongside men in lower-level municipal and county organizations while separating them from men at the state level and above. It was less than the Democrats were doing. Nor did it satisfy the more conservative women in the party, such as Livermore and Sabin, who continued to urge, quietly, in party meetings, equal representation by doubling the number of seats on any given committee. Still, as the presidential election of 1920 took shape, New York Republicans had registered about 1.5 million women.[30]

Neither party could ignore the doubling of the electorate, but some of what Republican women were demanding was anathema to the leadership. The faction led by Henrietta Livermore, however, sought to work within the party, not take it on like Miss Hay and Mrs. Vanderlip. The way to translate those potential votes into positions of authority, she assured Pauline Sabin, was to prove to the leadership that women could be trusted, starting by accepting Wadsworth, whom party bosses had made clear they had no intention of discarding.

Meanwhile, Senator Wadsworth conceded that the time for debating Prohibition and suffrage had ended. The first was part of the Constitution and the latter would soon be.[31] He would not oppose either one. When asked if he supported suffrage, though, he replied, "Well, I haven't been converted to it yet, but it will soon be in the same position as Prohibition. I opposed both reforms, but I believe in upholding the Constitution. I voted for the Volstead Enforcement act because I believe that, having passed Prohibition, Congress should have the power to provide for its enforcement." Despite this change of heart, long-term suffragists and Prohibitionists continued their opposition to Wadsworth's candidacy.

In February, Sabin went to Carnegie Hall for the state Republican convention, technically an unofficial meeting, yet important for establishing the candidates and ballot measures to be voted on later, in the party's state primary.[32] Much of the discussion centered on opposition to the Treaty of Versailles while supporting creation of a world court, smaller government, and lower taxes, but New York Republicans found time to endorse "speedy ratification of the suffrage amendment." The conventioneers did not debate the plank, but merely ratified it, in a style of governance women found offensive.[33]

For her part, Pauline Sabin served on the Committee on Delegates; she was the only woman in a room with forty-one men, selecting the people who would represent New York at the Republican National Convention in June. The committee nominated four of the state's leading GOP politicians. The choice of James W. Wadsworth Jr. as a delegate-at-large, "to be voted for at the Primary Election April 6, 1920," brought three cheers from the crowd; it was a boisterous vote by the party faithful. Henrietta Livermore was named an alternate delegate-at-large; obvious to all, it was a choice designed to placate women, but at least it gave women, and their causes, a voice amongst a sea of men.[34] Henrietta's selection also granted her the position of chair of the Women's Executive Committee of the Republican State Committee.

Following the convention, the women got to work. As a vice chair of the Republican Ways and Means Committee, Sabin traveled around the state, holding classes to educate women on the important issues and the stances of the candidates, hoping to persuade her audiences—most of whom remained uncommitted to either of the two national parties—to join the GOP.[35] Only enrolled party members could vote in the primary and therefore play a critical role in the election. She had to avoid any hint of partisanship and try to convince her audiences of her party's commitment to their issues, running the gamut from social justice, social welfare, and public health to international peace. The needs of her party trumping her personal beliefs, she would have to cite the successes of her party's progressive wing without letting her eyes roll. Ironically, the sublimating, compromising nature of being a party member was one of the main reasons many women feared political parties. Women's clubs were altogether different, went this way of thinking, and thus the prickliest questions directed at Sabin would come from members of the LWV, the Congress of Mothers, the WCTU, or one of the other national women's clubs. Rather than address the unique concerns of each group, Sabin advocated for party unity, focusing on her main goal: raising campaign funds.

Meanwhile, the New York legislature began debate over its light-beer-and-wine bill, which would allow the manufacture and sale of those products, in defiance of the Volstead Act, which detailed the agencies and mechanisms for enforcement of national prohibition and the penalties for violation. After a little more than a month of debate, the light-beer-and-wine bill passed on April 24, but sat in limbo awaiting decisions from the Supreme Court on the constitutionality of the Eighteenth Amendment and the possible limits of its restrictions.[36] New York was not the only state where people thought the Volstead Act should be amended. So far as public opinion can be determined in an era before scientific polling data, most Americans had thought that voting for the Eighteenth Amendment would eliminate saloons, that scourge on society and family life—not their right to have a drink.[37]

Chapter 2

Walking the few blocks from her office to the GOP state headquarters in the Hotel Stowell again and again, Mrs. Arthur Willebrandt eventually earned the right to volunteer for the party, although she was given menial errands, not tasks befitting an experienced attorney and political operative.[1] Even peripheral involvement at the GOP headquarters allowed Mabel Walker Willebrandt to cultivate relationships with leaders in politics, business, and law and to serve as a link between the party and politically active club women. Being a link in a chain involved, of course, holding on to two sides. The local party organization had accepted her, at least in part, because it needed its female volunteer to bring in the women's vote for its slate of candidates. Unfortunately, the highest-profile contest in the election divided California Republicans. The California presidential primary in May pitted the state's sitting U.S. senator, Hiram Johnson, against a political newcomer, Herbert Hoover.

Club women and progressives in general leaned in the direction of the candidate with a national reputation but an unknown political philosophy. Herbert Hoover was a hugely successful mining engineer and had won fame for organizing international relief efforts for the millions of starving Europeans displaced by the vast destruction of the Great War. Orphaned at the age of nine and raised primarily in Oregon, Hoover, armed with a degree in civil engineering from Stanford University and rare abilities to assess potentials in and manage ore extraction, had catapulted himself into the ranks of the fabulously wealthy. Onto such a biography many Americans, from both political parties, had grafted their own beliefs about Hoover, putting him in the sweet spot in American politics, that of a draftee for president by acclamation instead of a political candidate by desire. Having let his interest in the Republican nomination be known, Herbert Hoover had enjoyed moderate successes in the primaries as an Independent, showing strength among Democrats as well, in March and April. His decision to enter the California primary in May as a Republican represented an important strategic decision, reflecting his belief that voters desired a change from the policies of the Democrats.[2]

Mabel Willebrandt chose to back Senator Hiram Johnson in the primary. Senator Johnson had helped found the Progressive Party in 1912 and had run as Theodore Roosevelt's vice presidential nominee in that election. The Roosevelt/Johnson ticket, a third-party insurgency, had endorsed women's suffrage as well as a host of other reforms for which women's clubs had organized, such as eliminating child labor, creating food safety standards, and establishing ballot measures—referendums, initiatives, and recalls—allowing voters redress. The Progressive Party had failed in the election, but the spirit survived in some areas of the country, especially in Los Angeles, and its standard-bearer was Hiram Johnson. In his years as governor (1910–1916), Johnson's reforms had curtailed the influence of the lobbyists of the seemingly all-powerful Southern Pacific Railroad, among other improvements in the structure of California's government, propelling him into the U.S. Senate in 1916. When

Johnson offered himself as a presidential candidate in 1920, his strength was his national reputation and his belief in Progressivism as a political force. Although his campaign centered upon the denunciation of the League of Nations, Johnson had a strong domestic policy message: government had to improve the common good at the expense of the power of the captains of industry.

Her backing of Johnson placed Willebrandt at odds with many members of the women's movement, who had not abandoned the ideals of world peace embodied in the League of Nations and the World Court as quickly as Senator Johnson.[3] A leading activist, Katherine P. Edson, informed the senator that his attacks upon the league "would be fatal as far as the woman's vote in California was concerned." In addition, many club women were unimpressed with Hiram Johnson's record on women's issues. He had steered clear of the vote to ratify the antiliquor amendment and had appeared ambivalent toward efforts to win suffrage in California in 1911, but in serving as chairman of the Senate Committee on Suffrage, he had advanced the Nineteenth Amendment through the Senate on its way to ratification in the states.[4] In many meetings of the organizations devoted to women's rights and social justice to which she belonged, Willebrandt heard her friends commend Johnson for his commitment to the good-government side of Progressivism, while condemning him for his lack of leadership on moral issues, such as creating a public defender's office, a women's court, and a process to rehabilitate fallen women, and the revision of the community property law.

Choosing a side in the contest between Hoover and Johnson, therefore, represented no idle game. The traditional path to success for male attorneys had opened, slightly, for women. President Wilson's administration had appointed to high office two prominent women who had campaigned for him. If her candidate won, there was a real possibility of advancement for Willebrandt. On the other hand, backing Johnson risked alienating important female political leaders.

On the reasons for her decision, Willebrandt kept her own counsel, leaving no direct statement for posterity. However, while Senator Hiram Johnson's record on women's issues may have been checkered, he was a proven commodity, having won his campaigns for governor and for the Senate by wide margins. Whether he won his state's presidential nomination or not, the old curmudgeon would remain California's senior senator, his dour face ready to unleash a stream of vituperation upon any who dared disagree with him. While Herbert Hoover had filed the requisite forms to put together a campaign committee, had informed the world he was a Californian, and had stockpiled a formidable campaign fund, the famous engineer had little at stake—if he won the primary, he was expected to blow into the Republican National Convention that summer claiming to be a viable compromise choice in a year featuring six contenders for the Grand Old Party's nomination. If he failed, little would be lost. Hoover made it a race, though. He and Johnson spent tens of thousands of dollars in Southern California, an area much more progressive than the north, where the power of San Francisco's pro-business elite, which had once ruled the state, faded as Los Angeles' population grew by leaps and bounds.

The winds of change blew Mabel Walker Willebrandt's way in May, when Senator Johnson glided to a comfortable win over Herbert Hoover in the Republican primary. Papering over the widening rift between conservatives and progressives in the GOP, Johnson insisted his victory had been a referendum on the Treaty of Versailles and the League of Nations, and he positioned himself for the Republican nomination by attracting conservative, and predominantly male, Republicans, who opposed Wilson's diplomacy. Neither Johnson nor Hoover had once mentioned Prohibition.[5]

n mid-May, the chairman of the New York Republican state committee announced the names of those who would serve on the executive committee overseeing the fall campaign. Balanced between male and female, the committee included Mrs. Sabin and her friend Mrs. Henrietta Livermore. Seeking party loyalty over personal biases, Pauline hosted leaders of several prominent women's groups, none more important than Mary Garrett Hay, who served as president of the Women's City Club of New York and probably had registered more women in the state than anyone else.[6] Despite her enmity for James Wadsworth, Miss Hay pledged her party loyalty. Days later, the state chairman announced that Senator Wadsworth would head the state's delegation to the Republican National Convention.

In early June, at a gala at the Waldorf-Astoria Hotel, Pauline Sabin had the pleasure of announcing that "the New York City women members of the Ways and Means Committee of the Republican Party is the first to complete its quota of money to be raised for campaign purposes this year." She stressed "the fact that we have completed our quota before the convention begins proves that the women are giving for the party and not for the election of any particular candidate," an effective way of endorsing the party's choices while sidestepping the growing gender divide within her party.[7]

The following day, Friday, June 4, she departed for the Republican Convention in Chicago; she was listed officially as an alternate delegate but known to have secured a voting position, and had talked her Charlie into traveling with her.[8] The couple decided to spare Mr. Sabin, a lifelong Democrat, the ebullient partisanship filling the train cars of the "GOP convention special" leaving the following day and chartered to bring New York's thundering herd of conventioneers to Chicago. Those 255 delegates and alternates gathered at New York's Grand Central Station for their two o'clock train, cheered by a crowd of friends and supporters. All seemed in a festive mood as reporters sought to capture one moment in a new age. "Scorning wardrobe trunks, hat boxes and all the other paraphernalia usually considered indispensable by women travelers," as one reporter explained it, "the seventy-five women took only suitcases," making light of the ladies' choice, missing the significance of their action in a society where rich women were expected to change outfits four to six times daily. For the inquisitive reporters, the seventy-five female delegates had a message. They were not going as women, or asking for any special treatment or designated cars; they were going as "Republican voters," expecting to mingle with their male counterparts during the long trip. Declaring the day of "petticoat politics" over, the women explained that they "want no distinction made between them as voters and their husbands, and fathers and brothers and sweethearts who have been voting for years." Their slogan, "Not what we can get, but what we can give," to which all of them had pledged, was inscribed on their banners and emblems, "and also on their hearts."[9] The reporter assured his readers, though, that despite their protestations to the contrary, women like Henrietta Livermore could never be imagined "looking like proverbial 'frumps,' no matter what sincere resolutions they had made," a twist on the popular perception of politically active women as matrons of morality with all the style of a spinster. With the final stragglers, mostly the main leadership, climbing aboard as the whistle blew and the conductor bellowed, "All aboard!" the next step forward in the republic's history started west.

The female delegates from other parts of the country resembled those of New York. The women had come, wrote one perceptive female reporter, "believing that they were about to write a fresh page in American history." Yet their situation was hardly conducive to bold strokes: none of the delegates down on the floor had ever been a delegate before; three-fourths knew little of practical politics; only

10 percent had attended a previous national convention; "and nine-nine per cent. [*sic*] of them had brought to the convention not only zeal for their party and their particular candidate but a superb vision of what they, as members of their party, could contribute to the great task of re-establishing confidence and contentment in a nation more or less disrupted by war."[10]

The national committee stayed at the Congress Plaza Hotel, where the New York State Committee had two parlors reserved for their own use. None of the members could say how long they would be in Chicago; they would be released only after a nominee was selected and the convention adjourned. The New York delegation was full of disagreement, and the discussion sessions in their two parlors seemingly never ended. Senator Wadsworth, appointed chairman of the delegation, instructed his delegates to vote unanimously for Dr. Nicholas Butler, president of Columbia University and his dear friend. But the delegates were not interested in wasting a vote on a candidate who had no chance of winning, however much they respected Butler personally. Remaining loyal to the leadership fit Pauline Sabin's political proclivities, a tendency sure to establish an alliance with the senator. She and Jim Wadsworth surely began to address each other by their first names in the course of the feverish discussions, if they had not done so already.

On the eve of the convention's opening, the Supreme Court rendered its decision on the State of New Jersey's challenge to Prohibition, rejecting the state's contention that the Eighteenth Amendment was unconstitutional because it had not been ratified properly by several states, enacted statutory regulations that the Constitution had reserved for states, and sought to restrict personal behavior. Without comment, the court proclaimed it constitutional, ending any future challenges on the question. Elihu Root, one of the nation's preeminent attorneys, a public servant of great distinction and a guest at Pauline Sabin's first wedding, had failed. Doubtless, Root's

close partnership with Wadsworth would have produced a telegram informing the senator of the ruling, effectively ending any
discussion of Prohibition at the convention.

The delegates arrived at the Chicago Coliseum, the castellated
entrance on Wabash Avenue welcoming the throngs, on the morning of Tuesday, June 8; all were determined to make their respective
votes count.[11] According to one observer, the women participants
fell into a few classifications. A few came "because it was the fashionable thing to do." The overwhelming majority of women fell
between two groups, one wearing campaign buttons of rival presidential candidates and enjoying the hospitality extended at each of
the candidates' hotels, the other wearing their hearts on their sleeves.
The second group wanted to contribute, asking for meetings, conferences, and directions from their leaders on how to solve the problems of their communities, only to find there were no provisions for
such engagement. The top brass were closeted away, cutting the
deals, determining the future of the party. The women chosen to
serve on the committee of one hundred, appointed by Chairman
Hays months earlier, felt the sting of disillusionment most keenly,
for their mandate had been to serve as advisors, a task for which they
had prepared with care, yet they had no one to advise. As a member
of this group, Pauline Sabin could only have been enraged at
being patronized, ignored, and insulted. The committee held two
meetings, the upshot being a request that the Republican National
Committee increase its executive committee from ten to fifteen
members—seven men, seven women, and Chairman Will Hays—
and to give a leadership position, such as the vice chairmanship, to
a woman.[12]

Chairman Hays took the podium to welcome the party faithful,
and his confident pronouncements into the microphone echoed
through the vast reaches of the hall bedecked with flags and bun-
ting. Delegates held placards but not their tongues, the constant

murmur pushing each successive speaker to shout louder as the first order of business, agreeing on the planks of the party platform, began. Over the next three days, resolutions were made and the intent of the party's leadership, solidly conservative, seemed to peek through the generalities used to express them. Senate Republicans were not going to approve anything remotely resembling the League of Nations, which they believed would compromise the country's independence, but party leaders agreed to stand "for agreement among nations to preserve the peace of the world," balancing the competing interests within the party and a noisy antiwar movement, led predominantly by women, within the nation.

Having dispensed with the burning issue in foreign policy, the party produced a domestic agenda reflecting the values of the conservatives, a set of planks under the heading of ending "executive autocracy and restoring to the people their constitutional government." The Wilson administration "has used legislation passed to meet the emergency of war to continue its arbitrary and inquisitional control over the life of the people in the time of peace, and to carry confusion into industrial life" just as society and business sought to rebound from sacrifices necessitated by the Great War.[13] The burdensome oversight and intrusion into business by the federal government was detailed, the resulting planks calling for cutting taxes and regulations, unequivocally conservative positions.

Mrs. Maude Wood Park, president of the League of Women Voters, was allowed to address the committee of resolutions and to insert planks into the party platform,[14] including making "the woman's bureau in the Department of Labor" permanent, and addressing one of women's biggest political objectives by declaring "the Republican party stands for a Federal child labor law and for its rigid enforcement." Other requests included appropriations to continue the campaign against the spread of social diseases and for education in sex hygiene.

The Committee of Resolutions inserted every plank the LWV submitted, except the three it wanted most: support for the Sheppard-Towner Bill, a federal program for maternity and infant care; federal aid for reducing illiteracy; and regulation of the marketing and distribution of food. The conservative leadership opened the door to more legislation put forward by the women's movement by recognizing that the twelve million wage-earning women "have special problems of employment" and demanding, among other things, "federal legislation to limit the hours of employment for women," "equal pay for equal work" for those employed by the federal government, and, more ambiguously, the promise of "an enlightened measure of social and industrial justice." With that seemingly benign recognition of women's right to equality in the workplace, the party had inadvertently stepped into a deeply buried schism in the women's movement in particular, and in the labor movement in general. The party's assertion that "the federal jurisdiction over social problems is limited" would not suffice to contain all the ambitions it had set loose.[15] The federal government's latest and most extensive intrusion into the autonomy of the states, Prohibition, went unmentioned at the convention in Chicago, the home of gangster Al Capone.

On the morning of Friday, June 11, the conventioneers were treated to the speeches of party leaders nominating the various presidential candidates, the bloviating measured in hours, an unfortunate tendency given the withering heat. Unlike the men, women gave short speeches. After one leading contender's name and qualifications had been put forward, Corinne Roosevelt Robinson, sister of the recently deceased Theodore Roosevelt, delivered the seconding speech as red and green feathers floated down from the rafters of the barnlike arena. Her presentation offered such a welcome change that, as one female journalist wrote, "all the Presidential candidates were thereafter desirous of having women speak for them. Mrs. James W. Morrison, who seconded Herbert Hoover's nomination, was the old fashioned motherly type." She held the attention even of those well to the back, the chatter and clatter dying away. "It was difficult to believe . . . that she was the type of woman who had marshaled 8000 women in a suffrage parade in Washington and had worked effectively for suffrage for years, at the same time rearing a fine family of five children."[16] The speaker who rose to nominate the senator from Ohio kept his remarks blessedly short and had a bit of fun, leaning over the podium to holler directly at the delegates on the floor, "Say, boys—and girls, too—why not nominate Warren Harding?" The improvisation tickled the audience's fancy, causing a stir as conventioneers "rose and cheered and began to march in the aisles, saying 'that's right we are all boys and girls, the girls are in politics now, too.' "[17]

The first ballots were cast that afternoon, a great moment for all the female delegates. Over the course of four ballots, the candidacy of Senator Hiram Johnson failed to catch fire, but he and Dr. Nicholas Murray Butler remained in the running, the latter having no reason to thank the New York delegation, which splintered to other candidates "before a shot was fired," as the Republican committeeman from New York conceded.[18] The party's front-runners split votes over several ballots, their supporters unwilling to yield to one another. As the convention adjourned for the evening, it was clear that a compromise candidate would be required if the first ballot of the following morning failed to produce a clear majority.[19]

That night, a group of Republican senators met in the Blackstone Hotel, away from the party's headquarters, and chose Senator Warren G. Harding of Ohio, then presented their choice to Chairman Hays and other key leaders in the wee hours of Saturday morning. Given Senator Wadsworth's prominence as head of the New York delegation, the largest in attendance and the greatest prize to secure, word of the compromise candidate must have passed like wildfire to the New York caucus held at nine fifteen a.m. Saturday.[20] In the first few ballots of the morning, the conventioneers proved obstreperous, unready to kowtow, although Dr. Butler conceded early and released the delegates pledged to him, but by the end of the ninth vote, everyone in the bleachers knew the tenth would be the finale. Wadsworth pushed his New York delegation to fall into line as he switched horses, producing a convincing tally for the GOP nominee, Senator Warren Harding.

During the course of the convention, the realities of the party machine demolished the ideals of the women's movement. They accepted the presidential nominee, grudgingly, his selection less offensive than the "steam roller on which the party machine rode him [Harding] straight over the other candidates . . . On that last day, the wheels ground into their very souls." The women would vote the ticket, but the zeal, the desire to put their shoulders to the wheel, was gone. As the *New York Times* put it, "They left for home dazed, benumbed. Their future performances for the party hang in the balance."[21] Their party had not recognized the voice of the people in choosing its nominee, much less given the female attendees a meaningful role in the proceedings. The whole process seemed a sham.

Chapter 3

As the Olmstead trial approached, Prohibition director MacDonald sought to eradicate not just the liquor trade, but liquor consumption. MacDonald promised that "any man who carries a bottle on the hip places himself liable to restraint by injunction brought in the federal courts. This provision of the Prohibition law is the only instance I know of in jurisprudence where an injunction may be brought to enjoin a man from committing an offense. The man who totes liquor on the hip is classed as a public nuisance in federal law." MacDonald's assessment hit on one of the finer points of the Volstead Act, and the earlier Washington State law, which established the manufacture and sale of alcohol as crimes, but not its consumption. MacDonald sought to prevent consumption by curbing the possession of liquor, making criminals of citizens who had not violated the federal law.

He also promised moonshiners they would not be treated as they had been by the revenuers of old. Now prosecution would be pursued vigorously, with jail time and the threat of government seizure of all personal property associated with moonshining. MacDonald extended the threat of property seizures to include "any vessel, boat, cart, carriage or automobile used to transport liquor . . . It does not matter who may own the vehicle used in transportation. The liveryman who rents a team, or the garage proprietor who sends a car out may lose it if the passenger has 'a half pint on the hip.'"[1]

MacDonald's warnings came the same day that news of the federal court's crowded docket was reported. One hundred and fifty cases against suspected violators of the National Prohibition Act were on the court's May calendar, along with many others of more traditional fare, making the month "one of the largest in the history of the United States to district court."[2] Of course, the case against Roy Olmstead and Thomas Clark, representing smuggling on a major scale, the indictments against them having to be reset because additional civilians had been added to the conspiracy, was featured, while a number of lesser trials would have to be put off until the fall, a disturbing sign that the federal court system was being overwhelmed by the new statute.

In early June, the bootlegger cops and their cohorts pled guilty, Olmstead and Clark each receiving a 500-dollar fine for importing 1,072 quarts of liquor with a street value of roughly 21,500 dollars at 20 dollars a quart; it was a slap on the wrist more than a deterrent to further criminal activity.[3] Though individuals continued to be convicted for producing or peddling small amounts of liquor, reports of liquor rings operating throughout the Northwest disappeared from the newspapers.

The 20th Century Limited returned the Sabins to New York on June 14, ahead of the rest of the Republican delegation. In the afternoon, Pauline attended her regularly scheduled Republican women's meeting and was asked to speak. She declared that the party's presidential nominee "is satisfactory to East and West alike, and he has a good clean record which cannot be challenged in any particular." A reporter for the *New York Times* quoted her at length, which was appropriate given her various offices within the party; included in the article was her assurance that all Republican women "will stand united" for their party's presidential nominee, despite the ongoing fight over the reelection of Senator Wadsworth.[4] Other female leadership agreed. A week later, Henrietta Livermore related her experiences in Chicago at a tea held for one thousand women at the Vanderbilt Hotel in Manhattan. She described how the party leaders had turned to women often for their opinions, and excitedly illustrated how involved women had been in the proceedings, her presentation leading up to the big announcement: the national committee had promised to create the positions of vice chairman, assistant secretary, and assistant treasurer, each position to be filled by a woman. The national committee would also expand from ten members to fifteen, and include women.

Whether Mrs. Livermore got it wrong or the reporter did is unclear, but her pronouncement suggested membership on the "national committee" determining all party policies, though it was actually an executive committee formed to oversee the Harding presidential campaign, or, more correctly, to handle those tasks delegated to it by the nominee and his close advisors. Senator Harding and Chairman Hays insisted that New York's national committeeman, Charles Hilles, be named chairman of the executive committee and that Hays approve the other members.[5] Charles Hilles had worked with Pauline Sabin, had a house in the Hamptons not far from the Sabins, and knew her as a proven fund-raiser and organizer of women's votes. The day after his own appointment, he sent Pauline a note acknowledging certain promises he had made to her. He said Harriet Taylor Upton had accepted his appointment to the committee, and reported that he'd told Chairman Hays he himself wouldn't serve unless Henrietta Livermore was also named to the committee.[6] He had, therefore, delivered all Pauline had insisted of him, a recognition of her ascendancy in the party.

Pauline's party work continued. On July 11, she hosted a luncheon for sixty at her summer home outside Southampton.[7] It was a small affair by Sabin's standards, likely the kind of summer garden party a society woman was expected to throw for her friends and acquaintances. Safely appointed to the Suffolk County Committee, she invited area committeemen as well as "many from the smart set in Bay Shore and Easthampton," observed one attendee.[8] Cultivating the "smart set" and showing gratitude to her fellow committeemen satisfied personal goals, among them abandoning the meaningless "pink tea parties" to which her mother and grandmother had been consigned.[9] A squall sent everyone into the ballroom, elaborately if hastily decorated for the occasion. Her friend Henrietta spoke, as did the chairman of the Republican state committee, before Senator Calder took the podium. Sabin and her female friends served the guests refreshments on the porch after the speechifying, presenting each one with a portrait of the GOP's nominee, Warren Harding.

Ten days later, James Wadsworth invited reporters to his home in upstate New York, to hear his reply to the attacks made against him by the ASL. He declared himself ready to explain his vote against the Nineteenth Amendment and to take his candidacy to the people. Identifying the key issues, he emphasized the question of "whether or not irresponsible and reckless agitators can succeed in their efforts to terrorize men in public life into abject submission to their will and thus destroy popular government." Wadsworth's list continued, naming the important national and international debates of the day, including "the growth of the bureaucratic system and its tendency toward State socialism; [and] the enforcement of National Prohibition Amendment."[10] Prohibition, and responsibility for its enforcement, passed from a state to a federal issue with the Supreme Court's recent denial of New Jersey's challenge to the Eighteenth Amendment, rendering null and void the light-beer-and-wine bill enacted by the New York legislature earlier in the year.[11] New York's challenge to Prohibition had failed, pleasing the WCTU and ASL, but also encouraging violation by those who would not be denied their alcohol or good times.

Wadsworth's ongoing travails were an issue on the eve of the state convention,* party leaders knowing a certain segment of the party was up in arms about him. As far as the *New York Times* could discern, the anti-Wadsworth faction of the party represented an alliance between the Prohibitionists, suffragists, pacifists, and those who disliked a party run by its most powerful, entrenched members.[12] Various segments of the women's movement could lay claim to membership in each of the opposing groups, but they did not function as a united front. Nevertheless, a significant portion of the electorate seemed to stand against Wadsworth.

The GOP's second "unofficial" convention of the year met in Saratoga Springs on July 25. The first had established a series of planks and selected delegates to the national convention. This second convention, "unofficial" because the primary chose "official" nominees, would endorse preferred candidates. The GOP hoped to dismantle the direct-primary system if it won the governor's office and control of the legislature. The attitude of women on this subject became an object of much discussion at the convention, since women, particularly those from the city, did not like the party leadership naming a slate of candidates without discussion or approval from all convention delegates. The State Committee, which included

---

* The reader will recall that the Republicans held an "unofficial" state convention in February of 1920, also. The word "convention" appears to have had a broad meaning, designating any gathering of delegates put forth by respective county committees.

four women, Mrs. Sabin among them, declared that the eleven hundred delegates to the convention should decide upon the candidates and the platform, rather than allowing backroom deals like the one that chose candidate Harding in Chicago.

Wadsworth, upon arriving in Saratoga Springs, confessed he did not know whether he should ask the convention to endorse him, while he tried to figure out how to allay the opposition "of Republican women who form practically the only stumbling block in his way."[13] Jim certainly sought the opinion of Pauline and others in the female leadership, and secured a measure of comfort in advance of the vote. "Certain women made a demonstration against Wadsworth," observed Charles Hilles, "but in the main there was a fine feeling for him."[14] Mary Garrett Hay and her supporters presented their resolution against Wadsworth, but he was endorsed as the candidate overwhelmingly, with 988 votes of 1,103 cast.

Wadsworth's willingness to accept the verdicts on the Eighteenth and Nineteenth Amendments made a good impression at the convention and in some of the news reports. Most pundits believed a majority of the state agreed with Wadsworth's opposition to Prohibition, but that included Democrats, a contingent he could not rely upon in the general election. As for suffrage, he had represented a vocal minority opposed to it, but as of late July, its ratification was taken for granted and it was no longer worth arguing about. Whether he should be punished was a question taken up by the *New York Times*, whose political reporter decided no. Already, the tactics of the ASL were breeding resentment, the group's attacks upon Wadsworth viewed as out of touch and generally helpful to the senator, although not of great importance.[15] As far as suffrage went, the *Times* reporter felt the time had come to let "bygones be bygones," because the great debate had ended, for practical purposes.[16] Since Wadsworth had represented a vocal and large minority, could women show "broad-mindedness, a spirit above political grudges, revenges, punishments?" The reporter reasoned that the even temperament of women, along with their higher moral code, which had been justifications for the Nineteenth Amendment's passage, would serve them well in granting forgiveness to Wadsworth now. Henrietta Livermore urged the women's state Republican executive committee to see themselves as the key to a Wadsworth victory, but she worried, "The greatest work of the campaign will be overcoming the inertia and indifference of those who have a vote."[17]

In the summer of 1920, the battle in California over Proposition 13, the Community Property Law, began to heat up, as each side strove to get its message into the newspapers and before voters. When quoted in the newspaper, most of the proponents, the club women, toed the new line—that this initiative was not about women's equality, that Proposition 13 merely granted women limited testamentary rights while protecting a husband's control of community property during his lifetime.[18] Journalists, however, noted the issue caused "women to line up against men," in what one reporter deemed a "Sex War."[19] In June, the Bankers Association, speaking for the opposition, asserted that "the reason and principle underlying our community property laws and justifying the control over and power to dispose of community property by the husband, is his legal and moral obligation to support the family. This obligation does not rest with the wife except in rare cases."[20] The husband's control of community property therefore must be "undisputed." The bankers were concerned that under a new definition of community property a wife preceding her husband in death would be able to dispense her half of the estate to her children or grandchildren, effecting the immediate withdrawal of half of the husband's capital, forcing the estate into liquidation. While the bankers' concern raised an ostensibly reasonable objection, its expression degenerated into arguments that such actions would destroy families, and held women accountable, as always, for preserving family bonds and security.[21] As for the "Sex War," one male estate specialist claimed, "Few women care to accept, or are qualified to assume, the responsibilities these proposed changes would impose . . ."[22]

To win over progressives and Republicans, the Women's Legislative Council published a pamphlet coauthored by Mabel Walker Willebrandt. The pamphlet explained the issue in markedly dispassionate language, befitting the suspended law's modest goal. It struck at the critics' major claim first by conceding: "The husband is the business partner and has the right to manage and control it [the community property] during the existence of the marriage relation . . ." The change in the definition of community property would come into effect only upon the death of one of the spouses, allowing the wife to will her half of the joint estate to her children or grandchildren or her husband, but to no one else without her husband's consent, while imposing a similar restraint on the husband. As to the effect upon a husband's business when his wife passed away, Willebrandt's legal training could be seen presenting the evidence. California was one of only eight states using the community property model, and the only state to completely deny wives testamentary rights. In none of these eight states, nor in the other forty, had the issue caused widespread problems in business. Suggesting an ulterior motive of the initiative's opponents, the pamphlet pointed to the banking industry, particularly the trust departments and those companies deriving "a large part of their income from the handling of estates." At present, these trust companies charged a fee on both the husband's half and on the wife's half, upon the death of the husband. The new law would prevent trust companies from charging a fee on the wife's half of the property, a provision costing them half of their income from estates in probate. The current statute was, Mabel and her coauthors concluded, "backward."[23]

For all the talk of the Nineteenth Amendment at the state and national conventions, full ratification waited upon one more state to pass it and make it the law of the land. Tennessee seemed the best bet. The state's governor, Albert Roberts, and James Cox, the Democratic presidential nominee, both wanted to claim the final victory for women's suffrage. Cox's willingness to support the amendment, with Rogers' endorsement, urging the Tennessee legislature to pass it swiftly, forced the Republican nominee to get involved. Harding expressed his support of women's suffrage to the chairman of Tennessee's state party and Carrie Chapman Catt, head of the LWV and a leading suffragist organizer for more than thirty years, but he also equivocated when provided the opportunity, allowing that legislators should vote their consciences.[24] He would not concede the voting power of the women's movement to the Democrats or alienated conservative elements within his party to achieve victory in November. On August 18, 1920, Tennessee's legislature voted in favor of the amendment, bringing to fruition a dream set in motion more than seventy years earlier.

Oddly enough, the California Republican Party held its convention in September, well after the national convention and a scant two months before the general election. Male members of the state committee took the opportunity to dislodge some of the prominent club women: those who had become too controversial, too radical in their thinking, for a party swerving toward its conservative side.[25] The leadership looked past the prominent suffragists and Prohibitionists, the women who had for decades torn at the barriers delimiting the lives of women, and chose Mabel Willebrandt for the state committee. Certainly, her relative youth, which meant she'd missed controversial battles, helped, as did her impressive academic accomplishments, and her membership in many important women's clubs. By keeping her head down and her rhetoric cool, Willebrandt had taken another step forward, gaining the chance to mingle with some of the most influential men in her party, such as Frank Doherty, a Los Angeles attorney and a key ally of Senator Hiram Johnson. She had become the female voice of the Republican Party in Los Angeles.

August was the season for American aristocrats to travel abroad, but the Sabins would have to miss this year. Pauline's steady work and party loyalty leading into the Saratoga Springs convention resulted in her selection as the campaign committee's treasurer, an appropriate position for the vice chairman of the New York City Republican Ways and Means Committee. In addition, she was campaign manager for the nominee for state comptroller.[26] Sabin's organizations, the Women's Division of the New York County Republican Committee and the Women's Executive Committee of the Republican State Committee, planned to host the party's nominee for governor, Nathan Miller, twice before the election, just weeks away. The offer was quickly extended to all the GOP candidates, but most could not make it. James Wadsworth, hoping to shore up some measure of support from women, made sure he did, and both he and Miller were warmly greeted. Much of the discussion, including the reading of a telegram from Warren Harding, focused on President Wilson's postwar policies, which Harding characterized as "a real menace to the American republic in the centralization of Government . . ."[27] Such themes united Republicans, male and female, in common cause. Afterward, Henrietta Livermore issued a statement declaring that many of the Republican women who had opposed Wadsworth had dropped their campaign against him in light of his overwhelming victory in the primary. "Policies, laws and reforms rank first and the person to accomplish them second," she said, and Republican policies benefited women more than those proposed by the Democrats.[28]

Wadsworth's detractors managed to cut into his vote total, but not enough to make a difference. He won handily on Election Day, riding a wave of Republican victories that carried the White House, the Senate, and the New York governor's office, where Nathan Miller unseated Al Smith. A reporter for the *New York Times* noted that Miller, who advocated for rigid enforcement of the Eighteenth Amendment, received fewer votes than Wadsworth, a vocal opponent of Prohibition; this suggested that Miller's stance tainted him with urban voters more than Wadsworth's positions on Prohibition and suffrage did with women.[29] If so, it confirmed the danger of assuming that women cared more about women's issues than about the viability of their parties and candidates.

I n Los Angeles, female activists took heart in the great political victory of the suffrage movement as they looked to the next horizon: the community property law. By one estimate, there were thirty-seven speeches describing all of the referendums given at fourteen women's clubs the week of October 17 alone. Willebrandt spoke at five club meetings that week in favor of the community property bill, while retired judges and others, all men, took the opposing view.[30] Willebrandt focused on facts, reading letters from attorneys who worked in the seven states with laws similar to Proposition 13, offering evidence that the law was functioning properly. She must have noticed, however, the absence of many club women, most especially the members of the WCTU.

One of the main reasons the women of the WCTU had advocated for total Prohibition was an economic one. Leaders of the

WCTU wrote incessantly of their desire to "protect women and children" from the economic insecurity resulting when working men drank away their week's pay. Cutting off the sources of beer, wine, and rum would ensure workers would come home after work, their paychecks in their pockets, ready and able to fulfill their duties as fathers and husbands. The deeply religious women who wore the white ribbon of membership in the WCTU wanted to restore this ideal family structure, not advocate radical solutions such as divorcing deadbeat husbands or creating career tracks for young women. The WCTU's initial support of the community property law had likely been won by family-friendly statements like "When the wife keeps the home in order, rears the children and attends to their needs, economizes, and manages to conduct the family, she just as truly earns the community property as the husband."[31] However, as the depth of the change contained in Proposition 13 and the unequivocal hostility of the business community toward it became clear, the WCTU backed away from it.

On November 2, the voters of California overwhelmingly rejected the Community Property Law.[32] The law would remain as before, denying a wife any legal authority, as one debater phrased it at the time, "to make any provision for her children" upon her death.[33] Several organizations within the California Federation of Women's Groups, including the Women's Legislative Council, had much larger memberships than the WCTU, but the council, clearly, had failed to convince women, and enough progressive men, of the law's benefits.

Bearing witness to the low membership and influence of the WCTU and like-minded organizations, the voters of Los Angeles rejected a local ordinance directing law enforcement agencies to enforce the Eighteenth Amendment. Statewide, voters also defeated the Harris Act, legislation to force California to implement the Volstead Act. Only one year earlier, they had voted for the ratification of the Eighteenth Amendment; the success of the Drys was proving ephemeral. A total proscription of all alcoholic beverages, what people called "bone dry," was not what Angelenos wanted, nor did the citizens in San Francisco, Oakland, or the state capital, Sacramento. The legality of Prohibition, the wisdom behind it, and the ability to enforce it were becoming contentious issues. The author of the Los Angeles ordinance, Dr. D. M. Gandier, opined that full public acceptance of Prohibition would take a generation of successful enforcement to create, a life span sure to be filled with controversy.[34]

Just days after the election, Sabin, Livermore, and the other members of the Republican Women's State Executive Committee met to plan next steps. They decided to hold a victory dinner in December and invite Republican women from across the state.[35] The New York women were not the only ones looking ahead. The Women's Joint Congressional Committee (WJCC) was established at a meeting on November 22, 1920, in Washington, D.C. Representatives of the League of Women Voters, the General Federation of Women's Clubs, the National Council of Women, the Women's Trade Union League, the WCTU, the Congress of Mothers, the PTA, and the National Consumers League attended the meeting and agreed to be part of the new organization. Maud Wood Park, prominent in the League of Women Voters, was selected as chairwoman of the WJCC.[36] The coalition of so many groups gave the appearance of a united front, regardless of party affiliation, a sharp contrast to Sabin's efforts to work within the Republican Party framework.

She was soon called upon, in mid-December, to speak on behalf of Republican women, when the Lord's Day Alliance, a group of unknown origin and composition, announced its plan to oppose the showing of motion pictures on Sundays, an extension of blue laws often favored by defenders of the family. Interestingly, the opponents of blue laws included a diverse mix: Al Smith, Catholic organizations, the Motion Picture Theatrical Association, the president of the Women's Republican Association of New York, and Pauline Sabin. Sabin declared, "I am heartily opposed to any legislation that will deprive the public of a wholesome entertainment on Sunday. It is very logical that the Motion Picture Theatrical Association should champion the cause of the people in this respect. I sincerely indorse [*sic*] them in this fight."[37] Her statement seemed in opposition to the family values she typically espoused, but it actually made perfect sense: the Lord's Day Alliance was launching a broader effort to have the federal government censor motion pictures, a level of intrusion Sabin's conservative leanings could not abide. The censorship call soon faded from the news, but recognition of her willingness to hold firm on Republican values rather than being baited into taking the "women's" position raised her profile, again.

On December 15, she held another gathering at her home, this time with the governor-elect, Nathan L. Miller, and state party chairman George A. Glynn in attendance, along with other members of the state committee, to present Henrietta Livermore with a silver tray in honor of "her leadership . . . fairness, [and] her loyalty to . . . the cause of Republicanism." Miller "promised to women full cooperation in all state political enterprises [and] urged them to visit Albany often to give him the benefit of their suggestions and advice."[38]

Sabin's and Livermore's efforts to firmly secure a place for women in the Republican Party specifically, and in national politics generally, reached an apex that winter in the establishment of the Women's National Republican Club (WNRC) on February 17, 1921.*

---

* Newspaper coverage in 1920 mentions women's Republican clubs on many occasions, although it is unclear if these referred to the same group. The author has chosen to use the date used by the WNRC on its website.

Taking inspiration from the LWV, the WNRC was created as a place where women could learn about the issues of the day. Although the club's political bent was evident in its title, and its location on Thirty-ninth Street was not far from the party's headquarters, the group eschewed any formal or legal connection to the GOP machine.[39] Yet its stated purpose must also have been a reaction to the direction the women's movement was taking, especially the initiatives being run through the WJCC.

Mabel Walker Willebrandt had several victories to celebrate, not least her appointment to the California State Republican Central Committee. Where she had once been rebuffed as a volunteer, she now met with prominent politicians, barristers, and power brokers—all male—within her party. A Republican had won the White House; another had joined Senator Johnson as a U.S. senator from California. Her ascendance was occurring at an auspicious moment in history. Yet from her place on the central committee, she would have perceived her party's lurching away from Progressivism as a definite concern.

At her desk and lost in thought one afternoon, she was brought back to the moment by the ringing of her telephone. She lifted the receiver and instantly recognized the irritable, staccato voice of one of the judges in whose courtroom she had often worked. "I just wanted to tell you I think I've been all wrong about you women. You're much better on juries and in court than I thought you would be." Willebrandt managed to maintain her hold on the phone and withhold a burst of laughter. "You women lawyers have some sort of society, haven't you?" he continued. "Well, I will come to your next meeting. Yes, I should like to meet 'em all and tell them what I have just told you."[40] Perhaps, she allowed herself to think, changes were happening faster than she realized.

B y March, Harry Daugherty, longtime political advisor of the new president, Warren Harding, had received from the newly elected and entirely unprepared chief executive his reward for his years of stewarding the "empty suit" to ever higher levels of office. His prize: the post of attorney general, despite emphatic advice from nearly everyone Harding spoke to about Daugherty, all of them urging him to place his old friend in a position better suited to his abilities.

Daugherty's first task was filling prominent staff positions, none more important than assistant attorney general, second in command and responsible for prosecuting violations of the nation's newest law, the Volstead Act. Hiram Johnson was a major force not just in the California party, but within the GOP nationally. As such, he expected the new administration to look to him as it began to fill federal jobs in California, such as postmasters, customs inspectors, Prohibition administrators, and U.S. District Attorneys. Johnson, looking ahead to a reelection campaign in 1922 and recognizing he had fewer close allies in the southern part of the state than he liked, solicited his friend Frank Doherty's ideas about who among their allies should receive one of the patronage jobs located in or around Los Angeles.[41] Sometime in late May or early June 1921, Mabel Willebrandt met Frank Doherty for the first time, and learned that he had begun lobbying for her appointment as the new U.S. assistant attorney general. He had heard that Daugherty intended to nominate a woman to succeed Annette Adams, the first woman ever to hold the post, and he doubtless knew of or perhaps had even witnessed Willebrandt's indefatigable drive and superior ability. She met the qualifications for the job, having presented cases before federal courts, and she had the gifts of persuasion, earnestness, and keen insight.

In political terms, it was crucial that Mabel be a Mrs. and not a

Miss. Doherty would have asked about Mr. Arthur Willebrandt, recognizing the public scrutiny Mrs. Willebrandt would receive. Her marriage had failed years earlier, her husband a deadbeat. They had not, thankfully, divorced; she had left him behind, but not the union, not the name, not the ring. In public opinion, divorce compounded the sacrilege of a woman taking a man's job. Men had families to feed, while women worked only to earn "pin money" for little luxuries.

Doherty took it for granted that she supported Prohibition, just as Hiram Johnson understood it to be a "woman's issue." Mabel Willebrandt did not view Prohibition as a war between God and Satan as women of the WCTU were wont to offer, rather she believed in the sanctity of the Constitution. So she wasn't passionate about Prohibition. That was okay. Hiram Johnson enjoyed the occasional drink and disliked the ASL heartily. As Johnson's emissary, Doherty mainly needed to know if Willebrandt was ambitious; was she up to the job of assistant attorney general of the United States? She affirmed her desire to attain that lofty rank, one so far above what the few thousand female attorneys in America in 1921 could ever hope to attain.

Frank Doherty had surely passed his recommendation of Willebrandt to Hiram Johnson by June 24, 1921, when the *Washington Times* ran a story holding up Clara Foltz as the likely assistant attorney general. Foltz had become the first female attorney in California and was also the sister of newly elected senator Samuel Shortridge, famous for her activism, a single mother of five who in 1878 had authored the bill to change California state law allowing women to become members of the bar, and a longtime leader in the suffrage movement.

By almost any measurement, Clara Foltz's credentials and experience outweighed Willebrandt's, but Doherty would have fortified her in advance, telling her of Foltz's many enemies, including California's senior senator, Hiram Johnson, who thought appointing Foltz would be "unfortunate and embarrassing," Foltz siding too often and too publicly with his political opponents.[42] She had also angered prominent club women when, as assistant district attorney, she denied the existence of the "white slave trade," or prostitution rings, in Los Angeles, and suggested that women engaged in the world's oldest profession had chosen of their own free will. College-educated women in particular, the demimonde of which Willebrandt was an acknowledged leader, took a dim view of Mrs. Foltz's "old fashioned ways and pompous style."[43]

With the support of key party officials growing behind Wille-brandt, Senator Shortridge offered to endorse her if she could first secure the endorsement of his sister. Willebrandt hastily arranged a meeting with Mrs. Foltz, showing her the telegram with Short-ridge's offer and letting her know Mabel "would not presume to ask" her brother, Senator Shortridge, for his support, expecting him to "urge her [Clara's] appointment."[44]

Looking at Mabel, Clara, noting the open collar, the short hair and shorter hemline, the absence of a frilly hat, could see how times were changing. The effect was less formal and ladylike than her own appearance, but Willebrandt's light makeup kept her from looking too rebellious. Having confronted all her career the stereotype of being a dowdy, unsexed spinster because of her activism, the veteran understood the importance of her dress, of her constant references to being a mother and cooking and cleaning.[45] Foltz had always in-tended her career to inspire younger women, to open opportunities for them, to convince America that women were full citizens, and here before her sat the result. The renowned seventy-two-year-old leader of the women's movement liked what she saw.

Other considerations factored in, of course. Foltz had also just embarked on a secret get-rich-quick scheme.[46] She may have seen little reason at her age to sacrifice a successful practice to move to

Washington, D.C., to administer the controversial antiliquor law, a job almost certainly destined to destroy the career of the person who held it. The evidence was everywhere. In her former hometown, San Francisco, the city supervisors reprimanded "two police captains for having actively enforced National Prohibition while on duty." The California state legislature wanted to amend the laws to allow the sale of light wines and beer, and voters in Los Angeles had rejected an ordinance to require local police to enforce Prohibition, leaving the task to federal agents.[47] Yet the position of U.S. assistant attorney general was a prize not to be quickly scorned.

Clara Foltz made her decision on August 3, and sent a telegram to Daugherty removing herself from consideration and recommending Mabel Walker Willebrandt for the position. Ten days later, Willebrandt heard from the man himself, the new U.S. attorney general, via telegram. He informed her of Johnson's recommendation of her nomination as assistant attorney general, but said she also needed the support of the other senator from California. "If you desire to do so," he proffered, "you may come here to talk the matter over."[48] She decided to go to Washington and chase down this opportunity. She would begin with a visit to Senator Johnson on Monday morning, taking his counsel on whether to pay a call at the office of Senator Shortridge, whom she did not trust, before visiting the attorney general.

Willebrandt bought a rail ticket, a serious gamble on her part given it cost upward of four hundred dollars, excluding meals and accommodations. On the day she was to depart she heard that Senator Shortridge had informed the attorney general of his approval of her appointment. She wasn't going to the nation's capital to discuss a possible job; she was going to talk to her new boss.[49]

Of her thoughts of the five-day trip, only fragments remain. The Southern Pacific Railroad's steam-powered locomotive headed south out of Los Angeles, skirted around the southern end of the massive mountain ranges on California's eastern border, stopping often to replenish the engine's water supply, and turned northeast at El Paso before pounding across her native state of Kansas. As farmers' fields and rural communities flashed past, so too must have scenes of her youth, as the daughter of two dreamers who had eked out a living on the flat prairie. Her parents, David and Myrtle Walker, had tried their hands at a number of occupations in many different locales, usually establishing a newspaper in an emerging community, only to fail, time and again, and move on to the next perceived opportunity. To pay her tuition, Mabel set type in her father's newspaper presses. The grown woman, the successful attorney, rode the train with her Bible on her lap, often opened to one of her favorite verses, a reminder of a youth spent worshipping at any church within walking distance, and of parents whose love and encouragement had never set boundaries on her ambition, their itinerant life a model of a stubborn desire to try, and try again. As ably explained by Willebrandt's biographer, no woman in 1921 could have watched the vast land pass her window and assumed that the new job would give her actual power, that her opinions would be valued by her bosses or her directions followed by her male employees, or that she would be paid anything close to what the male assistant attorneys general earned.[50] She knew she would be a token, yet there were grounds to dare for more.

A relentless club woman, Mabel worried less about whether she would be treated as a token and more about making another critical step forward, toward women's equality. Her success could set fire to the web of prejudices, buried deeply into American culture, that dismissed women as unfit for serious endeavors. To become the standard-bearer for millions of women placed a heavy responsibility upon Mabel Willebrandt's shoulders, so heavy the Southern Pacific Railroad should have charged her for the extra baggage.

Chapter 4

President Warren G. Harding was inaugurated on March 4, 1921, but he and his advisors had begun the chore of staffing his cabinet and other important posts shortly after his election in November. As a longtime Republican member of Congress, Senator Wesley Jones of Washington knew the president would need his help in enacting his legislative agenda, and in return Jones expected to have a say in filling certain jobs in his state. Senator Jones considered the post of the state's federal Prohibition director one of the most important, especially given his ardent support of the Eighteenth Amendment. He announced he would "recommend no man for a Federal position as Federal attorney or marshal, or to any position that had to do with the enforcement of Prohibition, until I had a written pledge from him that he would stand by the enforcement of the law."[1] That pledge helped Jones avoid some of the mistakes made by others in his position; his criteria for judging potential officers, though, would have been improved vastly if he had demanded not just fealty to the law, but experience in law enforcement.

The new position of federal Prohibition director in each state was not subject to the rules and regulations of the Civil Service Commission. Put another way, there were no minimum qualifications. Senator Jones could nominate anybody he pleased; send the name along to the federal Prohibition commissioner, Roy Asa Haynes, in Washington, D.C.; and expect it to go through. This is exactly what occurred.

In late July 1921, Prohibition director Donald MacDonald received the letter he had been expecting, relieving him of duty and naming Roy Lyle to take his place. MacDonald released the letter to the press, sending reporters in search of Lyle, a former librarian and real estate agent, who had not yet received official word.[2] Jones knew Lyle through the Young Men's Republican Club of King County, and knew he was a supporter of Prohibition, a member of the Anti-Saloon League, and a Methodist as well as a Republican— an almost perfect candidate. The leaders of the Women's Christian Temperance Union and the Anti-Saloon League supported his nomination because Lyle was a reliable Dry, a qualification lacking in so many men better qualified because of their experience in law enforcement. Lyle's superiors in Washington, D.C., instructed him, and other state directors, to hire agents "of unquestioned integrity, firm conviction and patriotic purpose" rather than seeking "to pay political obligations."[3] In other words, they needed to be Dry, first and foremost.

Roy Lyle took the job, announcing, "The booze runner, the bootlegger and the skulking flouter of our dry laws must go."[4] He said he appreciated how difficult his new job would be, although "the people of the state [have] thrice expressed themselves in favor of Prohibition, even as high as 5 to 1," so he expected the support of every law-abiding citizen and the cooperation of every law enforcement official. More such declarations followed, none accompanied by substantive proposals, as Lyle set the bar for his success as the complete elimination of the use of alcohol as a beverage, a bar far higher than the police set for laws banning other vices—like prostitution and gambling—and a goal that ignored the fact that some alcohol, for medicinal or industrial uses, for example, was still legal.

Roy Lyle's enthusiasm and expectations buried some harsh realities. The Pacific Northwest District, the Twentieth, encompassed the states of Washington, Oregon, and Alaska, containing more than 800,000 square miles, and was one of the largest districts in the country, with seven distinct, sometimes idiosyncratic judicial districts before which cases would be brought. The climate, geography, and topography of the Twentieth Prohibition District presented another set of problems with its extensive jagged coastlines, high mountains, dense forests, heavy rain- and snowfall, and generally poor roads to navigate. Lyle was allotted eleven agents for the state of Washington, and another eleven were assigned to cover smuggling activities between the states of the Twentieth District, adjacent districts, and Canada. The agents enforcing Prohibition district-wide would have little communication with Lyle or the state agents he controlled; they preferred to work in the shadows, developing their cases without interference, even from their fellow agents. This created unnecessary competition and, often, resentment between state and district agents.

Only eleven days after he started his job, hardly enough time for Lyle to be seen as capable, a group of thieves broke into the Prohibition Unit's "secure vault" and removed 3,500 quarts of liquor with a street value of $35,000, a fantastic sum of money to most readers of Seattle's daily newspapers.[5] The details of the heist made a poor impression, with little "security" in evidence as the truck backed in to haul away the prize—a process that had taken hours—and a Prohibition agent caught wondering aloud why the bottles, held for evidence for a trial long since completed, had not been destroyed. The fact that much of the liquor had been seized originally from a gang led by former Seattle police officers Roy Olmstead and Thomas Clark helped make the theft look suspicious to the community. Director Lyle demonstrated little control of the situation and little force of personality.

A great sigh of relief came two weeks later, when Lyle's men, working in conjunction with local police, U.S. Customs officials, and an investigator from the Internal Revenue Bureau's Special Intelligence Unit, sent from the bureau headquarters in Washington, D.C., found the cache of stolen liquor and caught six men "red-handed."[6] Lyle believed the men were just employees working for "the king bootleggers," whom he did not identify, but the specter of Roy Olmstead was raised in a newspaper story about the incident. Lyle praised his fellow law enforcement officials for their help, particularly Seattle police chief William Searing, with whom he released a joint statement: "We were working to clear the Police Department and Prohibition office because aspersions had been cast on individuals of both services. Our investigation has failed to show any police officer or [Prohibition] official was in any way connected" to the theft from the unit's vault. While the suspects were first held at the Immigration Detention Center, a federal facility over which Lyle had some authority, the center had not been built to handle prisoners, and Lyle was grateful when the police allowed him to place them in the county jail.

The spirit of cooperation began to strain, however, when a week later Lyle ordered the arrest of Patrolman C. H. Parker. He had been under suspicion since the first break in the case, having walked the beat around the warehouse from which the liquor was stolen, and Lyle promised more arrests related to the robbery. He needed to generate good news; Prohibition agents were on trial for manslaughter in Spokane, and one of his sting operations had netted nothing but bottles of water.[7] For his part, Parker, the arrested patrolman, told a reporter, "I am not worrying," perhaps displaying an insider's knowledge of how difficult it was to get a bootlegging conviction, especially against a Seattle policeman.

With the assistance of revenuers from the Seattle office of the Internal Revenue Bureau, additional arrests were made, but in late October, the wheels started to come off the case. The district attorney reported that Attorney General Harry Daugherty had ordered him to delay the trial until the new district attorney, Thomas Revelle, took office. The outgoing district attorney alleged that Roy Lyle had gone behind his back and contacted Daugherty directly, assuming Revelle's commitment to prosecution would be more vigorous. A delay was granted, but at a cost: the men arrested by the revenuers were freed because the revenuers had failed to prove any connection between their suspects and the other thieves. For the others, the six arrested at the site and Patrolman Parker, delays resulted in two missed appointments before the grand jury—a violation of their right to a speedy trial, claimed their attorney.[8]

M abel Willebrandt's predecessor as the assistant attorney general responsible for Prohibition was Annette Abbott Adams, another Californian whose selection had reflected both the decision to reward women for carrying the torch of Prohibition and to hold them accountable if it failed. The Volstead Act, as the outgoing AAG described it, had been left as an infant on the Justice Department's doorstep. "As a woman I could not refuse to offer it shelter and neither did I want the men to think it was too big for me to undertake, so from the day of its christening, I mothered it." Yet it had been a thankless task. "The tendency on the part of men is not to share with us what they already have but to invent new fields for us. They want to have a welfare department for us where we can mess around. This [Prohibition] will be a new toy for us to play with." She did not believe the women's movement should settle for such limitations, and she recommended that women continue to "bore from within."[9]

Willebrandt met with Attorney General Harry Daugherty and his staff several times during her first week in Washington. Daugherty thought having a woman might have a "wholesome effect" on his department.[10] Daugherty wanted Willebrandt to focus on prosecuting tax fraud and those arrested for violating the Volstead Act. To her primary tasks, Daugherty added reviewing all cases involving war risk insurance, pensions, prison cases, the interstate commerce commission, and commerce and labor laws. She was granted a staff of three attorneys, one secretary, and two stenographers.[11]

After granting his endorsement, he sent Willebrandt to meet the president. Warren Harding had the stern visage, the commanding presence, and the resonant baritone of a president. Talkative and friendly, the president may have taken his time, seeing if she were the right sort, before expressing his concern: "There is only one thing against you—your youth."[12] Rather than responding that thirty-two was old enough, she smiled winningly and promised to "outgrow" it, Mr. President. Her quip, combining calmness and humor, muted his concern.[13] Daugherty wanted her to start immediately, and she agreed, postponing a return to California to "close her affairs."[14] She announced to the press that she would not grant interviews for at least a week, and one reporter declared, "A woman who is not ready and willing to talk or be photographed has been found."[15] The cheap jest hid a wise move, though, for someone who had undertaken an enormous leap in her legal career. She had to find a place to live, a difficult task for a single woman in an unfamiliar city; acquaint herself with her staff, all of whom would be men who had never had a female boss; worry about her parents, now elderly, living in a rural farming community; and begin sending out her thank-you notes, the never-ending work of successful and assiduous politicians.

Among the congratulations received was an unsigned letter from a "friend." On her law firm's stationery, the author implored her to "gaze upon the heading . . . the dignity and simple import conveyed by the simple announcement—'Law Office,'" before regretfully acknowledging the dream of that law firm had come to an end with her appointment. The letter could have been written only by Fred Horowitz, her law partner who wished to become much more. The letter indicated how much he struggled with his emotions, first insisting Los Angeles was "the only place on earth you belong," and deploring the idea of a fine lawyer becoming a politician, before concluding with well-wishes in the form of advice: "Hold fast to that which is good [and] yield to no one."[16] Unlike most other letters, she held on to this one all her life.

Director Lyle got just the kind of district attorney he had hoped for when Thomas Revelle took the oath of office on October 22 and assumed control of the government's criminal prosecution team in western Washington. "There is no more reason for condoning violation of the Prohibition amendment than for condoning murder," Tom Revelle stated, making his case for imposing maximum penalties on bootleggers and rumrunners. He decried public apathy, even from those in support of the Eighteenth Amendment, stating, "If the Eighteenth Amendment is not enforced it is easy for other laws, even the constitution itself, to fall into disrespect. One law cannot be made a joke without the whole system of law enforcement feeling the effects of that disrespect."[17] Quietly, Lyle agreed with the district attorney's every word; he was eager to put violators behind bars, rather than the predominant practice of issuing fines, which allowed bootleggers and rumrunners quickly to return to their illegal pursuits.

In his conversations with Tom Revelle, Director Lyle came to understand that some of the problems in prosecuting bootleggers were created in his office. Obtaining search warrants, collecting evidence, and taking statements from suspects were key steps in building a successful prosecution, but Lyle had no experience with any of those. The former real estate agent needed a legal advisor on his staff to help train his agents in the proper techniques for making arrests and gathering evidence, ensuring every case had been properly constructed before passing it to the DA's office. Simultaneously, Lyle received word from his superiors in Washington to move the headquarters of the Prohibition Unit out of Tacoma to Seattle, where it would be closer to Revelle's office, the U.S. district court, the headquarters of the Anti-Saloon League, and the WCTU—and the biggest, most brazen bootleggers in the state. Several agents would remain based in Tacoma, while two stenographers would move into the new suite of offices leased by Lyle in the Thompson Building, at the corner of Fourth Avenue and Cherry Street in the heart of downtown Seattle, near many of the city's hidden, and not-so-hidden, speakeasies.

Lyle announced the appointment of William Whitney as assistant director and legal advisor, and asked him to direct enforcement efforts.[18] Assistant Director Whitney would prepare the evidence on liquor cases for presentation to juries, thereby becoming a critical cog in Lyle and Revelle's plan to obtain the harshest penalties possible for violators. "Heretofore we have had difficulty, through the lack of legal knowledge on the part of agents, in securing proper presentation of evidence to the United States attorney's office. I feel that we are fortunate in securing a man of Mr. Whitney's undoubted ability."[19]

Neither Lyle nor DA Tom Revelle doubted Whitney's commitment to the cause of Prohibition, which matched Revelle's own intensity, or the force of Whitney's personality, which far exceeded Lyle's quiet demeanor. Whitney also had experience managing a workforce of dozens of employees, having served as chairman of a busy draft board during the Great War and leading the Young Men's Republican Club of King County; he was one of the few honestly Dry men to have held the position in decades.[20] Given that his qualifications and his closeness with Senator Jones both exceeded Roy Lyle's, it can be surmised that the only reason Jones had not appointed Whitney to the director's position was the public embarrassment of Whitney's alleged affair with a former secretary, which resulted in a charge of alienation of affection by her husband. Taking over the leadership of most functions of the unit, Whitney pushed Lyle, his nominal boss, aside. Roy Lyle, it was generally agreed, had neither the backbone nor the training to impose his will against the driven, angry, and ambitious Bill Whitney.[21] So the administrator quietly stepped aside, deferring to Whitney's direction.

Whitney intended to be an effective enforcer of public morality, putting the bootleggers behind bars, rehabilitating his reputation and getting ahead in the world in the process. He dived in, relishing the opportunity to hire agents—men loyal to him, men full of fight, men ready to become agents in a world of intrigue. "In selecting Prohibition agents," he advised, "the color of the man's hair or his stature may be reasons why you don't want to appoint him because these things might make him a marked man."[22] So far as he or his boss Lyle knew, there was only one way to catch a bootlegger—in the act, allowing the agent to go on trial and say, *I saw this man, at this time and in this place, selling booze.* The problem was, the leaders of the liquor smuggling and distribution rings usually left the physical movement of liquor to working stiffs, thereby avoiding prosecution, a practice frustrating to the leaders of the Prohibition Unit.[23]

The fact that Canada was dripping wet, its export houses selling unlimited quantities of alcohol to all comers so long as they cleared Canadian customs, loomed paramount in all discussions of how to shut down the smugglers. Lyle arranged a meeting with officials of the provincial government of British Columbia, seeking to gain some cooperation. The officials of British Columbia took care not to give any interviews to the press, since the majority of Canadians felt that Prohibition was ludicrous, and it had resulted in a windfall of profits for Canadian businessmen and for their government's coffers; taxes collected on liquor bound for the U.S. were in the range of forty thousand dollars per week. Unnamed Canadian officers were quoted as saying their "hands were tied under existing laws."[24] Happy to announce something that sounded like cooperation, Canadian officials and Prohibition officials in several western states announced they had agreed on "booze restrictions" and planned to require "the consent of officials of the Canadian province involved before American liquor is permitted to enter Canada."[25] Readers could be forgiven for scoffing at the idea that enterprising rumrunners were trying to move liquor *out of* America.

Although they could do little about the legal purchase of liquor within their sovereign borders, Canadian officials allowed the Americans to review Canadian customs records, thereby divulging the names of smugglers and the frequency and amounts of their purchases.[26] One record described a "speedy launch which runs from Vancouver to Birch Bay," an inlet featuring a shallow beach just south of the border. "This boat drops its cargo of liquor in sacks in eight feet of water at a point just off the beach and departs. The sacks are recovered by grappling hooks at a convenient time from a small boat . . ." Lyle was informed the boat made three trips per week carrying as many as fifty cases per trip. Deliveries to Birch Bay avoided the U.S. customhouse at the border crossing; it was a handful of miles to Bellingham but a long drive south to the big market in Seattle. Lyle summarized the situation for his mentor, Senator Wesley Jones, who noted one of the many absurdities in the Volstead Act. "It certainly is a peculiar situation," Senator Jones observed, "where permits are given for the purchase of liquor in one country on the condition that the purchaser will undertake to export this liquor to a country where its manufacture for beverage purposes is prohibited." Jones expressed his confidence in Lyle's ability to "meet the situation along the border," and pledged "to seek the state department's aid in an endeavor to end the issuance of permits in British Columbia to export liquor to the United States."[27]

In order to make an arrest, Prohibition agents had to catch men in the act of violating a provision of the Volstead Act—manufacturing, smuggling, or selling alcohol fit for consumption. This meant they had to work undercover and ingratiate themselves with the violators, not just to catch them in the act of breaking the law, but to see if there was a way to be introduced to men further up the chain—the bigger dealers, the importers, the moonshiners. Whitney, the trained attorney, knew that his agents had to be taught the boundary, though, between entrapment and effective police work. All persons were to be presumed innocent until an officer received information to the contrary. Anytime an agent encouraged someone to break the law, the resulting case would be weak, if not thrown out altogether. When an officer had reasonable grounds for suspicion, he was free to "disguise his person, change his name, deny his purpose or do anything else within law and morality that will make an opportunity for a law breaker to reveal his unlawful intentions by unlawful acts." If asked by a bootlegger, an officer could participate in a criminal act to obtain evidence, so long as he received approval in advance from his superiors and he did not surpass the result sought.

While Whitney could instruct his men in the basic principles of the law, he had no training in police work. Professional standards of investigation, surveillance, evidence gathering, warrants, searches, and seizures were entirely lacking, but then, the situation was similar for members of the Seattle police force, who received little, if any, formal training. New policemen learned by walking a beat with an experienced man. Whitney's unit had no experienced men, nor did it provide anything in the way of guidelines for addressing these fundamental problems. Most cases came down to eyewitness testimony, the most important of which was that of the arresting officer, who would produce, as evidence, a bottle or sample of a defendant's illegal beverage.

Almost no aspect of the unit's work, because so much of it demanded legal assessment or preparation of paperwork, escaped Whitney's attention. He served as probation officer for persons given suspended sentences. He worked with the district attorney and his assistants on the issuance of search warrants and production of witnesses at trial; he appeared at trial to explain or corroborate testimony and investigative methods; and he examined all matters regarding collection of taxes, assessments, or civil penalties "arising in the enforcement of the National Prohibition Act and the revised statutes relating to intoxicating liquor."[28] Each year this workload related to hundreds, and later thousands, of investigations undertaken by the Prohibition Unit in Washington. It might seem that little was left for Lyle, but he managed to stay busy coordinating investigations and arrests with the myriad international, federal, state, and local law enforcement agencies whose paths crossed in defense of the Eighteenth Amendment.

Director Lyle attended the state sheriffs' convention in late January of 1922 to foster better relations and make plain his plans for increased enforcement efforts. Lyle got a little carried away onstage, though, and began promising to declare any building in which intoxicants were sold a public nuisance and padlock it. The Volstead Act granted him the authority to shutter hotels, rooming houses, and restaurants for up to one year, and the threat got the public's attention. The next day, reporters wanted to know more about this plan. "I don't know yet how far I can go with this," he responded, admitting that he needed to consult with Whitney, "but the owners of buildings have been warned."

Lyle's inexperience and ignorance extended to other key aspects of the problem. Police officers, sheriffs, and his own agents had found it hard to stop vehicles they suspected of being used to transport spirits. Lower court rulings to the contrary, lawyers informed Lyle and the sheriffs that "strict enforcement" of the laws governing the use of motor vehicles "furnish legal reasons for stopping automobiles and examining their contents without search warrants." Lyle promised the sheriffs that his agents would continue to stop cars without warrants.

Finally, he promised a harder line against bootleggers making "pistol plays," or brandishing guns when confronted or chased by law enforcement. "When a bootlegger draws a weapon," Lyle warned, "he should be made to realize he is inviting the Prohibition officer to shoot." Otherwise, apathetic citizens could expect a "big tragedy" forcing them to awaken "from lethargy to a full cognizance of the prevalent lawlessness." "We mean business," said Director Lyle. "We are going out to get these fellows now."[29]

M abel Willebrandt's confirmation raised no questions; her nomination was submitted before the Senate on September 22, 1921, and approved five days later.[30] After taking the oath of office, she had to answer questions from a reporter, who asked about her goals. "It would be presumptuous in the extreme," she replied, "for me to say I came into the office with some glorious scheme of reform. I am here as an assistant to Mr. Daugherty and his views and his policies will be carried into every decision of this office." Returning to her office, she signed an official communication denying a prisoner of Leavenworth a commutation in his sentence, looking past the grieving family to the evidence of his guilt.[31] With that decision, the word began to get around that the old idea of women being guided by their emotions rather than by facts did not apply to the new assistant attorney general. Sometime soon thereafter, Senator Johnson called to congratulate her. Did she notice that, as one of the senator's friends once admitted, Johnson found taking "serious women seriously, especially in politics," difficult?[32]

The urgent demands of her duties forced Willebrandt to postpone, again, a return to California to settle her affairs. She had three cases to present to the United States Supreme Court in November. At the same time, she had to prepare for the Supreme Court's bar test. A handful of women had been admitted to the court already, yet the test was to be feared. One of the court's newest members, Associate Justice James C. McReynolds, had objected publicly to the notion of women becoming attorneys, his overt misogyny complemented by his pronounced hatred of African-Americans and Jews, his hostility toward the latter on public view because of the two Jewish justices on the court. He had a reputation for leaving the bench when female attorneys rose to argue their cases.[33] As Willebrandt was learning, playing politics meant more than answering to the Republican Party and the men who had helped secure her new position. It required balancing the perceptions of a male-dominated world—some friendly, some hostile, all unsure of what to expect from Mabel Willebrandt.

Pauline Sabin spent much of 1921 building the membership of the WNRC, arranging speakers (primarily male politicians) to educate women not just on the issues of the day but, more importantly, the rules of the political game. Women had shown political will in getting the Eighteenth and Nineteenth Amendments enacted, but she felt they needed to shed their one-issue agendas and embrace the concerns and legislation adopted by the Republican Party if they wanted to gain the respect of the party leadership and assume a permanent role in determining the future direction of the party.

When the New York state legislature went into session in February 1922, Pauline Sabin announced, "I've joined the ranks of the lobbyists," as she journeyed to the state capitol in Albany to press legislators to pass the Livermore Bill, requiring political parties to give women 50 percent of all party management positions and thereby speeding up the pace of change.[34] The Livermore Bill passed, the power of women in New York politics burgeoning.[35] A few days later, she joined her husband for a journey down to Washington, D.C., for the state dinner given by President Harding in honor of Chief Justice William Howard Taft of the Supreme Court. Senator Hiram Johnson of California and the other leading lights of the Republican Party attended as well. Despite Charlie's prominence in the banking community, he was a registered Democrat; clearly, the invitation had been made to *Mrs.* Sabin, perhaps as an acknowledgment that her stature was growing beyond New York.

I n late March of 1922, Mabel Walker Willebrandt wrote her parents about a speech she had presented to the Women's Bar Association of New York, complaining in her letter that her effort to say something important had been ignored. A local newspaper reporter wrote that she was "a beautiful picture in a black spangled gown," who had "laid a silken scarf aside as she arose to speak." The reporter had included something of her speech, complimenting her delivery, but the article had irritated her: "Why the devil they have to put on that 'girlie girlie' tea party description every time they tell anything professional that a woman does, is more than I can see."[36] Among the topics stirring within her was the Supreme Court's recent refusal to hear *Blum v. Wardell*, allowing the curiously Californian definition of community property to stand, a sour defeat for her.[37] A month after the decision, the Women's Legislative Council of California dissolved, its work unfinished and, seemingly, unattainable.[38]

Perhaps owing to her frustrations, Mabel Willebrandt allowed herself a rare evening off in the Big Apple after her speech at the bar association. She joined some friends for a ginger ale on the rooftop of the Amsterdam Hotel, and after midnight they headed off to a club called the Plantation, at the corner of Broadway and Fifty-first Street, to see its famed cabaret depicting the life of the "negro from a hen roost to a Mississippi flat boat."[39] If she witnessed any of the patrons topping off their glasses with a hip flask, as was likely the case, she ignored it, knowing that consumption of alcohol did not constitute a crime in itself.

The small fine assessed against Olmstead after his arrest convinced him the risks he had taken were well worth any penalty, and that he could gamble more. He gathered investors, retained an attorney, hired an office staff, and instituted a simple code of ethics: forbid employees from carrying firearms, never water down the product, and never deceive suppliers or customers.[40] Behind his easy smile and glad hand was the trustworthiness that had always drawn people to him, that ability to know what he could accomplish at the moment and never overpromise. Olmstead aimed to be the most honest rumrunner and bootlegger in America, and he was confident that profits would ensue.

Roy Olmstead and Tom Clark operated primarily through a company called Western Freighters, though they also worked with a larger company called Consolidated Exporters. These entities, both duly licensed Canadian liquor exporting houses, provided the financing and created the contracts for shipping tons of spirits to Vancouver, British Columbia, from around the world. At the docks, stevedores loaded as many as thirty thousand cases at a time into the holds of their steamships: the *Prince Albert*, the *Tuskawa*, and the *Coal Harbour*. As the ships made their way to the twelve-mile limit, cases were broken and bottles placed in more manageable gunny-sacks before being unloaded to midsized boats, which then proceeded along the coasts of Oregon and California to make other rendezvous. The midsized boats brought their loads lumbering into the Strait of Juan de Fuca at night, meeting up with the faster gas launches at various points, most often one of the coves along the coast of Discovery Island, in Canadian waters. The fast boats then made the run down the Puget Sound.[41]

With every shipment, Olmstead, who handled the Seattle area, and Clark, who received shipments in California, collected handsome profits in cash and became ever more successful international businessmen. Early in 1922, they expanded. Eschewing the expense of buying or leasing another ship, they decided to move their products aboard freight cars of the Oregon-Washington Railroad & Navigation Company. Loading train cars in Seattle for the trip to the big markets down south first required that the bottles of King George Scotch, Haig & Haig, and Old Taylor Whiskey be pulled from their muslin sacks and stuffed into barrels with sawdust for padding, a process completed on one of the islands in the Puget Sound. Part of the trick was to match the weight of each barrel of alcohol with that of a barrel of salted herring. Olmstead's ships docked right along Seattle's waterfront, his agents bribing stevedores, railroad workers, and another set of customs officials to move the barrels off the ships and onto the railcars. Soon, Olmstead and his confederates were sending a train south about once a week.

Some of the railroad agents in Olmstead's chain, however, became greedy and tipped off hijackers, who on May 10 attempted to steal six barrels, marked "salt fish," stored at the railroad freight warehouse in Seattle. The ensuing confusion came to the attention of William Whitney, and his investigators spent days surreptitiously watching and following the shipment of salt fish, building their case. On May 19, Prohibition Director Roy Lyle announced that his men had coordinated with the Prohibition Unit in San Francisco on a major bust, seizing "barrels of the finest kinds of whiskey and wines" in warehouses in Seattle as well as in San Francisco. The liquor seized in the raid in San Francisco was valued at over $100,000, although the trap there had been sprung poorly and one truckload of Scotch had escaped in a car chase through the business district.

Lyle described the enterprise behind these shipments as "the operations of a whiskey ring financed in Seattle." From the financiers to the "expert packers" in the islands of the Puget Sound to transfer men working at Seattle's docks to the railroad freight houses, the Prohibition agents had found a flood of bribe money. Thousands of barrels of the finest whiskeys and wines "had poured openly into Seattle from the islands of the Puget Sound and trans-shipped here by railroad to Portland, San Francisco, Chicago, Kansas City and Eastern points." This liquor cabal had been moving the contraband along the railroad "virtually on a weekly schedule," so well had this outfit greased the wheels of any suspecting law enforcement official.[42] Lyle's description clearly distinguished this gang of unnamed bootleggers from the several smaller, less sophisticated groups his men had arrested of late.

In the days following the bust, Olmstead and Clark felt the Prohibition Unit getting closer. Men in the rail yards and warehouses were being questioned. On May 24, Prohibition agents nabbed one of Olmstead and Clark's key organizers, in part because the man had looked out of place in the village of Anacortes, a bustling little port in the middle of Puget Sound, where he was driving a fast, gasoline-powered boat, "well dressed" and with "the appearance of a retiring but prosperous business executive." Director Lyle crowed in the press, outlining the tentacles of this underground enterprise, with its fictitious shipping bills and paperwork, and promised more arrests shortly. "The operations of the liquor ring are declared to be the most extensive ever uncovered on the Pacific Coast."[43] In the ensuing days, the unit arrested men in Seattle and San Francisco and interrogated scores of others. Roy Lyle's goal, along with rolling over the workers and getting them to name their employers, was to uncover the location where the bottles were repacked between Victoria, British Columbia, and Seattle, Washington. Lyle also suspected that Olmstead and Clark maintained another location somewhere in Seattle and used it to repack the bottles for shipment on the railroad.

Whitney was getting closer than Olmstead could have expected, and was speaking with Elsie Potter, the rumrunner's bookkeeper, in early June of 1922. Elsie told him about several "liquor caches," which he located, confirming her value.[44] Years later, the government claimed Elsie had been a paid informant who provided evidence regularly.[45]

Still, Olmstead and Clark were open for business. In early June, their rum-running boat, the *Zambesi*, brought down three hundred cases. They set their men to repacking the sacked bottles into pine boxes for loading onto a railcar, where the bottles would be hidden under a load of furniture. Thomas Clark and his associates then boarded the steamship *President* for the trip to Los Angeles, and held a little party in Clark's stateroom. Among the passengers invited to join in was Leonard Regan, who worked for Whitney's unit. Regan had stepped aboard at the last minute "with $13 in his pocket and no baggage," surely snickering up his sleeve at the invitation to join Clark's party.

While the steamer sailed, Whitney's men seized the railcar loaded with whiskey, a cargo valued at $66,000, and held several workers at the warehouse for questioning. Using the "wireless," Whitney arranged to have the ship met by six agents at the dock in Los Angeles. Agent Regan greeted the local agents at the dock, and decided to tail the suspects instead of effecting an immediate arrest. At Clark's "palatial" villa—rented for four hundred dollars per month, a sum significantly greater than most workers' entire monthly paycheck—they found a small quantity of liquor and arrested Clark and his two accomplices.[46] Clark's high living helped convict him in the newspapers. How else but bootlegging could a former cop earn such fabulous sums of money? The suspects were held on bail of ten thousand dollars each, although the only charge against them was "possession and transportation of a small quantity of liquor found in the palatial home."[47] Director Lyle traveled to Los Angeles to develop a conspiracy case against Clark while Whitney hunted for Thomas' partner, Roy Olmstead.

Chapter 5

On May 3, 1922, anti-Prohibitionists, led by several labor organizations, held a rally at Madison Square Garden calling for modification of the Volstead Act, barely two years old. Some ten thousand people came, undeterred by a downpour outside. Senator James Wadsworth, unable to attend, sent a letter, read to the assemblage, describing Prohibition as a "terrible mistake" aggravated by "an enforcement act so severe in its provisions that it is proving impossible of enforcement." Without providing details, he urged "that the whole Prohibition situation should be revised and a sane effort made to place it upon a respectable basis." Other speakers claimed the Eighteenth Amendment never would have passed if politicians had not gone "to sleep," refusing to believe a sufficient number of states would make it the law of the land. Loud cheers echoed through the arena when speakers claimed the right to drink alcohol as inalienable or a "physiological necessity." Even if all the country's drinkers could magically be exterminated and replaced with "Simon-pure Prohibitionists," "within two weeks the Mexicans would be on the Hudson River with a flock of mudscows and capture New York City," so weak was America's fiber without liquor.[1]

Olmstead was not one to hide from an arrest warrant, though he did take care to avoid capture for a week, allowing time to put some of his affairs in order. Whitney's agents raided the home of Thomas Clark's sister, finding dozens of cases, some in the basement, most in the high grass behind the small frame house. Whitney's agents arrested two men there, and Whitney claimed that he had seen Olmstead there himself. At five p.m. that same day, Olmstead was arrested in the office of his attorney, John Dore, and charged with "transportation of liquor." Importantly, he had not been arrested by Whitney, nor charged with a weightier offense, nor thrown into the Immigration Detention Center. The next morning, Roy Olmstead posted a one-thousand-dollar bail.

Whitney now had many suspects—stevedores from the freight yards, a dealer in used furniture, and a few others who seemed to be important operatives in Olmstead's smuggling ring—but the connections between the suspects were tenuous, based upon hearsay and circumstantial evidence. The fifty cases of booze found in the backyard of Clark's sister's house would seem damning, but the house was owned by relatives of Clark, none of whom lived there or had a connection to the smuggling operation. A big bust at Point Lobos, just south of San Francisco, netted eight men and fifteen cars, which Lyle insisted had to be a part of the Clark-Olmstead ring. He had been told the shipment had come from British Columbia, the seized cars had Seattle plates, and the fifteen hundred cases of liquor were all bonded, brand-name products—only Clark and Olmstead were known to deal in large quantities of such quality. After a short exchange of pistol shots, about two dozen men and one woman had fled.[2] Whitney put all of his men to finding the fugitives, surely suspecting that the woman was Elsie Potter, the one who kept Olmstead's books. He had to find her—and the books—to make his case.

When the federal grand jury convened on June 26, Whitney downplayed his hand to reporters, admitting his investigation into the ring operating between California, Seattle, and British Columbia was still "incomplete."[3] For his part, Lyle believed that some of the men in his custody were going to divulge important information. One suspected smuggler, upset that his employers had not gotten him out on bail, assured Lyle from his jail cell he could provide the key details about the "Seattle liquor ring" in exchange for a grant of immunity from prosecution, but Lyle passed on the offer, confident in the evidence he had collected.

Lyle's investigations in Los Angeles and San Francisco uncovered a few facts. The fast boats with which the smugglers had attempted to land their cargoes at Point Lobos had cleared Canadian customs with false manifests. The ships were "declared to have arrived in Mexican ports without liquor," according to the Mexican consul, "and obtained false clearance papers to show upon their return to British Columbia."[4] Lyle told reporters that, on the basis of the false manifests, he had asked the Canadian government to seize some of the boats engaged in this trade, but he knew that the Canadians were unlikely to expend much energy unless the matter was deemed detrimental to the Crown's interests.

Roy Olmstead confidently strode into court on July 7, 1922, dressed in a fine suit, offering a smile toward friends and foes, his preliminary hearing presided over not by a judge but by a U.S. commissioner; this was a not-uncommon occurrence given the growing length of the court docket. William Whitney explained that his men had tailed Olmstead to the house occupied by Thomas Clark's sister. Olmstead had not been apprehended there, but agents had found forty-eight cases of whiskey at the residence. The occupants of the home had been arrested, with Whitney charging that Olmstead had personally "conveyed [the] liquor" to them. Whitney hoped to establish a connection not just to the cases of liquor, but to Clark. Whitney charged both Clark and Olmstead with coordinating the shipment of alcohol confiscated in Los Angeles and Point Lobos, but offered no hard evidence, proffering Olmstead's arrest two years earlier as proof of his guilt.

Whitney then admitted that his star witness—a woman whose name he refused to divulge, an associate of the bootleggers who knew everything and could connect the conspirators—had disappeared. Whitney asked the court for a three-week continuance, though he admitted he was not absolutely certain he could locate the witness. The court asked him to detail what information, exactly, she would bring. Whitney refused to provide any specifics, claiming that releasing such information would harm the government's case. The U.S. commissioner immediately threw out the case and ordered Olmstead's one-thousand-dollar bail returned. Whitney vowed to haul Olmstead before the next grand jury.[5] But his complete defeat—with the dapper Olmstead, known by all of Seattle as a bootlegger on a massive scale, strolling out of the courthouse a free man—raised public doubt about the Seattle Prohibition Unit's competence and greatly boosted Roy Olmstead's arrogance in flouting the law. Whitney would not see the mystery woman again for a number of years. Whatever interest she had expressed in helping him had dissipated quickly because she had begun a relationship with Olmstead.[6]

The grant of suffrage and imposition of Prohibition, the aim of women activists for so long, left the groups claiming to represent women asking: What next? Only two years after its formation, the League of Women Voters questioned its necessity. Many women working in other organizations also questioned the need for the

LWV. Seeking to validate its existence, the League asked the WNRC to take the affirmative to the following question: "Resolved, that the League of Women Voters should be abolished." After a spirited debate among the members, Pauline Sabin declared that the question suggested the League "considers the question of its existence a debatable one," a point which the club would not help the League decide.[7]

Pauline Sabin revealed more of her thoughts on groups devoted solely to women's issues when she concurred with the decision of Theodore Roosevelt Jr., Acting Secretary of the Navy, to prohibit use of the Naval Radio Service to broadcast speeches made by members of the National Woman's Party at the dedication of their national headquarters in May 1922. Roosevelt declared that the naval radio system, the only network in those early days of radio with the capacity to broadcast across the entire country, should not be used for political purposes. Roosevelt feared that allowing the Woman's Party to use the radio system would encourage other politicians and political groups to insist upon fair access, also.[8]* Roosevelt's decision and his reminder that the Woman's Party was a political entity prompted President Harding to cancel his planned appearance at the ceremony for fear of appearing to endorse an agenda of which he was unaware. Pauline Sabin sent a telegram to Roosevelt, a former beau, commending his decision, which he appreciated almost as much as he took pleasure in the Woman's Party's disappointment, saying he regretted "that circumstances prevented me from saying what I really felt about them."[9]

Roosevelt did not spell out what he would say about the National Woman's Party and whether his seemingly negative attitude toward

---

* The Radio Act of 1927 set a standard along these lines by requiring radio, and later television, stations to grant equal time to candidates; that is, if one candidate or viewpoint was permitted on air, opposing candidates and viewpoints must be accorded the same privilege.

the group extended to women in general or just to women activists, but his cordial relationship with Sabin suggested he accepted women in politics at least so long as they worked within the mainstream parties. Sabin agreed, or at least she knew that setting themselves apart would only make it harder for women to be heard, would give men opportunities to exploit differences, and would weaken the political strength the women's groups held collectively.

The National Woman's Party, which claimed membership from the two major parties, was now seeking a twentieth amendment guaranteeing equal rights to women, bringing them on par with men in all matters. Many women, including Pauline Sabin, opposed this type of "blanket" amendment because it lacked specific definitions of equality, and failed to acknowledge that true equality would eliminate current protections for women in the workplace. The National Consumers League, a bipartisan group of men and women who had championed many of the workplace safeguards an equal rights amendment would dismantle, appointed Sabin, a longtime member, to the central committee responsible for arranging speaking engagements and educational sessions to promote opposition to the blanket legislation. Pauline hosted a gathering of three hundred women at Bayberry Land in July 1922 to hear Frances Perkins, the first woman appointed to an administrative position in the New York state government, speak on the subject.[10] Then in November 1922, Sabin presided over a conference that addressed the matter of "Why Women Oppose Blanket Legislation" and was sponsored by the National Consumers League.[11] The proposed amendment had little chance, but it foreshadowed the splintering of the gender-centric interest groups that had brought the Eighteenth and Nineteenth Amendments to passage. Gaining their political voices, through suffrage, meant women no longer had to huddle together, separate from men, for support. They could join the political mainstream.

The issue of equal rights arose, again, at the New York Republican Convention in September, when representatives of the National Woman's Party tried to take credit for a party plank calling for legislation that would abolish discrimination against women, primarily in the workforce. Pauline Sabin fired back, "We have been working on that plank for several months. It represents our work entirely," referring to Republican women.[12] The National Woman's Party had wanted to go further, admonished Sabin, hoping to force their blanket legislation, "which would wipe out with one stroke of a pen all the inequalities between men and women." She understood that differences in education, opportunity, physical strength, and familial roles, obligations, and expectations varied greatly, making the imposition of equal rights inherently unfair, for the time being. Protecting against discrimination demanded equal and fair treatment, but did not insist that women meet the same standards applied to men. Insisting on equal rights before women had gained equal opportunity and political footing might permit employers to create unattainable goals for women, holding them back.

In October 1922, Sabin was appointed to the executive committee of the New York Republican State Committee, and also joined the newly formed Women's State Executive Committee.[13] Using the pulpit afforded her by her position as president of the WNRC, Pauline praised Governor Nathan Miller's achievements over the past two years and advised, "Women who are really interested in welfare work in this State would do well to inspect" his record "along welfare lines." She contrasted Miller's record with that of his Democratic predecessor and opponent in the upcoming election, Al Smith. Miller had pushed through legislation establishing a juvenile court, securing additional money for treating the mentally ill and physically handicapped, training teachers for epileptics, assisting blind citizens to become self-supporting, and providing nurses to expectant mothers to improve infant care.[14] Sabin predicted women in the state and in Suffolk County, her home, would give Miller a big boost on Election Day.[15] Miller agreed, charging Smith and the Democrats with offering the "bunk promise to give the people rum," to which women would stand opposed.[16] Both Miller and Sabin were wrong; the women's vote was divided, just what Sabin had feared, and a wave of anti-Republicanism in the state sent Al Smith back to Albany for two more years.[17]

R oy Olmstead's ability to elude conviction spoke to the difficulties faced by Mabel Willebrandt, whose Department of Justice could not trust the evidence and testimony collected by the Prohibition Unit. She vowed, after Olmstead's first trial, to take a more active role in cases against large-scale smugglers; she would direct her district attorneys to strengthen relationships with Prohibition agents, would guide their collection of evidence, verify the reliability of witnesses, and ensure the proper execution of search warrants.

Mabel Willebrandt's high profile and party loyalty placed her in great demand as the 1922 congressional campaign season began. Her old patron, Frank Doherty, was working for Hiram Johnson's reelection, and believed that "women occupying a position as important as hers [would] become the vogue among club women and she no doubt would be much sought after and looked up to. She has the courage to express her opinions and I believe would have no hesitancy in doing so."[18] Willebrandt pledged to aid Johnson in whatever way possible.[19] No sooner had Johnson asked her to campaign in California, however, than she informed him that pressing matters—notably the Haar case, which concerned an extensive smuggling operation in the southern United States and the possible corruption of Prohibition agents—would prevent her from making the trip for another month. Doherty suggested Johnson talk to Harry Daugherty, the attorney general and Willebrandt's boss, to impress upon him the necessity of her trip, which would serve, also, to quell rumors that the Harding administration opposed Johnson's reelection because of his opposition to Harding's nomination in 1920.[20] Dinner at Hiram Johnson's Washington, D.C., residence secured Willebrandt's timely assistance. In advance of her first California speech, Senator Johnson told her, "You may be interested in knowing that you had two great opponents for the exalted position you present[ly] hold, Clara Shortridge Foltz and Gail Laughlin. Both of them are perniciously active against us in California. I do not fear ten thousand such with Mrs. Willebrandt with me."[21]

Mabel fulfilled her obligation to Johnson with a series of speeches to women's clubs in August and September. At the end of her tour, another old friend, James Pope, warned her about political affiliations that came with strings attached. Pope did not consider her affiliation with Johnson a problem, but he recommended she stay so busy with Justice Department work that she would have no time for "political missions."[22] While she was obligated to Johnson, Daugherty, and Harding for their roles in getting her into office, Mabel Willebrandt always gave her highest allegiance to the causes that mattered most to women. At a speech before the Women's Branch of the Republican Party in October 1922, she stated that the GOP stood "for those things that have promoted nationally, and in State government, the ideals in which women are largely interested—the preservation of the home, safeguarding the educational and other rights of childhood, promotion of business and the establishment of economic security."[23] Her knowledge and accomplishments gave her credibility, but so did her femininity, a quality her secretary noted as a sharp contrast to her predecessor, Annette Abbott Adams, whom she regarded as "rather masculine and so terribly cold."[24]

Her boss, Attorney General Harry Daugherty, certainly trusted Mabel Walker Willebrandt. He told Harriet Taylor Upton, "I'll put her up alongside any several men—(In fact I've just done so in a recent matter) and she comes out ahead from sheer reasons and judgments & convinces me too!"[25] The admiration went both ways. Willebrandt wrote in her diary, "He's the only one with <u>sand</u>." She was contrasting Daugherty with Treasury Secretary Andrew Mellon, titular head of the Bureau of Prohibition, whose friends had become entangled in bribery accusations. Mellon had asked Daugherty to intervene, but Willebrandt opined in her diary, "Why should the A.G. [pull] Mellon's chestnuts out of the fire?" perhaps expressing her own frustrations with the treasury secretary, whose subordinates in Savannah continued to impede the Haar investigation. "I hope he refuses to protect Mellon," she wrote.[26]

Willebrandt noted in her diary that her "self dependence" had grown such that she no longer felt the "inward terror at the magnitude" of the job. But while crediting herself for growing into her myriad responsibilities, she admitted moments of uncertainty, especially related to the "dread shadow of deafness." Her partial hearing loss was a huge secret, unknown to anyone at the Department of Justice, let alone her boss. She had developed multiple strategies to mask her disability, but whenever she received a compliment, she thought to herself, "Damn you, you think that <u>good</u>, do you know what then <u>could</u> I do if I weren't struggling under the most horrible handicap that you do not guess.' In other words if I could use in intellectual energy that extra attention, and nerve, and willpower that I <u>always</u> exert to even <u>keep the drift of what's going on</u> what couldn't I do? It cuts so deeply to be thought stupid or appear so because you haven't heard & can't therefore make the connection."[27] The only thing worse, to her mind, was the sympathy she would get if people knew.

Willebrandt secretly hoped her service in the Department of Justice would afford her the chance to become a federal judge. Unbeknownst to her, the idea was floated to Senator Hiram Johnson in early 1923.[28] Johnson asked the opinion of Frank Doherty, Willebrandt's champion, who hesitated at giving his recommendation—not for a lack of faith in her abilities, but for the perception that might attach to Johnson's endorsement of her. Doherty regarded Willebrandt as "industrious, level-headed and with great possibilities," but balked at naming someone only thirty-three years old to a lifelong post.[29] Doherty worried, also, that Johnson might be accused of pandering to women voters, which might raise questions about the political motivations of all of his judicial recommendations. Perhaps, Doherty offered, a few more years of government service would erase any doubts about her credentials and the justification of her appointment. While Willebrandt was expected to honor political obligations, it seemed the arrangement did not run both ways. The point was set aside after Harry Daugherty let it be known that he felt Willebrandt could do more good in her current position than as a judge.

As the possibility of a judgeship receded, Mabel was torn between a request from her parents to resign by the end of 1923 and loyalty to the job and to Harry Daugherty, who was beset by failing health and mounting scandals. Given the circumstances, she did "not feel in conscience or honor, I could resign and wish upon him the perplexity of choosing a woman substitute." She recognized her position as the domain of a woman, a sort of birthright accorded for the decades of women Prohibitionists who had brought the Eighteenth Amendment to realization. Her resignation, Mabel believed, would produce "a much more serious complex in choosing a woman assistant than in filling any of the places held by men. With the Republican Party in the condition it is today, of course it would have to be another woman." Her loyalty to Daugherty clearly included the the GOP and, by extension, President Harding, but she questioned whether Harding could be renominated amid the escalating financial scandals. She liked the president personally, but, unwilling to campaign on his behalf, she vowed to resign if he was renominated.

If Harding resigned, Willebrandt feared Herbert Hoover would win the Republican nomination, "in which case I would certainly resign. I owe something to Harding and Daugherty and Johnson but, thank Heaven, I owe nothing to Hoover, and I do not have personal respect for him enough to do any campaigning."[30] Her old ally James Pope recommended she hang on through the 1924 elections, increasing her recognition around the country, but most significantly in California, where she planned to return, and where, Pope hoped, she would run for office.[31] A few months later, Harry Daugherty, reeling from the suicide of his trusted ally Jess Smith amidst more rumors of scandal, asked Mabel Willebrandt to "stay by me—no one ever lost by staying by me. I'm not going to resign unless I completely collapse. You've done so wonderfully so much better than I believed any one could do that no one can fill your place."[32]

Pauline Sabin's loyalty to the Republican Party, reflected in the organization she helped found, the Women's National Republican Club, occasionally put her at odds with speakers brought to the club. In late 1922, Sabin had rescinded an invitation to William Anderson, the New York State superintendent for the Anti-Saloon League, after Anderson made a "slanderous" attack upon Senator James Wadsworth. Anderson had charged Wadsworth with supporting Al Smith in the governor's race in exchange for a promise of support from Tammany Hall, still regarded as the headquarters for New York's Democratic Party when Wadsworth ran for reelection in 1926.[33] Anderson had been scheduled to debate Wadsworth on the liquor question at the club in January 1923.

Looking ahead to the 1924 governor's race in particular, Charles Hilles stressed the importance of securing the women's vote by utilizing the skills of Mrs. Henrietta Livermore and Mrs. Pauline Sabin, who knew "the problem," which he characterized as exaggerating the "oscillations of the pendulum of politics unprecedently [*sic*] and unexpectedly."[34] To correct the situation, "women must be 'domesticated' in politics until they cease running wild, organization work must continue in season and out of season," the effort "as essential as any work we may undertake." Surely, Pauline Sabin would have encouraged Hilles to use *The Republican Woman*, a newsletter created by Sabin and Florence Wardwell, to reach women across the state.[35]

A few months later, Pauline Sabin questioned the faith placed in her, telling Hilles she could not "fathom" Mrs. Livermore's "attitude in some instances," her views differing to such a degree that Sabin judged, "One of us is certainly lacking in political acumen and I am beginning to think that I am the guilty one."[36] The admission could be read as a polite rebuke of Mrs. Livermore, one of Sabin's role models and one of the few suffragists who had proudly worked from within one of the established parties. Pauline's confession to Hilles suggested she knew which woman he would support, but the issue resolved itself when Livermore announced her resignation as chairwoman of the state's women's executive committee.[37] Charles Hilles advised George Morris, the state's party chairman, to ask for the input of the women's executive committee, keeping in mind that the woman selected to replace Livermore must be in tune with Morris and with "a real taste for politics, some experience at the game, enthusiasm to impart to others and the ability to organize."[38]

Days later, Pauline Sabin was named to the newly formed Women's Advisory Council to the Republican National Committee, a group first proposed two years earlier. Sabin and other women appointed to the advisory council, one from each state, could not be granted full status as members of the national committee, composed only of men, until the next national convention, which was a year off. As the title denoted, the women would offer advice to the committeemen from their respective states, and in doing so exert influence in the selection of delegates for the national convention in June 1924, where they fully expected to receive all rights and privileges accorded the men.[39] Sabin characterized the appointment as "a test rather than an achievement," explaining, "There are still many men who seem to think women merely wanted the right to vote, that now they have it, they will lose interest as if it were some fashion or a dress fad."[40] On the contrary, Sabin declared, "Women are taking politics seriously," and they were "going to stay interested, seriously interested, more than many men realize." Sabin did not naively believe women could "direct the political affairs of the nation," there being much to do, learning "the whole business from the ground up." Taking a page from her own experiences, she advised women to start at the bottom, learning the political "machinery" in district and county organizations, moving up to state committees and, then, onto the national scene, whether as candidates or leaders in the party. She felt "very strongly" that women should follow that path through the established political parties, "taking advantage of existing machinery, at least while we are educating ourselves politically, instead of trying to scrap what we find before we have anything adequate to put in its place." She had been told on several occasions by men that they expected little of women, assuming they would "do sudden, rash, illogical things." Staying within the parties would demonstrate to suspicious men that women were serious, willing to learn, and eager to help. Sabin was opposed to the single-issue organizations, predominantly female. Men would not take women seriously until they considered all legislation equally important. "If we are to help the organizations," Sabin instructed, "and have a part in them, we must take up the work of the organizations," performing, at first, "hard, quiet, efficient work, work of real value."[41] Seven months later, in February 1924, Sabin and her fellow Republican women adopted a resolution favoring the McGinnies Bill, which would grant men and women equal representation on state committees. "A woman's vote counts for as much as that of a man," Sabin declared, "and for that reason we should have equal representation."[42]

M abel Willebrandt's early efforts to bring down large-scale smugglers revealed a significant challenge: her Department of Justice was reliant on evidence and testimony collected by the Prohibition Unit, a Treasury Department agency over which she had no influence and whose employees had little, if any, law enforcement training. Compounding the disconnection between the two agencies, the Treasury Department sometimes assigned its Intelligence Unit to lead investigations when illegal income was identified and could be assessed tax penalties. A secondary mission of the Intelligence Unit concerned the investigation of Prohibition agents suspected of corruption, a situation that impeded investigations, because Prohibition agents were fearful were they were being surveilled while building cases against bootleggers and rumrunners. While she could not directly instruct Prohibition and intelligence agents in methods of investigation and the building of airtight cases, Willebrandt repeated her instructions to district attorneys, reminding them to guide agents in proper methods of evidence gathering and verification She hoped a spirit of cooperation would emerge, especially as the case of Willie Haar and his associates, known as the Big Four, in Savannah, Georgia, presented the opportunity for a big win.

However, Mabel Willebrandt received reports in early 1923 that more than a lack of cooperation in the Haar case was preventing it from going forward. An Intelligence Unit agent alleged systemic corruption among the Prohibition officials in Georgia and South Carolina, preventing the collection of evidence and the ability to catch smugglers in the act. The agent also accused U.S. Attorney Charles Donnelly with being a Wet, suggesting he was disinclined to dig deeper into the activities of men who could quench his thirst.[43]

Willebrandt's doubts about her underlings must have increased when she visited the federal prison in Atlanta, a few hours from Savannah and the planned future home of Willie Haar and his associates. Escorted by the prison warden and local officials, she took a "lovely moonlight ride" during which mint juleps were offered for refreshment. When liquor was offered to one of the top law enforcement officials in the country, Willebrandt must have been thinking about the difficulties she faced not just in Georgia with the Haar case, but in similar pockets of rebellion across the United States.

Seeking clarification and support, she contacted David Blair, commissioner for the Internal Revenue Bureau. Blair believed his agents understood the importance of cooperating with the U.S. Attorney's office in Savannah, and appreciated the interwoven relationship between tax evasion and liquor violation charges. He assured Willebrandt that any and all evidence gathered would be shared.[44] He noted, however, that his revenue agents "must adhere to their specific field" because their "commissions restrict them to it," and offered, "Other branches of the service, and other Departments, are especially concerned with matters beyond the scope of tax determination."[45] This was disingenuous, because he oversaw the Prohibition Unit as well as the Intelligence Unit, and had the authority to insist on cooperation between the two, had he desired to do so.

Blair's equivocating aside, information did pass from revenue and Prohibition agents into the hands of a special prosecutor sent by Willebrandt to Savannah to prepare the cases against Haar and his coconspirators. Linking the tax case to the liquor law violations sharpened charges of conspiracy against the Big Four.[46] In June 1923, Willebrandt's team succeeded in convicting two of the Big Four, and she was happy to have ended the "political chicanery and pull" that had kept the bootleggers out of jail for so long.[47] Two months later, a grand jury issued indictments against seventy-two of Haar's coconspirators.[48] To complete the conviction and end the criminals' appeal, Willebrandt had brought witnesses to Washington, away from Haar's influence peddlers, to tell the truth, finally. She took great pride in breaking through the corruption, which Willie Haar's brother had characterized as covering everyone in Washington except for Robert Crim, Assistant Attorney General for the Criminal Division, and that "damned woman." Willebrandt called "it some of the highest praise I have received."[49] Later, the agent from the Internal Revenue Bureau's Intelligence Unit who had refused to cooperate with the U.S. Attorney was prosecuted for his interference.[50]

Convictions like that of the Haars did much to slow smuggling and generated good press, but Mabel Willebrandt wanted cases with potential to establish legal precedents, giving definition to the National Prohibition Act, closing loopholes, leaving rumrunners and bootleggers with less room to operate and district attorneys with more charges and higher penalties to assess. The case of George Remus, a big-time bootlegger out of Cincinnati, provided just such an opportunity, his case having wound its way through the courts for two years by 1924. Remus had owned numerous distilleries, all of which obtained permits to produce liquor for industrial and medicinal purposes, but Remus sold much of the output illegally through a vast network stretching from Ohio across the Midwest and the South, using his former wholesale warehouses as distribution centers for smaller bootleggers. In late 1921, Prohibition agents had arrested Remus and several associates on permit violations. In April 1922, as a grand jury in Cincinnati convened to assess the charges against Remus and his associates, Harry Daugherty directed Willebrandt to conduct "any kind of legal proceedings, civil or criminal, including grand jury proceedings and proceedings before committing magistrates, which district attorneys now are or hereafter may be by law authorized to conduct."[51] The newness of the Volstead Act, recently amended for clarification on the finer points of enforcement, and the seriousness of big cases like Remus', warranted deeper involvement from an assistant attorney general than might usually be expected, a development that became more routine than extraordinary over time.[52]

In May 1922, Remus and his associates were found guilty of violating the National Prohibition Law, but they appealed.[53] The Circuit Court of Appeals finally affirmed Remus' conviction on the Prohibition violations in June 1923, sending Remus to the Atlanta Federal Prison for two years. Willebrandt was "exuberant" over the result. She made particular note of the court's opinion that it was not necessary to prove that the "acts alleged" to have been committed by Remus and his coconspirators were actually committed.[54] Remus set the wheels in motion for the illegal sale of liquor, authorizing over-production from his distilleries, providing trucks and railroad cars for distribution, maintaining contacts around the country to receive illegal liquor, receiving payments, and paying employees to perform the illegal work. The court's ruling, which would be applied in thousands of other cases, determined that Remus did not have to carry, make, or deliver illegal liquor to be guilty.

Willebrandt was pleased with the conviction, but it applied only to the production, sale, and distribution of liquor; Willebrandt had hoped to develop a case against Remus for failing to pay fees required under his permit to sell liquor legally. The judge in the Cincinnati case had quashed the counts regarding internal revenue statutes prior to the start of the trial, charging that the penalties imposed in the National Prohibition Act superseded any earlier laws and penalties concerned with liquor taxation.[55] Shifting gears, Willebrandt devised a strategy to charge bootleggers with income tax evasion on the profits they received from their illegal activities, an approach that would be used to its greatest success in bringing down Al Capone some years later.

Looking for additional means to weaken those networks, she

landed on the idea of issuing injunctions to halt operations at establishments where liquor violations occurred. She described the use of injunctions as a "very effective weapon for wholesale elimination of places running contrary to Prohibition law."[56] While happy to add another weapon to fight rumrunners and bootleggers, Mabel Willebrandt knew it should not have taken nearly three years since Prohibition's enactment to devise a system for effective enforcement.

I n the summer of 1923, Roy Olmstead's network of customers came to include some of Seattle's finest and most exclusive men's clubs. These clubs could afford to pay top dollar so long as what they received was top-shelf, making them, in other words, Roy's ideal clients. Though primarily a rumrunner, unloading his wares to bootleggers at the wharf, Roy had always done some bootlegging. Making regular deliveries to the Arctic Club, situated just around the corner from the Prohibition Unit's headquarters, certainly tickled the fancy of the Olmstead gang. It also encouraged a belief that anything was possible. Olmstead strode boldly about town, fashionably dressed, his pockets full of cash, and greeted anyone in his path, even fervent Prohibitionists, exhorting them not to take life so seriously. One reporter credited Olmstead with the "power that goes with good liquor, easy to get, and good money, easy to give."[57] The so-called King of the Bootleggers appeared to have the easy life to which he had always aspired.

But while the money was flowing in, it flowed out just as quickly. Employees' salaries, petty fines, and payments for boats and delivery vehicles consumed most of the revenue. Not making enough money to pay for his equipment, even as large sums passed through his business, provoked Roy. He began planning the moves it would take to build a more profitable business.

Anti-Prohibitionists achieved a victory in June 1923, when Governor Al Smith signed a bill repealing the Mullan-Gage Act, New York's "baby Volstead Act," which had committed the state to enforcement of Prohibition by state and local authorities. The law's revocation did not nullify the Volstead Act, but it did relieve local law enforcement agencies from pursuing cases or making arrests for violations of the national Volstead Act. Local authorities would cooperate with federal agents when formally asked, and were not to turn a blind eye to liquor violations when spotted, but police would not undertake concerted efforts to enforce Prohibition, and local courts would see their dockets cleared of any liquor-related cases. Women in particular took the news hard, feeling betrayed for believing Smith's promise to uphold the Eighteenth Amendment.[58]

On June 26, 1923, President Harding gave a speech, his last of any significance, offering strong statements on the importance of adhering to the laws of the land, particularly the Volstead Act, as "the most impressive mark of a civilized community." Harding stressed that disregard for the law was driven by a "small and a greatly mistaken minority" who believed the Eighteenth Amendment would be repealed. He saw the challenge not as an "issue between wets and drys, not a question between those who believe in Prohibition and those who do not," but "an issue of whether the laws of this country can be and will be enforced." The president vowed that they would, and he called on local and state governments who had abdicated their responsibilities for enforcement to the federal government to reconsider what could "prove one of the historic blunders of political management" and predicted that "neither of the great parties will see the time, within the lives of any who are now voting citizens, when it will declare openly for the repeal of the

Eighteenth Amendment."[59] Harding would be dead in two months, but Mabel Willebrandt felt hopeful at his vision.

M abel remained married to Arthur Willebrandt, but she had had no involvement with him for several years, the issue never discussed in public circles. In the intervening time, a relationship with her law partner, Fred Horowitz, had grown to be more than a friendship, but not something easily categorized by Mabel herself: "The years of association to you have been built up [sic] protons (positive electricity) and to me electrons (negative) and I further wonder whether yielding to our natural attraction would prolong or intensify our electrical energy—or lessen it."[60] Considering her feelings and intentions for Fred, Mabel, separated but still legally wed, wondered, "Why should society be so cruel. Why should I care what it thinks. Is that strength or numbness."[61] Contorting her emotions further, Mabel questioned, "Why should I so fiercely refuse at slavery. Why when I'm so tired & perplexed at the world so yearn to yield my wrists to manacles that I know I most fiercely hate." Clearly, her experience with Arthur Willebrandt had tainted her belief in the institution of marriage, but not in love and companionship, though neither conviction brought her any closer to a decision about Fred.

Mabel's mother, Myrtle, could read the doubts and unhappiness in Mabel's letters, and cautioned her daughter to be "very careful" in any decision to marry, referencing a potential suitor in the East Mabel had mentioned. Myrtle feared marriage to an "eastern" man would require her to "change inside," and chase "soap bubbles" of "ambition, wealth, power" that would float away. Myrtle advocated finding a man back in the West. Later that fall of 1923, Myrtle pressed her daughter to resign and return to California, suggesting Mabel's desire to stay in politics for the hope of a judgeship was not worth the sacrifice.[62] Mabel appreciated her mother's concern, but

the subtle pressure could not have made her choices any easier, especially as another court opening went to someone else. A few months
later, Mabel described herself as "a pawn fate had marked for a different move."[63]

Like a nagging sprain to his ankle, questions and concerns about
William Whitney reemerged in the fall of 1923, forcing him to
play defense, hobbling his efforts to manage his agents as he saw fit.
In early September, two agents of the Internal Revenue Bureau
(IRB), men nominally allied with the Prohibition Unit, began investigating Lyle and Whitney's office.[64] The IRB agents paid particular attention to requests for travel reimbursements submitted by
Whitney and his men, the agents combing through court records to
determine which payments had been made to agents of the unit.
They looked into the auditor's books, examined the warrants issued,
and even opened old case files looking for patterns that might betray
an intent to defraud the government. Director Lyle, while concerned, was the type to put his faith in the righteousness of the
work. His legal advisor, though, had as much trust in the "special
representatives" of the IRB as he did in the officers of the other law
enforcement agencies with whom his office worked, which was
none. Whitney and his trusted agents made no attempt to cooperate
with the investigation.

The hard line taken by Whitney only made his situation worse.
On September 11, 1923, the district attorney for San Francisco,
John Williams, arrived in Seattle to make a "detailed survey of
the law enforcement situation in the Pacific Northwest," focused
specifically on "obtaining closer cooperation between all federal
agencies and state, county, and city officials." Williams' presence
generated interest from reporters, who got him to announce, "There
is an abnormal situation in Seattle. I do not know of any place in the

United States where a similar situation is to be found. As I understand it, the office of the Prohibition director has a legal advisor, who in Prohibition cases fixes the crime the person arrested shall be charged with. This is unusual as the district attorney is the legal advisor of the Prohibition director."[65]

Williams' point seemed clear to the reporters: legal advisor William Whitney was an unnecessary cog in the wheel of justice; the Prohibition Unit needed to focus on catching the bootleggers and leave prosecutions to the Justice Department. Yet Williams must have noticed that Whitney and Revelle worked in lockstep. Revelle had too many cases and needed the extra support provided by Whitney, a trained attorney who kept abreast of the evolving legal situation surrounding Prohibition. On the other hand, Whitney did not trust most of his law enforcement partners in Seattle, seeing the U.S. Marshals' office rife with men who opposed Prohibition, the Coast Guard littered with drunken sailors, and the city and county police departments filled with wayward officers. Whitney had no interest in working with agencies he viewed as corrupt and rarely passed up an opportunity to impugn them.

Senator Wesley Jones, responsible for most of the federal patronage jobs in Washington State, including those of William Whitney and Roy Lyle, rushed to stem the rising tide of criticism, declaring, "Before any man was appointed in this state as United States Attorney, marshal, collector of customs, collector of internal revenue, or commissioner of immigration, each assured me that regardless of his personal views on Prohibition he would cooperate to the utmost in enforcement of the Prohibition law. I hope each has done so."[66] The senator did not rule out problems, but laid the responsibility at the feet of underlings—"deputies," he called them. "If any deputy is winking at or condoning violations of the law," Jones would not "hesitate to ask for his removal." The promise sounded good, but it avoided the issues surrounding Whitney—that his agents were overzealous, that false reimbursement requests for travel had been filed, that he had failed to cooperate with other agencies, and that one of his job titles, legal advisor, was unnecessary.

Before the IRB agents even submitted their report finding no direct evidence of wrongdoing,[67] Senator Jones claimed "that any interference with Director Lyle or his administration will be playing directly into the hands of wet interests in the state of Washington," and furthermore, "Sincere Drys have no complaint against the director." His preemptive statement suggested Jones was less concerned about the veracity of any charges against the Seattle Prohibition Unit office than he was about the perception of misconduct they created. The perceived threat to the Prohibition Unit brought forth a powerful response from the senator's allies in the war to end the consumption of alcohol. The WCTU, ASL, YMCA, Seattle Federation of Churches, and other religious organizations quickly sent telegrams of support for Director Lyle "and his agents" to Jones in Washington, D.C., with copies for the local papers.[68] These organizations rose as one to declare "a conspiracy exists to defeat enforcement of the Prohibition law in this state by discrediting federal officers in charge of enforcement."[69]

Roy Lyle had spent more than a year encouraging citizens to support the law of Prohibition. This was not exactly the same aim as William Whitney's.

Chapter 6

Pauline Sabin found a political ally in Senator James Wadsworth, their conservative values meeting on common ground, but her continued support of Prohibition put her on the opposite side of the fence from Wadsworth and even her own husband, though it did lend her credibility with most women, placing her in the role of trusted liaison between the two factions. In October 1923, the League of Women Voters asked Pauline, who had remained a member of the group even after her caustic statements about the LWV in 1922, to join a delegation slated to meet with James Wadsworth to "express to him satisfaction in his stand in favor of the World Court." Pauline supported U.S. membership in the World Court, but correspondence with Wadsworth showed a great deal of apprehension. She judged, "There is no doubt a very large majority of Republican women" who endorsed the World Court, feeling "it is a Republican measure," but Pauline felt "damned if I do and damned if I do not" regarding her participation in the meeting, perhaps sensing ulterior motives in the LWV's desire to have her participate. Wadsworth and the LWV clashed on several issues, dating back to his opposition to Prohibition, suffrage, certain child labor restrictions, and equal rights amendments, all measures overwhelmingly favored by women. Pauline asked Wadsworth, whom she had taken to calling "Jim," to give her "some general idea of what you are going to say to them because it is needless for me to say I'm going to stand by you, but I do not relish the idea of having them spring something on me for which I am unprepared!!!" Any advice or warning from Wadsworth went unrecorded, but Sabin, already politically astute, sensed the best way forward was through the middle. She would join the delegation "as an individual, not as the President of the Women's National Republican Club or as the Associate member of the National Republican Committee," begging the organization's "cooperation in making this fact understood should any publicity be given out on this matter."[1]

The meeting between the LWV delegation and Wadsworth appears to have gone off without a hitch, but just days later Pauline reported to Jim on growing agitation over the child labor amendment. The Women's National Republican Club had not proffered an opinion on the amendment, but Pauline knew the membership was split, with all opposed to child labor, but many "equally opposed toward cluttering up the Federal Constitution in any more amendments." Before someone or some group asked the club's position, Pauline wanted Jim Wadsworth's opinion on the proposed amendment and on how the WNRC could best state its position. If the club came out publicly opposing the amendment, a position held by Wadsworth and many leading Republicans, "we will undoubtedly have many resignations from the club, and have most of the women's organizations down on us and it seems to me we must have something to offer in its place."[2]

Wadsworth believed the child labor amendment was unnecessary, since all but a few states had their own child labor laws, and he recommended instead that groups endorsing child labor legislation attack the states where none existed. On a deeper level, Wadsworth opposed the amendment because it sought to impose a "police statute into the Constitution." Wadsworth charged, "That is exactly what we did in the case of the Eighteenth Amendment and we made an awful mistake," enacting the only amendment granting the federal government police powers, a license which had existed only for investigation of mail fraud previously.[3] The WNRC, clearly influenced by Pauline and her correspondence with Jim Wadsworth, took a diplomatic stance, issuing no opinion on the child labor amendment, allowing members, as individuals, to choose their side.[4]

Wadsworth teamed with a Democratic counterpart, Representative Finis Garrett of Tennessee, to propose that any future amendments to the Constitution must be ratified a second time if changes in a state legislature had occurred since the first vote.[5] Supporters of the Wadsworth-Garrett measure suggested the Eighteenth and Nineteenth Amendments, both of which Wadsworth opposed, might have failed if the proposed bill had been in effect. Legislative bodies, "composed of comparatively few men," judged Wadsworth, could not be expected to withstand "the modern machinery of propaganda" when its full weight was brought down upon them.[6] Wadsworth's references to "propaganda" were directed at the ASL, WCTU, and similar single-issue organizations that beat state legislators over the head with threats of public shaming when their votes were made public, a common practice during the fight to get the Eighteenth Amendment passed. Few men could withstand charges of opposing family stability in favor of the saloon. Similarly, proponents of a child labor amendment threatened political retribution.

The Wadsworth-Garrett proposal moved in fits and starts, from subcommittee to committee hearings in both the Senate and the House, with discussion extending from January 1923 into the spring of 1924. Pauline Sabin traveled to Washington, D.C., along with

Alice Chittenden, who had replaced her as president of the WNRC, to submit to a House committee conducting hearings on the amendment the results of a poll taken at the club. Chittenden provided the testimony, reporting that an overwhelming majority of the club's membership, which drew women from thirty-seven states, supported the Wadsworth-Garrett amendment, seeing it as restoring stability to the Constitution, which had undergone too many additions of late, and granting the people, not state legislatures, greater influence in the constitutional process.[7]

The Wadsworth-Garrett amendment's proposition concerning the requirement that one house of the state legislature be elected after the U.S. Congress submitted an amendment to the states for ratification left many scratching their heads. Wadsworth argued that state legislators elected prior to congressional approval of an amendment did not reflect current realities in a constantly changing political landscape where voters might have selected different candidates if they had known legislators would consider certain amendments.[8] This argument failed with many congressmen, who observed that change was inevitable and trying to stay current meant you might never get ahead. People also misconstrued the Wadsworth Garrett provision as allowing a popular vote to decide an amendment's fate after a legislative vote. That provision had grown from Wadsworth's experiences in his home state, where popular opinion, dominated by New York City's wetness, had failed to overcome ratification of the Eighteenth Amendment by the state legislature, dominated by Drys from upstate, rural districts. Wadsworth-Garrett's attempt to allow for second chances smacked of sour grapes, dooming its passage in Congress, but its illumination of excessive calls for constitutional amendments appeared to stymie the efforts of those supporting the child labor and equal rights proposals.

Shortly after the defeat of the Wadsworth-Garrett amendment proposal, the movement to draft a child labor amendment arose, much in the way Wadsworth had warned; the movement attempted to put into the Constitution strictures governing the ages at which children could be employed and the types of industries in which they could work. The senator walked a fine line trying to explain his opposition, which was not based on the intent of the amendment— for he found no fault with protecting children—but on the manner in which protection would be mandated, regulated, and enforced by the federal government, overreaching its authority and the intent of the founding fathers. The proposed child labor amendment, much like the Eighteenth and Nineteenth Amendments, were "whittling at the structure framed by the founders of this Government," warned Wadsworth, and "if we whittle long enough, we will destroy it."[9]

When the movement to draft a child labor amendment failed, many women blamed its downfall on James Wadsworth, who could not convince women that he did not oppose suffrage, Prohibition, and protection of children out of misogyny, but on constitutional grounds, where he saw states holding the authority to determine what happened within their borders. Most women did not agree, failing to see how a patchwork of differing laws and conditions from state to state best served half of the population. Pauline Sabin, though very much a Wadsworth supporter, was probably concerned about the same thing.

While the political positions of Sabin and the WNRC remained in nearly constant debate, Pauline did take a moment's respite to enjoy a significant achievement, the opening of a new clubhouse for the WNRC in February 1924. Having outgrown two temporary locations, the Women's National Republican Club had purchased a permanent home in May 1923, in the heart of one of Manhattan's best shopping districts and convenient to Grand Central Terminal and Penn Station.[10] Club members from thirty-eight states had subscribed $257,000 in bonds for the building's purchase.[11] Mrs. Warren Harding had purchased the first bond.[12] Pauline Sabin regarded the building and its acquisition as a "milestone in the history of feminism," the building "indicative of the permanency and importance of the place which women are achieving in political affairs." When the new headquarters opened, the five-story building contained meeting rooms, a library, a lounge, two dining rooms, and fourteen bedrooms for visiting guests, all rooms decorated with early American furnishings, evocative of the Federalist period, Pauline's skills as an interior decorator on elegant display.[13]

At its opening day reception on February 11, 1924, the new home of the Women's National Republican Club hosted sixteen hundred people. The following day, President Coolidge, the vice president who had become president upon Harding's death, attended a reception at the club, and was greeted by more than one thousand people on the street outside.[14] Belying his moniker, "Silent Cal," the president did not remain mute while at the club, taking tea and chatting with members, impressed with the headquarters, the organization, and its president, Pauline Sabin.[15]

In early 1924, Mabel Willebrandt learned she had been denied another appointment to the federal bench, but she could live with it, knowing she would have had to compromise her integrity to get the position. Hiram Johnson had suggested she go to California's junior senator, Sam Shortridge, and ask for his endorsement, hinting that placing herself in Shortridge's debt would seal the deal. Willebrandt told Johnson, "Ten judgeships would not be worth it. I have to respect at least anyone of whom I will ask a favor." She did not regret her decision, but missing another opportunity to return to California and her family hurt.

Attorney General Harry Daugherty had managed to hold on to his office into early 1924, despite numerous calls for his resignation amid a new scandal involving a speck of a place called Teapot Dome in Wyoming. Daugherty vowed to fight, calling Mabel Willebrandt back to Washington from a conference in Chicago. Willebrandt decided that President Coolidge was owed, if not allegiance, a certain amount of faith, since he had asked Daugherty to stay on after Harding's death despite being fully aware of the enemies facing the attorney general. Willebrandt felt that Coolidge would be "a yellow livered, dishonorable craven" if he failed to give Daugherty all his support. Regarding the scandals that swirled around Daugherty, Willebrandt declared that the attorney general "had no more official opportunity to know of the mistakes of the administration for the past few years than Coolidge did." Rather, she charged Coolidge with being "closer, officially, to the mistakes being made" than Daugherty because the vice president had greater access to Harding and his cabinet than the attorney general did. (In fact, Harding and Coolidge had very little interaction, Harding remaining close to Daugherty and the rest of the "Ohio gang" that had secured him the presidency.)

Willebrandt was inclined to stay on, believing Coolidge had an excellent chance for reelection and fearing her departure would send a political message damaging to the Republican Party.[16] Two days later, her inclination had changed, and she told her parents if Daugherty was forced to resign, she would follow suit rather than work with those who'd brought down her boss, a man who had earned her trust through continued support and confidence in her abilities. Willebrandt's loyalty to Daugherty blinded her to the facts; the attorney general and his cronies had taken advantage of their positions to secure financial gain at public expense. Less than two months later, evidence mounting against him, Daugherty resigned, admitting nothing. As per her earlier vow, Willebrandt resigned, unofficially.

Harlan Fiske Stone assumed the position of attorney general on April 9, 1924, and promptly asked Mrs. Willebrandt to continue in her work. Loyal to the cause she had inherited, she agreed, though she judged Stone "not so loyal nor lovable a man as Mr. D."[17] She agreed to a request from her old boss to speak at a women's club meeting in Marion, Ohio, Warren Harding's hometown, in support of Daugherty's bid to be a delegate to the Republican National Convention—he hoped Mabel's appearance would demonstrate that he had not been "crooked"—but she did not relish the opportunity. She was tired. In the previous weeks, she had made numerous speeches in the Northeast, prepared two cases for the Supreme Court, and appeared before a congressional hearing in addition to her usual workload; she was working so much that her secretary took on the task of writing Mabel's parents on her behalf.[18] The appearance for Daugherty added another chore, but, more than that, she was fed up with people who instead of being "for Prohibition are for politics first." Daugherty had given Willebrandt free rein to pursue enforcement, but others—Roy Haynes, the Prohibition commissioner; Wayne Wheeler, head of the ASL; and Andrew Mellon, treasury secretary and nominal head of the Internal Revenue Bureau—played a game, each trying to hold on to his place on the board, often at the expense of sound policy. Willebrandt charged, privately, "More skullduggery can be unearthed [in the Treasury Department] than in all Washington put together."[19] Willebrandt chose to remain as assistant attorney general to serve the greater good, rather than personal ambition, in the hope that Washington culture would change, and believed that if vice were to be eradicated "women must use the scrubbing brush and soap."[20]

After elections for the New York state assembly in the late fall of 1923, in which the Republicans had lost several seats, Charles Hilles proposed a meeting among party leaders to set a course of action, not only for the upcoming legislative session, but for the 1924 elections. The meeting would select the "Big Six" delegates, as Hilles called them, to the national convention, with two positions reserved for women, one from the New York City area and one from upstate.

Hilles advised leaders from the southern area to talk with their "women associates" to gain a consensus, but he clearly favored Pauline Sabin. Similarly, he saw Henrietta Livermore as the logical choice from upstate.[21] Hilles appreciated Sabin's political acumen and value to the party, regardless of her sex, but he was, at heart, a politician and hoped the appearance of diversity would define the Republican Party as the more inclusive. After the "Big Six" delegates, including Pauline Sabin, were set, Hilles proposed the selection of alternate delegates, who would also attend the convention, representing the diversity of the state of New York; he suggested "colored," Jewish, and Irish representatives, and also allowed political bosses in Syracuse, Buffalo, and Albany to offer candidates. He recommended that Sabin be among those consulted in framing the party platform, which Hilles advised should focus solely on national issues, with the hope that much of it would serve as the basis for the platform adopted at the national convention, a not-unreasonable hope given New York's influence upon national elections, whether it was the production of political leaders or its large electorate.[22]

While Hilles' "rainbow" coalition might have given a picture of unity, campaign efforts divided along gender and racial lines. Sabin spearheaded the party's drive to bring women to vote for Republican candidates.[23] Her status meant men in the party sought her advice on women's issues, their views on matters of general interest, and the selection of women for roles in the party leadership and the discussion of candidates and strategy.[24] Pauline appreciated the idea behind dividing the electorate into distinct groups, securing votes by addressing the unique interests of each group, but she knew, if women were to play a larger role in party politics and leadership, they needed to be more than a special interest group. Unfortunately, stepping ahead of women's issues proved difficult, even for someone as politically astute as Pauline Sabin.

The taint of Prohibition touched Pauline Sabin on April 4, 1924,

when Izzy Einstein and Moe Smith, perhaps the most famous Prohibition agents in the country, raided a garage she owned, seizing
fifteen thousand dollars' worth of liquor. The raid seems to have
occurred by accident; the agents were merely looking for a parking
space when they were tipped off that the garage "was full of liquor,"
at which point they entered and found Samuel Carter, the Sabins'
chauffeur, who said he alone owned the liquor.[25] Despite Carter's
claim of sole responsibility, a newspaper saw fit to criticize Pauline,
calling her a "misrepresentative of the nobler class of women,"
who could be "aptly termed the representative of the bob-haired,
bandit Mrs. Cooney [a convicted bootlegger] and other women
criminals or law-breakers of the Commonwealth, by her avowed
advocacy of opposition to the law."[26] Despite her association with
many anti-Prohibitionists, Pauline had always supported Prohibition publicly. Strangely, the newspaper did not assign any responsibility for the liquor to Charles Sabin, who openly *opposed* Prohibition.
A week later, the same newspaper printed a halfhearted retraction
of its criticism after "a friend" reported a "probability" that Mrs.
Sabin was unaware of the liquor in her garage. The paper offered an
apology "for the injustice done the accused," if indeed Sabin did not
know about the liquor in her garage.[27] The paper did not, however,
mention Pauline's support of Prohibition, leaving readers to wonder,
perhaps, where she stood. For her part, Pauline never addressed any
of the paper's claims.

Nothing further about Carter's arrest appeared in the papers and
any stain attaching to Pauline appears to have washed away, but the
criticism signaled her arrival as a recognized party leader.

The success Roy Olmstead was enjoying did not go unnoticed.
William Whitney and his agents had been busy interrogating
men arrested for peddling bottles of alcohol or for transporting

small amounts, and were trying to connect those "bottlemen" to their suppliers. The assembled evidence, much of it hearsay, indicated a large, well-organized conspiracy for distributing liquor throughout the Pacific Northwest. Conspiracy charges, as Whitney well knew, carried the maximum penalties under the Volstead Act. The key was to convict what Whitney called "the higher-ups," the executives of the operation, and he had a plan to do so: force enough of the petty criminals to testify to build up a body of evidence. Of all the men engaged in transporting and selling liquor, Whitney explained, "there are but a few men now engaged in the liquor business who are still importing, and doing their own distribution." Refusing to offer names, Whitney declared, "Our office is rapidly closing the net upon some of the biggest men now engaged in this character of law violations."[28]

The reappearance of "Miss Potter," the bookkeeper whom William Whitney hoped would bring Roy Olmstead to his knees at the 1922 trial before her mysterious disappearance, would have brightened prospects of convicting the "King of the Bootleggers" in 1924, if she had not emerged from hiding on the arm of Olmstead. Whether Elsie Potter had told Roy of her conversations with William Whitney is uncertain, but her relationship with Olmstead had begun about the time she vanished. Had she purposely led Whitney astray, offering false hope, at the instigation of her lover, or had Olmstead, upon learning of Elsie's betrayal, banished her, only to fall for her charms? In either case, they had become inseparable. Roy Olmstead's marriage had been over for a few years, probably since his first arrest in early 1920. Viola Olmstead had been satisfied to be the wife of a police lieutenant, not one of Seattle's most infamous rumrunners. Viola filed for divorce in January 1924, "alleging cruelty," bringing to an end their fifteen-year union.[29] Despite her discomfort with Roy's illegal activities, Viola wanted her share of the money he had made as well as custody of their two daughters. According to the state's community property laws, her interests were defined as "equal and unified," so her share amounted to what she could prove he owned, a difficult task; few documents showed the value of boats, trucks, and warehouses owned by Roy or the volume of profits derived from his illegal activities.[30] Whatever he offered, it proved sufficient. Viola disappeared from public life and Roy married Elsie a few months later.

Roy Olmstead needed more men for his burgeoning enterprise, but they needed to be men with talent. The emerging commercial radio industry and the potential uses of such technology interested Olmstead, and led him to Alfred Hubbard. Only recently escaped from his awkward teenage years, Al had built himself a reputation as a boy wonder of technology, backing up his moniker with a host of claimed inventions, including a form of an X-ray machine. Despite his slovenly dress, pockmarked face, and ill manners, the young man's confidence impressed Olmstead, who wanted Hubbard to build him a radio station. The two men, along with Olmstead's attorney, Jerry Finch, established the American Radio Telephone Company with the aim of building a one-thousand-watt broadcasting station in Olmstead's house, "because that was the only real estate any of us owned." Hubbard installed a studio in the building where Finch had his office.[31] They adopted the call letters KFQX and the station became operational in the spring of 1924, Elsie soon broadcasting, from the home she shared with Roy, bedtime stories for kids, using the pseudonym "Aunt Vivian."[32]

Mabel Willebrandt continued to involve the Justice Department in attempts to resolve the antiquated community property statutes in California. The DOJ in March 1922 had issued, certainly at Willebrandt's behest, a ruling that spouses residing in those handful of states referred to as "community property states" could file separate tax returns, a backhanded way of establishing a woman's legal right to her half of the marital estate. California, unfortunately, was not named as a community property state, given the unsettled nature of its definition of community property. The legal wrangling persisted until the end of 1923, when a superior court in Oakland, California, held "that the rights of the wife in her half of the community property are absolute . . ."[33] This ruling had enabled Senator Samuel Shortridge, whose sister Clara Foltz had been a leader of the California women's movement for decades, to threaten "Internal Revenue Commissioner Blair . . . to recognize the California community property law in the matter of federal inheritance and the submission of separate tax returns," or the senator would call for a thorough investigation and a fifty-million-dollar refund to the taxpayers of his home state.[34]

On March 27, 1924, Attorney General Harry Daugherty, perhaps repaying the loyalty of Mrs. Willebrandt, issued a statement that the federal government would recognize California as a community property state, ignoring the enormous tax implications of such a position. Secretary of the Treasury Andrew Mellon, on the same date, stated that henceforth, California would be governed by the same federal treasury regulations as applied to other community property states, allowing a wife to file a separate tax form and claim half of the gross income from the marriage.[35]

A few months later, however, the new attorney general, Harlan Stone, indicated he would reverse Daugherty's decision on California's status as a community property state because estimates of rebates due for alleged overpayment of taxes had grown to $130,000000, a sum large enough to bankrupt the federal government. But when Stone issued his final decision soon thereafter, he actually supported the opinion offered originally by Mabel Willebrandt. Stone told her he had started his study on the matter from the opposite position, but came around to her view, a fact that gave Willebrandt much satisfaction. Stone's "official" decision left "mine in full force and effect as the major pronouncement on the subject," Mabel proudly proclaimed to her parents.[36] Later courts and legislation would support Mabel's opinion and Stone's agreement, allowing for future challenges in states with unequitable community property laws. Having achieved their goal and feeling magnanimous, the women of California and Senator Shortridge dropped their demand for tax restitution, a concession to the greater good rooted in the hope of a brighter future for women.

Relieved that one victory had been achieved, Mabel Willebrandt refocused on taking down rumrunners. Uncertainty about U.S. rights to halt and seize ships on the high seas and a lack of cooperation from Canadian authorities had hamstrung efforts to make a dent in the rum rows scattered along America's shoreline, but Willebrandt saw a glimmer of hope in late 1923, when the U.S., British, and Canadian governments agreed on a treaty designating an acceptable zone in which the Coast Guard could board British or Canadian vessels and seize illicit cargo.[37] In addition, Canada and the United States agreed to share information on vessels cleared by the Canadians, but suspected of smuggling; Canada agreed to deny clearance to any vessel that it determined could not withstand the journey to its stated destination, answering charges that smugglers claimed destinations that realistically could not be reached given the size and fuel supply of their vessels.[38] For the first time, Mabel Willebrandt thought the smuggling of liquor into the United States could be stopped, as long as the federal government provided sufficient manpower and equipment to patrol the coasts.

Much of the Republican leadership supported the continuation of Prohibition, but some in the party, notably James Wadsworth and Nicholas Murray Butler, with both of whom Pauline Sabin had worked, challenged the law, first on its constitutionality and, by 1924, on its ineffectiveness. Butler became increasingly vocal, charging Prohibition had done nothing but "endow the liquor business by setting it free from taxation and from any measure of public control." Such statements resulted in calls for his resignation as president of Columbia University and demands that Republican leaders denounce him. The New York Women's Committee for Law Enforcement asked Pauline Sabin to give her views of Butler's statements and her own on the Eighteenth Amendment. Sabin said she favored "enforcing the law of the land, more than that, I am in favor of and advocate law observance," but she would not denounce Butler.[39] Perhaps it was in deference to Charles Sabin, a Democrat, who had supported the repeal of Prohibition almost from its inception, and served as an officer for the Association Against the Prohibition Amendment (AAPA), a group to which Butler belonged. The AAPA was composed, primarily, of rich men from both parties, who saw Prohibition infringing on individual liberties, establishing an impossible goal of imposing moral purity on an unwilling public. The organization's emphasis on the loss of revenue from the now-defunct alcohol tax and increases in personal income tax tarred the association with the interests of an "eastern elite," keeping the organization's influence low.[40] It is surprising no one ever asked Pauline about the opposing views of her husband on Prohibition, but they appeared to have no effect on the couple's relationship. Demonstrating her open mind and generosity, Mrs. Charles Sabin offered to serve on the General Reception Committee for the 1924 Democratic National Convention, organized in part by Charles.[41]

The nomination of President Calvin Coolidge for the 1924 campaign was not a foregone conclusion; although he'd unexpectedly become president a year earlier, his knowledge of and possible involvement in the corruption of the Harding administration was a question mark. Pauline Sabin, however, had no doubts, believing

Coolidge "a man of integrity and simplicity" the equal of whom had not been seen since Abraham Lincoln.[42] In fact Coolidge was proven innocent of any connection to the Harding scandals, and his famous reserve held an undefinable appeal for Republicans eager to shed the boisterous, unfettered abandon of Harding's "Ohio gang."

Pauline Sabin expected a large turnout from women in the 1924 elections; it was their first real opportunity to vote on a large scale, and they were eager to opine on a broad range of political issues. "The erroneous idea that women should be interested only in measures that affect women and children and not inform themselves as to the other political issues is defeating the very reason we wanted the vote—so as to take sex out of politics."[43] Harriet Taylor Upton, vice chairwoman of the Women's National Republican Executive Committee, identified 125 women as full delegates and twice that number as alternates, both significant increases over the number of women in attendance at the 1920 convention.[44] Pauline Sabin, a member of the party's national committee, was counted among them, along with Mabel Willebrandt, attending not as a delegate but as the highest-ranking woman in President Coolidge's administration.[45] The women's greatest hope was approval of their resolution for equal representation on the national committee. The Democrats had granted equal status to women in 1920, but the Republicans had neglected to make similar accommodation, failing to foretell the impending passage of the Nineteenth Amendment.

Before the convention got into full swing, Sabin hosted a tea, at the Shaker Heights Country Club in one of Cleveland's toniest suburbs, for prominent women from around the country to cement their call for full representation on the national committee and equal committee representation.[46] The New York delegation unanimously elected Sabin the state's associate member to the Republican National Committee, with Charles Hilles as the full member, and knew that Sabin's "associate" label would soon fall away.[47] Her "as-

sociate" status, a designation harkening to the days before passage of
the Nineteenth Amendment, was removed a day later when the Republican National Committee formally approved equal representation, the announcement generating loud applause and cheering from
both women and men on the convention floor.[48] Almost immediately following upon that vote, Sabin was appointed to the convention's subcommittee on policies and resolutions, which would frame
the policy language for the party platform.[49] A final honor and recognition of her ascent in the party came at the end of the convention, when Sabin was appointed to a "special body" to choose an
executive committee of fifteen members to serve as the staff to assist
the Republican National Committee chairman, William Butler, in
managing the Coolidge presidential campaign. By virtue of her role
in helping select the executive committee, Sabin would also serve on
that committee.[50]

The party conventions functioned as a good demarcation point
to assess the advances of women in politics. Anne O'Hagan Shinn,
a columnist for the *New York Times*, attended both the Democratic
and Republican conventions and observed many changes since the
conventions of 1920. In 1920, women and their exuberance at inclusion proved a novelty, but in 1924, they were "taken for granted as
normal political people," an evolutionary step welcomed by Shinn.
She listed the increased numbers of delegates, committee memberships, candidates, elected officials, and political appointees, recognizing that though some designations existed only as tokenism, even
that represented forward motion. "If women had come into politics
full-grown, brain-children like Minerva, perhaps their list of offices
and emoluments wouldn't seem very impressive," Shinn conceded,
"but for four-year-olds, kindergartners, toddlers, it doesn't make
such a bad showing. And it is even better as promise than as accom-
plishment."[51]

n early June 1924, the Prohibition Unit caught a break—a "fluke," Roy Lyle called it when told by William Whitney.[52] Whitney had met a man named Richard Fryant, who had worked for various telephone companies and developed the unique skill of tapping phone lines and listening to the conversations.[53] As luck would have it, Fryant knew Harry Behneman, whose odd jobs had afforded the opportunity to familiarize himself with the telephone exchange of the Henry Building, where Roy Olmstead's office coordinated liquor deliveries. The prospect of listening to Olmstead's unguarded conversations, of learning the entire conspiracy from top to bottom, including dates, times, and locations of deliveries, must have made William Whitney quiver with anticipation. It would provide the evidence of conspiracy that would put Olmstead and his cohorts away for a long time. Without hesitation or approval from Lyle, Whitney hired Fryant as an agent to tap Olmstead's phone and "gather evidence."[54] And Fryant asked Behneman to assist.

At nine a.m. on June 25, Fryant and Behneman entered the basement of the Henry Building and Fryant wrapped two wires around the lugs of the main Olmstead phone connection. The pair of wires led to a single earpiece.[55] Neither man had thought to bring a chair or a desk or much in the way of pencils and paper. Fryant listened first, and heard an order for liquor being placed. Another followed quickly.[56] Perched on boxes, they took turns: one wearing the earpiece, the other scribbling notes on the few sheets they had, filling every inch. Whitney stopped by and listened in that day, excited at what he heard.

Acting on information gathered that first day, two of Whitney's agents staked out the alley running behind the A-1 Hotel in downtown Seattle. At about three p.m., a car dropped Myer Berg, a top

Olmstead man, at the hotel's rear entrance and drove off. A second car pulled up as Berg reemerged in time to receive two packages of whiskey, which Berg carried inside. Having seen enough, one of Whitney's men walked over to the two bootleggers in the car and informed them they were under arrest. The men jumped out of the car and ran, the agent shooting after them to no avail. While the two made good their escape, Myer Berg walked back out of the hotel and into the arms of the two Prohibition agents.

Fryant and Behneman learned about the bust before Olmstead did; they were listening in as one of the men who had gotten away called his boss's office, blurting, "They got the load." A feeling of power must have come to the wiretappers. Even though the first afternoon's work had produced mixed results, they were now inside the biggest liquor ring in Seattle. But problems ensued. Transcribing the conversations word for word demanded more earpieces and more writers, but Fryant was reluctant to bring in another agent. Further, the conversations were shot through with nicknames, slang, and messages predicated upon mutual understanding. Worse, quite often neither Fryant nor Behneman could positively identify a particular caller. After a few days, Fryant told Whitney that they needed help in creating the necessary documentation to corroborate their evidence. Whitney ordered Fryant to meet with his wife, Clara Whitney, who had been trained in dictation.[57] Every second or third night, Fryant would give her his notes and she would begin to transcribe them into legible accounts. When time allowed, she then asked Fryant to read over her handwritten copies to make sure they were accurate.

On June 25, Roy Olmstead met with one of his coconspirators, Mark Fleming, to purchase some insurance. Fleming knew that Assistant District Attorney Clifford McKinney, Tom Revelle's second in command, wanted to get in on the liquor money. McKinney, tall and thin with the charm of the boy next door, had indicated he was willing to sell information about Whitney's unit, with which his office worked so closely, to the King of the Bootleggers. Roy handed Fleming three thousand dollars for McKinney.[58]

John McLean, Olmstead's dispatcher, warned him on July 1, "The Feds are watching the place," to which Olmstead replied, "Well, they might as well let down. They can't buck this gang. We are too strong for them." Olmstead's confidence took a hit the following day when Whitney's agents raided one of his warehouses. Olmstead wondered, "It seems strange that they got wise to that place so quick." McLean suggested they have the telephone company look over the lines, as they might have been tapped. Olmstead offered, "No, I don't think so; I don't see how that can be done."[59]

To be safe he brought in a repairman from the phone company to search for taps on the operation's phone lines. The repairman found and removed taps attached to three lines, but Olmstead called him the next day to report that the phones had been tapped again. It did not occur to Olmstead to question how the taps had been discovered without discovering the tappers; either Fryant and Behneman were out when the repairman arrived or an arrangement had been made to deceive the bootlegger. He decided to disconnect the primary number used to receive orders and directed one of his lieutenants to contact all customers in person and tell them not to use the line any longer.[60] Despite the concern over taps, Olmstead's men continued to use phones, some with new numbers. Perhaps the rumrunner believed the cryptic conversations, full of nicknames, numbers, and abbreviations, contained little that eavesdroppers could decipher.

On July 14, Harry Behneman went to William Whitney and demanded payment for his services or he would quit and sell what he knew to Olmstead. Whitney was confident he had no further need for Behneman's expertise now that the operation was up and running. Whitney offered him fifty dollars and told him to do as he pleased.[61] Behneman departed and, unnoticed, took his notes with him.

Chapter 7

Almost from its enactment, people questioned whether Prohibition could work. Four years in, Mabel Willebrandt observed that passage of the Eighteenth Amendment had brought "one bad effect," sowing the seeds of its possible ruin. Before the Eighteenth Amendment, twenty-three states had enacted Prohibition within their borders, and even those states without any restrictions on the manufacture, distribution, or sale of alcohol had organizations educating its citizenry on the dangers of alcohol to the family and society. After the amendment's passage, many states abdicated their responsibilities to the federal government. Equally disconcerting to Willebrandt was the seeming disappearance of the social reformers who had carried the Eighteenth Amendment to passage. Liquor remained "as a scientific, social problem, as well as one of respect for the law," she charged. As critics sought to answer whether Prohibition could work, Willebrandt believed it had not been given "half the kind of a trial nor half the earnest effort that can and must be put forward in order to succeed in the national undertaking." She attributed the failure to three factors: lack of assistance from local communities, inefficient coordination among federal agencies, and "entirely too much politics." The key to successful enforcement was community support. Willebrandt hoped communities and law enforcement at all levels would work together, efforts overlapping, with success in enforcement at the federal and local levels influencing public perception, which would reduce demand, pushing bootleggers from glamorous speakeasies to back alleys, "where no claim to respectability is made" and where politicians, eager to hold popular support, would be less likely to tread.[1] A concerted effort on all fronts would win the day, but it started with recognition that each citizen was equally responsible to national and local laws.

Willebrandt knew Prohibition could be made a reality if she had resources at her direction and disposal; she told a reporter for *Collier's* magazine, "Give me the authority and let me have my pick of 300 men and I'll make this country as dry as it is humanly possible to get it," and added, "There is one way it can be done—get at the sources of supply. I know them, and I know how they could be cut off."[2] The reporter believed her, proclaimed that she was "the one person in official Washington who could, and, if vested with proper authority, would make America almost bone dry," and dubbed her the "first legal lady of the land." That "almost" acknowledged the difficult task faced by Willebrandt and other defenders of Prohibition, even "if" she had all means at her disposal.

Willebrandt believed in the rightness of Prohibition, but also viewed her position as assistant attorney general as a stepping-stone to a judgeship. Articles like the one in *Collier's* served both purposes. Her old friend James Pope, who had advised her to seek her current position, had hoped she would find just this kind of publicity, "the right kind which is publicity of recognition," bringing her accolades not just for her work at the Department of Justice, but afterward, where "a much bigger and harder thing awaits you and that is to demonstrate that mental quality and strength is common to women as men and that discrimination on account of sex is wrong." Pope conceded, "There will always be the position that if women deserted the homes and became public personages the race would die out," but he recommended that Mabel continue letting the work speak for itself.[3] In due time, the rewards she sought would come.

Only a month later, on September 23, 1924, Mabel received recognition of her efforts, when Treasury Secretary Mellon authorized the transfer of more than $150,000 to the Department of Justice, permitting Willebrandt to direct investigations into large-scale smuggling operations. The money allowed the hiring of fifty investigators and legal assistants, positions that had not existed previously, to conduct work that would not otherwise have been undertaken. Just the day before, Willebrandt had talked to Internal Revenue commissioner David Blair, "telling [the Treasury Department] we'd fooled each other long enough batting the lace back and forth as far as pleasant promises were concerned and I construed inaction for this long period as negation." Mellon also promised to provide a "fast boat" and the cooperation of all treasury bureaus and units. Mabel could barely contain her excitement in passing the news to her parents, exclamation points liberally placed throughout her letter, faith restored in herself—"I'm so masterful and sure of myself and unafraid"—and in the importance of her work advancing "the direction of human endeavor and purposes."[4] That direction extended not only to "proper Prohibition handling of investigations," but advocating for appointment of women as U.S. Attorneys. The only thing that would have made her news better was the presence of family to share in the moment.

Willebrandt's yearning for family and something resembling a normal life led her to consider adoption. In October 1924, she paid her first visit to an orphanage; she was "eager" to find a child, unworried about family histories or problems a child might have, and joked with her parents that they had drawn a "lemon," but she allowed that things had worked out all right.[5] Willebrandt's dreams for a family did not, at least as an imperative, include a husband. Still estranged from Arthur Willebrandt, she gave Fred Horowitz, who offered her something resembling a proposal, the boot, letting him know she could not be had solely on his terms.[6] Trying to regain Willebrandt's trust, Fred traveled to Washington, D.C. She appreciated his visit, feeling that Fred recognized the "worthwhileness" of her work, the "magnitude" of her "power and the graceful things in the life about me," but saw no romantic future with him any longer, their divergent "aims and interests and mode of life" too much to overcome.[7]

Pauline Sabin announced in August that the WNRC would begin a program of training its members to become speakers, poll watchers, and "disseminators of facts regarding the Republican Party and its candidates."[8] The club would offer special classes to instruct its members, planning for them to take on duties in their own communities. Sabin's own advocacy was taking her to deeper involvement in the party, moving beyond speeches to high-level meetings with party leaders and backroom deals, away from her base in New York to key battleground states. Party leaders sent her to Maine in late August to assess Republican sentiment in advance of the state's elections to be held in mid-September (Maine was considered a barometer for national sentiment, as in the old adage, "As Maine goes, so goes the nation"). Sabin confirmed the party's fears that the governor's race would go to the Democrat, but she found Coolidge and national Republican policies held in high regard, presaging victory in November. While her assessment concerned overall attitudes toward the president and the party, from men and women, Sabin gave special credit to women for organizing in every county, hosting Republican speakers, planning well beyond the governor's race.[9]

With the presidential election approaching, Sabin granted a long interview to the *New York Times* about women and the campaign. She acknowledged it was hard motivating women to step from behind their husbands, but with an army of volunteers, she foresaw huge gains in the number of women voters. She believed attacks upon the Constitution, such as the proposed child labor and equal rights amendments, motivated women, "naturally more conservative," to recognize that the present "system of Government has brought safety to them and their little ones, that it has assured prosperity and they dread any attack upon that safeguard of our liberty." She found political work invigorating, wondering why women would want to talk about "pink teas and the latest style of dress when they can help to formulate policies which may influence the weal and woe of the nation." She saw most women becoming as interested in politics as herself, learning the game, soon being able to "teach their brethren." Calvin Coolidge, she predicted, would be in debt to women for his reelection. "It used to be a standing joke in the man-made funny papers," Sabin declared, "to poke fun at the woman's lack of understanding of baseball and politics. All the fine points were supposed to go over her head. Perhaps this was true in the past, but it is no longer true."[10] From now on, she forecast, women would become an increasingly significant piece of the political landscape and "a determining factor in every election."

Sabin filled a key role in Coolidge's reelection campaign, though almost no one knew of it prior to Election Day. Before the campaign began, the president created an Advisory Publicity Board to approve and monitor all speeches made by Republican spokespersons. Coolidge selected four men with backgrounds in journalism, placed them in offices in Washington, D.C., Chicago, and New York, and directed them to vet all speeches or advertisements to make sure they concentrated on the president and his administration's accomplishments in reducing government spending and taxes, bringing prosperity to the country; no reference to Harding's scandals would be permitted. This policy, carried to great effect, meant neither Coolidge nor party leaders answered charges made by the Democratic nominee, John Davis, or even *mentioned* Harding in any context. In the New York office, located in Republican Party headquarters, Sabin reviewed any speeches planned for spokeswomen from the party's Women's Division.[11] This brand of "censorship" led to boilerplate pronouncements, but kept voters focused on the issues and on Coolidge's credibility. The results spoke for themselves; President Coolidge achieved an easy victory, compiling a majority of 2.5 million votes over his rival.

Hoping to learn how much his conversations were overheard, Olmstead baited a trap. He set up a rendezvous with several associates with the stated purpose to move liquor stockpiles from the Olympic Repair Shop.[12] William Whitney, hoping to nab his big fish in the act of bootlegging, had his men stake out the Olympic Repair Shop early on the morning of September 11, 1924. Three cars, one driven by Olmstead, and a truck entered the Olympic Repair Shop before dawn, the door closing behind them. Outside, watching, Whitney waited just long enough for the bootleggers to begin their work before busting into the garage. They found Olmstead and his men standing in a circle, talking. Next to them stood two Cadillacs, their rear seats removed. Myer Berg saw Whitney and said, "You are just a little too early; if you had waited a half an hour you would have gotten a load of whiskey."

"I guess I will wait, then," replied Whitney.

"There is no use waiting now. You have made enough commotion out here—we have changed its course. It will never come here. You don't think we were fools enough not to leave a man outside to divert it if anything should happen."[13] A search of the shop came up empty.

The Olmstead gang had a good laugh, their question of who was listening answered.[14]

Falling into Olmstead's trap put William Whitney on alert. The rumrunner's apparent knowledge about the phone taps rendered them unreliable. Whitney decided it was time to go in for the kill.[15] The wiretaps had revealed the length and breadth of a conspiracy involving the importation of liquor from Scotland to British Columbia and the distribution from Vancouver to landings scattered from Seattle to San Francisco via oceangoing vessels, with delivery from smaller watercraft and trucks to customers within those communities. Raids on Olmstead's stockpiles around the city, with the subsequent arrests of some of his men, had connected more of the dots. Whitney, though, knew he needed to catch Olmstead redhanded, with the booze and with his business records, to seal his nemesis' fate.

On the evening of November 17, federal agents pulled up to Olmstead's elegant two-story home with its manicured lawn and hedges, several fine cars parked in front. Whitney had his men surround the house, and he heard the "sounds of merriment inside," a most encouraging sign, as he strode up the front walk. Whitney gave the signal and his men stormed in from all sides. The Olmsteads and their guests were seated at the dining room table, having all but finished their meal. The table bore no bottles of wine, no half-filled martini glasses or decanters of bourbon. This looked bad. Whitney ordered an immediate search. His agents went at it with vigor for over an hour, but they turned up not a single bottle of liquor, beer, or wine. Perhaps it was the smirk on Olmstead's face, or the desperation brought on by raiding the house of the supposed King of the Bootleggers to find it dry, but when the phone rang, Whitney went to answer it. Elsie stepped in front of him, telling him that now that he had finished his search, he "had no right to remain on the premises or use the phone." Whitney did not accept challenges from women lightly, and he nearly struck her in the face before lowering his hand and pushing her against the wall.[16]

Whitney picked up the receiver and said hello. Ed Engdahl, a longtime conspirator of Olmstead's whom Whitney knew, identified himself. Engdahl asked for Olmstead, and Whitney "told him he was not there." Engdahl, failing to suspect anything wrong, asked Whitney about others in Olmstead's "gang" before exclaiming, "We have got a bigger load of liquor coming in." He needed Olmstead to call him back.[17] The call excited Whitney, sparking an idea to mitigate the potential disaster of the raid. He began ringing up other members of Olmstead's gang and, impersonating one of Olmstead's associates, invited them over for a party. Whitney soon asked his wife, Clara, who was inexplicably along for the raid, to issue invitations as well, impersonating Elsie, and ordered another agent to impersonate Olmstead.* It was not long before cars began to arrive at the Olmstead home.

Whitney's plan did not work, though, because, of the eleven people who responded to the phony calls, only one arrived with liquor, and only one bottle at that. Efforts to browbeat the suspects, to search dark corners of the house, to prove this raid worthwhile went on hour after hour. Whitney discovered documents upstairs relating to Olmstead's business, and these he seized. Just after three a.m., more than seven hours after they had arrived, Whitney had his men drive the suspects to his office for more questioning from Director Lyle.

Lyle focused on young Al Hubbard, who up to this point had been mostly ignored. Lyle and Whitney wanted to know what his radio broadcasting set was intended for and pushed the young man to admit his creation played some role in the operation of the ring, to incrimi-

---

* Such action today by law enforcement would invite charges of entrapment.

nate Olmstead. Elsie was not broadcasting stories, Whitney accused; her words were a code "used by Olmstead to communicate with co-conspirators in Canada, Japan and at sea . . ." Hubbard declared that he knew nothing of rum-running. He was a radio "pioneer" and had been hired to build and maintain a radio station—nothing more. Lyle and Whitney believed enough of what Hubbard said to regard him as a possible witness against Olmstead, someone who could offer direct testimony because he spent so much time in Olmstead's home.[18] Within a few hours, Olmstead's attorney posted bail for the lot.[19]

Whitney knew he could convict his suspects for selling liquor, based on the tapped telephone conversations, but that would not represent the convincing victory needed to bolster the public's faith in the Prohibition Unit. On the afternoon of Friday, November 21, Lyle and three agents burst into the office of Jerry Finch, Olmstead's attorney, handed the surprised lawyer a search warrant, and proceeded to ransack the premises for any documents related to Olmstead. Finch argued that it was illegal for Lyle to remove them, a ready store of legal opinions buttressing his bluster. Lyle blithely handed Finch a receipt for the stack of letters, receipts, and memoranda his men carried out.

Finch took his case to the courts the next day, submitting a petition asking the federal court to take charge of the papers taken from his offices by the federal agents. He also contested the search warrant, which alleged that alcohol would be found on the premises and was believed to have been sold from there previously. Since no liquor had been found, Finch claimed the Prohibition agents had no legal authority to seize his documents.

Judge Jeremiah Neterer immediately denied Finch's motion, surely a poor harbinger of the federal judge's attitude for the upcoming case. Neterer stated, "If the raid constituted a crime, the attorney had other remedies." Besides, said Neterer, the seized documents were not in the court's possession, so it could not impound them "pending further hearing as to the right of seizure."[20] Put another way, the judge believed that the phone transcripts Whitney had shown the U.S. commissioner provided enough evidence for the raids, even if the raids themselves had found nothing illegal. Taking his complaint to the press, Finch lambasted Whitney as "an employee whose official designation is unknown to the plaintiff, but who has and assumes power equivalent and in some cases in excess of the powers of Lyle." The two agents were "actuated by 'hatred, envy and malice and imbued by too intense a zeal in the performance of their duties . . .' "[21]

The cries that James Wadsworth opposed women's issues gained steam, again, in early 1925 when he told representatives of the National Woman's Party that he would not support an equal rights amendment. He admitted some laws discriminated against women, but believed the proposed amendment "might result in the repeal of all laws that today are to the advantage of women," pointing to laws that protected wives from responsibility for the debts of their husbands. (As Mabel Willebrandt would have pointed out, protecting wives from their husband's debts meant, conversely, that wives had few, if any, rights to their husband's assets.) As if potentially offending half the population were not enough, Wadsworth proved the spark to new debates in the state of New York on the other issue always attached to him, Prohibition. Orville Poland, legal advisor for the New York branch of the ASL, facetiously suggested Wadsworth make himself aware of current newspaper reports claiming the senator would not use his influence to advocate for a state enforcement law to replace the Mullan-Gage Act repealed in June 1923. Poland reminded Wadsworth that the state's Republican committee had endorsed an enforcement law during the recent election season. The ASL lawyer would not "charge" Wadsworth with going against the party, but he insinuated as much. "There is no way for you to rid yourself of the unpleasant innuendo of these implications save by a specific denial of your intention to be a party, either by your action or lack of action, to the defeat of a State Prohibition enforcement law by reason of a failure to caucus," advised Poland.[22]

Arthur Davis, New York's ASL superintendent, added his voice, claiming Wadsworth held the power to determine the success or failure of the enforcement bill and the promises made by the Republican Party to get the bill passed. The state assembly had passed the bill on to the state senate, where twenty-six votes would secure its passage; twenty-nine Republicans served in the senate, but four of that number indicated they would oppose the bill, voting the wishes of their constituencies. Davis refused to accept that argument, declaring, "They should have thought of that before they ran on a Republican ticket at an election where the Republican Party promised a State enforcement law."[23]

Throughout, Wadsworth remained silent, annoyingly so to some Republican leaders, but he did lend his name to a publication of the Association Against the Prohibition Amendment during this time, making clear where he stood. Whether Wadsworth's influence was strong enough to sway one of the four state senators without doing damage to his own interests is unknown, but without his involvement, the enforcement bill went down to defeat in March 1925.[24] In a final stab at the perceived betrayal, Arthur Davis announced the ASL would "take every lawful and proper step to oppose the renomination and election of the leading exponent of the fundamental principles of the Association Against the Prohibition Amendment, Senator James W. Wadsworth."[25]

The charge that James Wadsworth controlled the Prohibition debate in New York represented a minor component of a larger contention by his opponents that he controlled all politics in the state, and the votes of all the Republican state legislators, who controlled both houses. It was an outlandish accusation, allowing the senator's detractors to focus all their frustrations with the Republican Party in one person rather than admitting rifts within the party. The promotion of personal freedoms, big business, and small government clashed with movements to create more protections—Wadsworth would say restrictions—whether applied to women, children, farmers, or minorities. Progressive Republicans had brought many changes, including suffrage and Prohibition, in the previous twenty years and many in the party, particularly women, wanted such change to continue. Wadsworth did not, and his unwavering opposition to legislation that might be termed progressive continued to create trouble for him.

The associate chairman of the Democratic State Committee, Caroline O'Day, called upon all New York women to oppose the "boss rule" of James Wadsworth, and charged the senator with directing Republican legislators to vote against anything supported by Governor Al Smith. At Wadsworth's command, Republican legislators ensured the death of bills to promote children's health and education, protect working women, and safeguard public morals, charged O'Day. She wondered, "What brutal system of forcible feeding was employed to make them swallow their own words and try to look happy," but it was clear to O'Day that Wadsworth had directed them through "secret pressure" to do just that. She insisted that the "boss" would not allow any Republican candidates in the 1925 election for state assemblymen who did not follow his edicts.[26]

Pauline Sabin remained silent while charges were thrown at her friend Jim Wadsworth, but accusations soon flew her way. In late May 1925, Sabin hosted an "unofficial conference" at Bayberry Land to discuss the reelection of George H. McDonald, chairman of the Republican Suffolk County Committee, and John Boyle Jr., the assemblyman from Sabin's district. A rift among the attendees formed, due to an alleged association between McDonald and the Ku Klux Klan, which claimed credit for getting him elected to his current position. Sarah Schuyler Butler—daughter of Nicholas Murray Butler—representing the Republican state committee, said that the state committee would not recognize McDonald or his associates. One newspaper account described Sabin as supportive of the county's "old guard," who wielded "great power with the party leaders not only in New York state, but throughout the country."[27] Another labeled her an "anti-dry," out of step with the majority of Republicans in Suffolk County, who would not "take kindly to having the whip lash snapped over them by a few wealthy summer residents of Southampton who are threatening not to recognize the regularly elected representatives of the party in the county in the matter of Federal or state appointments." Harsh criticism, also, followed Miss Butler, "daughter of a pronounced wet," who made an "intemperate speech . . . not likely to tend to party harmony in Suffolk." Pointedly, the paper warned that Suffolk Republicans supported the Eighteenth Amendment, implying that Sabin and Butler did not. The charges made against the two women diverted attention from the original issue: McDonald's possible relationship with the KKK, a group in favor of Prohibition. McDonald declared no allegiance to the KKK, but his refusal to disavow the group raised calls for his resignation. He declined, but the state committee revoked his privilege of assigning federal patronage in Suffolk County.[28]

The conflict did not end with the conference. After Pauline and Charles left the country for a summer in Europe, McDonald and his cronies put forth a candidate to challenge for her seat on the county committee.[29] Upon her return, Pauline had only two weeks to address the challenge, but her reputation in the county and her growing voice on the national scene brought her a slim victory. Unfortunately, McDonald and Boyle won, also.[30] A few weeks later, committee members, including most of the women, returned McDonald as county chairman, though his involvement in patronage decisions remained in limbo.[31]

etting passed over for federal judgeships had become almost routine for Mabel Willebrandt, but another rejection in February 1925 must have stung more than the others and let her know there was very little, if any, chance for an appointment so long as Calvin Coolidge sat in the White House. The President emphatically declared he would not appoint a woman to any government post if it was not already held by a woman. Katherine Philips Edson, a prominent player in the California Republican Party and a Willebrandt supporter, pondered, "How many women expect to get any place if everybody took that position? It certainly is a pretty good way to stop any progress."[32] Coolidge's decision came just weeks after Willebrandt had attended an event at the White House, noting, "I've been invited to the White House so often lately and all the officials are so fine to me that I can't help have a grudging enjoyment of it all," a marked change from the previous years in which she received far less recognition. Mabel showed "no disappointment" outwardly, upon hearing about the latest denial of a judicial appointment, but admitted to her parents, "At heart I care terribly," the frustration having "plunged" her into doubt "and a feeling that destiny is a thing one's dreams cannot deflect nor toy with as perhaps I have tried to do, unwisely."[33]

Willebrandt pushed forward. In mid-February 1925, she traveled to Cleveland "on a most intriguing mission," for which she would "need the wisdom of Solomon and the guiles of a serpent, the intuitions of H. G. Wells and the self control of Lincoln." She attended the grand jury hearing for two bootleggers indicted for conspiracy in 1921, but who had fled the country before trial. One of the men, Harry Grossberg, claimed he could not be indicted or convicted because his political influence extended to former president Harding, who had passed away eighteen months earlier. Grossberg's claim was based on an association with Sam Ungerleider, who had allowed Harding to purchase stock on margin. Before Harding could pay for the stock, he died and the stock promptly lost $170,000 in value. Attorneys representing the Harding estate and Ungerleider pled with Willebrandt for restraint in the matter regarding Sam, which she was willing to grant, but she did not feel the same about his brother, Abe, who had closer ties to Grossberg. Abe's books showed that payments for ten carloads of whiskey from Canada came from the same account from which President Harding's stock purchases had been made. "Imagine the arguments 'destroy the country's confidence,' 'smirching [*sic*] a dead president,'" she thought, agitated at the complication, but deciding it "was right to prosecute letting consequences be what they may." Unrecorded were her thoughts about her old boss, Harry Daugherty, Harding's trusted friend and frequent bagman, whom she had so staunchly defended. He would surely have known of Harding's ties to the Ungerleiders. Perhaps her decision to proceed was an admission that her blind loyalty to Daugherty had led her astray, and she had a chance now for redemption.

Willebrandt told Coolidge of her plans to proceed with the case, but he said nothing, forever holding his distance from Harding's scandals. Digging deeper into the case, Willebrandt learned Prohibition agents associated with the case had been dismissed or shipped to "some 'burying ground' as they call it like Butte, Montana." The Ohio Prohibition director, appointed by President Harding, approved permits, intended for industrial and medicinal purposes, requested by Warren Barnett, the law partner of a Harding campaign manager. Barnett collected twenty dollars per case of questionable liquor, and used the money to pay for graft and to reduce the million-dollar debt remaining from Harding's 1920 campaign. The former president had interceded in the Grossberg case in 1922, getting Secret Service agents to "cover up" the movement of money collected by Barnett.

Willebrandt relished the idea of bringing down Treasury Secretary Andrew Mellon, whose department oversaw the Secret Service. She regarded Mellon as "the full partner" in the Cleveland case, directing "his agents" to funnel monies into the campaign fund.[34] Such bold thoughts revealed her frustration with Mellon's lack of interest in enforcing Prohibition, which had made Willebrandt's job much harder. The grand jury returned numerous indictments, but none for the Secret Service agents or Mellon. Willebrandt's "personal assurance" that the cases would be prosecuted had secured the indictments, but the grand jury's reluctance to find against the Secret Service agents served as yet another reminder of how deeply politics extended into the daily machinations of Prohibition enforcement.[35]

District Attorney Tom Revelle informed U.S. Attorney General Harlan Stone on January 2, 1925, that some evidence against Roy Olmstead had been gained through wiretaps. He did not know who had "tapped" the wires and felt it was "better for me not to know," noting that wiretapping was a misdemeanor under Washington State law, but he believed the ends justified the means in this situation.[36] Two weeks later, Willebrandt appointed William Whitney as a special prosecutor in the Olmstead case, putting aside her usual "repugnance" to appointing special prosecutors to avoid the risk of losing the trial. She appreciated Whitney's expertise regarding the wiretapping evidence, but noted his questionable methods in the past, recalling an incident when the Prohibition agent "almost came to blows" with a U.S. Marshal.[37] Later, Senator Wesley Jones suggested Willebrandt attend the trial to provide "assistance."[38]

Rumor of the wiretapping leaked to the public, newspapers seizing on the salacious rumor. The *Seattle Times* teased: "Did the 'whispering wires' whisper your name?" Seattleites wondered if secrets exposed during the Olmstead case would "be the spark to set off a great explosion."[39]

Meanwhile, an avalanche of press coverage was making Olmstead a famous man—not a good attribute for the head of an illegal enterprise—and tending to convict him in the minds of readers and potential jurors. A lot of the leaks were true, of course, including the rumor he had bribed policemen not only to protect his shipments, but also to disrupt his competitors. Thomas Revelle predicted the grand jury would hand down scores of indictments after considering the array of evidence, the facts disclosing a massive conspiracy with "tentacles of the traffic reaching into Oregon and California" from British Columbia.[40] Revelle was right; the grand jury wasted little time finding just cause for the issuance of indictments covering smuggling and clandestine importation of liquor. Working late into the night, the U.S. Attorney's office issued warrants of arrest for ninety individuals, a staggering number in keeping with the promises made by federal law enforcement officials that they would expose a vast conspiracy.

On March 31, 1925, Mabel Willebrandt appeared before a Senate subcommittee investigating the efficiency of the Internal Revenue Bureau's operations. Willebrandt believed that different ideas about the best means of enforcing the Volstead Act hampered cooperation and decreased the effectiveness of enforcement between the IRB and her office.

The handling of revoked permits for legal alcohol production provided a glaring example of the disconnect between the two agencies, charged Willebrandt. The IRB issued permits for production of alcohol for industrial and medicinal uses, but many distilleries generated volumes in excess of permitted amounts, selling the surplus to bootleggers. When the IRB found out, they seized such distilleries and initiated legal proceedings. However, the IRB allowed the distillers to appeal a permit revocation, a process that could take six months, during which time the distiller could continue operations with little oversight. The seizure and appeal process clogged court dockets and pulled Willebrandt's district attorneys away from cases focused on big bootleggers and rumrunners. Willebrandt preferred injunction proceedings, which simply demanded that illegal operations must cease, and if they did not, fines and jail time could be assessed.[41] Executing an injunction placed the onus on the owner of the brewery rather than law enforcement. When asked by the Senate committee if attempts to convince the IRB to use injunctions had proven successful, Willebrandt explained that U.S. Attorneys had been told to use injunctions "vigorously," but she confessed those attorneys could make their decisions based only on evidence provided them by Prohibition agents, suggesting yet another disconnect between the agencies.

Willebrandt listed inadequate investigations by Prohibition agents where they should have dug deeper to reveal bigger conspiracies or where they did not collect sufficient evidence to make a case, necessitating additional investigations, often undertaken by the Justice Department's Bureau of Investigation, precursor to the FBI.[42] Inefficiencies in the building of cases by Prohibition agents led Willebrandt to conclude that Prohibition agents had little knowledge of the laws they were responsible for enforcing or of proper "tactics of investigation and the science of investigation."[43] Senator William King of Utah opined, "You may spoil some political jobs in that way," implying that some agents might fail training or educational exercises designed to improve their qualifications. Willebrandt wanted agents placed under civil service hiring guidelines, which would bring in better people without political obligations. Quoting from a recent *New York Times* article, she said of agents: "Many of them are well meaning, sentimental, and dry, but they can't catch crooks. The sole object of others has been to appropriate all the graft in sight, and they won't catch crooks." Attempting to lay blame,

Senator James Couzens tried to label Willebrandt as the "chief law enforcing officer of the Prohibition law." She quickly refused the appellation and the misconception that the Department of Justice had primary responsibility for Prohibition enforcement, reminding the committee that the Treasury Department annually received twenty-six million dollars specifically to enforce Prohibition; the Justice Department received no designated funding for its efforts, and made do with existing staff and attorneys whose work without Prohibition on their plates would be more than ample to keep them busy. Willebrandt answered all the senators' questions with statistics and specific case references, but felt attacked by veiled suggestions that she had it in for Treasury Secretary Mellon, overseer of the IRB. Publicly, Willebrandt admitted nothing but facts in discussing her knowledge of Prohibition operations overseen by the Treasury Department, but in private, she voiced her frustration to her most trusted confidants, her parents. She charged Senator Couzens, in the midst of a long-running feud with Mellon, with using her to "load his gun to shoot at his personal enemy Mellon, meaning also the whole bunch of conservatives who'd rather choke truth than to face a criticism."[44] She suspected the portrayal of her as opposing Mellon dimmed any remaining chance she had for a judgeship, but took comfort in knowing she had spoken the truth. Acknowledgment of her integrity came two months later when Senator King summarized what many had been thinking: "I feel confident that if it had been taken over by the Department of Justice in the beginning many of the evils which we are now seeking would not have existed."[45] Fellow committeemen agreed with King, but the idea would go nowhere for another five years.

The badgering questions and misperceptions of the senators tried Willebrandt's patience, but the greater hurdle to overcome was her hearing loss, still unknown to anyone outside her closest associates and family. The quick banter of congressional hearings, questions bouncing from one committee member to another, from one side of the rostrum to the other, not to mention chatter from the gallery, made it difficult to keep her secret. She had taken to using a hearing aid, which helped, but it required concealment, lest she show anything that could be perceived as a weakness.[46]

Willebrandt's apprehensions about her hearing loss extended to her personal life, as she wondered whether she could be a good mother. What if an occasion arose when she might not hear the sound of her child in danger? Willebrandt's mother lovingly scolded her, "If you say 'when I am deaf' you are forging in your body a deaf condition," knowing best how to prod her daughter, who always rose to a challenge.[47] Restored by her mother's faith, Willebrandt resumed her search for a child, finding "the dearest, wisest little two year old I ever saw" in August 1925.[48] The little girl, Dorothy, already adopted once, had come from a woman Mabel had assisted during her days as a public defender in Los Angeles.[49] While her schedule of trials and speaking engagements frequently pulled her around the country, Willebrandt, eager to hold tight to the new family she had craved, brought Dorothy whenever possible.

Never missing an opportunity to expand her political affiliations and raise her profile, Pauline Sabin entertained Charlie Sabin's Democratic friends and attended party events with him, charming the power brokers, impressing them with her knowledge on many subjects and willingness to compromise whenever convinced of the greater good. When the New York legislature created a commission in late 1925 to study the current structure of state government and make recommendations for combining various agencies and departments, Sabin was well-known to those, mainly Democrats, assembling the committee. Sabin was designated to serve on the commission addressing the Corrections Department, along with George Wickersham, a man with whom she would cross paths on the Prohibition debate. The Corrections Department committee made several recommendations concerning creation of new positions, elimination of others, and transfer of a hospital for "mental defectives" to the Department of Mental Hygiene.[50] By the end of the legislative session all of the recommendations had been approved.[51]

Sabin's experience in bipartisanship continued in late 1925 with her appointment as a vice chairman to a newly formed Department of Political Education under the auspices of the National Civic Federation, an organization formed in 1900 to foster better communication between labor and business interests. The department aimed to raise voter turnout by promoting "a greater realization of their duties and responsibilities." The executive council of the group included some of the biggest names from both parties, expanding the circle of influence in which Sabin operated, building her political résumé. Her friend Sarah Schuyler Butler joined her on the council, along with two men with whom she would do more and more work, Charles Hilles and Senator James Wadsworth. The Department of Political Education hoped to reverse the downward trend in voter turnout, which fell to about 50 percent in the 1920 and 1924 presidential elections. That number proved especially troubling when the assumption had been that granting suffrage to women would produce a significant spike in voter numbers; it appeared women tended to vote in the same middling percentage as men.[52]

Tom Revelle wanted a trial soon, but he knew the court's calendar was full for many months. On a more hopeful note, he stated, "We believe we have all of the evidence necessary to obtain a conviction," but he would not have been surprised if the attorney general—which meant in reality the assistant attorney general, Mabel Willebrandt—decided to send him experienced prosecutors to assist in trial preparation and prosecution.[53] Luckily for Olmstead, the lengthy court docket combined with a continual stream of motions from his attorney pushed the trial date to December 1925, eleven months away.

Although he remained free on bail, Olmstead found himself in a tough spot. The publicity and legal wrangling in advance of the trial had diminished his business, and newspapers had run his photo so many times he could hardly expect not to be recognized. The prospect of jail had not convinced him, however, to change professions. The fight to keep himself, his wife, and their friends out of jail demanded lots of money. Musings about rebuilding his liquor importing and distributing business received an enthusiastic response from his young radio inventor and houseguest, Alfred Hubbard, who wanted to do more than operate the radio station, fix engines, and repair boats. Olmstead, desperately in need of men, agreed.

Behind his deference to his boss, Al Hubbard hid a keen desire for money, and lots of it, along with the power and perhaps even the fame of Olmstead. That desire, better understood as a combination of brashness and jealousy, led Hubbard to the offices of the Prohibition Unit, where he offered his services, claiming Olmstead was "not the kind of man he thought he was."[54] The proposition must have quickened William Whitney's heart with possibility. Hubbard sold Whitney on the solidity of his friendship with Olmstead and his own trustworthiness, marrying his respectful and guileless demeanor with easy lies. He was the boy wonder, ready to set things straight, wanting "to be able to look the world in the face and say when the blow-up comes, as must inevitably happen . . . that he was a duly accredited employee of the United States Government while he was furnishing this information and working for the downfall of this enormous [smuggling] ring."[55] Hiring a friend and business associate of the King of the Bootleggers posed many risks, but Hubbard seemed like a weak personality Whitney could keep in check. In submitting Hubbard's application to Senator Wesley Jones, who controlled the Seattle unit's positions, Whitney assured, no matter what, Hubbard "could do no harm."[56] Jones hastily approved the application and Hubbard took the oath of office on October 2, 1925.[57]

With his confidence returning, Olmstead arranged to land a shipment at the Woodmont Beach dock on November 26, 1925. As he and his men, including Hubbard, began unloading 111 sacks, each protecting a case of whiskey, gin, or a popular cordial, three men approached unnoticed, guns drawn, and jumped into their midst, demanding, "Hands up!" William Whitney could barely contain his glee in reporting the arrest to the press. "It is the first time since Olmstead left a police force that he has been caught handling liquor directly," Whitney said before observing, "In his palmy days [Olmstead] never touched a load, just directed his subordinates. He evidently was forced to do the actual work because of many recent reverses which had hit his pocketbook pretty hard."[58] Being caught red-handed meant another grand jury, another indictment, and seemingly a lock on what would become a second conviction.

In due course, Hubbard had to answer to Whitney, Lyle, and Revelle. What had he been doing on that beach? Hubbard explained that he had learned of the liquor landing at the last minute and had no means to inform his Prohibition Unit superiors. To maintain his credibility with the criminals, he had played along, intending to inform Whitney as soon as possible. The plausibility of the story, along with the young agent's honest-to-gosh mannerisms, convinced Whitney and Revelle. They had hired Hubbard to get them inside the rum rings, to get them the evidence on the big operators, but they wanted some insurance while they tried to build a conspiracy case from the Woodmont Beach bust. Whitney decided to ask his bosses at the Prohibition Unit headquarters in Washington, D.C., for help, and he requested a special agent to work with Al Hubbard and to keep an eye on him.[59]

Chapter 8

During the 1925 Christmas season, Willebrandt, perhaps feeling a need to construct a traditional family for Dorothy, revisited Fred Horowitz's marriage proposal made a year earlier. However, she came to the same conclusions, placing even greater emphasis on the professional goals she hoped to achieve. She doubted his "love & satisfaction" could survive the "strain, social conditions & other circumstances out of my control." Should the marriage dissolve, as she suspected, "wrecked would be the fruits of all my sea of repressions and discipline and achievements so far," while Fred's "prestige and opportunities for a full life" would be unaffected.[1] Though she didn't say so, the specter of Arthur Willebrandt, her estranged husband, probably shrouded her thinking. A divorce from Arthur, the mystery man never spoken about by Willebrandt or revealed in the press, would need to be obtained before betrothal to Horowitz, marking one strike against her. A potential second divorce from Horowitz, should he realize her fears, might as well have been strikes two and three in Willebrandt's assessment of her future opportunities. She loved Horowitz, but could not trust his love would last and could not afford the damage to her career and standing that would accrue with another failed marriage.

Amidst congressional hearings, Supreme Court presentations, appearances at court cases around the country, and the administrative chores of her office, Willebrandt found time to be a mother to Dorothy, whom many took to calling "little Mabel," especially as the girl tagged along on her mother's business trips. Willebrandt took her to Seattle in January 1926 to peek in on the Olmstead case preparations, to Yellowstone National Park for a vacation in April of that year, and to New England in the summer for a slate of Chautauqua presentations she made.[2] She admitted frustrations with her daughter's "infinite capacities for naughtiness," but conceded she was "bright and original and responsible." Dorothy enriched her life, but Willebrandt still wanted more, judging, "I am in my life and profession a <u>man</u>." She craved a "family reaping vicarious pride in my success and being noticed for it, etc. But that—the forever not having that—is another liability of my sex."[3]

Pauline Sabin began 1926 by removing her name from consideration for president of the Women's National Republican Club, a post she had held for three years, during which she had increased the club's membership rolls and raised its political profile along with her own.[4] She would remain a member, but her duties with the Republican National Committee and plans to assist James Wadsworth in his reelection campaign demanded all her time. The success of Sabin's efforts to educate women through the club's programs could best be seen in her successor, Alice Chittenden, who had opposed suffrage for women out of fear that it would alter a woman's control over the home, but had come to see suffrage as granting political power to preserve the home rather than allowing men alone to determine its fate.

Transitioning from club organizer to political campaigner, Sabin hosted the WNRC's annual luncheon, held, as always, at the Waldorf-Astoria; she invited James Wadsworth and Nicholas Longworth—speaker of the U.S. House of Representatives and husband to Pauline's longtime friend Alice Roosevelt Longworth—to speak at the January 16 gathering.[5] On the same day, at the Hotel McAlpin, five hundred members of the Women's Christian Temperance Union met to hear several speakers attack inadequate efforts to enforce Prohibition. Carrie Chapman Catt, an old-guard suffragist and Prohibitionist, painted "a gloomy picture of immorality and crime" rooted in "extravagance and prosperity," of which Prohibition violations were but the most obvious symptom. Ella Boole, president of the WCTU, denounced James Wadsworth and the Association Against the Prohibition Amendment and called for a "campaign of education, agitation and legislation to show that America's financial leadership of the world is greatly enhanced by the benefits of Prohibition even under imperfect enforcement" and by opposition to any changes in the Volstead Act. As if on cue, Arthur Davis, the New York ASL superintendent, called for the "political annihilation" of Senator Wadsworth.[6] Back across midtown Manhattan, the two thousand attendees at the WNRC luncheon filling nearly the entire second floor of the Waldorf-Astoria heard Longworth defend Wadsworth and say it would be a "national disaster" if he were not reelected. The senator spoke next, condemning attempts to centralize more power in the federal government's hands, citing Prohibition as the keystone example of failed policies in that direction. He characterized the Eighteenth Amendment as the first "to say to the individual citizen, 'thou shalt not.'" In so doing, Wadsworth accused Prohibitionists and like-minded people of diverting "the logical and orderly development of the Constitution . . . to a new path and in the direction of a goal scarcely dreamed of by the liberty-loving people who founded the Government. So abrupt a change was this and so at variance with the age-old conception of constitutional law that we should not be surprised at this confusion, to use a mild term, which resulted."[7]

Orville Poland later saw fit to challenge Wadsworth's attack on centralization, saying that if the senator believed in states' rights so strongly, he should have no reason to oppose a state enforcement law, wresting responsibility from the federal bureaucracy so the state could regain its sovereignty.[8] Poland failed to mention that an enforcement law by the state legislature would never be enacted; Governor Al Smith had promised to veto it.[9] The true intent of bringing a vote to the New York legislature was to force Republicans—for all Democrats were considered Wet—to state definitively their position on Prohibition. If they voted for an enforcement bill, the ASL and WCTU would hold those legislators accountable in any future Prohibition arguments, using their vote as a cudgel to hold them in line. If they voted *against* an enforcement bill, they would be cast as radicals, defying the party platform. But New York's Republican legislators bridled at being defined by one issue. On March 22, 1926, five Republican state senators stiffened their backs and joined twenty-two Democrats, that party's entire caucus, to reject two enforcement bills.[10] Emboldened by the victory, senate Republicans pushed forth a resolution calling for a statewide referendum asking voters whether a petition should be sent to Congress requesting modification of the Volstead Act.[11] Republicans in the assembly sought to reassert their claim as the "dry" party, exposing any members choosing to vote against the party's promises. Both measures, the referendum bill in the senate and the enforcement bill in the assembly, moved in tandem through committee hearings and floor debates into mid-April, each seeking enough votes to set a tone for the most populous state in the country and for the Republican Party nationally. On April 13, the competing bills came up for votes in their respective chambers. The senate passed the referendum proposal, needing only the votes of twenty-two Democrats for victory, but also got eight votes from Republicans, unafraid of the ASL and WCTU's threats. The assembly passed the enforcement bill with the bare minimum—seventy-six votes to seventy-two—needed to send it to the senate.[12] The triumph of the enforcement bill held little joy for its backers, though, who saw no chance in the senate after that chamber's recent vote against a similar measure. They were right. Arguments that the public should have a say on the Prohibition question drew more votes, the referendum bill passing the assembly easily.[13] The bill moved to Governor Smith's desk, and on to a vote in November.

Great crowds of gawkers gathered outside the federal building on the morning of January 19, 1926, as the biggest case in the history of Prohibition, featuring the King of Bootleggers, opened.* Few of the members of the public jamming the halls made it inside the courtroom, with U.S. Marshals allowing entry only to those directly involved with the trial, and a few reporters. Forty-six defendants, many with their own attorneys, took up a sizable portion of the room. Another forty-four individuals who had been indicted had fled the country or pled to a lesser charge. If they had appeared, little room would have been left for the reporters.

When the clock struck ten, the bailiffs and marshals quieted the crowd, and attention focused on the door beside the imposing bench of Judge Neterer, guarded by a bailiff. On cue, the bailiff opened the

---

* The claim to being the "biggest case" was based upon the total number of defendants, as of that date.

door, and the judge stepped up to his seat above the proceedings as another bailiff rapped a gavel, crying, "Hear ye, hear ye, all rise . . ." The solemnity lasted only a moment, though, as Roy and Elsie Olmstead, accompanied by Roy's mother, entered the rear of the courtroom. The elderly Mrs. Olmstead found a seat with the audience; the couple took their seats behind their counsel. Roy, tall, relaxed, and unhurried, had made his point. He would not be cowed. The long-delayed "whispering wires" trial, set in motion by the arrest of the Olmsteads and their dinner guests in 1924, had begun.[14]

Everybody in the courtroom expected the prosecution team to open with testimony related to the "whispering wires," but Tom Revelle chose to establish the length and breadth of the conspiracy from Canada to downtown Seattle first. Through a series of witnesses, most of whom had been employed by Olmstead, Revelle established the day-to-day routine of a rumrunner—pickups, deliveries, corruption of local law enforcement—but none could provide direct evidence of Olmstead's participation in the purchase, transport, or sale of illegal liquor in the United States.[15] The brief sideshow completed, the main event began. William Whitney, the man who knew everything, took the stand.[16] With the hour of the "whispering wires" at hand, the prosecution began with questions allowing Whitney to reel off the successful raids, each yielding enough contraband to indicate a large commercial operation, Whitney specifying how each location fit into the Olmstead gang's scheme. The description of each raid allowed Whitney to spell out who all the conspirators were and what were their respective duties, and to name all the defendants.[17] The *Seattle Times*, describing his first day of testimony, said, "Whitney has relentlessly invaded the strongholds of the liquor dealers," and gathered the evidence against the conspiracy that had been "flooding Seattle with liquor and generating $500,000 a year in profit."[18]

After putting the conspiracy in context, Whitney held aloft the

775-page book that every spectator jammed into the courtroom knew contained the transcripts from the wiretaps.[19] Whitney described entire conversations he had heard over the "whispering wires" between men clearly engaged in taking orders and running liquor to waiting customers. Many of the callers had helpfully identified themselves, according to Whitney, with salutations such as "Hello, this is Johnny the Wop," and often included their locations. One of Olmstead's attorneys, George Vanderveer, objected throughout Whitney's testimony, claiming the Prohibition agent was providing hearsay evidence and relying on the book of transcripts for details of conversations he never heard. The judge, laying bare his bias and his assumption that Olmstead would be convicted, swept aside every objection and advised Vanderveer to raise the issues on appeal.[20]

Upon cross-examination, Vanderveer bore into Whitney, and badgered until Whitney admitted he had not listened to all the conversations but relied on the book his wife, Clara, had typed up from her notes, which, in turn, had been extrapolated from the "stenographic" notes made by Whitney and the other agents listening to the calls. Vanderveer hammered away with questions about the validity of the information transcribed: How long had the book been in existence? How many agents had listened to the phone lines or seen the original notes? How could an entire conversation be captured in longhand? Eventually, the defense wanted to know what had become of the original notes.[21] Whitney admitted he did not have them. Pressing, Vanderveer extracted an admission that Clara Whitney had edited the original notes, and she was also unaware of their whereabouts.

The prosecution next called Richard Fryant, one of the original wiretappers, to the stand. Fryant handled a number of the defense attorney's questions about the note-taking process well, until he was asked to state when the book of notes, the all-powerful "whispering wires" evidence, was completed. Fryant's answer—December 1925—

brought an audible gasp from the defense team. The transcripts had been completed one and a half years after the conversations had taken place, just prior to the start of the trial.[22] The disturbing revelation induced the judge, finally, to grant the defense's request to have the book introduced as evidence. Upon that small victory, the defense pressed Fryant about his ability to testify without the book, the agent quickly admitting, "There was such a volume of conversation" no one could recall it all, prompting the judge to allow the witness to refresh his recollections by consulting it.

The defense attorney wondered aloud at Fryant's description of himself sitting alone at the wiretaps and observed that he had not been alone, because Harry Behneman had been seated next to him. Fryant admitted that, well, yes, Behneman had been there but he never had possession of original notes—notes which might conflict with the typed transcript.[23] Like the Whitneys, though, Fryant had to admit he did not know what had become of those notes—or Harry Behneman.

Vanderveer's tactics gave Olmstead an air of confidence bordering on contempt for the proceedings. At one of the court's recesses, Revelle stopped to light a cigarette before leaving the courtroom. Olmstead, walking with the crowd, spied the light and steered over to him. "No hard feelings; gimme a cigarette?" Revelle shook one out of the pack for him. Outside the courthouse, Olmstead consorted with members of his "gang." He was a free man in the evenings; his operations continued, though reduced, resources focused on localized rum-running, selling wholesale to local bootleggers. Nights of hard work left many of his gang tired. The accused slept so much during court that one of the bailiffs opined, "They must go to night school, or something," surely triggering a chuckle from those still plying their trade.[24]

The success of the defense attorneys in attacking the prosecution's witnesses had turned the trial on its head, those witnesses unwillingly putting doubts into the minds of jurors unsure of the veracity of the "whispering wires" evidence. As the defense prepared to call its witnesses, looking to punch more holes in the truthfulness and trustworthiness of federal agents, news broke that raised the stakes for Whitney and Revelle. "Federal officials at Washington, DC," the story went, were "showing keenest interest in the Olmsted liquor conspiracy trial in Seattle." Citing only "authentic sources," the *Seattle Times* stated that if the government's case proved successful, the use of the "whispering wires" might become commonplace in Prohibition enforcement, though the newspaper's unnamed source warned that higher courts might take a different view of wiretapping, seeing it as an invasion of privacy. Further proof of the interest of decision-makers in Washington, D.C., was an announcement that Mabel Willebrandt, Tom Revelle's boss, would appear at the trial.

With Fryant dispatched, Vanderveer prepared to raise his defense, starting with Olmstead, but an unexpected phone call from Harry Behneman changed the course of his preparations. In hiding for the past several weeks, Behneman told the attorney of his role in the wiretapping, but, more importantly, produced twenty-seven pages of notes bearing Fryant's handwritten corrections and signature.[25] To Vanderveer and his defense team, the pages shone like rays of sunshine breaking over them. Behneman's notes, which had not been incorporated into William Whitney's "book," offered the promise not just of destroying Richard Fryant's version of events, but also of at long last creating a fulcrum upon which the whole 775-page edifice of "whispering wires" could be toppled.

Unaware of Behneman's reappearance, Revelle and Whitney felt secure in the strength of their case and eager to impress Willebrandt, who arrived in the Pacific Northwest for a working weekend as Fryant finished his testimony. She had come to inspect the federal penitentiary at McNeil Island and would make the trip north to Seattle on Sunday.[26] The two men's mood changed, most assuredly, when the Sunday newspapers carried the story of Behneman's return to Seattle and his readiness to appear in court.[27] On the train north to the Emerald City, Willebrandt may not have seen the Sunday newspapers, but Revelle, a worrier by nature, would have been concerned about her attitude toward this potential setback. A reporter caught the moment of their meeting: Revelle, a good foot taller than Mrs. Willebrandt, stooping slightly in his three-piece suit and bow tie as he gave "his superior officer" a firm handshake and a bouquet of flowers. She had no time for him at that moment, though, as she was hurrying to a breakfast being given in her honor at the University Women's Club by the local chapter of Phi Delta Delta, a women's law honor sorority of which she was national president.

As Willebrandt departed for her breakfast, an astute observer would have seen in her itinerary an indication of her priorities. Listing her visits to the penitentiary and the Women's Club ahead of a conference with Revelle and Whitney was the action of someone who refused to allow the intractable problems of Prohibition enforcement to distract her from other priorities—priorities where she could make a real difference. Creating a prison in which inmates were not just incarcerated but reformed and prepared for reintroduction into society, and encouraging women brave enough to excel in college to ignore the naysayers and negative employment statistics mattered more to Willebrandt.

In the early afternoon, she arrived at the new Washington Hotel to receive most of the local members of federal law enforcement: Thomas Revelle, Roy Lyle, William Whitney, U.S. Marshal Ed Benn, and William Bowling, in charge of the Department of Justice investigators in Seattle. These were serious men, the burden of a huge case on their shoulders, tired from weeks of grueling effort, their jobs on the line. They were undoubtedly eager for some "face time" with the boss, which probably made little impression on her beyond the way their interest in her approval represented her success in a man's world. The details of the meeting were not recorded, but more than likely, Willebrandt would have wanted to know if the case could be made without the wiretap transcripts, the question of whether they represented a breach of constitutional guarantees of privacy looming over their admissibility.

The reporters caught up with Willebrandt afterward, and asked about her trip. She extemporized at length about turning McNeil Island into a model penitentiary, one that reformed its inmates by putting them to useful work, such as an industrial program for canning fruits and vegetables. She praised the beauty of the Pacific coast as a good politician should, omitting any description of the women's event. It was fine for her to talk about reforming prisoners, but she knew her message to the young women was too controversial. At last the elephant in the room was addressed, when she was asked about the Olmstead conspiracy trial. Her answer astonished them. "I will not have the opportunity to look in on the Olmstead trial," she said flatly. "We all hope for the best, and the case is in most competent hands, Mr. Revelle doesn't need me."[28] Her eastbound train departed at five p.m. Sunday.

A letter to her parents written the day after she left Seattle showed other things on her mind. "I've fought at loneliness to the point when I knew I'd rather be married, no question of that, if my marriage could be a private affair in my life the way it is for a man," she lamented. "Unfortunately the things I most prize are tenderness and intellectual challenges. I don't expect to find both in anyone so far," discounting marriage to Fred Horowitz again. In lieu of marriage, even companionship, she had Dorothy and a desire to make sufficient "capital" that she could have financial security without a husband. She saw a life in California, "a home on a hill with mts. and sea from the windows, three children, a fair compensation, and a dignified community standing. That's all I want. Don't you think that's better than political office."[29] A judgeship would give her that, but she would not go "holding my hand out for political favors."

On Monday morning the trial resumed, the defense calling several witnesses to rebut specific allegations made by the prosecution before calling Harry Behneman to the stand. After establishing the basics—Did you know Fryant? For how long? Did you help him tap Olmstead's office phone number?—the defense counsel asked the witness when the tapping had begun. "June 25," came the reply—nearly two weeks earlier than Whitney and Fryant had testified—establishing a new timeline and unveiling a different narrative for the wiretaps. Olmstead's defense team would exploit the discrepancy upon cross-examination, citing it as an example of Whitney's ineptitude, never guessing the real reason was a calculated move by Whitney to ensure that nobody learned that Fryant had not been sworn in as a Prohibition agent until early July 1924 and had been working in an unofficial capacity before then. Behneman said the first time he saw anyone beside Richard Fryant listening to the phone lines was July 14, when Whitney visited for a short time. At this point, offered into evidence were the twenty-seven pages of notes penciled on brown paper and described as the original notes written by Behneman and Fryant in late June and early July 1924. They had traded the paper back and forth between them, the witness contended, as one endeavored to write what he had just heard while the other listened to the next call, sitting in the basement of the Henry Building, worried they would be discovered by a repairman from the telephone company. Leading his witness, the defense counselor asked how the names of the parties on the calls were identified, but the judge supported objections from Revelle, denying Behneman a chance to answer. Vanderveer, demonstrably frustrated, begged the opportunity to show that "names, dates, hours, whole conversations were deliberately filled in: that's the purpose of this inquiry." If Fryant retook the stand and admitted his handwriting appeared on these pages, Behneman's notes would immediately become the "originals." Any discrepancies between this scant record and Whitney's tome would undermine the "book's" validity and prove Fryant guilty of perjury. Vanderveer demanded Fryant's return. The judge allowed for Fryant's return to the witness box, but denied any questioning from Vanderveer, allowing only rebuttal testimony to Revelle because Fryant had been his witness. Fryant flatly refuted Behneman's assertions, leaving jurors to decide for themselves where truth lay.[30]

Stymied at so many turns, George Vanderveer presented his final motions in summation, moving that all wiretap testimony be struck from the record as a violation of privacy rights granted in the Fourth and Fifth Amendments to the Constitution, and in violation of statutes enacted by the State of Washington. Vanderveer moved, also, that the testimony of Clara Whitney and Fryant be struck, their recollections rooted in the 775-page transcription cherished by William Whitney, "the authenticity of which has now been disproved." Judge Neterer denied both motions.

After five grueling weeks, the case went to the jury, but not before the judge offered his view. He instructed the jury to regard the "whispering wires" transcripts as one source among many. "If you are convinced and believe the testimony, and believe that the parties talking were members of the conspiracy, if you find one existed, then you will conclude accordingly. The value of these telephonic conversations is based upon the identity of the voice of the person talking and the recollection of what was said, insofar as it is not corroborated by other evidence." Speaking to the challenges raised by the defense, the judge asserted the objections were an attempt to "influence your decision based upon something other than the evidence. In other words, that you should find for the defendants as a way of saying wiretapping 'will not be permitted!'" Making it clearer, Neterer declared, this "is no place to punish anybody for wiretapping, if an offense has been committed. There is no law in the United States against it."[31]

The doubts raised by Olmstead's attorneys about the reliability of the tapped conversations could not wash away the other evidence presented against him and his codefendants. Associations between the rumrunner and others clearly involved in the liquor trade could not be denied. The connections between Olmstead and these men hinted at conspiracy, especially after several defendants had admitted to selling liquor. The absence of a clear alternative to the government's presentation betrayed how completely Whitney had laid bare Olmstead's business. Explaining away job descriptions, such as those of truck drivers and phone operators and salesmen—jobs so clearly detailed by the prosecution and assigned to specific individuals—proved impossible. The fundamental truth, like acid, dissolved the defense's assertions into a confused mishmash. After seven hours of deliberation, the jury returned a verdict of guilty.[32]

The reporters now had their turn, aiming to capture the scene as well as the comments of the significant participants. Attorneys Finch and Vanderveer, exhausted and deflated, announced their intention to file an appeal to the U.S. Circuit Court in San Francisco and, if necessary, to petition the U.S. Supreme Court. In a real scoop, a reporter got Olmstead to offer a surprising opinion. "I am satisfied with the verdict," Olmstead said. "Twelve good, loyal American citizens did their duty as best they saw it. It was not the way I saw it. But they did their best. That is all."[33]

On March 1, 1926, Pauline Sabin hosted a meeting of the vice chairpersons, all women, from thirty-five of sixty-two New York counties, to garner support for James Wadsworth. The topic of

Prohibition took center stage, but Sabin reported the discussion proceeded in a "temperate manner," something she found pleasantly surprising given the intemperate criticisms typically lobbed at Wadsworth.[34] Her loyalty to Wadsworth and the party outweighed what she saw as petty differences over Prohibition and Wadsworth's past positions on child labor and equal rights. The larger issue, she agreed with Wadsworth, was expansion of the federal government, the resulting monolith subsuming states' rights and personal liberties. If she'd truly opposed Prohibition above all else, as some critics opined, Sabin would have had little reason to support the Republican Party or Wadsworth; the Democrats were definitely the anti-Prohibition party.

A month later, Sabin called another meeting of women leaders to seek their endorsement of Wadsworth's campaign. She admitted the senator's opposition to the Eighteenth and Nineteenth Amendments, "on conscientious grounds," but since passage of the Nineteenth, she contended, Wadsworth had encouraged full participation of women in the political process. Sabin did not address Prohibition further, but focused instead on his conservative values, the respect of his peers, and his growing reputation around the country, as evidenced by the support of the Speaker of the House of Representatives and President Calvin Coolidge. She believed most women would choose "courage" as the one quality they most admired in men, and while courage could be found in many places, Sabin appreciated the "courage of one's convictions," something she saw in Wadsworth but in so few other elected officials. With Sabin's arguments striking the right note, the women endorsed Wadsworth.[35]

Sabin recommended to Wadsworth that he refrain from dispensing interviews or materials about his stand on Prohibition, and Wadsworth agreed.[36] Sabin had a harder time avoiding questions—publicly, privately, and intellectually—about her own views. The situation came home in May, when the AAPA established a New

York Committee on the Referendum including her husband, Charles.[37]

n the spring of 1926, almost constant questioning of the desirability and enforceability of the Eighteenth Amendment and the Volstead Act culminated in the presentation before the Senate of eleven distinct resolutions to correct perceived inadequacies. The resolutions included plans to shift enforcement authority to local and state agencies, raise allowable alcohol percentages, tighten regulations on prescription issues, grant greater authority in seizure and control of property, establish a border patrol, allow each state to set its own definition of "intoxicating" liquors, advance a national referendum on the Volstead Act, and flat-out repeal the Eighteenth Amendment. With more than 150 witnesses, representing every side and angle related to the proposed resolutions, the hearings turned, largely, into a debate on two related questions: could the Volstead Act be enforced to satisfy the mandate of the Eighteenth Amendment, and, if so, what would it take to make that happen? Fiorello La Guardia, a representative from New York, a state generally regarded as one of the most lax in terms of enforcement, put it bluntly: "It is impossible to tell whether Prohibition is a good thing or a bad thing. It has never been enforced in this country."[38]

Senators, the public, and newspaper reporters anxiously awaited Willebrandt's appearance before the subcommittee holding the hearings, regarding her as one of the de facto experts on Prohibition enforcement efforts. She began simply by presenting statistics as proof of improving efforts—twenty-two thousand convictions and 4 million dollars in fines in 1922 increasing to thirty-eight thousand convictions and 7.6 million dollars in fines in 1925—but the senators were more interested in what remained to be done.[39] Without hesitation, Willebrandt stated her belief that Prohibition was enforceable, and offered recommendations to make the task easier for the Department of Justice. She considered the inability to assess penalties "commensurate" with the crime as the greatest deficiency in the Volstead Act, and she recommended modification of the Volstead Act to provide for prosecution of local and state officials failing to perform their duties, by either outright bribery, conspiracy, or turning a blind eye.

Willebrandt made clear that investigations and arrests occurred outside her department and oversight, but subcommittee members wanted her perspective on activities of the Prohibition Unit as it applied to the work of her office. As in past testimony, Willebrandt highlighted the convoluted separation of enforcement powers when asked about the number of search warrants issued. She could not answer, Willebrandt explained, because her department did not approve or issue warrants in Prohibition cases and her office had no control over the U.S. Commissioners of the Courts who issued them. While all federal courts fell under the banner of the Justice Department, commissioners reviewed evidence and made decisions on warrants independently, without supervision or guidance from above. In some locations, commissioners had little legal training, having obtained their positions as political favors, and granted warrants without adequate evidence. Coupled with insufficient training in evidentiary procedures for Prohibition agents, warrants with few verifiable facts did not hold up in court even after searches found evidence of violations. The greatest success rates of conviction came in districts where Prohibition agents cooperated with and received guidance from U.S. Attorneys. When asked if she could obtain better results if the Department of Justice had control of Prohibition agents, Willebrandt demurred, saying that was not a given. When pushed, she responded, "You are asking me to admit I am a bigger man than anybody else," prompting laughter from the committee.

Later, she conceded that with more agents, attorneys, and time, the law could be enforced, regardless of which department performed the work.

Willebrandt's answers seemed clear to everyone but Senator James Reed of Missouri, an outspoken opponent of Prohibition, who demanded to know if it was her judgment that the law could be "enforced so as to absolutely stop the manufacture and sale of intoxicating liquors." She replied:

> I am not a Utopian, but what I do mean to say is that the officers of the law with proper evidence and facts can try a case and get a conviction, and more than that, I mean that the violations of this law can be reduced to be probably commensurate with the violations of other laws.

Reed reminded her that Lincoln Andrews, the assistant treasury secretary in charge of Prohibition enforcement, had said in earlier testimony that the seizure of 172,000 stills in the previous year represented only one out of ten in existence. Seeking a comparison for argument's sake, Reed mused, "Do you think it is the same sort of a problem as horse stealing or burglary or highway robbery?" Willebrandt answered no, "because we are long past the time when so-called first citizens indulge in highway robbery, horse stealing, and burglary." Reed pushed again, asking whether she believed the law could be enforced to the same degree as any other. Willebrandt did, basing her assessment on the success of enforcement in locations where local law agencies did their fair part. When full transcripts of the hearings were published, Willebrandt's testimony was buried nearly one thousand pages deep; the testimony of Lincoln Andrews, who made similar statements about enforceability with additional agents and training, began on page forty-five. Roy Haynes, the commissioner of Prohibition, had not appeared at all.

On March 8, Judge Neterer sentenced Roy Olmstead to four years in a federal penitentiary and assessed him an eight-thousand-dollar fine. Olmstead wrote the verdict down in a little red book, his casual manner unflappable. A U.S. Marshal placed him in custody, but only until bail could be arranged. Mrs. Olmstead had her husband out that same afternoon, having sold their home for thirty thousand dollars. Their appeal had been filed in federal court, with a motion for a stay on jail time, so once bail was arranged, the Olmstead gang might spend as much as a year waiting for the U.S. Circuit Court of Appeals to offer a ruling, one that might send the "whispering wires" case back to Neterer or on to the Supreme Court. If they lost the appeal outright, Olmstead would have to serve at least two and a half years before he would be eligible for parole.[40]

Roy offered no comment to the press at his sentencing, perhaps at last, rather too late, realizing that allowing himself to become a public figure, maintaining an office downtown and a mansion in a fashionable district, had made William Whitney's job easier. A few days later, the Olmsteads held an estate sale to clear out their house. Roy absented himself while Elsie watched the throngs of people poke and prod through her belongings, and bravely kept up appearances for the reporters, making it sound as though downsizing to a smaller home would be good for them.[41]

The sale of his home and its contents may have been when Roy Olmstead divined the truth, one that tens of thousands of men in his industry faced: for all his efforts, he had created nothing of real and lasting significance. The money from rum-running and bootlegging had vanished; the superstructure of his enterprise broken; his reputation in the community, of which he had been so proud, irrevocably diminished. A convicted felon facing time behind bars had few respectable friends and no social standing. Whatever the long-term effects of his conviction, Olmstead needed money to appeal the decision to the Circuit Court and more money to pay for his defense of the Woodmont Beach indictment, still awaiting a court date. Like many convicted felons free on bail, especially those tens of thousands caught violating the Volstead Act in the 1920s, Olmstead went back to work in the only job that could get him out of the hole: running rum from Canada, humping thousands of cases on and off boats to the caches used by their distributors in town.

In one last gambit, Olmstead went to Tom Revelle's home and threatened the U.S. District Attorney. If two of Olmstead's operatives, recently caught by the Prohibition Unit, were indicted, Olmstead would go to the press about payments Al Hubbard claimed to have made to Whitney and Lyle, as well as bribes paid by Olmstead to Revelle's assistant, Clifford McKinney. Revelle, who knew nothing of these payments and alleged bribes, did not hear enough in Olmstead's threat to realize that Hubbard was playing a double game. Perhaps Revelle understood the threat to mean Olmstead would betray Hubbard's secret undercover work. By coincidence, William Whitney was at Revelle's house, and Revelle brought him in from another room. Whitney bucked up Revelle's courage and the two men refused to make any deal with Olmstead. As Olmstead walked out the front door, though, he probably failed to realize his exit meant Al Hubbard was home free. Like Revelle, Olmstead had missed any clues about Hubbard's true allegiances and actions.[42]

A few days later, on May 13, 1926, Revelle announced indictments for liquor conspiracy against nearly two hundred defendants, including Olmstead, stemming from the bust at Woodmont Beach. Roy Lyle, the region's Prohibition administrator so often in Whitney's shadow, spoke to reporters about the "smashing blow" these indictments dealt to liquor law violators in the Pacific Northwest, a comprehensive "take down sure to have national and international significance."[43] The next morning, the former King of the Bootleggers took a familiar trip across town and presented himself at the U.S. Marshals' office to be taken into custody only long enough to post bail.[44] Whitney knew it was time to announce the ace up his sleeve. The titular head of the Prohibition Unit stood up and shocked everyone by announcing, "Alfred M. Hubbard, 23 years old, long believed to be a confidential aide of Roy Olmstead, convicted liquor king, has been a secret agent of the federal dry office for some time." Pouring it on, Whitney delivered the startling news that "the cases which resulted in the liquor conspiracy indictments which the grand jury has just returned were all due to Hubbard's work."[45] In an impromptu press conference, Whitney's protégé stood before reporters and took questions. When asked what his other boss, Roy Olmstead, would say, Hubbard matter-of-factly responded, "Well, all I can say is Olmstead was doing wrong, wasn't he?"[46]

Chapter 9

The Republican Party in New York increasingly opposed Prohibition. The selection of U.S. Representative Ogden Mills, a confirmed wet, as temporary chairman for the upcoming state convention hinted at the evolving direction of the party. That Pauline Sabin served on the committee selecting Mills suggested her own views might have been changing also.[1] Pundits suspected Republicans wanted to tap a wet for the governor's race, mitigating Al Smith's wet position, forcing voters to choose their candidate based on something other than Prohibition. A leader of the New York ASL agreed with that assessment, charging "Mrs. Sabin" and others with trying to divide the "outlaw vote" with Smith, an impossibility, they charged, because the governor was "the bootleggers' hero."[2]

As the campaign moved into the fall, the national dividing line in the Republican Party over Prohibition played out in the state of New York. The presumptive Republican candidate for governor,

James Cropsey, a New York Supreme Court justice, wanted the party to endorse greater enforcement of the Eighteenth Amendment, something the state had not seen since 1923. Wadsworth, Sabin, and many other Republicans opposed the idea. Wadsworth remained hopeful of an alternative to Cropsey, and learned on a recent trip through upstate New York that Republican leaders there opposed Cropsey's plan to push for a change in Prohibition enforcement. So strong was their opposition, some of the leaders suggested they would vote for Democrat Al Smith in the general election if Cropsey's plan were endorsed.[3]

Days before the state convention, Wadsworth reiterated his opposition to Cropsey's proposal to secure a plank supporting Prohibition enforcement, but he preferred to set aside any measures concerning Prohibition until after the election, when results of the state referendum would reveal which way the wind was blowing.[4] As for presumptions that Cropsey would be the party's nominee for governor, Wadsworth refused to "discuss persons or candidacies of persons," leaving a decision on the party's candidate for governor to the convention delegates. Wadsworth's non-endorsement worked as a blow to Cropsey's candidacy, and he rescinded his name from consideration.[5]

As Cropsey's light faded, Congressman Hamilton Fish III picked up the torch for an enforcement plank. Wadsworth cared little, according to Fish, about the damage caused to the Republican Party and state candidates who might be tarred with his brush on the Prohibition question, and Fish warned that if the party slipped off "the rock of enforcement," or was "pushed into the quicksand of lawlessness and defiance of the Federal Constitution, its candidates on the State ticket will have no chance of election."[6] Fish's views reflected those held by many upstate party leaders and voters who questioned New York's defiance of the Volstead Act by the absence of state-mandated enforcement. Wadsworth conceded he could support a "moderate dry" as candidate for governor if that made him electable. Dry advocates suggested the term might apply to any candidate, wet or dry, who agreed to approve an enforcement bill if passed by the legislature, leaving the question, again, in the hands of voters who would determine the makeup of that body.

But the public was clamoring to know where each potential candidate stood on Prohibition. Sabin had managed to sidestep questions for much of the campaign, but in mid-September she endorsed the referendum vote, reminding people that its results carried no mandate to modify existing laws, its purpose only to inform the U.S. Congress of New York's satisfaction or dissatisfaction with Prohibition. She managed to avoid stating which way she would vote, but hinted at it in advising women to "register whether or not they thought the existing Prohibition laws are affecting among our citizens, the temperance and respect for law and order that every woman wished to have instilled in her children."[7] Sabin's carefully chosen words suggested a frustration with the law's inability to deliver on its promise.

Behind all the debates, arguments, editorials, and aspersions loomed a largely unstated question: did Wadsworth's call for repeal of the Eighteenth Amendment mean anything when no one believed Congress would allow a reconsideration of the amendment or that the requisite number of states would overturn the amendment?

Hoping to shore up support, Wadsworth traveled to White Pine Camp in New York's Adirondack Mountains to meet with President Coolidge, who was summering there.* Coolidge supported Prohibition and had made it known he would not involve himself in the New York elections, but the president recognized the need to keep

---

* Many presidents departed muggy Washington, D.C., during the summer, when Congress was out of session, for more temperate locations.

Republicans in power in the state.[8] Wadsworth did not receive an endorsement, but returned from the mountains with Coolidge's recommendation to nominate a moderate instead of a "wet" for governor.[9]

Perhaps sensing the growing angst over his candidacy and the problems it foretold for election, Wadsworth attempted to clarify his position, reiterating his desire that the Eighteenth Amendment be repealed, but equally stressing his hope that the saloon and private liquor traffic would not return. Wadsworth's greatest concern lay in "the fact that millions of people are resisting and 'nullifying' the Constitution today, due in my judgement, to the unsoundness of the Eighteenth Amendment." He urged repeal as a means to restoring respect for the Constitution, an issue "infinitely more important than the question of whether or not an individual may have a glass of beer." The amendment and the Volstead Act did not bring abstinence and it never would, but temperance could be attained with different laws, decided upon by the respective states. Declaring, "We all want temperance," he asked that discussion of solutions to the obvious failure of enforced abstinence be "temperate as well."[10]

The New York Republican State Convention began on September 27 in the new Madison Square Garden with 2,600 delegates and alternates filling only a fraction of the twenty thousand seats available.[11] After a preconvention conference, Wadsworth declared that a compromise on a Prohibition enforcement plank was at hand.[12] Compromise on Wadsworth's candidacy to retain his Senate seat, on the other hand, had not been reached. Many dry delegates supported Franklin Cristman and contended that "the plot to put up a wet ticket from Governor down, was hatched nine or ten months ago" by Wadsworth and his friends, setting a dangerous path for the Republican Party, not just in New York, but across the nation. "The questions of Prohibition and even of law enforcement become in a sense secondary issues, as compared to the whole nature of the

Republican Party from a free agent, acting for the highest good of all the people, into a servile tool of sinister and discredited interests which know no party and are only interested in their own aggrandizement."[13]

Regarding the Eighteenth Amendment "as a sacred part of our fundamental law," Cristman's supporters saw the nomination of Wadsworth "as so serious a menace to Republican principles and such a blow to Republican ideals, and of such serious and disastrous consequences to the future welfare of our nation, that we feel it incumbent upon us to hereby give notice that we reserve for ourselves complete liberty of action."[14] The agitation ended with Cristman's declaration of his candidacy on behalf of the Constitutional Party. With Cristman choosing to avoid party squabbles, Wadsworth handily won the nomination in a near-unanimous vote.[15]

Rather than adopt a compromise plank regarding the enforcement of the Federal Prohibition law, the party simply urged voters to give "a full expression" of their opinion of Prohibition by voting on the referendum.[16] Further dampening the spirit of the drys, the convention selected Ogden Mills as their candidate for governor.[17]

Wadsworth and his supporters had managed to keep an enforcement plank from the platform, but they did not go far enough, according to his Democratic challenger, Robert Wagner, a New York Supreme Court justice, who charged the senator with straddling the fence in hopes of keeping dry Republicans on his side. Wagner reminded voters that Wadsworth had voted for the Volstead Act, making him a "deserter" to the wet cause. Wadsworth had explained his vote many times, saying that, once Prohibition became law, he did not think it proper to leave it unenforced.[18]

The Wadsworth campaign sat in limbo, not wet enough to pull Democrat voters their way, and too wet for many Republicans, who drifted to Frank Cristman, whom Sabin regarded as unelectable. She sympathized with women who wanted to vote for Cristman, feeling "they must make their protest against Senator Wadsworth's stand on Prohibition," but she wondered if they realized such a choice was "throwing their vote to Tammany Hall, an organization far wetter than the Republican Party." Sabin implored, "Don't let it be said that the Republican women are not as loyal to their party as are their Democratic sisters."[19]

Cristman's campaign manager, S. E. Nicholson, warned that "national Republicans" supporting Wadsworth, "the pliant tool of the discredited liquor interests," threatened to split the national party much as Wadsworth's candidacy had done in New York. Sabin rushed to her friend's defense, broadcasting her message by radio across New York City. Wadsworth, she asserted, opposed the Eighteenth Amendment as a perversion of the Constitution that inserted a "sumptuous police statute" into that document, resulting in "contention and disrespect for the Constitution itself." Wadsworth, Sabin continued, had urged modification of the Volstead Act to end the "hypocrisy, corruption and contempt for law and the Constitution, so prevalent in the country today." He did not oppose Prohibition for its aim, which he believed should be temperance, but its method, which forced abolition.[20] Sabin herself was nearing a similar view, though she was not ready to stand fully for repeal in the same way Wadsworth did.

As the congressional elections of 1926 approached, Mabel Willebrandt was forced into the role of political pawn. Samuel Shortridge, the junior senator from California, tried to secure her endorsement, promising Willebrandt a judgeship, according to Hiram Johnson, the senior California senator so instrumental in Willebrandt's appointment as assistant attorney general.[21] Relations between Johnson and Willebrandt had soured two years earlier when she supported Calvin Coolidge for the Republican nomination rather than Johnson.[22] Matters were not helped by Johnson's attempts to get Willebrandt's assistance in the hiring and firing of personnel in federal prisons, to no avail. Explaining the situation to Harold Ickes, a Johnson supporter in 1924, Johnson granted Willebrandt had "performed the duties of her office with fair success," but averred, "I know she has been more successful in obtaining publicity." Johnson claimed to "have no criticism" of Willebrandt, but accused her of abandoning him when he "was on the political toboggan and practically dead." He assumed credit for "everything politically that she is," but she had since become "a devotee of power, and worships at the shrine of the prevailing dynasty."[23]

Willebrandt fed Johnson's suspicions when she suggested to her old friend Frank Doherty that Shortridge might have more political clout than Johnson. Doherty regarded Shortridge as "dishonest," and predicted any association with the junior senator would irrevocably damage Willebrandt's relationship with Johnson.[24] In a letter to Doherty, Johnson pointed out that Shortridge was a "wet" and Mrs. Willebrandt the "leading 'dry' in the nation." If "she would sell her principle" for a judgeship, Johnson threatened to "retract everything that I have said concerning the very fulsome recommendation I gave to her" when advancing her name to Harry Daugherty in 1921.[25] Choosing to remain silent on an endorsement of Shortridge but not openly opposing him left Willebrandt in limbo, with a supposition that after the election Shortridge would hold her silence against her, preventing her appointment as a judge.[26]

Pauline Sabin debated Eleanor Roosevelt over the merits of their respective candidates—Sabin for James Wadsworth and Roosevelt for Democrat judge Robert Wagner—at a rally hosted by the Women's City Club. As the election neared, she hosted Wadsworth at Bayberry Land, escorting him on a speaking tour through surrounding Suffolk County. Wadsworth spoke on many topics, hoping to demonstrate that he was more than a one-issue candidate, but questions about his Prohibition stance could not be held at bay. Sabin took the flak, turning the subject from Wadsworth's personal views to the Prohibition referendum, which would offer voters the chance to express their sentiments, determining, in large part, the course that Wadsworth would take. That "certain organizations," presumably the WCTU and the ASL, urged their members not to vote on the referendum amazed Sabin. "It seems strange to me that any woman should not want to register her opinion on this vital question. The question before the women today is whether they feel that the present Prohibition laws are winning their respect."[27] Sabin turned the tables on Wadsworth's opponents, explaining that they possessed the means to decide the fate of Prohibition in New York without factoring Wadsworth into the equation. If New Yorkers opposed Prohibition, they could vote against the referendum without using their vote against Wadsworth, who, other than on the issue of Prohibition, represented most of the values held dear by Republicans.

Sabin's prediction that votes for Frank Cristman were votes for Tammany proved accurate. James Wadsworth lost to Robert Wagner by 127,718 votes, with Cristman receiving more than 220,000, enough to have put Wadsworth over the top.[28] For all the heated accusations about Wadsworth's anti-Prohibition sentiment, the cloud of doubt cast on the strength of the senator's convictions on that position might have done more harm than Cristman's vote pulling. New York's voters overwhelmingly approved the referendum calling for modification, voting three to one in favor.[29] Despite the seeming mandate for modification, Prohibitionists in New York did not blink. Cristman's campaign manager called the referendum a "straw vote" designed to distract from wet candidates. Arthur Davis, superintendent of the Anti-Saloon League of New York, claimed the "real referendum lay in the defeat of United States Senator James W. Wadsworth," his loss advancing "the cause of Prohibition in the nation to a greater extent than any event since the adoption of the Eighteenth Amendment."[30] Such comments failed to reflect the reality, that not only had New York, the most populous state in the country, endorsed modification of the Prohibition laws, but so had five other states—California, Illinois, Montana, Nevada, and Wisconsin—with a combined population of about twenty-four million people, representing almost a quarter of the nation's inhabitants.[31] While popular votes against the existing law carried no legal authority for change, the votes in those six states constituted a significant shift in public opinion. Still, when asked about sponsoring a bill for modification of the Volstead Act, Wadsworth said such a bill had no chance even to get out of committee hearings.[32]

Mabel Willebrandt's 1926 ended with uncertainty, frustrations in her professional life motivating deep reflection as the New Year approached. She could admit that "most any other man or woman would jump at the opportunities of my office," which provided a "fair salary," travel, and "worthwhile and interesting work" but so far had not proven the stepping-stone she had hoped it would be. Willebrandt had learned, "It takes lots longer for a woman to get to the same place so far as good results for public office is concerned than it does a man."[33]

Pauline began 1927 at a three-day national conference, a first of its kind for women, in Washington, D.C. The dates of the conference coincided, probably by no accident, with gatherings of the General Federation of Women's Clubs and the WCTU, being held in the capital at the same time. Members of the three groups, some of whom might have belonged to all three organizations, ran into one another repeatedly during the week. Pauline and Charles Sabin, along with prominent women from all three conferences, attended a dinner hosted by Secretary of War Dwight Davis and his wife honoring President and Mrs. Coolidge.[34] Knowing his friend Charlie Sabin, a Democrat and fellow prominent member of the Association Against the Prohibition Amendment, might have trouble fitting in with a stuffier, Republican-dominated crowd, James Wadsworth suggested the Sabins stop at his house on the way to the Davises' for "a little fortifying against the strain of the evening."[35] Who can say whether Jim meant political or liquid reinforcement? The following night, the Sabins and two thousand other guests, including many of the women from all three conferences—and Mabel Willebrandt—attended a state reception hosted by President and Mrs. Coolidge honoring the judiciary.[36]

The convergence of so many women, representing so many groups, with so many varying interests, inflamed Sabin's frequent concern about a "feminine bloc," represented largely by the old guard of suffragists, working outside the established parties.[37] She urged women to consider a candidate's principles and positions on *all* issues, not the "pet" concerns of narrowly defined interest groups.[38] An editorial in the *New York Evening Post* recognized Sabin's approach as granting her "more real power than those who remain outside in purely feminist" organizations. The paper saw groups focusing on women's issues "bridging the gap between the pre-suffrage era and the era of full political understanding and practice by women," but hoped women remaining outside the parties would not be "set aside."[39] Months later, Sabin repeated her admonition, applauding Republican women for sticking with the party to achieve "the greatest good" possible "by the women cooperating with men," urging women to do their share of the work, hoping that effort would result, one day, in the election of women to political office in proportion to their numbers.[40]

While Sabin attended the Republican women's committee conference, a Long Island newspaper editorial placed James Wadsworth's poor showing in Suffolk County squarely upon her shoulders. Sabin and her like-minded sisters were "disloyal to the cardinal principles" of the Republican Party, undermining any claim they had to be leaders within the party; the "women of wealth and culture" lacked the "high and worthy ideals" needed to "keep in close touch with the thousands of women in the lowlier walks of life and present to them the unselfishness and holiness of their mission."[41]

The argument that many of the women becoming active in party politics came from the upper class was valid, but this was an issue particular to Suffolk County, where wealthy denizens of Manhattan had built large estates in the past ten years, changing the rural character of the area, its former agriculture-based economy, and its politics.

Questioned by Congress about expenditures, particularly for undercover agents, Assistant Secretary Lincoln Andrews argued that such work was necessary to ferret out information about bootleggers and their vast conspiracies, and to build cases, like that against Olmstead's liquor ring, over a long period of time rather than making arrests at the first sign of illegality. "A limited number of Government employees, every one of them known to the criminal element, operating in broad daylight and in the view of all, can not [sic] hope to defeat unknown, intelligent, and unscrupulous men," charged Andrews. The assistant secretary did not see any need for undercover agents to "engage in any illegal practices or entice others to do so," but acknowledged that without them, "Prohibition enforcement will be handicapped almost to the point of failure." Hoping to clarify the distinction between acceptable and unacceptable involvement by undercover agents in criminal enterprises, Andrews supplied an example, seemingly ripped from William Whitney's playbook: could an agent go to work for a rumrunner and participate in criminal acts to build a case? No, because that smacked of entrapment and grand juries might refuse to indict. Entrapment was not just the act of enticing a citizen into committing a crime, but the equally illegal act of "placing in his hands the instrument of the crime and then proceeding against him because of his possession or use thereof."[42] Rather, Andrews hoped that undercover agents could build cases by observing criminal acts or learning of proposed acts and passing the information to their superiors.

On the first of March 1927, Al Hubbard dropped by the headquarters to meet with Lyle and Whitney and tell them he had been offered a bribe by some whiskey runners desperate enough to approach a known Prohibition agent hoping the right amount would ensure his assistance. Hubbard said he could make another big case if allowed to accept the bribe and pretend to offer protection in exchange.[43] The idea of accepting a bribe scared Whitney, perhaps recalling the recent admonition of Assistant Secretary Andrews, so he sought the counsel and approval of Tom Revelle. Agent Hubbard and his partner, Richard Fryant, would need to make several runs on the ships from Vancouver to Seattle, they told Revelle; they might need to help unload cargo; and they would almost certainly need to accept bribe money to convince the suspects of their legitimate criminal intent. But the catch would be worth the gamble: a dozen or more men and several boats, including one of the newest and fastest. Whitney asked Revelle "whether or not they should take up the work," the district attorney answering, "This is the kind of work we should be doing."[44] Years later, Whitney claimed to have

told "Mr. Revelle I would have nothing to do with the case independently and Mr. Revelle stated that he would take the entire responsibility and would direct the case himself."[45] For an indomitable
Prohibitionist like Whitney to hesitate testified to his misgivings
about Hubbard.

Whitney's reluctance to back Hubbard's potentially illegal activities, conducted in secret, contrasted sharply with his approval of
brutal tactics employed openly against those violating the Volstead
Act. Neither Whitney nor Revelle thought that the beatings and
shootings of smugglers and moonshiners were unwarranted. Whitney liked his agents to be tough men unafraid to smash a speakeasy
to bits or beat a bootlegger into submission. Revelle agreed that
some offenders "deserve a good killing," and admired his friend's
dedication to enforcement, but he had warned Whitney that when
his men went too far, it hurt their public image.[46]

On April 1, 1927, a bill to reorganize the Prohibition Unit and
Customs Service took effect with both agencies raised to the
status of a bureau, on a par with the Internal Revenue Bureau.[47] Roy
Haynes would remain as commissioner of Prohibition, but Lincoln
Andrews and Andrew Mellon would formulate policies and issue
directives to field personnel. Lincoln Andrews granted Haynes final
authority on matters of enforcement, but Haynes was expected to
confer with Andrews before making decisions. On the surface, it
appeared Haynes had regained some of the powers usurped from
him previously, but the need to consult with Andrews seemed another mitigation. As the changes were implemented, letters of opposition that Mabel Willebrandt had written to various senators
during debate on the bill became known to the public. She believed
the new arrangement scattered responsibilities, endangering successful enforcement with too many cooks in the kitchen.

The administrative changes formalized a scheme begun in Seattle shortly after the end of the Olmstead trial when Alf Oftedal of the Internal Revenue Bureau's Intelligence Unit walked into Revelle's office carrying a letter from Assistant Secretary Andrews of the Treasury Department announcing Oftedal's appointment as chief coordinator of Prohibition enforcement action on the Pacific Coast.[48] Andrews had given Oftedal and his special agents authority to take over any investigation or involve themselves in any manner Oftedal deemed in the best interest of enforcement, placing the Seattle office of the Prohibition Unit in a subservient position. Revelle recognized the threat to William Whitney, who had been investigated by the Intelligence Unit previously over allegations that some of his methods skirted the law. The district attorney took his concerns to Assistant Attorney General Willebrandt. He believed Oftedal was more interested in investigating federal forces for corruption than in pursuing rumrunners, a situation sure to generate friction with Whitney, who had told Revelle he would not cooperate with Oftedal. Revelle hoped that Willebrandt could force cooperation between the Intelligence and Prohibition Units, agencies over which she had no authority, but such efforts should not put Oftedal in a position superior to Whitney or Lyle. "The best thing for this territory," advised Revelle, "is for all parties to keep their hands off Roy Lyle and Bill Whitney and give them sufficient men and money, and we will make this district one of which men can be proud."[49]

Al Hubbard marched into Tom Revelle's office on April 29 to report that he and his partner, Richard Fryant, would assist in the delivery of two hundred cases of whiskey from British Columbia aboard the speedboat *Zev*. The rumrunners had invited Hubbard and Fryant along to shield the shipment from any enforcement agencies they encountered. Hubbard volunteered to ride on the *Zev* with the rumrunners while Fryant waited with some agents at the rendezvous point, Samish Island, to seize the landing party upon arrival. Once the two agents had the suspects under control, Fryant would call Revelle, who would lead several U.S. Marshals to one of the gang's Seattle homes to arrest six others Hubbard had fingered in the conspiracy.

Hubbard brought the ship down as planned on Saturday, and Revelle got his call about three a.m. Sunday. He and the deputies raided the designated home, but no one was there. Revelle smelled treachery and the stench increased when he heard from Fryant that Hubbard and the *Zev* had not arrived at the rendezvous point and neither did those expected to take delivery from the *Zev*. Hours passed, the fate of the *Zev* unknown. Revelle alternated between concern for Al Hubbard, fearing his true intentions had been discovered, and anger that he may have been double-crossed. Finally, the boat turned up in Anacortes, at the U.S. Coast Guard base several miles south of the rendezvous point, with Hubbard in command.

Hubbard delivered an inspired account of the night's events. When the *Zev* had docked at Samish Island, Hubbard's use of the light to signal Fryant had aroused the rumrunners' suspicions, and they turned on him in a foul mood. "Seeing that the game was up," Hubbard had pointed his pistol at them and placed them under arrest, promising to shoot them if they did not comply. He manacled one man to the ship's wheel and used rope to bind the other. Fearing the comrades of his two captives were on the island and would attempt to board the *Zev* and overpower him, he cast off, fired the engines, and set off into a nasty storm. He piloted the craft to Anacortes and turned the ship and crew over to the guardsmen for safekeeping. Although he believed the bust would have been bigger had some of the suspects not been tipped off, Revelle was thrilled, calling it "a wonderful piece of work."[50] The *Seattle Times* hailed it "as a heroic capture."[51] Whitney, in Washington, D.C., under scrutiny by his superiors, read the news of Hubbard's work and sent his protégé a fulsome and enthusiastic note of congratulations, declaring, "You have justified my every confidence in you," promising to get the *Zev* for Hubbard's future efforts.[52]

In the week that followed, though, the men arrested on the *Zev* claimed Hubbard had extorted thousands of dollars from them. Tom Revelle discounted the assertions as a feeble attempt by the men to save themselves, until one of Senator Jones' closest friends, an attorney representing the men caught in Hubbard's *Zev* sting, told Revelle that "Hubbard and Fryant had received between eight and ten thousand dollars" in bribes. The attorney was offering to have his clients tell the whole story, to get affidavits from their partners in Canada, but Revelle refused the offer, saying he would not hold up the statements of rumrunners against the statements made by agents. A few days later, Fryant told Revelle he had personal knowledge that Al Hubbard had taken bribes from rumrunners to remain silent about their operations. Worse, Fryant claimed he and Hubbard had passed one thousand dollars to Whitney as evidence in a previous case, something Whitney had failed to share with the district attorney.

Wanting to get out ahead of the problem, Revelle wrote long letters to his boss, Assistant Attorney General Mabel Willebrandt, and his benefactor, Senator Wesley Jones. From Willebrandt he asked for an investigation, stressing at great length that it should not be conducted by agents of the Internal Revenue Bureau's Intelligence Unit. Knowing Willebrandt thought highly of the Intelligence Unit, yet respecting her as a "true and good woman," he pled for her to understand that the IRB's work "would not be received with full credit in this district." Rather, she should ask the Bureau of Investigation in the Department of Justice to send agents to Seattle.

In his letter to Senator Wesley Jones, Revelle asked if he would meet with Willebrandt and convince her of the wisdom of using the

DOJ's agents to investigate. Somewhere out there, Alf Oftedal's Intelligence Unit, already at work, would relish the chance to investigate Hubbard, seizing upon anything implicating Whitney and Lyle. Revelle believed in the honesty of Whitney and Lyle, but worried that if the accusations made against Hubbard proved true, "the enemies of this work and this great movement would shout and yell and ridicule." "And yet," Revelle admitted, "if we don't meet the situation and at once prove the truth or falsity of these charges, and that they should break some other way, then we would be all accused of covering these things out."[53]

I n the spring of 1927, the Women's National Republican Club sent a survey to its members to gauge their attitudes about Prohibition and, more importantly, Prohibition laws and enforcement. Only 107 of almost a thousand respondents were satisfied with existing laws; the rest were split nearly evenly between favoring outright repeal and modification of the law to make it effective. The overwhelming majority of women, 817, felt there had been no improvement in public morals and an almost equal number saw disrespect for the law on the rise. A majority said crime and drinking had gone up as a result of Prohibition.[54] The *New York Evening Post* said the survey offered "one more proof that the 'woman vote' cannot be ticketed and counted upon to be different from the 'man vote.'"[55] The *Philadelphia Ledger* suggested women's "indifference" at the voting booth might change in the 1928 election, as Prohibition, a women's issue, seemed likely to become a major factor in the campaign, giving "politicians some uneasiness."[56]

Muddying the waters for career politicians, who were busy trying to assess the sentiments and voting preferences of women, the Women's National Committee on Law Enforcement, in conference

shortly after the WNRC released its survey results, issued a reminder that the survey was small and did not represent the views of
most women. Ella Boole of the WCTU echoed those comments,
touting the voting strength of her organization's 300,000 members.
Mrs. Edward White, vice president of the General Federation of
Women's Clubs, had not heard about the survey, despite claiming to
be a "fairly prominent Republican" in her state. Mrs. White and
Mrs. Boole joined with others at the conference to endorse a resolution protesting the WNRC poll and any suggestion that it represented the sentiments of women.[57]

After a winter and spring of rum-running, Roy Olmstead's luck
finally ran out. On May 9, 1927, the Circuit Court of Appeals,
by a vote of two to one, upheld the Olmstead convictions. The circuit
court had reviewed only the assertion that wiretapping was unconstitutional; Olmstead's defense team did not submit a list of the
many flagrant violations of court procedure by the prosecution, perhaps because they feared the wrath of Thomas Revelle, who was
about to prosecute a second case against Olmstead. Revelle dismissed the opinion of the dissenting judge, who saw wiretapping as
a violation of the Constitution, which "was 1000 miles away from
the real law in this case."[58] But the dissenting opinion provided a
glimmer of hope to Olmstead's defense team, who promptly issued
an appeal to the highest court in the land, allowing Olmstead, once
again, to avoid jail.

The circuit court's decision affirmed Revelle's reliability and honesty in Willebrandt's mind, making her decision to initiate a DOJ
investigation of the *Zev* affair much easier. Revelle's request had
read like an admission of guilt by association, but she trusted her
district attorney's motives and integrity. While Willebrandt's acqui-

escence pleased Senator Jones, any investigation held the potential to expose the unconventional methods of the Seattle Prohibition Unit office and, specifically, William Whitney.[59]

On July 29, 1927, two agents from the Department of Justice interviewed Al Hubbard about the rumors that he and Agent Fryant had taken bribes and had turned over $1,000 to Whitney as evidence. Hubbard denied the charge, but he didn't fabricate a believable story with which to protect himself. On his agent's salary of $155 a month, he admitted to paying his first wife $150 a month alimony, along with an earlier cash settlement of about $3,000. He had spent $800 on the ring for his second wife and $2,500 on his own ring. As the two investigators plied him for more details of his financial situation, Hubbard could not keep his hubris in check, and he bragged that he owned a boat and several expensive cars. Hubbard's candor, inexplicable to his interviewers, revealed the tawdry charade he was playing upon Olmstead, Whitney, their respective organizations, and so many others.[60]

Chapter 10

Calvin Coolidge welcomed fifteen newspaper correspondents into his summer White House office, inside the Rapid City, South Dakota, high school on August 2, 1927, the fourth anniversary of President Warren Harding's death, and handed each a neatly folded slip of paper with the following statement: "I do not choose to run for President in nineteen twenty-eight." One reporter asked: "Is there any other comment?" to which Coolidge replied, "None," sending the correspondents scurrying to telegraphs and telephones to report the bombshell. Prior to this "press conference," neither Coolidge nor anyone in his administration had even *hinted* at such a decision.[1] Twenty minutes after dispensing the notes, Coolidge left his office, greeted a chief from the Sioux Indian Nation, climbed into his chauffeured car, and returned to the South Dakota State Game Lodge in the Black Hills, where he was spending the summer. Before he reached the lodge, news of his abdication had spread around the country, touching off rampant speculation about the president's reasons and likely successors.

Mabel Willebrandt discreetly visited Seattle in late August 1927. After checking into the Olympic Hotel, she had Tom Revelle pick her up and drive around the city for half a day. Careful to be evenhanded, Revelle offered background on the Hubbard situation; he stressed his trust in Whitney and Lyle, but he was anxious to know the truth of the accusations thrown at Hubbard. Willebrandt readily agreed that he had to stand his ground and fight before she put her finger on the key problem, the one that would destroy the careers of so many of those involved: she asked if he "would have to depend upon the testimony of Hubbard in the trial of some of these big conspiracy cases."[2] A sharp pang of worry knifed his heart because the answer was, of course, yes, Hubbard would have a vital role in the second Olmstead trial and in the *Zev* case. In the end, Revelle stated his belief that the young agent could be trusted.

Just days later, Willebrandt, trying to vacation in Yellowstone National Park with Dorothy, received an urgent telegram from Revelle, who was concerned about reports in the local papers and the wire services that, according to the Prohibition Unit's headquarters in Washington, D.C., an investigation was under way into the possible corruption of his district's Prohibition Unit. Revelle had hoped the investigation would remain a secret until its results were conclusive. When his boss didn't respond, Revelle sent a second, frenzied telegram two days later: "Such interviews and publicity thereof will of necessity reflect upon every agent to be used as witnesses in pending conspiracy cases and in large measure destroy their credibility before jury." Hoping to control the damage, he asked Willebrandt, "Wire to those responsible for such publicity to discontinue same?" Advised two days later that based upon the DOJ's investigation Agents Hubbard and Fryant were to be suspended, Revelle wrote Willebrandt, "Suspension will result in failure" in the *Zev* case and the pending trial against Roy

Pauline Sabin and her sons, 1922.

Above: Pauline Sabin fulfilling her duties as a Republican leader at the Suffolk County Fair, 1922. GETTY IMAGES

Right: Mabel Willebrandt, circa 1920. LIBRARY OF CONGRESS

Mabel Willebrandt (*center, to the left of President Coolidge*)
as the only female member of the "little cabinet,"
composed of the top assistant for each executive department.

Radio station KFQX, the alleged source of "coded"
messages to rumrunners, inside the Olmstead home.

Roy and Elsie Olmstead seemingly unfazed by his indictment in 1925.

Left: William Whitney. NATIONAL ARCHIVES AND RECORDS ADMINISTRATION

Right: Mabel with Dorothy shortly after her adoption. LIBRARY OF CONGRESS

Left: James Wadsworth emphasizing a point. LIBRARY OF CONGRESS

Right: Al Hubbard before he became the talk of Seattle, circa 1924.

Senator Wesley Jones,
William Whitney and Roy Lyle's benefactor and protector.
LIBRARY OF CONGRESS

Mabel Willebrandt giving her future employer, Louis B. Mayer,
and his family a tour of the White House.
GETTY IMAGES

Mabel Willebrandt taking center stage at the 1928 Republican
National Convention as chairman of the credentials committee.

GETTY IMAGES

Mabel Willebrandt posing with James Good, Herbert Hoover's campaign
manager in the western states (*left*), and Walter Newton, head of the
Republican Speakers Bureau (*right*), after her controversial speeches in Ohio.

CHICAGO HISTORY MUSEUM

Two of the more than one million Women's Organization for National Prohibition Repeal members out in the streets advocating for repeal.
GETTY IMAGES

Al Smith; John J. Raskob, Democratic National Committee chairman; and Pauline Sabin at the 1932 Democratic National Convention joining in bipartisan support for repeal.
THE ASSOCIATED PRESS

Olmstead. "Convinced conspiracy on hand to defeat trial of these cases. Defeat of trial of cases can never be explained in this district. All believers in law in this district will believe action deliberately planned to save large rumrunners and grafters." Though this was a Treasury Department matter, he had faith in Willebrandt's ability to influence the outcome. "Can you not stop such action until I will be able to confer personally with [Prohibition Commissioner James] Doran?"[3]

Willebrandt ignored Revelle's request to be summoned to Washington, D.C., but promised to wire "Washington your views" although DOJ department policy, and basic logic, dictated "we cannot demand Treasury Department keep men in their department if they have lost confidence in them." She supported his aggressive moves to prosecute pending cases, promised to "back your office in trial," and concluded with a carefully worded warning: "It has uniformly been my experience in many situations similar to yours in many parts of the country, where similar fears were expressed of loss of cases because of dismissal of agent, the case can be won anyway if the testimony is true." Put another way, she was not joining the growing list of officials who were protecting Al Hubbard, nor did she think it wise for Revelle to do so.

In late August, Roy Lyle received a phone call from Dr. James Doran, Prohibition commissioner, informing him that Hubbard and Fryant had been suspended. Lyle called the action "arbitrary" and had the sinking feeling the decision had been made days earlier. Defending his action, Doran put the onus on Willebrandt, who had reviewed the Treasury Department's files relating to the matter and endorsed the suspensions. Whether she had made her decision before or after her correspondence with Revelle was not recorded, but her advice to him, to remain aloof, suggested her inclinations and should have served as a reminder to the district attorney of where his loyalties should lie. Doran, whose bureau Willebrandt appeared to be running, cautioned Lyle not to let himself or his staff appear to defend Hubbard or Fryant, men Doran regarded with a great deal of skepticism.[4]

Pauline Sabin's stature in New York politics grew steadily as she proved herself a capable fund-raiser and campaigner, knowledgeable on a variety of issues, not just those relegated to the domain of women, and willing to take firm stands for her beliefs.[5] While loyal to the Republican Party, Sabin did not allow herself to become doctrinaire, holding so hard to the party line that her own opinions might have become obscured. Proof of her independence came in the off-year elections of 1927, when several amendments to the New York State constitution were proposed, including one that would extend the term of office for the governor from two to four years. Sabin was asked by a New York City radio station to participate in a debate with Eleanor Roosevelt on the proposed amendment, and each woman took the opposite position of her party: Sabin supported the amendment, saying it would allow the governor more time to govern than campaign. Mrs. Roosevelt insisted voters would become uninterested if forced to wait every four years for an election of significance.[6] The debate showcased the growing influence of radio to inform and shape political discourse. The station asked its listeners to phone, telegraph, or mail their votes for the winner of the debate. Listeners gave the edge to Sabin by a hefty margin, but voters at the polls defeated the measure.[7]

The second Olmstead trial opened on October 17, 1927, nearly two years after his arrest at Woodmont Beach, but the King of the Bootleggers was not in the courtroom. He had elected to hide out, believing his absence might make things easier for his codefendants.[8] Thomas Revelle would not try Olmstead in absentia, but he would not delay the trial, either; Olmstead's case would be separated from the rest and saved for a later day.

Revelle had his star witness, Al Hubbard, recount the events of Thanksgiving Day of 1925 at Woodmont Beach and name all those involved in the planning of the operation and their roles in Olmstead's liquor ring. Hubbard moved quickly, following Revelle's lead, perhaps hoping to jump over questions that might arise should the defense counsel have the time to consider for more than a few seconds any of Hubbard's answers. But, already shaky in his recollections and demeanor, Hubbard wilted under cross-examination when he had to admit his recent suspension from the Prohibition Unit. No doubt a seed was planted in the jury's mind that Hubbard had something to hide.

Knowing how Hubbard's testimony would be attacked, Revelle called to the stand Prohibition agent Russell Jackson, Hubbard's partner on that night, to corroborate Hubbard's version of events. Revelle had seen Agent Jackson "hobnobbing with the defense counsel" and heard rumors that Jackson was no longer loyal to the unit, but Whitney, as usual, had faith in his men, and Revelle had no other option. When Jackson took the stand, though, Whitney watched in horror as his own agent testified that when he and his comrades rushed the beach, they "found Hubbard there laying planks on the wharf" to aid in the landing. When the agents arrested the smugglers, Jackson asserted, "Hubbard turned to Olmstead and said, 'Roy, they have caught us this time.'"[9] Revelle was dumbfounded, unable to think up a plausible excuse for Hubbard's actions.[10]

The trial moved much more quickly than the first involving the Olmstead conspiracy. Only a week after the trial began, both sides rested their cases and the jurors quickly reached their verdict. Fourteen of the thirty-six defendants were found guilty. Revelle was incensed at Jackson's betrayal and angry at a verdict that let off so many guilty men (in his assessment "everyone at trial was guilty as charged"). The trial had demonstrated how others—the jury, the press, the public—could easily see Hubbard's undercover work as a criminal enterprise, a scheme that implicated not just the Prohibition Unit but Revelle himself. Yet there was no easy way to rectify the problem. Revelle confided to Willebrandt, "Personally, I am very strongly convinced from our experience here in the last two or three weeks, that even though Hubbard and Fryant took money, yet there is no possible hope of ever successfully trying them for the same."[11] Revelle had just admitted to the assistant attorney general of the United States that he had used crooked agents to convict the bootleggers and he could not now prosecute the agents without undoing the convictions.

"Because of the undercover influence that is manifestly active and vigorous in the city against him," he informed the attorney general's office, "I will not be very highly justified in using him in any other cases except the *Zev* case."[12] His plan to use Albert Hubbard in another trial, a violation of the ethics he so often proclaimed, indicated just how lost the U.S. District Attorney for the Twentieth District had become. He would do anything to win the upcoming *Zev* case.

On November 8, Olmstead returned to Seattle and turned himself in, ready to face the charges.[13] Broke (and having forfeited his bail by missing the trial three weeks earlier), he had to sit in the county jail, waiting for an opening in the court docket.[14] It was the first time he had spent more than a few hours under lock and key since his arrest in 1925, but his incarceration lasted only a week. Hubbard testified to the rumrunner's role at Woodmont Beach, with Whitney adding that Olmstead said he had been caught "red-handed." Olmstead denied all charges and claimed Revelle had offered him a presidential pardon if he would tell a grand jury about bribing city and county officials. Revelle, forced to take the stand, admitted to meeting with Olmstead, but denied any promises had been made. Confirming Revelle's fears about the perception surrounding Hubbard, the judge's instructions to the jury included an admonition not to rely on the statements of government agents who lacked any corroborating evidence or witnesses. After only four hours of deliberation, Olmstead was acquitted. Revelle called the ruling the "grossest miscarriage of justice since I have been in office."

The infamous rumrunner left the courtroom technically free, but bound for the county jail until he was able to repay the bond he had skipped on two lesser charges. On November 21, 1927, the Supreme Court declined to hear the "whispering wires" appeal, indicating they saw no compelling constitutional question in the wiretap case.[15] Olmstead would have to serve the four years and pay the eight-thousand-dollar fine meted out to him nearly a year earlier. Whitney and his comrades were ecstatic at this final victory over Olmstead. After a brief reprieve orchestrated by his attorney, Olmstead, clad in a coat and tie as usual, carried his suitcase down the dock and onto the ship ferrying him to McNeil Island Federal Penitentiary on November 29, 1927.[16] Arrested in late 1925, the King of the Bootleggers had been out on bail for years, his presence around town a sign of the breakdown in the federal justice system.

He went with his characteristic smile fading from his lips, and gave one last quote to surprised reporters and onlookers: "I'm not complaining. I violated a law, and that is always wrong; now I'm going to pay the penalty society demands for such violation. It is my own fault."[17]

The long-awaited victory over Olmstead would have had some salutary effect on Whitney's reputation within the government as well as in the "dry" community, but it did not remove the taint attached to him. Reorganization of the Prohibition Unit required all employees to reapply for their positions and take a test to confirm their capabilities. Lingering charges of improprieties in Whitney's expense accounts and his approval of the use of excessive force by his agents meant he would need to do more than just pass a test. James Yaden of the Civil Service Commission arrived to interview Whitney; more than anything else, he wanted to know the role Whitney had played in hiring Al Hubbard and directing his activities. Casting aside personal responsibility, Whitney implicated Roy Lyle, Senator Wesley Jones, District Attorney Thomas Revelle, and Prohibition Commissioner Roy Haynes as approving the hiring of Al Hubbard, and offered a 1925 letter from Lyle to Haynes as proof of their roles.[18] In that letter, Lyle had expressed faith in Hubbard's character, and if he was wrong, "in no way could the government suffer even if it should be felt that he might double cross the government. Hubbard would never be in possession of any knowledge of what the government intended to do in any case, and would not know what plans the government had anyway."[19]

Having absolved himself from the hiring of Hubbard, Whitney defended his agent's work. The "boy wonder" turned undercover agent had produced almost immediate results, providing Whitney with information to make the second Olmstead case. Whitney professed to have trained Hubbard to avoid any instigation of criminal acts, but merely to "follow along . . . We always told Hubbard not to initiate any of the illegal actions."[20] As proof that he had often discussed such instructions and Hubbard's progress with Revelle, he submitted three large volumes of documents concerning Hubbard along with his application to the CSC.[21] As Whitney awaited his fate, he confided to Jones that if his application failed to pass muster with the CSC, "I will have wasted seven years of sacrifice and be in a worse position than I started . . ."[22]

As the campaign season began early in 1928, Pauline Sabin was a presumptive delegate to the national convention given her standing as a member of the Republican National Committee. New York was allowed seven delegates; the state Republican committee decided two would be women and assigned the task for their selection to the county vice chairpersons, who were women. Sarah Butler was the other presumed female delegate, but women from "up-state" counties, all those outside of greater New York City, resented the control exerted by party leaders based in the city, and wanted three rather than two women delegates including one from upstate. Hoping to avoid conflict and any appearance of division in the party, Sabin and Butler removed their names from consideration as delegates, Sabin declaring, "An individual, or the personal ambitions of an individual, are of no consequence compared to the importance of having an harmonious party."[23] The vice chairwomen selected Sabin and Florence Wardwell, of upstate Otsego County, to serve as delegates, a compromise possible by virtue of Sabin's party loyalty and graciousness.[24]

The five male delegates-at-large included James Wadsworth, though he no longer held office or an official party position and his prominence resurrected the debate over his views on Prohibition and whether he would support the presumptive presidential candidate, Herbert Hoover, or a movement to draft Calvin Coolidge at the national convention, an effort hinted at by critics of party leaders, particularly Charles Hilles. Perhaps attempting to soothe Wadsworth's detractors, he and Nicholas Murray Butler announced that they would not advance any initiative that would divide the wet and dry Republicans at the national convention.[25]

The differences between the female delegates, Sabin and Wardwell, reflected a division not only within the state Republican committee, but also the national Republican Party, over the candidacy of Herbert Hoover, President Coolidge's handpicked successor. Sabin and other state party leaders refused to endorse any candidate until the convention, and they got the state committee to agree that its delegation would not campaign for any candidate in advance of the convention. Ignoring the state committee's instructions to remain unpledged, Wardwell openly supported Hoover for the party's nomination months before the national convention.[26] Like-minded women taking their lead from Wardwell threatened to vote for Al Smith if Hoover failed to get the nomination as a result of the New York delegation's refusal to endorse him. Sabin challenged Wardwell's claim that Republican women overwhelmingly supported Hoover and charged her with disloyalty to the state party organization.[27]

The Women's National Republican Club called a "mock" convention for April 24, at the Waldorf-Astoria Hotel in Manhattan, suggesting a gathering intended to mimic the upcoming Republican National Convention in three months, but in truth mocking and, in some instances, skewering convention traditions, political opponents, and public perceptions of women in politics. Sabin played a small role at the mock convention, allowing those less familiar with convention proceedings to seize the reins and join in the fun. At one point, Sabin appeared as a "telegraph boy" failing in "his" duties to deliver a copy of a speech to its author and being scolded for caring more "about the cut of your uniform than you are with these serious proceedings," another jab at those who sought to define women in politics by appearance over substance.[28]

Mrs. Edward Van Zile, opening the mock convention, chided, "Only legal and qualified voters shall participate on a Republican primary or caucus for selecting delegates, but the delegates, though legal, need not be qualified." Van Zile also declared a policy of nondiscrimination based on "age, color or even for membership in the League of Women Voters." "Above all," she admonished, "let the delegates realize that the front we present to the enemy should always be marcelled, manicured and massaged," generating extended applause and laughter from the assemblage, which had grown tired of reporters who never failed to describe the wardrobe and appearance of female, and only female, political speakers. On the matter of law enforcement, the convention's "platform" teased, "Freedom cannot be appreciated unless there is some tyranny from which to be free. It is the historic duty of Government to furnish that tyranny; the Republican Party will see that the Government does its duty, having full confidence in the traditional ability of the American people to do the rest." In a moment of seriousness, Mrs. Coffin Van Rensselaer reminded the assembly that women had been invited into political decision-making only recently and needed to seize their opportunity more fully: "In the hands of women have been placed the fireside and all its influences; the guardianship of the beauties and delicacies of life, and the upraising in health and independence of the youth and, in a large measure, through these influences, the control of that elusive thing, the real power back of democracy— public opinion."[29]

President Calvin Coolidge's announcement that he would not seek reelection opened the field to many candidates, most of whom began jockeying for position in early 1928. Mabel Willebrandt stirred the pot in April when she announced her support, "unhesitatingly," for Herbert Hoover, the secretary of commerce, believing him the Republican candidate most supportive of Prohibition and most able to ensure a victory over the presumptive Democratic candidate, Al Smith, a renowned opponent of Prohibition. She made the announcement at a national gathering of the WCTU, an audience interested only in Willebrandt's view of Hoover as a defender of Prohibition. She pronounced Hoover "the answer to those who said Prohibition cannot be enforced." Willebrandt went on, "Prohibition is not being enforced and as a result the wets are saying that it can not [sic] be enforced. If you elect Mr. Hoover he will enforce it." Calling her "the fountainhead of Prohibition," the *Washington Post* wondered if Willebrandt meant she had been "hamstrung" by the Coolidge administration and would continue to be so if anyone other than Hoover were elected. The newspaper suggested Democrats might want to get Willebrandt before a Senate committee to explain her statements, but warned her "forceful" personality might be pushed to list the impediments to successful enforcement, in the process embarrassing elected officials who had opposed appropriations or changes in the law that might improve enforcement conditions.[30] The newspaper could not have described Willebrandt's seven-year dilemma any better: she had become the public face of Prohibition enforcement and been asked frequently to comment on its successes and failures, but she had no control over Prohibition agents or budget appropriations, a fact that she increasingly highlighted.

Willebrandt soon pointed to one failing that might hinder effective enforcement: the absence of women on juries. She took particular aim at New York, where "it seems incredible that fear of her [woman] persists," adding, "It amounts to saying that any kind of man is a better juror than the best woman, for as a matter of fact, in many districts, we are only getting the least responsible men on juries." Willebrandt did not claim "for woman any superiority" over her male counterparts, but insisted that women were not "inherently unfit" simply because of their sex or preconceptions of their "emotional" tendencies. Where women had been used as jurors, they were "superior intellectually and educationally to the men," many of whom remained available only after other men of quality secured excuses to avoid jury duty. Women jurors forced jury commissioners to reevaluate the lists of male jurors, some of whom Willebrandt regarded as career jurors, establishing relationships with police and court clerks to secure frequent listing for trial service, a situation that produced jurors who could be swayed by political favor making.[31] Willebrandt's pointed jabs underplayed a subtler commentary, one that would be echoed by others, including Pauline Sabin; most men acknowledged that Prohibition had been carried into existence by women, but the refusal of those same men to allow women to serve on juries hampered the effectiveness of the law.

Reversing itself in early 1928, the Supreme Court decided to hear the *U.S. v. Olmstead* appeal, filed as *Olmstead v. U.S.*, on the question of whether the wiretapping of phone lines violated the Constitution, specifically the Fourth and Fifth Amendments.[32] The decision scared those in the Prohibition Unit and its allies, pushing Senator Wesley Jones to write to Willebrandt about the urgency of defeating the appeal.[33] The assistant attorney general replied to the powerful senator, but only to advise him that Revelle would file the brief in advance of oral arguments scheduled before the nation's highest court on February 20, 1928.[34] The immediate effect of the court's decision was to grant the release of Roy Olmstead and most of his co-appellants on bail, after they'd endured just over two months in the pen.[35]

In mid-March, Special Assistant Attorney General Norman Morris, one of Willebrandt's trusted aides, arrived in Seattle to oversee a grand jury investigation into Agents Al Hubbard and Richard Fryant. Willebrandt had not informed Revelle; Morris just walked into his office. Revelle was "just sick over the matter," and Whitney felt betrayed because Willebrandt had promised "that she would not present this matter until all the important cases were tried."[36] Revelle still had defendants to be tried as part of additional, albeit smaller, cases against Olmstead. Hubbard was essential to those. He had just proven his value in the *Zev* case, in which six bootleggers from whom Hubbard had received bribes were convicted. Yet now he stood the chance of being indicted by the testimony of all the bootleggers the Prohibition Unit had ever convicted and by operatives of Alf Oftedal's Intelligence Unit.

In a few days, Lyle and Whitney heard "a persistent rumor" that Willebrandt intended to indict not just Hubbard, but also them and

Revelle. As usual, they turned to Senator Jones for help. Jones, however, declined to do anything that might be construed as interference in an official DOJ investigation. He trusted Willebrandt to be fair. Revelle, Whitney, and Lyle did not trust her, and they were sure the Intelligence Unit, in league with Willebrandt, would seek an indictment whether they had the evidence or not.[37] Their angst proved unnecessary, though, when the grand jury returned a "no true bill" on the charges against Hubbard and Fryant, having found insufficient cause for charges to be brought against them. Fryant was restored to duty within days; Hubbard's status was said to be pending.[38]

In the wake of his victory, and with the help of his mentors—Whitney, Lyle, and Revelle—Hubbard took a job as a deputy sheriff in Whatcom County, along the Canadian border. Perhaps the triumvirate thought a steady job in a rural setting would do the young man some good, or at least give them some relief. It did not last, though. Hubbard's aversion to rules and regulations may have prompted his firing a few months later, though it's more likely the separation was mutual, the freebooter wanting back into the action. Hubbard would stop by to see his friends at the unit, ask to be reinstated, occasionally ask for a loan (which Whitney granted), and on more than one occasion, he asked for one of his old bootlegging friends to be released from custody. "We knew Hubbard had slipped morally and was getting so desperate for money that he probably would take any course . . . ," Whitney claimed later.[39] It angered Whitney that Hubbard also visited the office of the Intelligence Unit, and made him fear what might result.

M abel Willebrandt's declaration for Herbert Hoover brought her deeper into the political infighting and machinations she had tried for so long to avoid. Whites in the South had voted heavily Democratic since Republican Abraham Lincoln had prosecuted "the War of Northern Aggression." The "solid South," which ever since had managed to deny most black and therefore Republican votes, found itself in a quandary during the Prohibition era, though, and Hoover hoped to exploit its predicament. Much of the South supported Prohibition, but the national Democratic Party had become increasingly wet, no more so than in 1928, when the party's presumptive candidate was New York governor Al Smith, who was candid about wanting to end Prohibition. Herbert Hoover hoped to make sufficient inroads with moderate, white Democrats to steal the South from Smith.

The myriad groups purporting to represent women—the League of Women Voters, the National Woman's Party, the General Federation of Women's Clubs, and the WCTU—held conferences in the weeks leading up to the Republican and Democratic party conventions. They set planks variously asking for "equal rights" for women; participation in the World Court; abolition of lame-duck sessions of Congress; child labor legislation; development of hydro-electric power at Muscle Shoals, Alabama; and creation of a federal department of education. Above all these measures, though, rode demands for increased enforcement of the Eighteenth Amendment and the Volstead Act. Specifically, the groups coalesced in support of the following plank in both political parties:

> The people, through the method provided by the Constitution, have written the Eighteenth amendment into the Constitution. The Republican [or Democratic] party pledges itself and its nominees to the observance and vigorous enforcement of this provision of the Constitution.[40]

On June 4, the Supreme Court issued its ruling in *Olmstead v. U.S.* Speaking for the five-to-four majority, Chief Justice William

Howard Taft dismissed Olmstead's contention that wiretapping without a warrant constituted an unlawful search and seizure. Taft asserted no rights had been violated because no personal residence or office had been entered, and, thus, nothing had been searched or seized. Congress could decide to grant telephone conversations protections similar to those accorded personal property, but the court would not overstep constitutional limits to make law.

Justice Louis Brandeis noted in his dissent that the Constitution's authors were thinking of search and seizure resulting from "force and violence" perpetrated by government agents; the founding fathers could not have foreseen technological advances, such as the telephone, allowing for government "invasions" of individual security. Brandeis equated a private phone conversation with a sealed letter, and claimed "the evil incident to invasion of the privacy of the telephone is far greater than that involved in tampering with the mails." Brandeis extolled the right to be left alone as the right "most valued by civilized men." Countering Taft's point that the court would not make law, Brandeis believed it was doing so by sanctioning the illegal actions of the federal agents who set up the taps in violation of Washington State law. "If the government becomes a lawbreaker, it breeds contempt for law; it invites every man to become a law unto himself; it invites anarchy." Rationalizing that the ends justify the means—that "the government may commit crimes in order to secure the conviction of a private criminal—would bring terrible retribution."[41] Justice Harlan Stone, formerly attorney general and Willebrandt's boss, agreed with Brandeis, as did Justice Pierce Butler, who regretted that the court's review was limited to consideration of the constitutional question. He had hoped for review of the controversy over the veracity of the evidence, the method of transcribing and retranscribing phone conversations substituting hearsay for eyewitness accounts posing as grave a threat as invasion of privacy.

Thomas Revelle rejoiced in the news, his long-running battle with Olmstead and his coconspirators, nearly four years in length, coming to an end. Two weeks later, on June 21, Roy Olmstead once again boarded the boat, now named the *Dorothy Willebrandt* in honor of the assistant attorney general's daughter, bound for the state penitentiary.[42] Within a few days, Revelle resigned as U.S. Attorney, moving on to private practice, his work done.[43]

Women's groups and candidates set up "lounges" at several locations near the Shriners' Ararat Temple, home to the 1928 Republican National Convention in Kansas City.[44] The lounges provided women opportunities to discuss issues and form opinions without the condescending or disapproving eyes of their male counterparts, many of whom had failed to bring women into their political circles and backroom discussions. With women comprising only about 10 percent of all delegates, the lounges offered spaces to find common ground, their voices banding together for greater effect; the *Kansas City Star* saw this happening, and forecast a burgeoning role for women in national party decisions.[45] Other newspaper accounts expounded on women's abilities to soften politics, subtly using "their verbal cutlasses and oral knockout punches that sting and wallop us effectually as any ever wielded by a masculine politico."[46] Another report heralded women's "press-wise" acuity, their willingness to always allow a photograph, grant an interview, or provide an opinion without couching the terms of such arrangements.[47]

Mrs. Henry Peabody, chairwoman of the Women's National Law Enforcement Committee, was charged with bringing to the convention the pledge to sustain Prohibition enforcement offered by so many women's groups. She made women's influence plain: "There are too many women who stand unequivocally for the Eighteenth Amendment for the politicians to ignore us. We don't care what else they put in their platforms, but the women's vote of this country is going to make certain that they insert a dry plank." Peabody claimed twelve million women behind her petticoats; all were desirous of seeing the Eighteenth Amendment remain the law of the land. Harking back to age-old arguments for Prohibition, one supporter put forth images of "weeping mothers whose sons have taken to drink and of the wives of liquor-wayward husbands," both of whose cries for help must be heard.[48]

Pauline Sabin hit the ground running in Kansas City, setting up an impromptu office in the Muehlebach Hotel, reputed to be the fanciest lodgings in the city, using her political connections to pull in support for alternate delegates from Florida and Mississippi, making long-distance phone calls, sending telegrams, and buttonholing delegates in the hallways to secure their votes or proxies. She approached it all "as smiling and pleasant as if she had a holiday ahead," according to a reporter for the *Kansas City Star*, rather than as the tough political fight it was.[49] Sabin advised, "Above all, [women] should keep their sense of humor and be impersonal in their political activities."[50] The day before the convention began, Sabin's backroom endeavors yielded fruit when she and her allies elected a slate of delegates favoring Charles Hilles for chairman of the New York delegation, defeating the previous convention's chairman, Ogden Mills, who had been regarded as being in Hoover's pocket.[51] Sabin and Hilles, her fellow national committeeperson, stated their intention to remain free of the debate over delegates, preferring to advance their calls for a movement to draft President Coolidge while denying they were anti-Hoover.[52] It was an important distinction, allowing Sabin, Hilles, and their followers to remain aloof from political squabbling and open to compromises on alternate candidates and divisive issues. Among those issues, Sabin planned to work for the appointment of women from all state delegations to convention committees, stating, "Women themselves must ask for this representation."[53]

Mabel Willebrandt made herself available in the week before the convention to any group who asked, so long as they supported Hoover, and flitted from one engagement to another and then back to the Hoover campaign headquarters in the Shriners' Ararat Temple to coordinate the next day's activities. Typical of her boosterism was a presentation made to two hundred women who would serve as "Hoover hostesses" during the convention, their job not only to greet delegates but to bring anyone outside the Hoover camp into its sphere. With the assistance of Mrs. Louis Dodson, manager of women's activities for the Washington Hoover for President Club, Willebrandt presented a sort of instructional skit wherein a hostess (Willebrandt) greeted a delegate (Dodson) opposed to Hoover, and offered counterarguments for every charge against Hoover presented by the delegate, who soon saw the wisdom of a vote for Hoover. One reporter described the scene: the hostesses listening attentively, "stowing away 'ammunition' for use next week along with cold drinks and wafers to win over the visitors to the cause of their candidate."[54]

Wrangling for political room and advantage in the southern states comprised an important part of Hoover's strategy, and one that required Willebrandt to play an even more important role at the Republican National Convention. Before the convention began, members of the Republican National Committee, which included Sabin, met to establish the order of events, designate speakers, and sort out quarrels over the legitimacy of certain delegates to represent their state committees.[55] For six days, the committee analyzed appeals, all from southern states except Wisconsin, where forces opposed to Hoover hoped to divide those state delegations.

Willebrandt's influence grew beyond sideline pep rallies when the party's national committee elected her chairman of the credentials committee, charged with collecting information on disputed delegates, the circumstances of their selection as delegates, and the legitimacy of their claims. While Sabin probably cheered the ap-

pointment of a woman to a prominent position, the choice of Willebrandt would have been disappointing by virtue of her political
leanings. Just days before, she had left no doubt of her allegiance
to Herbert Hoover when she chastised "those who attempt to cast
foreboding of his nomination through the desire to manipulate the
convention to their own personal desires."[56] As the credentials committee assessed the protests of contested delegates one by one, the
committee found in favor of delegates pledged to Hoover and
against delegates pledging support to other candidates, but not
before a final session running eleven hours, extending past midnight. Willebrandt needed several more hours to write a report of
findings, leaving her barely any time to change clothes, grab a cup
of coffee, and speed onto the convention dais a few minutes late for
her presentation.[57]

Despite her late night, Willebrandt looked "as fresh as a daisy,"
according to the *Washington Post*, and the audience listened "with an
intentness due rather to the novelty of feminine participation in its
routine work than to any interest in the report itself."[58] Her conclusion and call for adoption of the report were met with applause and
an "attaboy" from deep in the convention hall. Before Willebrandt's
recommendations could be seconded, let alone voted upon, Daniel
Hastings, a delegate from Delaware, asked for consideration of the
minority report of the credentials committee and requested a floor
vote on the status of questionable Texas delegates whose credentials
had been invalidated in the previous night's meeting. After lengthy
pronouncements from both sides of the debate, with Willebrandt
laying the legal foundation for the majority report, a floor vote was
called. The "yeas" sounded louder than the "nays," but those supporting the minority report asked for and received a roll call vote of
all 1,089 delegates. Votes against adoption of the minority report
and its findings won out by a two-to-one margin, ending the discussion and effectively ending any possibility that someone other than

Hoover would win the nomination.[59] The New York delegation, including Sabin, had voted by a surplus of twenty-eight votes to support the minority report, voicing their opposition to Hoover, but to no avail. Two days later, the New York delegation begrudgingly agreed to present a united front for the unavoidable nominee, and vote unanimously for Herbert Hoover. Sabin recognized the futility of continuing to advance a movement to draft Coolidge, preferring a Republican victory, regardless of candidate, to a Democratic one, especially as Al Smith loomed as the probable candidate of that party. Sabin "warned" her fellow New York delegates that their state "would be the scene of the hardest battle of the campaign," suggesting that any opposition to Hoover could be construed as support for Smith.[60]

With little fanfare, the resolutions committee, which generated the party planks from dozens submitted, endorsed the pledge, verbatim, for "vigorous enforcement" of the Eighteenth Amendment agreed upon by the women's groups.[61] Nicholas Murray Butler of the New York delegation had led an effort to keep the pledge out of the party platform, supporting instead a plank calling for modification of the Volstead Act, but it failed. Butler requested that a minority report concerning the Prohibition argument be presented by the resolutions committee, but the request was denied.[62] Unwilling to be silenced, Butler took his resolution to the convention floor, for all delegates to hear; in it he defined the Eighteenth Amendment, by making criminals of a large portion of the citizenry, as adverse to the Bill of Rights, which granted individual freedoms. Endorsing the plank put forth by the women's groups would be "a declaration for government-made lawlessness," and one "in support of these nationwide murders; of the invasion of the right of privacy, of search without warrant, and now of that habit of wire-tapping," a clear reference to the recent Supreme Court ruling on the Olmstead case. With the fervor of a minister, Butler insisted that his fellow Republicans rise "from the low places of cowardice and hypocrisy, come up to the heights of courage and vision and constructive leadership which our party has inherited and so often exemplified!" Challenging the delegates' convictions to Republican principles, Butler pled with them to choose "whom you will serve, the god of the founders of this Republic and the leaders of our party, or the Mammon of cowardice and bigotry and persecution."[63] Despite a fair amount of applause, Butler's words failed to sway the mood, and his motion was tabled without discussion, but Sabin put forth a resolution, adopted unanimously, to publish "a full and complete report" of the convention's proceedings, allowing Butler's pleas access to a wider audience.[64]

As the convention wound down, Willebrandt stood tall, having secured Herbert Hoover's nomination, increased her profile, and generated talk that she could climb higher in a Hoover administration. Scuttlebutt around the convention hall suggested Willebrandt would be named attorney general.[65] One highly regarded journalist, Herbert Corey, took matters a step further by issuing a "whimpering boom" for Willebrandt to be named Hoover's running mate, crediting her work to keep anti-Hoover forces at bay in the credentials committee.[66] Corey saw little chance for her nomination, but could find no other candidate with her intelligence and devotion to Hoover.

The day after Hoover's nomination and his acceptance, Willebrandt's parents, David and Myrtle Walker, could not contain their excitement over Hoover's triumph and the accolades given their daughter for helping to make it happen. The Walkers had come to Kansas City to watch Mabel work and had marveled at her stamina and celebrated her achievements along with everyone else.[67] For all the notice Willebrandt received, one newspaper account noted that her role, while significant, was of no assistance to women anxious to increase their standing in the party. Sixty-eight women had come to Kansas City as delegates, compared with 120 at the 1924 convention, a decline rooted in lingering misogynist attitudes in men, who largely determined the makeup of their respective state delegations.[68]

Willebrandt, in one of many speeches she made to women's groups in Kansas City the week before the convention began, seemingly excused the lack of progress for women in politics as their own doing, warning that women had to "earn their place" in one of the political parties if they expected "to give real service in government." She explained, "Only as they learn tolerance and accept disappointments and their victories with good sportsmanship can they expect to win political achievements on even terms with men."[69] So to women seeking higher roles in the political realm Willebrandt offered little advice beyond that they be patient, but within a year her own patience would be worn-out.

Chapter II

Pauline Sabin shocked many of her friends and fellow Republicans when she announced, just days after the Republican convention closed, that she no longer supported Prohibition and would work for repeal of the Eighteenth Amendment. She had been a supporter of Prohibition, believing it would safeguard her children, as most mothers did, but enforcement of the Volstead Act increasingly trod upon civil rights, causing her to reassess her position. Closer to home, a recent episode involving a boy she knew, probably a friend of one of her sons, concerned her. Participating in a conference of students discussing the transition from prep school to college, the boy participated in a debate about drinking at college; the two sides discussed the effect drinking might have on athletics, academic standing, and personal reputation, but not once was it mentioned that Prohibition was the law of the land. To Sabin this lack of respect for the law was part of a dangerous trend with grave, long-term consequences. She believed many other women held the same sentiment and would support repeal and a return to a sensible plan of temperance. Women's participation at the polls and traditional view as the public's conscience could "do more towards bringing about a change in the conditions which exist today than any organization composed solely of men."[1] She admired the conviction of steadfast "dry" women, who supported candidates based only on the question of Prohibition (accepting, in some instances, officials who voted for Prohibition and its enforcement, but who enjoyed a drink in private company).[2] She no doubt hoped to find an opposing group of women who would vote, single-mindedly, for candidates favoring repeal.

Sabin's new position on Prohibition placed her at odds with the Republican presidential candidate, Herbert Hoover; party leaders; and many women, for whom she had become a role model. If the lack of mention in newspapers is any indication—and it should be, given how many times her name appeared in print in previous elections—Sabin's change of heart on Prohibition appears to have influenced her involvement in the 1928 campaign, nationally and in New York. Hoover did not come calling for assistance as Coolidge had done in 1924. No candidates for U.S. senator or representative put her on their campaign committees. No state officials employed her talents. Nevertheless, Sabin remained a party loyalist, supporting Republican candidates regardless of their stance on Prohibition, whenever and wherever she was asked—though sometimes she bridled at expectations placed upon her. She began a speech in Newport, Rhode Island, by acknowledging that the "so-called woman speaker" was "expected to talk about the political activities and reactions of her sisters," not "real issues." Vowing "to do just what is expected of me," she described the upcoming election as the "real test as to whether or not the majority of women of this country wanted woman suffrage." Only 40 percent of women had voted in the 1924 election, the result of poor leadership by women charged with getting their sisters to the polls. She predicted 1928 would be different, that Hoover's candidacy would produce a women's vote that would "amaze and astound the masculine element in politics."

Early proof came in the large numbers of women volunteering on behalf of Hoover, many donating money in addition to their time. Sabin
extolled Hoover's accomplishments and those of the Republican Party,
comparing them to the wavering, uncertain policies of the Democrats.
She provided examples of Republican superiority in handling tariffs,
the gold standard, and foreign entanglements, in doing so verging toward the "real issues" she had sworn off at the opening of her speech.[3]
Sabin had learned well how to circumnavigate expectations of women
in politics by sticking to so-called women's issues in the beginning and
concluding with deeper, "masculine" issues and never addressing the
elephant in the room, Prohibition and her recent about-face.

Two weeks after the Republican National Convention, the Democrats met in Houston to select their candidate, and, much like at
the Republican convention, there was little suspense. Despite his
loss in 1924, the party favored Al Smith again, in the hope that the
strength of New York's sizable electorate would give the party the
best chance for victory in November. At a seeming cross-purpose,
the convention delegates approved a platform endorsing continued
support for the Eighteenth Amendment, which their candidate did
not support and for which he did not allow any accommodation.

In the wee hours after Smith accepted his nomination, as New
Yorkers rejoiced in their governor's victory, Assistant Attorney General Mabel Willebrandt directed a series of raids on fifteen speakeasies hidden behind locked doors along Broadway; more than a
hundred patrons and employees were arrested. Willebrandt had sent
agents of the DOJ's Intelligence Unit from Washington to New
York City to team with Prohibition agents, who had no idea until
the appointed time that the raids would occur, Willebrandt hoping
to curtail any tip-offs from corrupt agents. To maintain a cloak of
secrecy over the raids, Willebrandt had an assistant in her office,

rather than the U.S. Attorney in New York, prepare search warrants and had them signed by a federal judge rather than a U.S. Commissioner, the usual procedure.

A *Washington Post* reporter wondered whether the timing of the raids had been chosen for political significance, to expose the rampant lawlessness allowed under Al Smith's governance. Willebrandt issued no comment on the raids, but Maurice Campbell, the state's Prohibition administrator, claimed he "didn't even know there was a political convention in session," adding, "I didn't know who was going to be nominated," an assertion beyond the pale either of stupidity or believability.[4] When indictments for conspiracy to violate the Volstead Act were handed to more than 130 people a month later, the public learned that Willebrandt had authorized the expenditure of $75,000 for use by undercover agents, operating since February, posing as "men about town, correctly garbed in evening attire," purchasing liquor at prices up to $22 for a bottle of wine and $2.25 for a cocktail ($298 and $30, respectively, in 2017 dollars).[5] In an effort to collect more evidence and secure convictions, Willebrandt directed issuance of subpoenas to many prominent New Yorkers, in the hope that they would provide additional information on the accused rather than come off as supporting lawbreaking. Her efforts backfired, though, when the district attorney, Charles Tuttle, halted the questioning of New York's social elite, calling the tactic a "fishing expedition" without foundation. Tuttle sent everyone home, announcing any additional interviews would be conducted without public notice or spectacle.[6] Intriguingly, Tuttle left the city unexpectedly two days later, leaving word he had gone to his summer home on Lake George, two hundred miles north of Manhattan, in the serene woods of Adirondack Park. Willebrandt placed one of her assistants in charge and directed him to continue the interviews, now focused upon local police.[7] She wasn't shed of Tuttle yet, though. Advisors to Hoover had given consideration to advancing

Charles Tuttle as the Republican nominee for governor, giving the appearance that Willebrandt had pushed around a presumptive candidate.[8] Interest in Tuttle for governor soon faded among the party's state power brokers, but the experience left a bad taste in Willebrandt's mouth, souring her further on political gamesmanship.

James Doran, Prohibition commissioner, and his top aide, Alf Oftedal, had come west in mid-June for meetings in San Francisco, Portland, and Seattle. In the Prohibition Bureau's suite of offices in downtown Seattle, Doran started with encouraging words, promising his two top men in Seattle they would be retained in their present positions provided the Civil Service Commission admitted them, a matter in limbo and out of Doran's hands. Alf Oftedal then admitted that he had been wrong about Whitney and wanted "to let bygones be bygones." Oftedal now considered Whitney "one of the best men he had in the entire service."

During the commissioner's discourse, though, Whitney heard a great deal that disturbed him. Ongoing reorganization would require Whitney and Lyle to report to Oftedal, who could cherry-pick the most significant cases, leaving Whitney's office chewing on the tiny, the tenuous, and the troublesome. Whitney foresaw unnecessary and unproductive competition between the two units, their agents already distrustful of one another. "We may perhaps have to suffer with them [special agents] but we do not do it with good grace," Whitney wrote to Senator Jones. "[They] undermine the morale of our own agents . . ."[9]

Doran also announced the creation of a new unit for investigating allegations of professional misconduct, feeding fears Whitney carried with him always. His fears were confirmed just a few weeks later, when he began hearing rumors that Oftedal's agents were using bootleggers to discredit him. One of the bootleggers who had become friendly with the special agents bragged that he had been brought to Washington to meet Mabel Willebrandt and Doran, both of whom had promised him a presidential pardon, the very notion of which must have sent paroxysms of anger shuddering through Whitney. More than Oftedal, Whitney directed his anger at "the rather unfriendly attitude of Mrs. Willebrandt towards us."

Whitney believed Oftedal's agents and U.S. Marshal Ed Benn, whom Whitney had never trusted, had obtained statements from defendants in the Olmstead trials and sent them to Willebrandt. As luck would have it, Willebrandt was attending the American Bar Association conference in Seattle in July 1928, offering Whitney an unexpected chance to confront her. He approached Willebrandt while she attended a luncheon of the Young Men's Republican Club, a club he once had led, to ask for a few minutes of her time. She refused, telling him her schedule was already full. Whitney took this as proof she was in league with his enemies, Oftedal and Benn. He was partly correct, as he heard later from Mrs. Vincent, chairwoman of the WCTU in Seattle, who had met with Willebrandt for three hours, and from Tom Revelle, who had heard it from his successor in the office of District Attorney Anthony Savage: Willebrandt held him and Revelle responsible for the grand jury's refusal to indict Al Hubbard and Richard Fryant.[10] Worse, Roy Lyle had learned while in Washington, D.C., that Willebrandt "is more and more dominating the Prohibition Bureau, listening to the Intelligence Unit & now she and the Commissioner of the Internal Revenue Bureau David Blair are good friends & working together . . ." Blair and Willebrandt had cooked up the idea to divide the country into eight districts and provide each with additional attorneys to get more Prohibition cases tried and won. As before, Lyle and Whitney believed they should not be asked to answer to the leadership of the Prohibition Bureau. "The importance of our work and the results we are getting & would continue to get justify no change." Ignoring problems nationwide, they saw the change directed against them specifically as a move to take

Whitney's job as legal advisor. Lyle believed "Mrs. Willebrandt has been poisoned on Whitney and my office."[11] Considering all the forces he felt arrayed against him, Whitney confessed that his job was difficult, "one not agreeable except as we feel we are doing the public service."[12] His belief in his rightness was confirmed in early August 1928, when CSC finally approved his application and that of Lyle.[13] Lyle would remain as administrator and Whitney expected to be appointed to the newly created post of senior attorney.

After her big announcement, Pauline Sabin had committed her energies to the election of Herbert Hoover, but not without some hesitation. Prominent Republican women, including Sabin, met in late July to map a strategy for getting women in the eastern and southern portions of the country to the polls for Hoover, but controversy arose as soon as the conference began. Reference was made to the recent decision by Hubert Work, chairman of the Republican National Committee, to exclude women from an advisory group that would guide Hoover's campaign efforts in the eastern United States. Sabin called the decision a "grave mistake" and stressed that "if women are to share responsibility for the success of this campaign then they should also share in its direction and confidences." Sabin and others agreed to table the matter until they could present their case to Work, and moved on to strategies for getting women to the polls, adopting a plan perfected by Sabin in New York. Campaigning would be divided by congressional districts, with the greatest efforts devoted to areas classified as doubtful for Hoover. Sabin believed that votes for Hoover could be secured from Democrats, tilting the election in his favor. Applying the model to New York, Sabin explained that to take New York from its native son, Al Smith, party workers must increase the number of women registered to vote by 20 percent in every district. "It is our duty to see to it that women who have in the past stayed at home on Election Day shall go to the polls," declared Sabin.[14] Hubert Work, without a hint of irony for his refusal to involve women in running the larger campaign, expected a large turnout of women to favor Hoover, especially when they considered the "moral issue," alluding to Al Smith's anti-Prohibition stance.[15] Apparently, women could help, so long as they followed rather than led.

Many pundits believed women would, finally, after eight years of having the vote, turn out in greater numbers for the 1928 presidential election, probably determining the winner. Political parties, acknowledging the untapped power of women voters, attempted to win over the uninitiated or unaffiliated who were not entrenched like men were in their parties and beliefs. More significantly, the stark contrasts in candidates and issues between the two parties gave women something to care about more than in the previous two presidential elections. As a result, Eunice Fuller Barnard, a prominent journalist, saw politics invading the home: "The young mother, sewing beside her baby, may be listening at the same time to a candidate's radio speech. The factory girl conning her tabloids [i.e., reading her magazines] is balancing the rival masculine charms of the nominees and, also, perhaps, their labor records. Grandmother and flapper are debating the Prohibition issue." Barnard attributed the increased interest among women to "three factors which have been present in no previous election since women had the vote." First, the diametric opposition of the candidates in personality and on key issues revealed "undercurrents of feeling . . . about the moral issues of Prohibition, of religious intolerance and of the tenement against the log cabin as a birthplace for a President. These are all questions about the conduct of human life, of the sort women are used to considering and which they feel themselves equally competent with men to judge." Second, the rapid increase in the number of radio stations across the country, with ever-increasing range of broadcast, taking the "abstractness out of politics," bringing to "women who would never cross their thresholds to go to a political meeting . . . politics in the raw, with all the heat of emotion and personality about it." Such rawness came without the filter of reports from newspapers or husbands, allowing "the acute feminine ear" to hear a "candidate's humor, his dullness, or his adenoids." Lastly, Barnard saw the influence of more political education on women, the kind initiated by Sabin and the Women's National Republican Club, bringing many more women into campaign work.

Despite the very real possibility that women's votes could determine the election, Barnard saw old ideas about women voters setting the tone of efforts by the parties to secure their favor. On Prohibition, Barnard quoted Hubert Work, who looked "with confidence to women of all classes, irrespective of party affiliation, for support at the polls next November." Barnard found, however, that within the Republican Party, "most prominent women favor repeal or modification," citing a survey conducted by the Women's National Republican Club that revealed a margin of eight to one favoring a change. On the Democratic side, Prohibitionist women favoring Al Smith looked past his wetness, considering other issues of greater importance. Barnard's findings and suppositions challenged the masculine view of women as consistently and reliably dry, prompting a greater effort by male leadership in the parties to learn where they stood with women, according to Barnard. Each party tried to claim the greater allegiance and sympathy for women's concerns: the Republicans asserted that Hoover's experience as food administrator during the Great War provided him insight into issues of the homemaker, a designation he promised to list as an occupation in the federal census, and Democrats listed the legislation advanced by Al Smith promoting and protecting the rights of mothers, children, and labor.[16] Left unaddressed by both parties was the dearth of female candidates for local and state offices in the previous eight years, and the Republican Party's blatant refusal to allow women a role in planning campaign strategy for Hoover's election. Again, women's votes were in high demand, but not their opinions.

Days after Barnard's article appeared in the *New York Times*, the Republican Party announced its plan to put "a picture of Hoover in every kitchen," professing its belief that women could win Hoover the election. The party recruited Mrs. Thomas Winter, former president of the General Federation of Women's Clubs, to head the new effort, counting on her connections with those clubs to provide points of contact. They sent packets of postcards to club women, asking them to recruit one more woman to Hoover's side, in a sort of chain-letter scheme.[17] The Women's National Republican Club followed suit, announcing the formation of a "flying squadron" of fifty members, including Sabin, available to speak in homes for women seeking information about the party and Hoover. Another 280 women volunteered to work in the club, making themselves available to answer questions and register voters.[18]

James Wadsworth, the inveterate wet, jumped on Hoover's bandwagon despite the candidate's dry leanings. Wadsworth wanted the whole country wet, but he could not turn his back on his party, especially since he considered modifying the Volstead Act impossible if southern Democrats rode Al Smith's coattails to Washington in a Hoover loss. "Doubtless," Wadsworth offered, "there are some who wonder how a man who is utterly opposed to Prohibition can resist the temptation of voting for Governor Smith." Wadsworth might have considered Smith's views on modifying the Eighteenth Amendment if the governor's plans included a proposal to allow state control of liquor with the attenuating side effect of establishing state-run systems for distributing and selling liquor. Where Smith would trade federal control for state control, Wadsworth would not, calling, as he had since January 1, 1920, for the outright repeal of the amendment, state and federal governments removing themselves from any involvement in the manufacture and sale of liquor. If loyalty to long-held beliefs were not enough, Wadsworth noted the distance between Smith's proposal and southern voters, who would, in all likelihood, elect and reelect men to Congress who supported Prohibition. As Wadsworth saw it, "Governor Smith's own party, controlled as it is, is absolutely against him," his candidacy a "barren prospect." No president, charged Wadsworth, could initiate changes to the Eighteenth Amendment or the Volstead Act; only Congress held that power. Until such time as Congress or the public would rise against Prohibition, Wadsworth, like so many others, would cast his lot with his party's candidate, who supported Prohibition but promised an investigation to assess its successes, its failures, and possible adjustments—a glimmer of hope for anti-Prohibitionists who believed the investigation would reveal all of Prohibition's flaws and create a realization that change was needed.[19]

Sabin spoke frequently in September and October of 1928, advocating for Hoover's election, spending every other free moment soliciting campaign donations and organizing women's groups around New York to get out the vote.[20] One of her more inventive endeavors, and, perhaps, a dig at party leaders who had left women outside the main campaign apparatus, was a conference and clambake, the first of its kind to include women, 130 in all, held at Bayberry Land. Sabin noted it had been the habit of men to host "stag" events for years and it seemed appropriate to do something similar for women.[21] Only one man, W. Kingsland Macy, the Suffolk County chairman, spoke to the group; in his speech "women's issues" took a backseat to the economy, foreign relations, and reorganizing the federal bureaucracy.[22] Sabin's efforts and the plans she created had their effect, according to the chairman of the Hoover-Curtis Campaign Committee (Charles Curtis was Hoover's running mate), who claimed a new wave of women voters had "made up their minds to take a hand for the first time in electing a man who is keenly conscious of women's needs and the needs of the home."[23]

On September 6, 1928, Mabel Willebrandt wrote a letter to Hubert Work, chairman of the Republican National Committee, acknowledging the view of herself as a "storm center" swirling around Prohibition, an issue about which the Republican Party had not decided on its campaign tactics. Willebrandt wanted to help Hoover's campaign, but refused "to be haggled over and thus contribute to the indecision and confusion of a hard campaign."[24] Associates passed along rumors and innuendo, giving the impression "in some quarters that I am an unwelcome speaker." For those reasons, Willebrandt withdrew her name from the list of speakers available to campaign on behalf of Hoover and suggested that the "press of official duties" be offered as the reason she would not make appearances or speeches. Chairman Work denied her request, scheduling several speeches in Ohio, starting in two days.

Willebrandt's concerns proved prophetic. In her first speech, delivered before two thousand Methodists in Springfield, Ohio, a group reminiscent of those that had started and pushed the drive for Prohibition, she declared Al Smith a "wet" who would not enforce the Eighteenth Amendment and urged Methodist ministers to denounce Smith from the pulpit.[25] The Republican National Committee, uncomfortable with Willebrandt's strident position, provided the text of her speech to reporters, but made clear that "the publicity department does not attempt to censor the remarks of the speaker." Hubert Work did not address Willebrandt's comments, but issued a general rejoinder decrying all personal attacks made against the Democratic candidate, describing unspecified articles and letters as particularly "scurrilous."[26]

Two weeks later, at a conference of the Methodist Episcopal Church in Lorain, Ohio, Willebrandt charged Al Smith with "hiding behind his own church because he is afraid to come out and face the record that he has made as a champion of the liquor traffic." Her statement served as an answer to a speech by Smith in which he suggested Willebrandt was anti-Catholic. Willebrandt refuted the accusation, defining Prohibition as a moral issue, "long espoused" by all churches. Smith's assertions sought to turn that moral issue into political hay, hoping to divide the Republican Party between "drys" and "wets" to secure his election, but Willebrandt saw the New York governor's attacks as building stronger opposition, noting that both parties and all denominations favored Prohibition. "Religion has nothing to do with my attack upon him," she declared. Willebrandt regarded Smith as "the greatest force for disregard of the Prohibition laws in America," thus earning her opposition as a defender of the law.[27] A day later, in Warren, Ohio, Willebrandt attacked Smith for refusing to enforce Prohibition in New York and for his statements that the law could not be enforced under any circumstances. She commended Smith on his rise from humble origins "in the tenements of New York," but charged him with using "the forces of Tammany [Hall, the oft-cited corrupt seat of Democratic power in the city] and the underworld as stepping stones, with the inevitable obligations thereby imposed."[28]

After the speech, Willebrandt phoned George Akerson, Herbert Hoover's private secretary, and told him the meeting "went over wonderfully," with several Catholics congratulating her afterward. She felt that "religious intolerance was honorably and properly handled," and hoped she had defused criticism of her past statements and tempered the national debate over Smith's Catholicism, which many voters viewed negatively, believing his allegiance might lean more toward papal doctrine than the Constitution. All that mattered to Willebrandt, and all that she believed should matter to voters, was Smith's opposition to Prohibition. She blamed "wets at Headquarters" for stirring the opposition to her.[29]

And opposition there was. Walter Newton, head of the Republican Speakers Bureau in Chicago, had directed that all abstracts of her Lorain, Ohio, speech be recalled from Chicago newspapers before printing because Willebrandt had not been designated a "scheduled speaker" for the Republican National Committee.[30] Behind the scenes, Harriet Taylor Upton, the political veteran, counseled Hoover, heard nothing in Willebrandt's speeches as disparaging of Catholics, and was unable to see how any of her comments "might do harm." On the other hand, Upton admitted, "I do not offer my opinion as the effect all over the country politically of Mrs. Willebrandt's talks."[31] Pauline Sabin added her voice to the debate over Willebrandt's statements, saying, "I would rather see the Republican Party go down to defeat in November than to win as a result of religious intolerance."[32]

Mounting criticism, primarily from Democrats and "wet" groups, prompted Willebrandt to slip into Chicago for a meeting with Newton. She sequestered herself in the Blackstone Hotel, leaving instructions with the desk clerk to block all calls and visitors, but intrepid reporters learned of her arrival and asked Newton if Willebrandt had come to town at his "invitation." Newton demurred. "No, not directly," he said, "although I may have suggested that she drop in some time if there was opportunity." The reporters pressed, "Have you called her on the carpet?" Dodging, Newton answered, "I've found that I never have much success calling the fair sex on the carpet," adding, "If she wants to see me it is merely to talk over her engagements." He dispelled speculation that Willebrandt had been removed from the Speaker's Bureau's roster, listing several dates in October when she would give speeches in southern states.[33]

When Willebrandt arrived at Newton's office later that day, she held to her charge that Al Smith, not she, had injected religion and Prohibition issues into the campaign. When asked if she operated as a "free lance" speaker, as Republican Party chairman Hubert Work had avowed, Willebrandt deferred to Newton, who clarified his earlier statements, stating she "certainly has been speaking under the auspices of the speaker's bureau of the Republican national committee" and would continue to do so when asked. Perhaps to show there were no hard feelings, Willebrandt, Newton, and James Good, Hoover's campaign manager in the western United States, allowed a photograph; the assistant attorney general is smiling, her eyes averted from the camera, and she is flanked by the two men, Newton looking lazily at the camera, and Good looking somewhat disapprovingly at Willebrandt.[34]

With that, Willebrandt hopped a train for Washington, D.C., satisfied with the public display of support, but nursing her wounds at Work's noncommittal description of her efforts as "free lance." In a letter written during the ride home, she noted that she wouldn't contradict Work in the press for fear it would detract from the campaign, but that she emphatically had *never* made a speech on behalf of the Hoover campaign without it being arranged by the national committee. Further, she had asked the committee not to send her to Ohio and Pennsylvania, states where Hoover's support was questionable; she reminded Work of her letter of September 6, in which she asked to be excused from any speeches anywhere. In advance of her first Ohio speech, she had submitted the transcript to J. Francis Burke, counsel for the Republican National Committee and a Catholic, to ensure that none of her remarks would seem intolerant of Catholicism or any other religion. Similarly, she had submitted her Lorain, Ohio, speech in advance to the Speaker's Bureau, and had received no adverse comments. She concluded by saying she did not expect Work "to recall in the manifold responsibilities and hard work of this campaign" all of the events she related, but it was her "genuine opinion that great damage is being done the campaign by the picture of disorganization and lack of solidarity presented when you and your state leaders show hesitation, or express criticism of the Ohio speeches."[35] The party leadership's disavowal of the content of her speeches, while they continually returned her to the stump, suggested they were exploiting, if not actually creating, the controversy as a means to highlight Smith's Catholicism as a factor in his opposition to Prohibition. Using Willebrandt to deliver the message allowed the candidate to keep his distance from an unsavory topic while Willebrandt, unwittingly, planted seeds of doubt in the minds of voters, especially in states leaning Democrat. Her letter to Work hinted at such deception, but her commitment to securing the continuation of Prohibition overrode her trepidation.

Willebrandt returned to the campaign trail on October 8, giving a speech in Owensboro, Kentucky, focused on the dangers of Al Smith's anti-Prohibition stance. Calling to mind the reasons for Prohibition's existence, Willebrandt claimed Smith was "just one thing to women on the subject of Prohibition: the champion of the liquor interests and as such a menace to their homes and the welfare of growing children."[36] Democrats suggested the assistant attorney general was equating the Catholic Church and its membership with support of the liquor trade.[37] In her final speech before the election, Willebrandt called out her critics as "a shallow intelligentsia and those who hurl the epithet of bigot for political effect . . . Because of my unflinching opposition to those professional Catholic politicians, who have sought to mislead their coreligionists into the belief that loyalty to Prohibition is little short of heresy," she proclaimed, "I have been attacked as a bigot." She had no more time for false accusations, and she looked forward to a new era of tolerance led by Herbert Hoover, who, she believed, radiated "true toleration, Christian kindness and high idealism."[38]

The fear harbored by the Republican leadership that Willebrandt's comments might backfire and cast the entire party as a group of bigots proved unfounded. Hoover's personality, experience, and commitment to Prohibition brought him a substantial victory. Irving Fisher, a highly respected economist at Yale University, declared that the election produced two findings: first, voters firmly supported

Prohibition; and, second, so long as prosperity continued, the Republicans would dominate the White House and Capitol Hill.[39] While reliable statistics did not exist, Fisher attributed the "more firm establishment" of Prohibition, in large part, to women, who he judged were "undoubtedly an important factor" in Hoover's victory. Simon Michelet, president of the National Get-Out-the-Vote Club, estimated that as many as six million new women voters participated in the election, based on a sample review of voter registration across the country.[40] Still further proof of the burgeoning female voter class and its impact was verified by the Republican National Committee's Research Bureau, which conducted a survey after the election. The bureau concluded that "the militant support of Mr. Hoover by America's womanhood was a constant in every state," ensuring victory in states where the margin was close with Smith and generating huge majorities in others, serving as a mandate for the new president-elect. The bureau's report concluded that the "indifference or aversion to political activity which had characterized a large percentage of women ever since equal suffrage became a fact was overcome."[41]

Pauline Sabin had no doubts about the role of women in the election and declared, "It was the women's votes which helped more than anything to elect Mr. Hoover."[42] Four months later, she resigned her post on the Republican National Committee, saying only that she thought it another woman's turn to serve. When reporters asked if she had resigned because of her opposition to Prohibition, which stood in contrast to Hoover's calls for rigid enforcement, Sabin said only that she had quit for personal reasons.[43]

I n the early days of 1929, rumors circled around Mabel Willebrandt, some people suggesting she might resign, others recommending her for the position of attorney general. Several among those in the latter group posited that she was due the post not just in recognition

of her achievements, but as a reward for women, whose votes helped
Herbert Hoover to victory.[44] Publicly, Willebrandt denied any
thoughts of resigning, but privately, she hinted at the burden of
politics and how "the crucial campaign—tore the body, for others it
is broke over spirit, I guess."[45] She lamented the spotlight shone on
her during the election, sharing with her parents an article typical
of her critics, which spoke of "the delightful 'igloo of silence' into
which Mrs. W has gone since the election, hoping it may go on, and
on, and on. Well, with my enemies I hope, too, it may go on, and
have no desire . . . to stir up comment." Willebrandt did not want to
be chased from office, but she confessed, "Lately I don't seem able to
keep my heart high. I've got a cowardly streak I guess. I want to run.
I guess every hunted animal wants to hunt his hole to lick his wounds
and have his lair mates help him lick 'em too! Well, I just feel so
alone—no one interested to 'lick my wounds' of heart and soul!"

She had not raised the idea of resignation with President-elect
Hoover, but perhaps in a demonstration of his plans for Willebrandt,
he had "sent hints my way that he'd finance it if I'd go take over the
formation of a citizen 'army' nationwide, including Edison, Ford, etc.
to lead in <u>law observance</u>. It would be useful. It's alluring for the good
it'd do. The contacts would be fine—but I can't yet accept it." She
compared her plight to that of Job, the biblical character who, for all
his good works, encountered new challenges at every turn. When her
efforts at prison reforms were rebuffed in the U.S. House of Representatives, Fiorello La Guardia—"socialist, anti-Prohibitionist," in
Willebrandt's view, and thus an unlikely ally—came to her defense.
Writing to her parents, she paraphrased La Guardia: "I never approve
the Dept of Justice if I can help it, but you're right, you're uncovering
graft, and no one doubts your honor and effectiveness when they are
skeptical of most everyone else." Recommitting herself, she decided,
"I'll have to write a new book of Job, if these deliverances keep on,
I'll have the old man worsted!"[46]

n December 1928, Prohibition Commissioner Doran received a report made by an efficiency expert who had visited Seattle the previous month, investigating allegations of various improprieties committed by William Whitney, Roy Lyle, and other top agents. Doran was upset to learn that after one year the Seattle office still had not implemented the reorganization plan. Writing to Lyle, Doran inveighed, "I understand that you and your legal adviser are not inclined to favor the application [of the new plan, but] the secretary of the treasury has instructed me to apply the present classification law uniformly throughout the field service."[47] Lyle, who like Whitney believed that his relationship with Senator Jones was more important than taking orders from the head of his agency, sent Doran as hot a letter as the weak-willed administrator could write. Explaining that the efficiency expert had obviously filed a report "deliberately and intentionally untruthful," Lyle admitted he had implemented only those changes he deemed worthwhile, knowing better than the expert, who was, Lyle implied, a wet.[48]

Lyle forwarded a copy of the letter to Jones, adding another with even more attacks upon the efficiency expert, who "apparently came here thoroughly poisoned and especially antagonistic to Mr. Whitney." Dismissing the report, Lyle expressed his real concern: the expert had left Seattle headed for a meeting with Willebrandt. She was the enemy, Lyle pronounced: "Mrs. Willebrandt is, and has been for some time, doing everything possible that she could in a covered up way, to deprecate the personnel and achievements of many of the federal Prohibition organizations."[49]

f Mabel Willebrandt harbored any hope for the post of attorney general, it came crashing down when Herbert Hoover asked her to assess other candidates for the job. She performed the chore with her characteristic mixture of thoughtfulness and bluntness, telling Hoover, "<u>Your Attorney General will make or break your Administration.</u> Raised by the campaign to a high pitch of faith in you, the public expects too much from you and expects it too soon. The Prohibitionists are eager and hopeful and will not well bear postponement or disappointment. The religious extremists on both sides are ready to spring. Your Attorney General must be a <u>doer</u>. He must inspire faith. He must be over and above all other things, an executive with the ability to put morale into indifferent men." The statement defined all the strengths Willebrandt had exhibited in the previous eight years.[50] Given her parameters and the field of candidates presented to her, Willebrandt recommended Nathan Miller, former governor of New York, for whom Pauline Sabin had worked on his 1922 campaign. When Hoover picked William Mitchell, the solicitor general with whom Willebrandt had battled on tax case responsibilities, it proved a stinging rebuke of her opinions, and signaled the beginning of the end for the assistant attorney general tasked with Prohibition enforcement.

Willebrandt's mind and mood took a brief respite from her disappointment and indecision when she attended the annual Baby Cabinet dinner at the White House for the top assistants in each executive department. For seven years, Willebrandt had been the only woman there. At this one, the end of the road for most in attendance before the change in administrations, the twenty-seven male members of the Baby Cabinet paid Willebrandt "the loveliest tributes," prompting her to respond:

> In 7 years I have sat with you. The spirit that made you
> take me in, making me at all times without mawkishness
> feel one of you has been fine. It has not always been easy
> I know full well nor without sacrifice of your inclinations
> and convenience, but it has not gone unnoticed by me

nor unappreciated. You have been generous and sports-
manly and I thank you.[51]

Though she had made no final decision, her remarks had the ring of
someone on the way out.

As much as Willebrandt would determine her fate alone, a declaration of support from Herbert Hoover would have had great influence on her decision. *The New Yorker* wrote that Willebrandt "will
unquestionably be one of the administration's major problems." The
magazine assumed Hoover would not want her back, but pondered
what would become of "the personification of a national phenomenon." And, despite a decidedly negative tone in the article, the magazine wondered, "There must be a niche somewhere for the conscience
of a country which, as its votes and biological statistics show, wants
not only liquor but also a law against liquor."[52]

Ten days later, Willebrandt got her answer. Hoover called her at
home, asking, "Anyone on the line?"—an acknowledgment that most
phones were connected to party lines, accessible by anyone of the
"party," usually consisting of a building's residents or several homes
on a street, with busybodies often hanging on the lines, listening for
gossip. Willebrandt answered, "No, it is clear." Then Hoover said, "I
would have had you over were it possible to avoid comment and speculation. I just wanted to tell you the new atty genl [William Mitch-
ell] is a friend of yours," clearly trying to mitigate her past tribulations
with the man. Hoover continued, "I say that because maybe when
you see him you might not think so but he is and we want you to stay
on." Taken aback, Willebrandt said nothing, so Hoover continued,
"At least for a while it will be best for you. You deserve the recognition it will mean and the work desires it and needs you."

Reporting the call to her parents, Willebrandt revealed, "I was
intensely hurt that he asked me that way. It is part and parcel of the

many back stairs methods he adopted of dealing with me and with the drys during the campaign. The courteous thing would have been for him to ask me to come to his home and talk to me face to face. I think it goes to prove the thing I have feared, and my instinct has told me long ago that fundamentally he doesn't feel on a level with women nor deal with them as much as men. That he could put it off with just a phone call and a patronizing comment hurts me bitterly. The real truth is that he needs to have me stay for a while, but instead of saying so frankly he put it that I needed it—as tho he were doing me a great favor."[53] Willebrandt would not complain anymore, but she struggled to "see how I can go thru the next few months."

Her task got no easier when Hoover invited her to a dinner at the White House shortly after his inauguration. Hoover "was most cordial," and asked Willebrandt if Attorney General Mitchell had talked to her about the president's plan to resolve bureaucratic logjams in Prohibition enforcement. Mitchell had not discussed the matter with her, though a week had passed since the president had asked his attorney general to do so. Believing Mitchell incapable of delegating authority, Willebrandt felt "just as tho I had been pushed out on a limb, can't get down and no way back because of the heavy responsibility." In addition to her sense of abandonment, she confessed, "The wretched thing is that I personify Prohibition. The anti-Hoover forces wish to break him on Prohibition and to do that any pretext is seized upon to discredit me."[54] With such a view of her predicament, Willebrandt could have seen only one way out, despite her deep commitment to a problem unresolved.

On February 11, 1929, more than six months after he had been led to believe his reappointment was imminent, William Whitney received word that he had been appointed senior attorney.

"You and Lyle are now fixed," Senator Jones proclaimed, adding, "I have no fears as to the outcome."[55] Lyle's and Whitney's fears and fantasies of betrayal over the previous two years had continued up until the moment Whitney opened his letter from Assistant Secretary Lowman. A second letter, from Alf Oftedal, contained the respect due to Whitney for all of his achievements, noting his efforts to convict rumrunners and to "break down a number of the outstanding obstacles to enforcement," surely a reference to the numerous convictions his work had wrought.[56] The letter would have been worthy of rejoicing had it not been for one word: "probationary."[57] That uncertain status required Whitney to prove himself worthy, a condition he would have considered odious and sure to spark visions of devious schemes rising against him again.

In April, Al Hubbard came to the Prohibition Unit offices and asked to see Whitney. Hubbard began, with a chuckle, to tell his former boss about two of his acquaintances who had been caught bootlegging. As his story continued in a roundabout way, hilarious to the storyteller, Hubbard dropped a hint. If these two men were freed, there would be a substantial reward from an unnamed, but clearly nefarious, benefactor. Whitney saw no humor in a bribe, only insult, and he ordered Hubbard "to get out and stay out."[58] After Hubbard exited, Whitney became concerned about his former protégé, and the wisdom of having had him so involved in undercover work where corruption was an easy and lucrative offering.

Rebuffed and desperate, Hubbard believed he had another card to play. He took the long train trip to Washington, D.C., and found his way to the office of Assistant Attorney General Mabel Willebrandt. They sat down together on May 15, Hubbard surely donning the mask of an innocent, distressed youth, struggling perhaps to hold the facade as he met the unblinking eyes focused upon him. The boy wonder explained to Willebrandt that he had participated in a huge conspiracy, under the direction of his boss, William Whitney. At some length, and with telling details invented as he spoke, Hubbard explained that he delivered bribes of thirty to fifty thousand dollars to the senior attorney, with lesser amounts paid to Roy Lyle and top agent Earl Corwin. As the man at the center of this conspiracy between the King of the Bootleggers and the leaders of the Twentieth Prohibition District, Hubbard provided dates, locations, quotations, and more. Much of what he told her was true, after a fashion, making the lies difficult to spot.

Hubbard wanted to help Willebrandt convict these men and suggested she designate him an investigator for the DOJ, so he could begin collecting evidence. As he was a former Prohibition agent, Hubbard's direct testimony could not be ignored. He could be shown the door, but something had hit the mark. After he departed, Willebrandt got in touch with a friend at the Bureau of Investigations, a man she had recommended for the job of director of the FBI, J. Edgar Hoover. She asked Hoover to open an investigation into the allegations, the last action Willebrandt would take in the trials and tribulations that had affected Seattle's Prohibition office almost since the day Prohibition had begun.[59]

Sensing the end was near, Willebrandt sought to set Prohibition on the right path, fixing those things she could and advocating for change where she could not. Pushing for the transfer of the Prohibition Bureau from the Department of Treasury to the Justice Department stood at the top of her list. Willebrandt listed numerous failures in enforcement, administratively and in the field, under Treasury's watch, especially the alcohol permitting system, designed to provide alcohol for legitimate industrial uses, but so often corrupted. "One reason why," she charged, "is because from the start there has been an absence of legal sureness in granting and revoking permits. Almost everything done is the result of compromises with permittees." Treasury's close relationship with representatives of permitted liquor operations, distillers she referred to as a "little cabinet" within the Internal Revenue Bureau, had only grown over the years, especially after the appointment of Dr. James Doran in 1926 as Prohibition commissioner. Doran had worked as a chemist for the distillers prior to Prohibition, leading him toward leniency in dealing with his old friends. "Small wonder, then, that the Treasury Department has never been able effectively to control the diversion of alcohol and other intoxicating liquors," charged Willebrandt.[60] She begged Mitchell to advance statutory changes to strengthen oversight of the permit process, stiffen penalties for violators of all offenses, and promote transfer of all enforcement functions to the Department of Justice.

Mitchell took his time, but two weeks later he told Willebrandt he had become convinced of her argument to move everything into the Justice Department. At almost the same time, she learned President Hoover had decided *against* the move. She insisted upon an audience. She and Mitchell met in the president's study on a Sunday afternoon, attempting to sway Hoover with charts and data for an hour and fifteen minutes. His counterproposal to provide more agents and attorneys for her office would be "spectacular but of little real value in conquering crime," Willebrandt argued.

Hoover would not be turned. Willebrandt believed that his recalcitrance was rooted in fear that the legislation needed to effect a transfer could not be passed in Congress. She left the meeting "discouraged," tempted "to indulge the emotion 'to make them sorry' by resigning in such a way as to let the truth—cowardice plus the power of the alcohol trade—out," but she resolved to pray on it first. The next day she awoke "with the <u>confidence</u> that I must resign and insist that they accept my resignation, not because I couldn't have <u>my way</u> doing things but because such indefinite postponement of steps necessary for anyone to do the job scientifically and well and I simply couldn't permit myself to do it less than that way after 8 years in public office and by pledge of last summer's campaign." Her soul relieved, she had "never felt so happy." She talked to Mitchell immediately, who said, "It would be a blow to have me go and he wouldn't give up but <u>understood</u>." The next day, Willebrandt spoke to one of the president's aides who relayed the message to Hoover, who reportedly said, "Of course if she can't see that it's right she must be allowed to go," asking only that she delay her resignation until he could designate a replacement.

Within a matter of days, Willebrandt accepted a sizable retainer to represent a fledgling air transport company, AVCO, and agreed to write articles for *Ladies' Home Journal* and *Good Housekeeping*, which paid enough for her to buy furniture and law books for the private practice she would open upon leaving the Justice Department. The new work would provide her the stability she craved, erasing any doubts about resigning. Willebrandt got equal satisfaction knowing Prohibition would stay in the spotlight as speculation swirled around who would be her replacement when "they [Hoover and Congress] wanted just to forget it."[61] Her only regret was that she would not be "taking a hand in the greatest achievement of this agency," the trial and conviction of Al Capone on tax evasion charges, an area of the law in which she had excelled.

As Willebrandt cleared her desk of lingering cases in preparation for a life outside government service, the first of the defendants arrested in the speakeasy raids in New York City in the summer of 1928 came to trial. Both Helen Morgan and Texas Guinan, prominent "night club hostesses," were quickly acquitted. In Morgan's case, a juror told a reporter the jury felt Morgan "was only earning a living, that the law was wrong, and that no conviction was possible under such circumstances." A reporter for the *Washington Post* suggested that distaste for the newly enacted Jones-Stalker, or Jones Five and Ten, Act, (its primary sponsor was Senator Wesley Jones of Washington) might have clouded the jury's decisions.[62] The law, enacted only a month earlier, raised potential penalties to ten thousand dollars and/or five years in prison for each violation of the Volstead Act, but allowed judges to use discretion in sentencing, determining if the violations in question constituted "casual or slight violations" or "habitual" abuses.[63] The reporter also suggested a recent edict from Willebrandt reflected the handwriting on the wall. She had asked for stiffer penalties almost from her first day in office, but, fearful that acquittals would embolden new violations of the Volstead Act, directed her U.S. Attorneys to use discretion in applying the Jones Law, bringing charges under it only in cases where conviction was a certainty.[64] Willebrandt had gotten the stick necessary to punish large-scale violations, but it had come with a distinction—casual versus habitual—that made prosecutors, judges, and juries uncomfortable with the weight of their responsibility and the repercussions of making that distinction. For all intents and purposes, the new law came with a bark, but little bite.

Mabel Walker Willebrandt submitted her formal letter of resignation to President Herbert Hoover on May 26, 1929, after nearly eight years, three presidents, and three attorneys general; having brought down high-profile bootleggers and rumrunners—Roy Olmstead, Willie Haar, George Remus, Al Capone—and overseeing the convictions of tens of thousands of smaller operators, but never having stemmed the tide of alcohol flowing through the country. She felt it possible to stem that flow, but had never been given the tools. Willebrandt reminded Hoover, "The solution of the problem of lawlessness is in your hands."[65] President Hoover accepted her resignation with "deep regret," granting, "The position you have held has been one of the most difficult in the government and one which could not have been conducted with such distinguished success by one of less ability and moral courage."[66]

Chapter 12

The day after announcing her resignation from the Republican National Committee, Pauline Sabin met with fifteen women to iron out their plan to end Prohibition; they needed to adopt a temporary name, elect officers, rent an office, outline a basic organization, and arrange for a meeting, a sort of national convention, in Chicago on May 28, 1929, barely a month away.[1] Contacting the vast network of friends and political operatives she had cultivated over the past decade, Sabin got commitments from women in twenty-six states to establish state organizations and assurances from women in fifteen states that they would attend the Chicago meeting. Sabin and her friends, particularly in New York, began talking to their friends and friends of friends, drumming up additional support and publicity, generating pamphlets to spread the word of their aim: to "promote temperance and restore respect for law."[2] Almost as important to Sabin as ending Prohibition was letting men know that Ella Boole of the WCTU did not speak for all women, a claim she frequently made and which had been repeated in the press many times in the previous eight years.

At the meeting in Chicago, the women agreed on a name, the Women's Organization for National Prohibition Repeal (WONPR), a bit long, but reflective of their intent and origins. The group also adopted a structure, surely rooted in Sabin's experiences on the Republican National Committee; they established a "skeleton organization" with a national advisory council composed of members from every state, with state advisory councils directing local efforts. Each state council would form committees on membership, publications, investigations (to compile statistics on Prohibition's negative impact), and legislation (to attend hearings). The WONPR would assess no dues and all work would be conducted voluntarily. The WONPR presented no specific policies at the meeting, preferring to collect opinions and thoughts from its mushrooming membership, and reporting, "Women in all sections of the country are welcoming this opportunity to voice their protest and to help bring about the real temperance we all desire." As if plucked from the WCTU or ASL literature of twenty years earlier, Mrs. Courtlandt Nicoll declared, "We stand at the cross roads today where one sign points to anarchy and demoralization of the very fibre of our national character, the other sign points to bring about a change in the law and the recovery of those principles on which the nation was founded."[3]

Sabin understood "that we have a powerful group opposed to us in the W.C.T.U. and the Methodist and Baptist Churches. They have certainly put the fear of God into the Republican members" of the New York legislature and U.S. Congress.[4]

Sabin's organization catered to women exclusively, because she saw women's concerns at the heart of Prohibition, their actions over a long period bringing the law to fruition. For that reason, "surely, it is the duty of every woman to face the question fearlessly and to lend her part in its final judgment." Taking that position made her appear to stand in opposition to her long-standing pronouncements that women needed to shed themselves of women-only issues and work from within the established parties, but Sabin saw things differently. Prohibition was "a problem which the American people, regardless of party or creed, must solve," she reasoned. The WONPR was not a new party; it would work to increase the number of politically active women regardless of their party affiliations. Sabin knew that repealing Prohibition could not be accomplished by one party, or by women standing alone. However, many women had never yet cast a vote and thus were uncommitted to parties, politicians, or other anti-Prohibition organizations, like Charles Sabin's AAPA, all of which had complicated relationships with one another and with public perception. The WONPR could step into the debate without baggage. "Temperance," which had been the battle cry of the Prohibitionists, "must come from within," charged Sabin, and the extreme of abstinence demanded by the Eighteenth Amendment and the Volstead Act could not be compelled of people. Prominent among her critics was the WCTU, which of course had "Temperance" in its name rather than "Prohibition"; Sabin found it hypocritical of the organization to ignore the obvious contradiction of legislators voting dry but allowing themselves a drink. She found it difficult "to understand the frame of mind and the elasticity of conscience which can condone such obvious dissimulation." Even if Prohibition could be enforced, at a great cost, Sabin said she would still oppose the law because it was "contrary to the spirit of our fundamental Constitution."[5]

The WONPR's earliest networking activities spread from women Sabin had known in the Republican Party to the women's auxiliary branch of the Association Against the Prohibition Amendment (AAPA), to which Charles Sabin had belonged since its inception in 1918. Other members of the AAPA among Pauline Sabin's circle of friends and political allies included Nicholas Murray Butler and James Wadsworth. The AAPA opposed the Eighteenth Amendment because it damaged the economy; the alcohol tax had brought in about 30 to 40 percent of all federal tax revenue prior to the amendment's enactment, and personal income tax rates were raised to compensate for the lost revenue.

Much of the public, as a result, viewed the AAPA as a group of rich men devoted to lowering their taxes rather than to personal liberty or concerns about increased crime and alcoholism rates. The AAPA had made little progress, and its membership fluctuated wildly, from an alleged high of 770,000 in 1926 to a low of 11,000 in January 1929, after the group's president purged the membership roll of anyone who had made little or no financial contribution.[6] Charles Sabin's involvement with the AAPA gave Pauline a window into its activities, informing many of her decisions on the WONPR's organization and solidifying her determination to be inclusive of women from all backgrounds and every section of the country, encouraging local and state organizations in grassroots efforts, forgoing any required dues, making a far more democratic organization than the AAPA. Still, Pauline saw value in maintaining an association between the WONPR and the AAPA, and she sent her group's declaration of principles and plan of organization to the AAPA leadership for comment. The AAPA's leadership had one overarching recommendation, namely that the WONPR provide clear definitions of the organization's intent and policies so that prospective members would be left with no confusion about what they were supporting: full and complete repeal of the Eighteenth Amendment.[7]

Congress and Prohibitionist groups tried to assert a strong connection between the WONPR and the AAPA, citing the men's group's provision of an office and secretary to the WONPR when they began in 1929. But the WONPR's rapid expansion forced them into bigger offices and a larger staff, which they arranged without AAPA involvement.[8] Years later, Pauline Sabin was asked about a connection, specifically whether the AAPA provided any funding to the WONPR, but she refused to give an answer, saying financial matters were private and had long since passed being of interest.[9] Regardless of any behind-the-scenes association, Sabin and the WONPR set their own agenda, secured new members at a rate never experienced by the AAPA, and extended their arguments deep into the middle section of the country, something never accomplished by their male counterparts.

M abel Willebrandt's exit from office came so unexpectedly that an article written by her and published in the July 1929 issue of *Ladies' Home Journal* still listed her as the assistant attorney general. She had prepared the article, "Smart Washington After Six O'Clock," before resigning, never hinting in the piece that she would leave. In it Willebrandt discussed the changing social scene as the nation's capital became increasingly devoid of alcohol, "the ribaldry of the cocktail shaker, the exchange of home-brew recipes and the florid eagerness for false stimulation" fading in inverse proportion to the ascendancy of Herbert Hoover and his strong moral influence. She allowed a glimpse into her private life, a mystery for much of the eight years she served in Washington, with stories of dinners hosted by Supreme Court justices and cabinet secretaries, where intellectual discourse proved more stimulating than alcohol, the absence of liquor at a party "a social achievement" establishing a "reputation for successful entertainment without cocktail, highball or liquors." Willebrandt declared, "There is no such thing any more, if indeed society ever achieved it, as graceful drinking." She knew of congressional get-togethers in the past where liquor was proudly served, but she doubted the practice continued. The wealthy and powerful had begun to see themselves as contributing to the crime and corruption necessary to bring liquor to their tables, realizing, "It may have been clever and smart to serve a thing forbidden and costly if the dregs in the glass were not so repulsive and disillusioning."[10]

A month later, "The Inside of Prohibition," a series of twenty-one articles written by Willebrandt, began appearing in newspapers across the country, in which the former assistant attorney general addressed the question that had dogged her since she took office in 1921: were the Eighteenth Amendment and the Volstead Act enforceable? She would "not discuss the wisdom of adopting Prohibition as national policy," leaving others to determine the fate of the amendment; when "people are sure whether or not we can actually have Prohibition enforcement, then they will decide whether or not there shall continue to be a Prohibition amendment and Prohibition laws."[11] Throughout the series, Willebrandt offered specific instances—arrests, trials, conversations—where state and federal agencies failed to fully enforce Prohibition, either for corruption, ineptitude, or lack of effort. In making that argument, she returned to familiar themes. "Hundreds" of Prohibition Unit agents appointed through "political pull" put enforcement in charge of men "as devoid of honesty and integrity as the bootlegging fraternity."[12] During her tenure, she saw no change in the problem of corrupt agents, and she charged that the "government is committing a crime against the public generally when it pins the badge of police authority on and hands a gun to a man of uncertain character, limited intelligence or without giving systematic training for the performance of duties that involve the rights and possibly the lives of citizens."[13] The situation had improved slightly, she admitted, after 1927 when Prohibition Unit agents were put under civil service regulations, but problems at the administrative level, an area still governed by political appointments, had continued to hamper her efforts to establish training requirements for all agents. She charged Lincoln Andrews, the former assistant treasury secretary in charge of the Prohibition Unit from April 1925 until July 1927, with putting "in office men who were temperamentally and in every other way unfitted for the task to which he assigned them," adding, "It will take many a day for law enforcement to recover from the setback it suffered under General Lincoln Andrews."[14] Corrupt or incompetent leadership, within the Prohibition Unit, the Department of Treasury, and Congress, made it easier to divert alcohol manufactured legitimately under permit to illegal distributors. Such leaders placed no restrictions on the number of permits that could be issued, the volume of alcohol that could be produced under permit, or the businesses that could purchase alcohol. Even when Prohibition agents suspected a purchaser might be involved in illegal trafficking of spirits, they had no legal authority to inspect the alcohol in question or inquire of its uses. Willebrandt believed these diversions to be the single greatest source of illegal alcohol in the country.[15]

She did not shy from accusing Prohibitionists, either, notably the Anti-Saloon League, of failing to support the Eighteenth Amendment; she accused them of having "rocking chair-itis," leaning "back in complacent enjoyment" of past victories. The absence of "quiet, steady, forceful education on the value of temperance, community by community," formerly promulgated by the ASL and WCTU, opened the door for anti-Prohibitionists to create doubt, focusing on the crime and corruption brought by Prohibition.[16]

Willebrandt had understood from the beginning that it would take time to clarify the laws of enforcement and establish permissible methods of search and seizure and the penalties to be assessed. When "harmony of interpretation could not be obtained in lower courts," cases advanced to the Supreme Court, where she had argued nearly 80 cases and submitted certiorari (i.e., sympathetic) briefs in another 278. Several of those cases would have far-reaching implications beyond Prohibition. In *U.S. v. Carroll*, the court ruled that automobiles could be stopped and searched and incriminating evidence seized without a search warrant if law enforcement officers had sufficient reason to believe the vehicle's occupants had participated in criminal activity. In *U.S. v. Marron*, the court ruled that business records could be seized without a warrant if thought to reveal illegal operations. Previously, such records were regarded as self-incriminating and, therefore, inadmissible as evidence. Crimes of omission came under scrutiny in *U.S. v. Donnelly*, where the court determined that federal agents and attorneys could be found guilty of violating the Volstead Act if they failed to pursue cases against known violators. The *Grace* and *Ruby* cases found British rumrunners guilty when two ships anchored in international waters allowed smaller boats to be lowered from the main vessels and used to shuttle liquor to shore with the aid of a boat sent from the mainland.[17] Court rulings gave Prohibition agents and policemen more means to secure arrests and collect evidence, resulting in more arrests, but inadequate penalties did not prove a sufficient deterrent.[18] The recent passage of the Jones Five and Ten Law, she believed, with its higher fines and longer jail terms, would go a long way to slowing bootleggers and rumrunners, giving courts the freedom to assess sentences commensurate with crimes.

Willebrandt reminded her readers that only 305 out of 2,540 counties nationwide had declared themselves "wet," making repeal of the Eighteenth Amendment "almost an impossibility." Only thirteen state legislatures would need to oppose repeal to keep the amendment in place should a serious opposition movement arise. Willebrandt admitted gains in anti-Prohibition sentiment as demonstrated by the repeal of state enforcement laws in New York, New Jersey, Montana, Nevada, and Wisconsin, but saw a reinvigorated effort at education and resistance from traditional temperance and Prohibition organizations during Al Smith's presidential campaign. Women's interest in sustaining Prohibition had been revived, in particular, though Willebrandt observed a difference between single and married women: the "modern girl" was willing to share a flask with her escort, but "the moment that girl marries, she likely will, whether consciously or not, become a supporter of Prohibition, because she will always be unwilling to share any part of her husband's income either with a bootlegger or saloon keeper."[19] If women were not enough to hold Prohibition in place, the American people's characteristic desire to "accomplish the impossible" would.[20]

Enduring his time on McNeil Island, subjected to the penitentiary's rigid structure, Roy Olmstead had begun to change. The desires and goals that once had driven him had begun to drop away. He had become interested in the Christian Science religion. Into his contemplations of its tenets—including the belief that the material world is an illusion blinding humans from the truth of spiritual reality—about a year into his sentence, stepped an unexpected guest. Entering the visitors' room, Olmstead saw Tom Revelle waiting. The former district attorney had just learned of the bribes the rumrunner had paid to Clifford McKinney, Revelle's former assistant, and he wanted to make sure Olmstead knew that he had never known about the transactions. Revelle admonished Olmstead not to tell him anything now, or anyone else, for that matter, warning that additional charges could be brought against him. As the conversation ended, Revelle buried his veiled threat by proclaiming, "God bless you, my boy, you don't know how I've suffered for you. I've thought of this many, many times and I want to see you out of this trouble."[21] Olmstead made Tom Revelle not a single promise.

The October 4, 1929, headline in the *Seattle Post-Intelligencer* read, "Mysterious Investigation of Seattle Prohibition Office" in large block letters across the top. The investigation had been announced by none other than J. Edgar Hoover of the FBI. Assistant Attorney General Howard T. Jones, "temporarily filling the position left by the resignation of Mrs. Mabel Walker Willebrandt," stated that "many complaints from the Seattle district have been forthcoming for a long time." The news surprised Roy Lyle, but he would not back down, declaring, "I am not afraid of anything—there is nothing here to investigate." Going on the offense, both he and Whitney attributed the investigation to the work of locals "seeking to discredit enforcement of the Prohibition law here," aided by imprisoned bootleggers seeking pardons. Al Hubbard, whose work with Olmstead and then with Lyle "had brought him considerable publicity," according to the newspaper, had furnished the FBI with a great deal of information. Lyle cautioned readers to remember, "Hubbard is a dismissed Prohibition agent," but the account mentioned that Hubbard had been "exonerated" by a federal grand jury before concluding with a reminder of the two previous investigations of the unit by the Internal Revenue Bureau's Intelligence Unit, whose report "was never acted upon," leaving readers to ponder why.[22]

Privately, Lyle and Whitney were furious, considering the latest investigation unfair and even ridiculous, based as it was on "the alleged evidence" from prejudicial and criminal sources. While this "fake investigation" would subject them again to "the personal discomforts and injury and serious interruption of our work," the real issue was attacks on honest and efficient officials by "the unscrupulous and treacherous opposition of an enemy, not without but within the very government itself." These forces were intent upon destroying enforcement of the Volstead Act "through discrediting the efforts of the personnel." This point was echoed by many drys throughout the country. Failing to maintain the dignity of the office and the confidence of the public, agents of the Prohibition Bureau would lose the ability to gather evidence and tips from the public, and to win cases in front of juries.[23]

Along with the anger, there was great pain for both leaders of the Twentieth District. As Lyle put it to Senator Jones, "I am very resentful and bitter, as I feel I am justified in being because of these unwarranted attacks, yet in my own conscience I feel gratified in having had the privilege of doing my bit for my country in what I honestly believe to be one of its greatest contests and its greatest crises." Whitney made it plainer, telling Jones, "It does seem more than passing strange that we can get no action on such matters, but when any scoundrel and crook or Prohibition violator goes to any unit that can possibly investigate the Prohibition office a statement of the crooks are excepted [*sic*] as facts and they immediately start to harass Prohibition enforcement officers."[24]

Pressing upon Whitney as much as his perceived enemies was the very real possibility that the Prohibition Bureau would be transferred from the Treasury Department to the Department of Justice, home to the FBI now investigating him. Senator Jones had received assurance from President Hoover that the bureau's leadership supported the transfer, leaving Whitney "dumbfounded." He believed Mabel Willebrandt and Alf Oftedal, both of whom had resigned after only six months under Hoover's presidency, had clouded the president's thinking.[25] Whitney assaulted the notion that moving the bureau into the DOJ would somehow make everything "Lily white." Exhibit A was the DOJ's investigation into his own office. Swinging wild punches, he asserted that the U.S. Attorneys and Marshals had been the source of more corruption than the "carefully selected and civil service administrators," the garbled syntax an attempt to paper over his own problems.

Finally, on November 1, 1929, President Hoover named his replacement for Mabel Willebrandt: C. A. Youngquist, the attorney general of Minnesota and a friend of Attorney General William Mitchell and Andrew Volstead. On assuming the mantle, Youngquist said, "I am dry politically and personally, but I am not a fanatic on the subject," a clear sign of change in the government's approach to Prohibition.[26] At the same time, Mitchell hinted at moving all functions under the Department of Justice's umbrella, an idea long advanced by Willebrandt. As the legislation came before Congress, a House committee asked Willebrandt to appear and offer her comments on the proposal. She asked to be excused from the proceedings, saying, "Out of courtesy to those who are discharging the responsibility of enforcing the law I would prefer that you hear their views rather than mine."[27] Congress relented and Willebrandt did not appear before the committee.

Without the crushing demands of her former position, Mabel Willebrandt could give time and voice to the plight of professional women, a subject which had greatly influenced her acceptance of the job as assistant attorney general. In late September 1929, she had given a radio address advising women on how to achieve success in business or professional endeavors. She advised women not to yield their feminine sexuality to mannish appearance or allow men to exaggerate women's successes or failures using misperceptions about their defining characteristics. Willebrandt assigned some blame for those misperceptions to "self-conscious" behaviors that led women to believe failures resulted from conspiracies or prejudice against them rather than the typical mistakes or bad judgment of a novice. Neither did Willebrandt excuse men from needing to grant young women the same "right to make mistakes" as young men and for believing that women harbored inferiority complexes preventing them from reaching greater heights.[28]

In a magazine article printed in February 1930, Willebrandt went further, declaring: "Women have no fair chance in the business world yet. To say that they have is just 'Pollyana talk.'" Beyond doing her job well, a woman must "walk the tight-rope of sexlessness without the loss of her essential charm," pursuing "an impersonal fight against constant efforts to sidetrack her." Willebrandt granted, "Every woman wants a home," but men couldn't "sympathize with the pioneer spirit of the modern girl he marries," couldn't allow her to work outside the home without fearing questions or ridicule from his peers. Women could not overcome such prejudices without the help of a husband committed to preserving his wife's freedom, self-respect, intellectual acumen, and economic independence. Doing so, Willebrandt asserted, would produce a true "home" instead of the "outgrown 'manly' theory of 'my wife can't work for a living!'" Without a job, or some other outlet outside the home, she foresaw only desperation and anger for a woman. Even in instances where women, on their own or with their husbands' blessings, entered the workforce, they must be prepared to have their credentials and capabilities challenged by male bosses and colleagues. Maintaining "a subtle attitude of confidence and resourcefulness, revealed through quiet, restrained and womanly dignity" would slowly melt "stubborn prejudice." She expressed great hope for the future, but warned, in the interim, the successful woman was "bound to look back with yearning and perhaps with regret at dead hopes—the boy she loved but rejected because in his masculine egotism he demanded without understanding her free spirit's sacrifice— the children she could have had—the companionship she missed."[29]

If readers could have glimpsed the past ten years of Willebrandt's diaries they would have seen the roots of every declaration she made in the article. Her struggles with Fred Horowitz's ego coupled with the social stigma of a divorce and remarriage had convinced her to remain alone, seeking contentment in her career. Mabel Willebrandt would have great success in her professional life, achieving the financial stability she craved, and a certain amount of fulfillment with Dorothy's adoption, but her failure to find a sympathetic companion, a desire for which she expressed many times in her diaries and personal correspondence, served as the unstated example in her article.

As President Hoover's National Commission on Law Observance and Enforcement (better known as the Wickersham Commission after its chairman, George Wickersham) began its investigation into the effectiveness of federal Prohibition enforcement, several members of the U.S. House of Representatives, feeling empowered by potential change, advanced a series of proposals to amend the Constitution in relation to the Eighteenth Amendment. The proposals, variously, would have allowed the federal government to regulate the manufacture, sale, transportation, import, and export of alcoholic beverages; created a federal permitting system allowing manufacture and sale of alcohol; returned the decision to manufacture or sell alcohol to the states, individually; set a date for a referendum on repeal; or repealed the Eighteenth Amendment.[30]

On February 12, 1930, Pauline Sabin appeared on the first day of hearings on yet another proposed amendment to modify the Volstead Act. She came "to refute the contention that is often made by dry organizations, that all the women of America favor national Prohibition." She believed women had been significant in securing enactment of the Eighteenth Amendment, but their hopes of strengthening a weak will had not worked as desired: "They have seen an alleged moral reform debauch public and private life." Increases in crime, government expenditure on enforcement, prison population, death from alcoholism, and drinking among teens, Sabin declared, brought increasing dissatisfaction with the law. Worse were the lawmakers, in Congress and state legislatures, who were "notoriously wet in their personal conducts, but continue to vote under the whiplash of that political cabal called the Anti-Saloon League." Sabin called for the end of the hypocrisy that was "rapidly becoming our national characteristic" and "remedial" legislation to "replace the present era of lawlessness, corruption, hypocrisy, and killings with honesty, temperance, and sobriety." The assembled gallery applauded.[31]

After dozens of women, claiming to represent millions of women, had spoken against any modification of the Volstead Act or the Eighteenth Amendment, Sabin requested a chance for rebuttal, which was granted, but she could not appear on the appointed day because she was in Cleveland attending to the details of the WONPR's national conference, so she sent Elizabeth Harris, prominent in the Washington, D.C., chapter of the WONPR, in her stead. Harris took issue with the women favoring Prohibition and claiming they represented a majority of women throughout the country. She refuted claims by Mrs. Henry Peabody, president of the Women's National Committee for Law Enforcement, and Mrs. John Sippel, president of the General Federation of Women's Clubs, who said they represented twelve million women, by saying, "That Mrs. Jones is a member of a reading club, of a women's club and parent-teacher association does not make Mrs. Jones three women with three votes for or against Prohibition!" Harris reported on the receipt of numerous complaints sent to the WONPR and to newspapers across the country from women, many associated with clubs Peabody claimed for Prohibition, stating their offense at the suggestion that any of the groups in question had polled its membership regarding Prohibition. Returning to a familiar WONPR theme, Harris concluded there could be no response "to those who confined their statement to excited declaration that never, while the nineteenth amendment stood, could the Eighteenth be repealed."[32]

Away from the hearings, the WONPR attacked—if the use of statistics and hard questioning could be regarded as attacking—the WCTU and other women's Prohibitionist groups, challenging their assumptions that Prohibition was succeeding. At a forum headlined by Ella Boole and Pauline Sabin at the Women's National Republican Club, Boole shied from the obvious failure to slow the liquor trade, saying success could be measured by the "disappearance of the saloon," downplaying the existence of speakeasies as solely a New York City phenomenon.[33]

The Women's Organization for National Prohibition Reform's first national conference in Cleveland in April 1930 created a "Declaration of Principles" labeling Prohibition as "fundamentally wrong." National Prohibition destroyed "the balance" between state and federal authority, ignored the fact that only "moral sense and the community conscience" could promote abstinence, and produced "disastrous consequences in the hypocrisy, the corruption, and the tragic loss of life and the appalling increase of crime which attended the abortive attempt to enforce it." The WONPR called for the repeal of the Eighteenth Amendment and the enactment of state regulations "forbidding the return of the saloon," driving "crime-breeding speakeasies" into extinction. Noting that the Eighteenth Amendment had been enacted by votes in state legislatures, the WONPR urged Congress "to submit to conventions of the people" (a nod to Jim Wadsworth's failed amendment), ensuring a true mandate would be heard.[34]

While Pauline Sabin had pulled the WONPR's initial membership from her extensive political and social contacts, most of the women lacked any experience in political organizations. Typical of the membership was Bessie Gardner du Pont, former wife of Alfred du Pont. Bessie attended the convention in Cleveland as part of the Delaware delegation, "utterly unprepared . . . for the responsibility we were entrusted with."[35] She had never attended a convention of any kind or belonged to a women's club, and she knew little of the convention's purpose beyond what she had learned in reading the newspapers and "from a short morning's study" in the local library. She was exactly the kind of woman—previously uninvolved, her opinion not registered—that Sabin hoped to attract to the WONPR.

Sabin followed the convention with a radio address, explaining the identification of the WONPR as a "wet organization." She had no objection to the term for the purpose of distinguishing between her members and those who were satisfied with the current Prohibition Law, but said, "Literally, our organization is as far from being wet as many of our so-called Prohibitionist legislators are from being dry. Our organization stands for temperance, for wise and honest government, for better social conditions, and for the protection of the right of the individual to life, liberty, and the pursuit of happiness." Editors at the *New York World*, a publication with Democratic Party leanings, applauded Sabin's clarification, advising its readers to discard old definitions of wet and dry, and to understand that a "wet to-day is a man or woman who is opposed to national Prohibition."[36]

Sabin submitted to almost any request, from wets or drys, to speak about the dangers of Prohibition and of liquor; she hoped to illuminate the WONPR's calls for repeal without a return of the saloon, a distinction that escaped many people. She proposed that after repeal, national Prohibition would remain in effect for one year while state legislatures passed bills to regulate liquor traffic within their boundaries and devise laws "forbidding the return of the saloon." She believed "the people" in each state knew what measure of Prohibition or restrictions best suited their desires. The organization had members who "never have drunk intoxicating beverages," and, "undoubtedly," there were members who did.[37] That divide did not obscure the group's objection to the Eighteenth Amendment, which infringed on personal liberty and did more harm than good. Responding to the charge that Prohibition had not been given a "fair trial" in New York, a WONPR representative cited government statistics to demonstrate that law enforcement had done little to curb drinking or the illegal traffic in liquor, even in states where the law had been supported. Between 1920 and 1930, federal expenditures increased from 3.7 million dollars to nearly 29 million dollars, seizures of stills had increased nearly twentyfold, seizure of illegal liquor had grown from 153,000 to 32,000,000 gallons, deaths from alcoholism had increased 300 percent, and arrests for alcoholism had risen 125 percent, but none of those factors had stemmed the tide of liquor washing over the country or the burgeoning criminal enterprises needed to keep the booze flowing.[38]

On May 14, 1930, Senator Jones informed William Whitney that the attorney general had decided to empanel a grand jury to determine whether indictments should be handed to Whitney, Lyle, Revelle, or any other Prohibition Bureau staff for bribery and corruption.[39] As the grand jury convened, the U.S. Senate passed the transfer bill, placing the Prohibition Bureau within the Department of Justice. Whitney's worst fear had come into being. Not only did his job now reside in the department accusing him of wrongdoing, but with all the attorneys employed by the DOJ, his position might be unnecessary.[40]

On May 26, 1930, the grand jury indicted Lyle, Whitney, Clifford McKinney, and two others for conspiracy to violate the National Prohibition Act and for conspiracy to violate the statute against accepting bribes. Former U.S. Attorney Thomas Revelle was not named. Whitney, always the main target, faced an additional indictment for the crime of perjury. All men were suspended from duty, effective immediately.[41] "We never had a chance," lamented Whitney. "It [the investigation] was never intended to give us a chance." The coldest indignity came when Whitney was held in the city jail for want of a five-thousand-dollar bond. Lyle, ever the saintly figurehead, had been released on his own recognizance. McKinney's whereabouts were unknown, Revelle's former assistant having fled more than a year earlier, leaving his wife and children behind.[42] The following day, yet another disgrace befell Whitney when Senator Jones, his confidant and fellow Prohibition champion, stated he would allow repeal or modification of the Volstead Act if that was the will of the people, a statement unthinkable a few years earlier.[43]

The government had had years, as many as sixty investigators and agents, and tens of thousands of dollars, Whitney charged, to create its case. He and his codefendants had "scarcely a dollar." With all the negative publicity, the local newspapers aligning against Prohibition, "we cannot get a fair trial." Whitney estimated he needed three months to prepare for the trial, seeing not only his personal reputation at stake, but the larger import of this trial, and declaring, "This case will be tried on the wet and dry issue." If the forces arrayed against Whitney succeeded in getting him convicted, he concluded, "then the future of Prohibition is utterly hopeless."[44] According to Whitney, if he could be convicted, every "vigorous official" would be intimidated by the forces within law enforcement as much as from without, and begin to relax enforcement lest they incur the same wrath.

Whitney prepared for the trial just as his opponents had. He sought out the inmates at McNeil Island Penitentiary, hearing a great deal of damning hearsay about the work of the FBI investigators. Unnamed sources told him that bootlegger Chris Curtis had been paroled five days before the grand jury to induce his testimony. Curtis was willing to testify to any accusation made against Whitney and his colleagues, including the charge that Curtis had paid a six-thousand-dollar bribe to Lyle, through Hubbard, with the money directed to Senator Wesley Jones' 1926 campaign fund.[45] Confirming Whitney's suspicion that former assistant attorney general Mabel Willebrandt had always been out to get him, Jones confided, "I think that the reason why Curtis was paroled was because the department felt that it was under obligation to do so because of a promise made by Mrs. Willebrandt in connection with some trial about the same time when he was indicted."[46] While Whitney had always blamed Willebrandt for a significant portion of the attacks against him, he now hedged a little, accusing former U.S. Marshal Ed Benn, Alf Oftedal, and the warden at McNeil Island Penitentiary of intentionally misleading Willebrandt to further their own ends. She, in turn, had spread that prejudice throughout her department, including the FBI, which had produced the report used to indict Whitney and his colleagues. Summing up his predicament, Whitney wrote, "This case actually simmers down to this: not only must we prove ourselves innocent, but we have got to convict the very government itself. It's a pretty big task."[47]

The most embarrassing, painful, and egregiously unfair period of Whitney's life, his trial for conspiring with Roy Olmstead, began on Monday, August 11, 1930. Entering the courtroom where he had spent so much of the past eight years trying to convict bootleggers, rumrunners, and moonshiners, this time as the defendant, was to know betrayal—a perfidy capable of twisting his years of hard work into the end of his career, while all of Seattle and most of Washington State watched. Alfred Hubbard, whom Whitney had trusted, befriended, and ultimately staked his own career upon, arrived with great fanfare in the courtroom, mingling with bootleggers, Prohibition agents, and gawkers alike; smiling and backslapping; wearing his unofficial designation as "one of the most important government witnesses" like a crown. Whitney filed through the crowd alone, without his codefendants in tow, leaving them to find their places in the defendants' chairs while he took his customary seat at the counselors' table, though this time for the defense, not the prosecution.

Called as the first witness, Hubbard approached the stand. The years of lavish meals and abundant alcohol showed in his rounded face and thickened frame; the years of playing fast and loose in his flashy attire, a gaudy, rakish style favored by successful bootleggers across the country. He had dressed, according to one observer, "as fastidiously as a theater usher," his panama hat ringed with a red band, his black-and-white shoes setting off his dark suit. Hubbard reveled in the spotlight, having sought it since he had metamorphosed from a kid hawking lies about his inventions in radio, X-ray machines, and other electrical wonders into a double agent in 1925, freeing him to make large sums of money by playing both sides, a freebooter living on a knife's edge, the last great pirate of Puget Sound. Still identified as "a former inventor and electrical wizard," Hubbard viewed the trial as his path back into the big leagues, fancying his testimony worth an appointment to one of the federal agencies overseeing Prohibition. His greed for cash, power, and notoriety was never more apparent than when he began unwinding the most outrageous reinvention of himself and of Olmstead, Whitney, and the other defendants, mixing into this new version of history a slew of bald-faced lies intertwined with dashes of truth, told utterly without conscience, without concern for the damage he was wreaking upon men he had called his friends.[48]

Hubbard's testimony about bribes, their amounts, and dates, came tumbling out haphazardly, clearly made up as he went along. He claimed he had collected a total of $140,000 to $170,000 to bribe Whitney and his alleged coconspirators, reserving a 10 percent commission for himself. Reporters, upon hearing the volume of liquor passing through Olmstead's network, calculated the revenue that should have been generated for Olmstead, and asked the perfectly obvious question, as one headline put it: "Where did all of the millions of dollars supposed to have been handled by Olmstead and other liquor rings go?"[49] In the coming days' testimony, Hubbard would step over his "facts" repeatedly, unconcerned that dates, places, and amounts did not jibe with earlier testimony. At one point, he claimed to have built radio stations upon Whitney's direction, "presumably for Prohibition work, but really to tip off the boats about the Coast Guard."[50] Whitney had implied as much about Elsie Olmstead's broadcasting station in the first Olmstead trial, to little effect. If the witness was recycling and repackaging old charges to give shape to his new conspiracy tale, no one seemed to notice.

To buttress Hubbard's testimony, the prosecution introduced key documents: Lyle's letter authorizing Hubbard to use any boat he chose as part of his undercover investigation; and two letters from Whitney, one that began, "Dear Al, I guess you are still my pal . . ." and describing Hubbard's bust in the *Zev* case as "the most spectacular and bravest thing ever done in US in Prohibition enforcement." Another seeming nail in Whitney's coffin was the glowing letter of recommendation he had provided Hubbard after Hubbard's termination. Whitney skipped over his doubts about Hubbard, touting his "initiative and ability as an investigator," which had resulted in "some of the largest and most important conspiracy cases ever tried . . ." The praise went to ever loftier heights. For example, Whitney had written, "I have known him quite intimately, and I have not known him to do a dishonest act, but have found him always actuated by a desire to assist the government in to [*sic*] run down the criminal."[51]

The moment the government prosecutors stepped back from the bar, announcing the end of their questioning of the witness, the defense attorneys sent their best interrogator, A. R. Hilen, to destroy Al Hubbard. In his hands, Hilen held transcripts from previous trials at which Hubbard had testified. Terse and intense, Hilen fired questions at Hubbard, allowing only no-nonsense answers, quickly revealing that every piece of testimony offered by Hubbard in earlier trials stood in direct opposition to the story he had just spent days telling. Using the witness's own words like a hammer, Hilen forced Hubbard into a series of confessions. Admitting to perjury, the witness explained, "No, I wasn't telling the truth then. I was wearing Whitney's collar at that time—but I'm not anymore."[52] The defense team turned, at last, to Hubbard's motivation for making these charges, asking him if he had been pushed by Ed Benn, one of Whitney's nemeses. Provoked at last, Hubbard, with some heat, "insisted that Mrs. Mabel Walker

Willebrandt was the only person who urged him to tell his story."[53] There was nothing else to ask, the statement hanging in the air as proof of Whitney's years of suspicion, though Willebrandt was not called to testify to the claim and never commented upon it. Hubbard was excused and left the courthouse a free man despite having admitted to years of graft, bribery, and rum-running.

Whitney took the stand nearly a month into the trial, anxious to unravel the specious case against him and his comrades. Led by his attorney's questions, he disproved many of Hubbard's specific allegations using official expense reports and time sheets to explain how money came and went and to verify his whereabouts on days in question. Whitney mocked other charges as "a figment of his [Hubbard's] imagination." He admitted paying for a speedboat for Hubbard's use and investing in a radio station, but he said friendship, not conspiracy, drove him to put the boat title in his own name and help with the station, both more expensive than Hubbard could manage on his own. Ultimately, Whitney had to admit that, regrettably, he had trusted Hubbard to an exceptional degree. That trust had created a tangled mass of hearsay and lies and half truths. Whitney's trust did not equate to duplicity, but his faith in Hubbard did call into question his judgment. Whitney described the moment in April of 1929 when he had finally shown Hubbard the door after the boy wonder had offered him a bribe to let a load of liquor slip through. Wrapping up, Hilen gave Whitney a chance to conclude his days of testimony with a flat, unequivocal denial that he had "received a penny of corrupt money" from Hubbard, the "pay off man for the Olmstead organization."[54]

Thomas Revelle, next on the witness stand, supported Whitney's version of events in quick order, but the prosecution was anxious to put the former district attorney in the hot seat, hoping to reveal him as another link in the conspiratorial chain, even though Revelle was not on trial. The questioning began with Revelle's trip out to McNeil Island to see Olmstead and warn him not to tell reporters he had paid protection money to Clifford McKinney, Revelle's former assistant. Revelle admitted he had gone to meet Olmstead, but confessed nothing more about their conversation. Hoping to lead Revelle into a trap, the prosecution read from Olmstead's affidavit recalling the conversation, in which the former bootlegger quoted Revelle: "God Bless you my boy, you don't know how I've suffered for you . . . I want to see you out of this trouble." The audience burst into laughter.

The government prosecutor questioned Revelle about the wisdom and legality of allowing the Prohibition Unit to be complicit in smuggling huge quantities of liquor. Despite the prosecution's attempts to portray each of Revelle's affirmative replies as shocking, Revelle calmly explained that the ends justified the means.[55] He and Whitney had needed a man on the inside, and having one came with risks. They had used their best judgment and won several large conspiracy cases because of it.

Hoping to cast a wider net around the alleged conspiracy, the prosecution presented correspondence between Revelle and Willebrandt, revealing Revelle's shifting confidence in Hubbard's motives and veracity. In August of 1927, then U.S. Attorney Revelle had tried to block an investigation into Hubbard and had sent a series of telegrams to Willebrandt explaining that an inquiry would do harm to the DOJ and Prohibition enforcement as a whole. In one missive, he pled that suspending Hubbard would have weakened the Olmstead conspiracy case, which had been built largely with tips and information provided by Hubbard. Revelle had begged Willebrandt to recall him to Washington, D.C., so he could provide further explanation to her and Hubbard's superiors in the Treasury Department. Willebrandt had reminded him she had no authority over the Treasury Department and their possible suspension of Hubbard, but offered, "Our office will back you in all steps that may become necessary to trial . . ."[56] Revelle had followed up with his boss on September 10, 1927, citing rumors that "Hubbard and Fryant have accepted bribes and have been interested parties in [the] smuggling of whiskey," the truth of which Rev-elle could only guess.[57] A month later, he had changed his view, confessing to his boss in Washington, "Personally, I am very strongly convinced from our experience here in the last two or three weeks, that even though Hubbard and Fryant took money, yet there is no possible hope of ever successfully trying them for the same." This cor-respondence, which Revelle acknowledged, contradicted his earlier testimony that he had not believed reports of Hubbard's improprieties when they were first made known to him.[58] Revelle told the court he would not have put Hubbard on the witness stand in the second Ol-mstead case if he had had any doubts of his honesty, but his correspon-dence with Willebrandt recorded something different.

The prosecution had proven that Revelle, and by implication Whitney, had conspired to keep Hubbard out of jail long enough to use him as a key witness in several big conspiracy trials even though they knew he was deeply compromised as an agent, his testimony unreliable and largely unverifiable. The two had violated their oaths and the law. To have their sordid business on display, for the public to learn how they had been duped by Hubbard and allowed him to blossom into a freebooting pirate, must have caused the former dis-trict attorney and the former assistant director of the Prohibition Unit in Seattle the ultimate embarrassment.

After additional witnesses impugned the reputation of Hubbard, it appeared the defense would move to its summation, but Hilen had one more trick up his sleeve. He called Senator Wesley Jones to the stand, causing a clamor from the crowd. Although the senator's prom-inence had been tarnished at the recent Republican state convention, where participants had openly mocked him for his shifting stance on Prohibition, he still held the respect of most people in the state and certainly the court's curiosity. The prosecution wanted to know his role in the hiring of Hubbard as an undercover agent. "My advice was sought," Jones recalled, and "I was asked to see if it could be done."

Jones had seen the value in having a man inside the Olmstead organization, though Lyle and Whitney had told him they "didn't know
if they could depend on Hubbard, but they thought they could and he
couldn't do any harm anyway." Jones testified that he went to see Roy
Haynes, Prohibition commissioner at the time, but "I can't say that I
recommended the appointment"; he had merely explained the request
and "left it up to Haynes," a transparently disingenuous claim. How
could he have gone to the commissioner's office and explained the
plan without Haynes concluding this was an idea the senator endorsed?[59] Jones' support of the men he'd chosen to run federal Prohibition enforcement but disavowal of their hiring of Al Hubbard left
most Seattleites questioning either the senator's judgment in tapping
Whitney and Lyle or his involvement with Hubbard, a predicament
epitomizing the prosecution's assertions of ineptitude, confusion, and
duplicity among Seattle's federal Prohibition forces.

Closing statements began with the prosecution's lead attorney,
Assistant Attorney General Leslie Salter, declaring, "It was impossible to entertain the theory that Hubbard could have hoodwinked
either man [Roy Olmstead or William Whitney] and that it was
therefore apparent that an alliance had existed between Olmstead
and the law-enforcement officers." Hubbard was a "callow youth,"
Olmstead a "master mind of bootleggers," William Whitney an "astute attorney." Salter reminded the court of the "undisputed evidence that vast quantities of liquor had been brought into Seattle
during the period of the conspiracy . . . [many of the] circumstances . . .
admitted by the defendants themselves . . . ," but he offered no specific facts or documentary evidence, relying on the "he said, she
said" litany of witness testimony.[60] Charles Moriarty, another defense attorney, reminded the jury of the contradictions strewn about
by the prosecution's witnesses, leaving a trail of so-called evidence
so convoluted that finding a conspiracy amidst the tangle would be
impossible.[61] Moriarty seized upon a key point conceded by the

prosecution: Roy Olmstead, the King of the Bootleggers, currently resided in a cell at the McNeil Island penitentiary.[62] The defendants had convicted Olmstead in one of the most significant cases in Prohibition history and had indicted him twice more, obtaining a second conviction—hard facts to reconcile with the prosecution's insistence that Whitney and Lyle conspired with the man they sent to prison. Moriarty believed Whitney and Lyle had become "victims" of anti-Prohibition sentiments sweeping the city of Seattle, the state of Washington, and the entire country, which was increasingly wet and intolerant of the rigid law enforcement practiced by the Prohibition Unit in Seattle.[63] The defense got a little extra help when the judge instructed the jury to carefully weigh the testimony of convicts, ex-convicts, coconspirators, and those admitting previous false testimony. Judge Norcross took particular aim at "witnesses for the government [who] admittedly were co-conspirators," their testimony "a polluted source to be viewed with suspicion."[64] After only a few hours, the jury returned a verdict of "not guilty" for all defendants, ending the last piece of business begun by Mabel Willebrandt before her departure from government service.

Despite his exoneration, Whitney would not return to work for the Prohibition Unit. The trial had revealed all his faults—poor judgment, rash decision-making, distrust of his superiors—which when combined with his lack of remorse left the commissioner of Prohibition no alternative but to fire him.[65] Lyle, Whitney's boss in name only, was seen as subordinate to Whitney and was spared, the government offering him a position as a liquor permit inspector.[66] Always seeking the last word, Whitney opined that his banishment came because "perhaps I have taken this work too seriously," and the absence of serious people, he predicted, would prove the undoing of Prohibition.[67]

Chapter 13

Mrs. James Doran, whose husband had served as commissioner of Prohibition, assembled a recipe book for nonalcoholic drinks, including one from Mabel Willebrandt. Her recipe, Portia's Punch, included one small bottle of red Concord "California pure concentrated grape juice," two bottles of ginger ale, one thinly sliced lemon, and a half cup of chopped mint leaves.[1] Willebrandt submitted the recipe just after accepting a job with Fruit Industries, representing California grape growers.[2] Fruit Industries hoped that retaining the former assistant attorney general might improve an awkward relationship with the federal government, which suspected the company of playing both sides of the Prohibition fence. Many customers used the company's concentrates to ferment wine, drawing the ire of "gangsters," who had threatened to disrupt distribution of the juices. The company asked the government for protection of its salesmen and distributors, claiming it had no control over the actions of its customers.[3] Willebrandt's decision to work for Fruit

Industries had been fueled by her desire to support California grape growers who had suffered under the weight of drought and the expanding economic depression, but it smacked of hypocrisy to many in the Prohibition camp.

The Anti-Saloon League offered Willebrandt an opportunity to explain her seemingly contradictory position—working for an alleged winemaker while claiming to support the Eighteenth Amendment—at a meeting attended by many prominent in the Prohibition camp. To sustained applause from the 450 in attendance, Willebrandt professed her support for Prohibition, saying that she saw "an irresistible upward reaching, a spiritual flame, that can't be argued with" from the American people, among whom she saw "no weakening" of support for the Eighteenth Amendment.[4] She did not mention the alleged illegal use of her client's product to make drinkable, intoxicating beverages.

The congressional elections of 1930 brought a flip in the balance of power between wets and drys, opening the door to the day when wets would gain the majority necessary to approve legislation allowing state legislatures to reconsider the Eighteenth Amendment. In the House of Representatives, five states—Nebraska, Oregon, South Carolina, Tennessee, and Washington—with long histories of favoring Prohibition elected candidates favoring repeal. The electorate in three states—Illinois, Massachusetts, and Rhode Island—stated their preference for repeal in referendums on the issue and Massachusetts overturned its state enforcement, or "Baby Volstead," law, bringing the number of states refusing to enforce Prohibition to eight, representing 25 percent of the total U.S. population. In another eighteen states, the two major parties inserted repeal planks in their platforms. New York's legislature had gone so far as to pass a resolution stating their desire for the U.S. Congress to call state conventions for repeal of the Eighteenth Amendment, the position advocated by the WONPR.

Pauline Sabin resigned from the Women's National Republican Club in November 1930, apparently after the club's membership voted to support the continuance of Prohibition. She had been much less active in the club's business after her resignation as president in 1925, but, as she was a founding member, her influence and the cachet of her name were still considerable. The executive committee suggested that Henrietta Livermore, another founding member and the current president, contact Sabin to ask if she *truly* intended to resign from the club.[5] Livermore must have convinced Sabin to remain a member, because three years later she submitted another letter of resignation.[6] There was no changing her mind the second time.

A t the WONPR's second annual convention, held at the May-flower Hotel in Washington, D.C., in April 1931, representatives from thirty-one states met to hear of their organization's progress and the plans going forward. Sabin characterized the "growth of the sentiment" for repeal as "so inspiring, so convincing, that it sounds more like a song of triumph than the plain and simple annals of an organization." She charted that progress in surging membership, the increased number of avowed wets in Congress, the refusal of many states to expend funds on Prohibition enforcement, and the Wickersham Commission's near "complete indictment of the workings of the Eighteenth Amendment." Behind it all, Sabin saw the WONPR's insistence that candidates state their views on Prohibition and directing its membership to vote only for those candidates supporting reform, regardless of party affiliation. Moving forward, the organization would enlist "an army of women so great that its backing will give courage to the most weak-kneed and hypocritical

Congressman to vote as he drinks," saying, "Women will prove to them that the ballots of an aroused people are irresistible in the achievement of a fundamental project."[7] The WONPR endorsed all efforts to bring repeal, but balked at any plans for modification of Prohibition that might "leave the matter still in the hands of Congress and therefore liable to be a football in successive political campaigns." The organization wanted state legislatures to vote on repeal and they wanted the president and Congress to make that happen. The convention's attendees voted unanimously to send its resolutions to the president, leaders of Congress, and leaders of each party.[8]

Sabin had a quiet summer in terms of WONPR activities. Perhaps she was simply recuperating from surgery she underwent for an ear infection two weeks after the convention; certainly she was developing strategies for the big push that would come in 1932.

On May 12, 1931, Roy Olmstead, dapper as ever in a gray suit and tan overcoat, stepped from the McNeil Island launch onto solid ground, vowing never to return to the prison from which he had just been released, his sentence served in full, minus six months for good behavior. He didn't know what he would do, but vowed he would not return to bootlegging. He bore no grudges, relishing the chance "to do what I like."[9] Elsie met him at the dock and the two faded into the crowd and obscurity, though the Supreme Court's ruling in his case, in which they approved wiretapping over privacy rights, would prove a rallying cry in the anti-Prohibition crusade.

The WONPR represented a different kind of lobby, reported *Vanity Fair* in August 1931, and it was disorienting to congressmen comfortable with groups seeking favors for specific industries, labor interests, or those hoping to force their beliefs on other people. The

WONPR, by contrast, wanted nothing for itself and did not advocate a moral agenda; the "Sabines"* wanted merely "to correct a nauseating abuse of political authority . . . by ceasing to dragoon the public in the interest of a law which nobody loves." Ebbing membership in the WCTU and ASL, combined with economic misfortune, benefited the Sabines, "beautiful, cultured, and practical to their finger-tips," who approached congressmen with a single question—Where did they stand on Prohibition?—treating a dry "as a future friend" and a wet "as a valued ally." When votes arose on Prohibition-related measures, the Sabines mobilized their membership, sending telegrams to allies and prodding "future friends." They also instituted a "social lobby," hosting receptions, teas, and dinners for the wives of congressmen, many of whom were anxious to fit in with Washington society. "Dirty work," *Vanity Fair* called such efforts by "young, pretty and intelligent women . . . to employ their wiles to ingratiate themselves."

Such descriptions sound sexist today and probably offended the WONPR's leaders at the time, even though the magazine acknowledged the political acumen of their approach: nonconfrontational, inviting, and entirely effective. With the WONPR leading the charge for repeal, *Vanity Fair* believed the movement in "capable hands," a "cultured, charming and temperate body of women, who do not propose to let the country be ruined or their children debauched in the name of American womanhood."[10] The "Sabines" were usurping the WCTU claim that they represented women.

Testing the political deftness portrayed in *Vanity Fair*, the WONPR sent a letter to each congressman and senator in September 1931 asking if he would vote in favor of a bill to send the question of

---

* A nod to the legend in which the Sabine women halted a war with Rome by standing between the two factions.

repealing the Eighteenth Amendment to state conventions, where the people would decide its fate. The organization did not ask whether he opposed or favored Prohibition, but only whether he would permit the people of the country to vote on whether the amendment should be sustained or repealed.[11] Sabin announced the early results on December 1: nearly 60 percent of the respondents favored submitting a repeal referendum to the states. Of 251 respondents (almost half the House and Senate membership), 149 supported the proposal for submission, 49 opposed, and 53 refused to commit either way.[12] Sabin announced at a meeting of the WONPR's Executive Committee the votes of each congressman, identifying those opposed to any reconsideration of the Eighteenth Amendment and placing a target upon them in the 1932 elections, a tactic borrowed from the Prohibitionist women of yesteryear.[13]

As the anti-Prohibition tide rose, moderate politicians, those most likely wet in orientation but unwilling to challenge their constituencies, offered various schemes to modify the Volstead Act to allow manufacture and sale of "light" wine and beer containing less than 3 percent alcohol. Sabin and the WONPR opposed any modification, believing it "disastrous for us to think for a moment that we have thereby effected a real and lasting reform of [the] Prohibition problem." "National Prohibition will continue to plague, disorganize and demoralize the country as long as it remains in the Constitution," declared Sabin.[14] The organization would accept nothing less than full repeal, the uncompromising simplicity of that position gaining steam. By the end of 1931, after only eighteen months of existence, the WONPR had recruited four hundred thousand women to their cause, more than the WCTU could claim at any time in its fifty years of existence. The WONPR's membership included women from all forty-eight states, representing all manner of professional experiences and women classifying themselves simply as housewives, dispelling the "silly slander that the movement for

Prohibition Reform is a leisure-class movement, maintained chiefly by 'smart' or fashionable women."[15]

I n November 1931, a federal court in Kansas City ruled that the sale of grapes, grape juice, or grape concentrate that could be fermented constituted a crime under the Volstead Act. Specifically, the court ruled against sales to consumers in their homes, where the process of fermentation was described and suppliers such as Fruit Industries provided bottling services after the fermentation period had passed. Fruit Industries immediately announced it would no longer sell its products door-to-door, would offer them only in grocery stores with-out instructions or mention of fermentation on the labels.[16] Much as Mabel Willebrandt had avoided the question of whether her employer operated as a de facto bootlegger, Fruit Industries sidestepped the issue, asserting that their salesmen had done nothing more than provide advice and that they could not control the ultimate use of their product. Willebrandt made no statements on the ruling.

P auline Sabin knew supporters of repeal resided in even the driest states, their voices and votes buried beneath a vocal minority declaring the supremacy of abstinence over temperance. In November 1931, the WONPR had established an Anti-Prohibition Institute and an associated School of Public Speaking. The institute sought to educate the organization's members and other interested parties in the "fundamental arguments" for repeal of the Eighteenth Amendment and the return of liquor control to the individual states. A series of lectures would be presented twice a month through March of 1932. The School of Public Speaking was organized to develop additional speakers to carry the repeal movement, using the information acquired from the Anti-Prohibition Institute lectures, to clubs and organizations around the country.[17]

Seeking to expose the fallacy of a unified dry front, Sabin traveled to so-called dry states to gauge the level of support for repeal. In January 1932, she and Mrs. Courtlandt Nicoll, the WONPR's vice chairperson, traveled to Colorado, Nebraska, Minnesota, and Ohio, the birthplace of the temperance and Prohibition movements. Sabin's belief proved prophetic a few months later, when the newly formed Dayton, Ohio, WONPR chapter registered twenty thousand members in two weeks.[18]

Holding to the same theme of spreading the word, and making the WONPR a truly national organization, Sabin would need to attract supporters in the Deep South, a region known for its conservative values, its disdain for anything originating up north, and its devotion to the Democratic Party. She had some familiarity with the region, though, having spent considerable time in South Carolina at the Sabins' winter retreat, the Oaks, located a short distance from Charleston. Sabin called for a meeting of the executive committee of the WONPR in Charleston to formulate a plan to gain traction in the South. Representatives from twenty-six states, including women from several southern states, attended the Charleston meetings, which produced a resolution disputing old arguments by dry leaders that twelve million members of women's organizations endorsed Prohibition, having drawn that number from the combined membership of groups comprising the Federated Women's Clubs. The WONPR countered that many anti-Prohibition women belonged to those clubs and their voices were lost in such false statements. Hoping to disabuse critics branding the WONPR as a group of society ladies, Sabin presented results of a survey of the organization's membership revealing that 37 percent identified as housewives, 19 percent as clerical workers, and 15 percent as industrial workers.[19] From Charleston, Sabin and five WONPR officers traveled to Atlanta, where the Georgia WONPR chapter sponsored a luncheon for Sabin, and later an evening of speakers, in the packed ballroom of the Biltmore Hotel, which even the mayor attended.[20]

Shortly after the southern tour ended, Sabin got an opportunity to measure the success of the WONPR's efforts, when a vote on the Beck-Linthicum Bill, which proposed an addendum to the Eighteenth Amendment allowing each state to vote on whether to restore its authority to regulate the manufacture and sale of liquor within its borders, was scheduled in the House of Representatives for mid-March.[21] The WONPR's members understood the bill had little chance of passage, but the vote's importance lay in forcing Congress' members to "go on record" for or against Prohibition, something that would prove useful in the fall elections.[22] Drys, or at least those proclaiming themselves dry, defeated wets by a margin of 227 to 187, with the votes favoring the bill split almost evenly between Republicans and Democrats.[23] It was the first time a full vote in the House had considered the Eighteenth Amendment since its passage.

The WONPR's southern tour continued to generate press coverage in the region into the summer—another sign of changing attitudes, believed Sabin. In June, the *Baton Rouge Advocate* asked Sabin to profess her views in contrast to those of Clarence True Wilson, a leader of the Methodist Board of Temperance, Prohibition, and Public Morals. She added a new argument to the case against Prohibition, noting the opportunity voters had to assist in economic recovery, as the Depression worsened, by "voting to eliminate the stupendous waste of money squandered in an endeavor to enforce the obnoxious Prohibition law." Sabin had begun the WONPR to challenge the "moral depression" wrought by Prohibition, but it had become equally important to repeal the Eighteenth Amendment to help heal the economic depression. The cost of enforcement, federally and locally, had been estimated as high as forty-nine million dollars, with conservative estimates on the loss of tax revenue set at one billion dollars, money that could greatly assist an economic recovery. Sabin believed the majority of Americans wanted repeal with new, responsible controls on liquor traffic, including taxation. They also wanted to rid the country of speakeasies, bootleggers, gangsters, and the Methodist Board of Temperance, Prohibition, and "Other People's Morals." For his part, Clarence True Wilson labeled the repeal movement a conspiracy of the rich against the poor, with the latter expected "to pay the rich man's taxes."[24] He offered no evidence of Prohibition's successes, only indignation that it be challenged at all; he was certain that the majority of people wanted Prohibition.

While the Republican Party had no doubts about its presidential candidate, and stuck with Hoover, the party was less sure of its chances. Party leaders considered many potential vice presidential candidates who could strengthen the ticket, especially as criticism of Hoover's response to the Depression grew. Hoping name recognition might do the trick, Charles Hilles, among others, proposed Theodore Roosevelt Jr. Roosevelt passed, noting his responsibilities as governor general of the Philippine Islands. Roosevelt did offer thoughts, though, on the pending campaign, particularly on the debate over Prohibition. The Republican plank attempted to play both sides, calling for repeal of the Eighteenth Amendment but allowing for state options to enforce Prohibition within their borders. Roosevelt agreed with the position, and opposed those groups, notably the WONPR, that sought full repeal without any compromise. He compared Sabin, his old friend and ally, to Ella Boole, the strident Prohibitionist, ascribing to both "venomous personalities and general irrationality."[25] Presumably he was referring to the single-mindedness of each woman, for whom one issue superseded all others to the detriment, in Roosevelt's mind, of the party. His harsh remarks echoed those he had shared with "Polly" several years earlier, when he had decried the politics of the National Woman's Party and its existence separate from the two mainstream parties. Polly had agreed with Ted then, and for several years after, believing women should work within the established parties. Now the scourge of Prohibition could not be reversed by only one party, especially if her party, the Republicans, lost.

Franklin Roosevelt, Ted's cousin and the presumptive Democratic presidential nominee, announced in February 1932 his commitment to returning liquor control to the states, a position he claimed to have held for a long time.[26] During the rest of the campaign he would barely mention Prohibition or the Eighteenth Amendment again, favoring discussions of the worsening depression.[27] Herbert Hoover continued to waffle on Prohibition, his attention focused on the economy, to his own disadvantage.

The WONPR, increasingly the loudest voice for women, and to whom men often deferred on the Prohibition question, drew like-minded groups to their movement. Sabin met with officials from the American Federation of Labor, who were interested in forming an alliance, hopeful that cooperation would "insure many wives of laboring men joining" the WONPR, which would bring "a great effect upon our Congressman and Senators," according to one official.[28] The American Hotel Association, eager to offer its customers liquor, offered to join in the WONPR's efforts and told its managers at member hotels to assist in any way possible.[29] The first step in expanding cooperation, visibility, and membership began with the National Reform Week, set for May 16 to 22 and arranged by the WONPR, with a goal to raise membership to one million. The organization planned "intensive" efforts in forty-one states and the District of Columbia, and Sabin announced this over the nationwide Columbia Broadcasting System. She reminded listeners that three years earlier, when she had founded the WONPR, women had feared speaking out for repeal, but the group's efforts since then and the continuing failure of enforcement to end violence or improve the lives of women and families had put the word "repeal" "on every tongue." Sabin declared, "We wear our wet tag proudly," comfortable in the understanding that "wet" did not "mean a person addicted to drink any more than 'dry' means a person who has forsworn the consumption of alcoholic beverages."[30]

Following National Reform week, the WONPR sponsored, in association with two other anti-Prohibition groups, an investigative survey seeking proof of the supposed benefits of the Eighteenth Amendment. Recent graduates of twenty colleges traveled the country in a specially outfitted bus, chasing down leads from the WCTU, ASL, Salvation Army, public health offices, and police departments to determine whether Prohibition reformed alcoholics and improved the lives of families in which alcoholism and drunkenness had been a problem. By midsummer, the bus had visited twenty states, and the students claimed they could find no former alcoholics who had reformed their ways because of Prohibition or families whose fortunes had been turned around by the abolition of liquor.[31] The students provided as little hard evidence as the Prohibitionist organizations that had fostered the rumors of miraculous rehabilitations, but their efforts did raise an important question: if Prohibition was meant to correct a social evil, where was the evidence of its success?

Going beyond the usual campaign posters and buttons, the WONPR sold all manner of merchandise emblazoned with the word "Repeal": donation boxes, thimbles, silk scarves, powder puff cases, and a spare-tire cover for an automobile.[32] The organization even commissioned a song to be played at rallies, the words sung to the tune of "Pack Up Your Troubles in Your Old Kit Bag and Smile, Smile, Smile," reminding supporters of their influence:

If all the women in the U.S.A.
Make their vote worthwhile;

Congressmen and Senators
Would know they weren't in style—SO
Each mother's son of them would vote repeal and
Smile! Smile! Smile![33]

Sabin continued to crisscross the country, bringing her wares along, speaking at rallies of increasing size, but no rally could equal the exposure she received in newsreels seen by millions in movie houses everywhere.[34]

Sabin returned frequently to the impact of Prohibition on women, for whom the Eighteenth Amendment had been passed. Before the Eighteenth Amendment, women did not drink, "children scarcely knew that drink existed," saloons could not be placed near schools, and a general sentiment favoring temperance prevailed across the nation. Sabin admitted she had "welcomed Prohibition" for the sake of her children, but her position changed after she saw the lawlessness and disrespect for law that followed in its wake. She warned, "Mothers know that today speakeasies are located next door to schools, homes, and public buildings," and nothing under the existing law could change that. She had a growing impatience with so-called "honest, intellectual women who still believe that Prohibition prohibits, and that it should be given further trial for the sake of our children, who need its protection," given the "glamour which attempted Prohibition has thrown about drink, making it even more attractive to youth." The consequences might not be fully known for a generation, but Sabin would not wait for what she viewed as a continuing downward spiral of higher rates of juvenile delinquency and relaxed morals. It was not only the youth, women, and home about which she worried, but the erosion of personal liberties by a federal enforcement bureaucracy that "permitted tapping of private telephone wires, search without warrant, trial without jury," substituting "governmental spying for individual self-control."[35]

On the eve of the Republican National Convention in June 1932, Mabel Willebrandt indicated she would oppose a proposed plank calling for a national nonbinding referendum on the Eighteenth Amendment. It was "hypocritical and dishonest," an attempt to appeal to people hoping for an economic rescue that might accompany repeal. Besides, she said, the referendum would produce no effect on the law or policy.[36] Any plank should be clear, whether wet or dry. If wet, then the convention should ask for a vote on repeal, letting the country decide definitively.[37] After contentious debate, the Republican Party adopted a plank favoring neither full repeal nor resubmission of the question in the form of a referendum; rather, it proposed an amendment to the Constitution that, "while retaining in the Federal Government power to preserve the gains already made in dealing with the evils inherent in the liquor traffic, shall allow States to deal with the problem as their citizens may determine, but subject always to the power of the Federal Government to protect those States where Prohibition may exist and safeguard our citizens everywhere from the return of the saloon and attendant abuses."[38] The Republicans hoped to straddle the fence, believing a position somewhere in the middle, no matter how ambiguous, stood a better chance than calls for outright repeal or no change at all.

After the failure of the Republican Party to include a plank for repeal in its platform, Pauline Sabin directed all WONPR members to send telegrams to the chairman of the Democratic National Convention urging the party to include a repeal plank in its platform at *its* convention.[39] Her commitment to the cause over party could be seen best in her appearance at the Democratic convention in Chicago at the end of June 1932. She made no speeches or public declarations, but a photograph of Sabin laughing with AAPA president John Raskob and Al Smith, a political enemy when she had served on the Republican National Committee, ran in papers across the country, saying all that anyone needed to know.[40] Not in the photo, but no doubt enjoying the moment from nearby, would have been Charlie Sabin, always the Democrat, finally working on the same political side as his wife.

Raskob also served as the Democratic National Committee chairman, wielding influence over the convention proceedings and the composition of the party platform. Franklin Roosevelt, soon to be nominated as the party's candidate, signaled he would accept any wet plank adopted by the convention.[41] Raskob had little trouble securing a vote on a plank advocating full repeal, for which convention delegates voted overwhelmingly, surprising even Raskob, according to the *New York Times*.[42] The Democratic Party was on the record for outright repeal.

Immediately following the Democratic convention, the WONPR's Executive Committee directed its members to vote only for congressional candidates supporting repeal of the Eighteenth Amendment, regardless of their party affiliation. If both candidates in a race supported repeal, women should vote their party loyalty (though the directive favored Democrats, since many Republicans were waffling on the issue). The executive committee also directed its members to vote for Franklin Roosevelt for president; although the president had no role in changing constitutional amendments, "through the prestige of his office" the president had "the power to wield directly or indirectly great influence over legislation."[43] Such a vote might prove a bitter pill for members who were lifelong Republicans like Sabin; they would be saddled with a Democratic administration, the first in twelve years, and it might undo more than Prohibition, but for Sabin, at least, it was unavoidable.

The choice for Republicans in the WONPR and other anti-Prohibition groups grew muddier when President Hoover admitted the failure of Prohibition in some sections of the country and announced his support for the type of amendment proposed in the party platform. Sabin applauded Hoover's acknowledgment of the failure of Prohibition enforcement and agreed with his abhorrence of the saloon, but she opposed a system where the federal government still held power over "the definition of a saloon" for the Constitution. Emphasizing her point, Sabin cautioned that a constitutional provision "prohibiting the return of the saloon would give to the Congress the power to legislate and would be an open invitation for all fanatics and hypocritical Drys to keep the pot boiling in the House and the Senate." Sabin and the WONPR would accept only "the unconditional repeal of the Eighteenth Amendment."[44]

Time magazine acknowledged the growing women's repeal movement, placing Sabin on its July 18, 1932, cover. The article described a meeting of the WONPR's executive committee as "the cream of the nation's womanhood" and reported that Sabin had pledged to fight for repeal "for the rest of her life." The magazine saw little hope for the cause, with the wealth of Sabin and her cohorts on the executive committee its greatest strength and greatest weakness. The WONPR might have success with the "smalltown [*sic*] matron" hoping "to ally herself, no matter how remotely, with a congregation of bona fide, rotogravure society figures in a cause about which she may or may not have profound convictions," but would struggle to attract the "populous class of rural women who also vote and who bitterly suspect, envy and hate the ground that women like Mrs. Sabin walk on."[45] The magazine's oversimplified portrayal of women embodied a point Sabin had been making ever since her election to the Suffolk County Republican Committee in 1920: women could not be simply classified into large groups believing one thing over another. While she had railed about single-issue women in the past, she counted on them now to gather around a single issue, one last time; to do the right thing.

Sabin understood that the WONPR's unwavering call for repeal over modification generated friction with other anti-Prohibition groups, which held positions on many other issues, making it difficult for them to abandon their respective parties and candidates. This was especially true of the AFL and American Legion. Sabin recommended to Pierre du Pont, leader of the AAPA, that a meeting of the United Repeal Council, a loose affiliation of the many groups opposing Prohibition, be called to discuss any concerns of the respective organizations; she thought it would be good to establish in which congressional districts the various organizations could work together, and she worried that without a meeting and a unified front, opposition groups might be able to exploit the divisions.[46] The members of the United Repeal Council repeated their desire for outright repeal, echoing the Democratic platform, but the council as a group refused to endorse Roosevelt. When asked to comment, Pierre du Pont said the council "will not be diverted from that issue [repeal] by extraneous subjects which have no part in its work."[47]

The council did not meet, but it designated the WONPR to send a one-question survey to all congressional candidates. The survey asked:

> If elected, will you support a resolution for the straight repeal of the Eighteenth Amendment and the restoration to each state of its power to regulate the manufacture, sale and transportation of intoxicating beverages within its limits, such resolution to be submitted to conventions in the several states for ratification or rejection?[48]

The WONPR received 607 responses, 553 yeses and 54 nos. Of the 553 positive respondents, 474 favored outright repeal and 79 favored repeal with qualifications.[49] Unknown was whether the respondents would make public statements to that effect (or win election).

As Election Day neared, Sabin's rhetoric became more intense; she called the divide over Prohibition "the most controversial situation which has ever arisen in this country and I do not except slavery." Prohibition represented "an attempt to compel a hundred million people to become total abstainers," something she regarded as impossible, sparking "resistance and derision," as evidenced by the successful illegal liquor trade. She attacked the Republican Party's plank that would let states determine Prohibition's fate within their borders but leave Congress the power to "rebuke" state actions if enough congressmen felt the Prohibition on saloons had been violated. Poking fun at the obvious contradiction, Sabin explained that Congress would be forced to establish a definition to answer the question, "When is a saloon not a saloon and when does a saloon become a speakeasy and vice versa?" She provided Webster's definition as "a place where intoxicating liquors are sold and drunk." Did that mean a hotel restaurant, a golf club, and the diner of a Pullman car could be classified as a saloon? Causing further headache was the Republican plank's provision for Congress to address "attendant evils" of the liquor trade, which could be applied to almost anything, putting the country on a path "far more uncertain and confusing than the Eighteenth Amendment itself." Sabin sympathized with her estranged Republican brethren who put party loyalty first, but she had no patience for those who failed to grasp the difference between the Republican and Democratic planks or the disastrous possibilities hidden in the Republican position. For Sabin, the choice between party planks and candidates came down to Republicans' trust in the federal government to control liquor and Democrats' trust in the American people to choose for themselves. When critics suggested that the Republican plank of modification presented "the easiest way out" because thirteen states would always block full repeal, Sabin said she refused to believe that the people in those states "prefer the reign of intemperance, corruption and lawlessness which exists under national Prohibition, than to be willing to admit they have made a mistake." Women, including herself, had pushed for Prohibition, believing it the path to temperance, but while they thought "they could make Prohibition as strong as the constitution, instead they have made the constitution as weak as Prohibition." Sabin's own loss of faith in the possibilities of the Eighteenth Amendment led her, as it did many women, to reconsider the starting point of the movement, temperance, which "always will be the woman's cause." Sabin wrote that the WONPR now represented that goal, not the WCTU, which had become the organization of intolerance, its motivations based in fear and their efforts ironically bringing crime and corruption to new heights, sowing "moral degeneration." Sabin conceded that the Eighteenth Amendment was "an experiment noble in motive," but declared, "Experiments have no place in the Constitution of the United States."[50]

A few days before the election, Mabel Walker Willebrandt reemphasized her belief that the Eighteenth Amendment could be "enforced, should be and ultimately will be obeyed." She lamented the plank adopted by the Republican Party and a recent statement from President Hoover advocating partial repeal for the sake of the economy, but respected "his view even where I differ."[51] It proved to be her final public statement on Prohibition; she would leave the debate and its results to those still invested in the political process. Willebrandt moved past politics and expanded her private practice, opening offices in Washington, D.C., and Los Angeles, helping to establish regulations and law doctrine concerning aviation, radio, international treaties, and labor relations. Her work with aviation companies engendered an interest in flying that led her to become a pilot and support the careers of young female pilots, notably Amelia

Earhart, whose round-the-world flight was sponsored in part by Willebrandt. Her friendship with Louis Mayer of MGM Studios brought actors and actresses as clients and entrée into a world far more glamorous than she had known before. Professional success gave Mabel Willebrandt a life of excitement and security, allowing her time and resources to counsel and assist young professional women and encourage them to push the glass ceiling a little higher, if not break through, much as she had done.

Franklin Roosevelt won the election in a landslide, American voters preferring his optimism to the failed policies and dour predictions of Herbert Hoover. Sabin was delighted that not only was Hoover defeated but also dry New York State politicians, opening the door for changes in the Republican Party.[52] Nationally, Congress saw the addition of thirteen wet senators and seventy-one wet representatives, giving wets a majority in both houses, though some stood for modification rather than the full repeal demanded by the WONPR. Sabin understood that modification might seem the easier and quicker path for many congressmen, but she and the WONPR would not be satisfied until the question of full repeal had been presented to state conventions. Looking ahead from "this hour of approaching victory," Sabin reminded her membership that getting Congress to allow reconsideration of the Eighteenth Amendment constituted only the first step toward repeal; three-fourths of the states, thirty-six of forty-eight, would need to reject the Eighteenth. She encouraged members to seek counsel from constitutional attorneys about how to create their state conventions, select delegates to those conventions, and define the procedures to ensure their votes were counted.[53] A week later, Sabin called a meeting of the National Executive Committee to outline the plan going forward.[54] She could not emphasize strongly enough the importance of getting

Congress to approve a ratification process employing state conventions rather than state legislatures, that is, the people and not career politicians. The convention proposal presented several problems, though, not the least of which was who would pay for such conventions. Until that question and the many others concerning location, selection of delegates, number of delegates, and voting procedures could be answered, Sabin recommended that the WONPR's members refrain from expressing any opinions on the matter and any discussion of modification proposals, but stick to their original, simple goal: repeal of the Eighteenth Amendment.[55]

Sabin knew that both the public and legislators needed to be educated on the means by which repeal would occur through state conventions, a device allowed by the Constitution but ill-defined. Some U.S. Representatives thought that Congress had authority to call those conventions, while others believed state legislatures were the only bodies that could call them.[56] Hoping to avoid the involvement of state legislatures, which were filled with career politicians serving their own ambitions, the WONPR established educational programs to make its members knowledgeable about calling constitutional conventions.[57] The organization did not take a formal position, but privately Sabin confided in colleagues that she hoped Congress would "set up the machinery" for state conventions; she believed repeal would be achieved more quickly that way than if left to state legislators, many of whom met only every two years.[58]

The new year, 1933, began with a challenge to the WONPR's goal of full repeal, when a Senate bill proposing modification of the Eighteenth Amendment passed from committee to the full Senate. The bill proposed to leave the federal government with control of defining a saloon and to allow state legislatures to vote on the revision of the amendment. Sabin urgently telegrammed state division leaders, calling upon them to direct their members to contact their respective senators and demand that they vote against the bill.[59] Any bill seeking modification, such as another to allow manufacture and sale of beer, could delay the chances of full repeal for years.[60]

A month later, Senator John Blaine of Wisconsin submitted a resolution to repeal the Eighteenth Amendment, hoping to leave his mark before relinquishing office after losing his seat in the recent election. The preemptive move sparked fears that the lame-duck session of Congress, still containing many drys, would defeat the measure, making it more difficult to resurrect in the new session beginning in March.[61] Sabin would not support the Blaine resolution, fearing that its provision granting Congress the power to regulate the sale of intoxicating liquors "would perpetuate the proved evils of the ghastly experiment which it pretends to end."[62] After a failed vote in the House and a filibuster against a vote in the Senate, with many members voicing Sabin's concern, Blaine consented to revisions in his resolution and stripped it down to its bones, leaving only provisions for full repeal, guarantees for states voting to keep Prohibition, and ratification of repeal by state conventions rather than state legislatures.[63] The changes proved the tonic and the bill passed in both houses on February 16, 1933. Mrs. Courtlandt Nicoll, speaking on Sabin's behalf, expressed the WONPR's satisfaction with the "first step toward ridding the country of the evils of national Prohibition."[64]

On April 7, 1933, at 12:05 a.m., a truck bearing a sign reading, "President Roosevelt, the first real beer is yours!" delivered two cases of beer to the White House. Just two days earlier the president had signed the Cullen-Harrison Act, put before Congress at his urging on March 13, which legalized the sale and manufacture of beers and wines containing no more than 3.2 percent alcohol.[65] It was a temporary response to America's demand for legal liquor based on the argument that "light" beers and wines could not be considered "intoxicating," the type of alcohol prohibited by the Eighteenth Amendment and the Volstead Act. While the Cullen-Harrison Act was greeted with great fanfare across the country, Sabin and the WONPR barely noticed, intent as they were on their goal of full repeal of the Eighteenth Amendment and restoration of the manufacture and sale of all liquor, regardless of alcohol content.

Once Congress had determined to organize state conventions, delegates had to be elected. The WONPR leaped into action again, directing its state-division chairpersons to organize committees in each county, with subcommittees in smaller districts, to advertise the upcoming elections, which would not coincide with any other ballot measures. The selection of delegates would in many ways determine a state's vote, and the various candidates made their leanings well-known. The WONPR set up committees to phone all members and ask them to call their friends and associates who were not members to publicize the dates of the election of convention delegates and determine whether anyone needed transportation to the polls.[66] Sabin advised against overconfidence, saying only twenty states could be safely counted as wet, sixteen short of ratification. At the luncheon in May she even distributed a color-coded map showing the status—wet, dry, or degree of lean to either side—of each state and the date of its election of delegates. One of the hurdles was that the legislatures in three states she considered "hopeful" for repeal had adjourned for the current term, and two were not scheduled to return until January 1934, nine months away. Without special sessions in those states to set election dates, momentum might be lost, allowing Prohibitionists to regain a foothold. She wasn't giving up on the eight states she regarded as "doubtful," but the WONPR's state and county organizations in those states were undermanned in the face of such a daunting challenge.[67] The election of a wet president and more wets to Congress in 1932 had suggested a popular mandate for repeal, but the constitutional necessity to ratify the proposed amendment in each state, many of which supported Prohibition, exposed the complex dynamics of American democracy, where

Idaho's 445 thousand citizens, regarded as leaning dry, had the same impact as New York's 12.5 million generally wet residents. That reality concerned Sabin, preventing her from relaxing even a moment.

The WONPR and its allies pushed, prodded, and challenged state legislators and decision-makers to seize upon the public's zeal and move quickly to elect state convention delegates and hold conventions, striking while the iron was hot. By late August, only three months since the luncheon where Pauline had warned about overconfidence and complacency, the end of Prohibition appeared imminent, so much so that she reflected on the end of the organization she had created. She hoped that it would fade away, quietly, forever, once the thirty-sixth state ratified the repeal amendment. The approach of the finish line brought on "a bit of melancholy" to see her organization "go out of existence without meeting once more."[68] She suggested that the organization hold a final, celebratory dinner in Washington, D.C., in January 1934, by which time she expected ratification of the Twentieth Amendment would be secured.

Her "melancholy" that summer had deeper roots, as Charles Sabin's health began to deteriorate, prompting doctors to suggest he take time off from Guaranty Trust, which was struggling to survive the economic depression engulfing the country. Pauline took him on a trip, but it soon became clear that stress had not been Charles' only problem. His condition worsened, sending the Sabins back home to their beloved Bayberry Land.[69] Charles died on October 11, 1932, ending a life in which he and Pauline were "completely happy," leading her to say, "Life without him seems very futile and utterly meaningless."[70] However, she had promised Charlie she would "carry on," so close to the goal they both sought.

Sabin's party to celebrate the end of Prohibition came a month sooner than she had forecast, as the dominoes had fallen faster than predicted. The thirty-sixth state to ratify was expected to be Utah, when its convention voted on December 5. Turning a conservative stronghold such as Utah from a probable "nay" (Sabin's map listed it as "doubtful" only a few months earlier) to a "yea" demonstrated the full reach of the WONPR's network and the effectiveness of its argument—moving beyond moral concerns, and appealing to constitutionally guaranteed freedoms rather than restrictions. The WONPR'S final soiree, scheduled for December 7, would be a bittersweet affair, though, with Pauline still mourning Charlie. She had soldiered on, but her friends in the WONPR felt her pain and made sure the celebratory party was full of humor, without any serious toasts or tributes to her incredible leadership that might make the evening emotionally difficult for their beloved leader.[71] The only serious note came in the dinner program's dedication to "Mrs. Charles H. Sabin; to the National Officers, State Chairmen, and the million and a half women who have untiringly and earnestly labored in the counties, the cities and even the smallest hamlets" and had sent Prohibition to perdition.[72] Whether Pauline enjoyed a drink after her long fight went unrecorded.

Acknowledgments

After years of working on World War II projects and feeling privileged for the opportunities, I felt my attention begin to turn slowly, fully revealing itself after I had completed *The Pacific*. The object of my curiosity, a dream taking shape over time, had been investigating the era of Prohibition. My appetite had been whetted in 1999 by Owen Patterson of Louisiana, who had sent me, unsolicited, a sheaf of information about his grandfather, a successful and ingenious rumrunner named Alonzo "Pat" Patterson. I included part of Patterson's story in a documentary entitled *Moments of Truth*, of which my father (the late historian Stephen Ambrose) and I were the executive producers. Alonzo "Pat" Patterson had considered himself an entrepreneur, one who repudiated the overtures of gangsters and thugs, who devised a means to avoid armed confrontations with law enforcement, who eventually proved himself, in the run-up to World War II, a patriot. The story intrigued me—centering not on machine guns, common thugs, or Al Capone, but upon a man who considered himself a good citizen and a lover of his country, despite his flagrant violation of the Constitution of the United States. To get at the truth about Prohibition and its enforcement and, in so doing, savor the absurdities it generated within American society, I began exploring the impact of the Eighteenth Amendment upon upstanding Americans. The investigation would take me far beyond my initial conceptions and generate for me a new understanding of Prohibition, one embedded in the women's movement, one distinct from and often at odds with the prevailing historiography of the era, much to my surprise and, admittedly, delight.

In the summer of 2011, I was ready to present to my editor, Natalee Rosenstein, a proposal for a radical new interpretation of Prohibition, one written as a narrative account, drawing out a few key figures from the dark, misunderstood corners to which they had been relegated and revealing how their lives illustrated the era's successes, failures, and farce. The gulf between an interesting proposal and a completed manuscript grew, much to my dismay, wide. I am most grateful to Natalee and to Penguin for their unswerving support for this project and its author. I could not imagine better partners. I also thank my agent, Brian Lipson, for being a great advisor and an even better friend.

Able to work only part-time, I would have needed many years to assemble the massive collection of primary sources forming the foundation of this book. My choice of a research assistant, John Schuttler, was all I could have wanted. Gifted and driven, he welcomed each new request as he welcomed the ideas I bounced off him: with the thoroughness and thoughtfulness of an experienced research historian, looking for sources I had not identified, until eventually I teasingly began to call him my unindicted coconspirator. Often, the websites of the various archives listed in the bibliography allowed me to pick and choose what needed to be reviewed. To avoid costly travel when possible, I asked John to hire local researchers to help. The assigned task may have required only a day or two, although on occasion it required more, but I owe all of these folks my thanks for their efforts to provide me detailed information on the selected boxes and files and then, following my review, to send me copies of the relevant material. They were (in alphabetical order): Maria Brandt, Heather Furnas, Eileen Glaholt, Glory-June Greiff, Warren Hower, Kevin Leonard, Michelle Reeder, Reeves Richards, John Warner, and Cynthia Wrightsman. My thanks also to my cousin Chris Clarke for his assistance deciphering legal definitions and procedures.

Among the organizations whose leadership and archivists extended themselves to help me were the following: Mrs. Catherine Lenihan of the Women's National Republican Club in New York; Kate Humble at the Maritime Museum of British Columbia (www.mmbc.bc.ca). Katy Hughes at the Royal British Columbia Museum (www.royalbcmuseum.bc.ca). Chris Adams with Discover the Past, a company he and his father run, took me on a Smuggler's Tour of Victoria, British Columbia, one fine August evening. Captain Brett Rosson of Highliner Charters guided me and my redoubtable "Gunkholer Crew" through the San Juan Islands, telling us about the winds, the tides, and the challenges and joys of operating a boat in the upper reaches of Puget Sound. James Ritter, founder of the Seattle Metropolitan Police Museum, a dedicated historian of the force, and a longtime peace officer himself, went well out of his way to help me understand the Seattle Police Department and allowed me to review the relevant documents and images he has so painstakingly assembled from the time period. The LeMay, America's Car Museum, in Tacoma presented a great wealth of information about the automobiles of the 1920s. I also relied upon the collections and staff of the Lewis and Clark County Library.

I thank Doug Mitchell, my friend, my brother, my mentor.

In the period of time needed to complete *The Pacific* and then the years devoted to researching and writing *Liberated Spirits*, my wife and I found ourselves fully challenged by various exigencies of life. Such challenges do not make us in any way unusual, but I wish to recognize the debts we owe to our friends, particularly Joel Christiansen and Brad Blickhan. On various occasions in the past few years I have had to call Brad or Joel and ask for huge favors: for instance, to fly down and help me break into the city of New Orleans when it was still under martial law, in the aftermath of Hurricane Katrina, so that I could rescue my research. At a certain point in each of those phone calls, the full import of my request cascaded upon me: the disruption to my friend's life, his work and his family, the freight of it tangling my speech until either Brad or Joel interrupted my apologetic ramblings with "When?" followed by "Yes. Let me check with my wife, but I think we can make that work." My wife, Andrea, and I have been blessed with other family and friends who have supported us when we needed it, but this acknowledgment section would be incomplete without the forthright inclusion of our dear friends, particularly the two men who for decades have been my big brothers.

This book is dedicated to Andrea Ambrose, whose gentle, true spirit is a miracle.

HUGH AMBROSE
Helena, Montana

Po∫t∫cript

Hugh Ambrose died on May 23, 2015, within a few months of completing this book. Hugh was the first friend I made when I started graduate school at the University of Montana in 1989. Our friendship ebbed and flowed over the next fifteen years as we each left Montana and careers took us in different directions, but when he asked me to do a little research on the germ of an idea for what would become *Liberated Spirits*, I didn't hesitate. As the germ grew, Hugh asked me to serve as his full-time research assistant. Over the course of nearly three years, many diversions slowing the work for both of us, Hugh and I talked or exchanged e-mail on an almost daily basis, he allowing my insights to inform his interpretations and his careful analysis guiding my search for the next, best piece of information. We were brothers-in-arms, and in any relationship between brothers, one leads more often than not, teaching, guiding, and giving more than the other. Hugh led more than he followed, but he always had the courage to take a step behind, to listen, to think, to reassess, and to be equally generous in his criticism and praise. Those gifts have served me well in completing *Liberated Spirits* for Hugh, his vision of its import and his unique approach to the discussion of the "noble experiment" of Prohibition intact.

I could not have attempted, let alone completed, this book, without the stalwart support of Hugh's wife, Andrea, who asked me the day after his funeral, amidst her tragic loss, if I could finish the book. I did not hesitate to commit fully to the effort. Hugh's drafts, outlines, and extensive notes and our correspondence and the reminders of our many conversations provided me ample guidance for completing *Liberated Spirits*, offering a capstone to Hugh's legacy for his family and many friends, so many of whom offered me their support. Prominent among those friends was Hugh's agent, Brian Lipson, whose faith in me, an unpublished research historian he had never met, bolstered my confidence and my intent. Finally, the gifts of time and quiet offered by my wife, Mary, and our three children, Aidan, Cara, and Tanian, gave me the opportunity to focus all my energies on this effort, and I don't think I can ever repay their sacrifices, but I will certainly try. They understand how much this work, which never felt like work, has meant to me. I don't say casually that I will never pursue an endeavor that means as much to me as completing *Liberated Spirits*. It has been an honor and I believe that it would have earned Hugh's praise, a thing never given lightly but, when tendered, a source of great pride and contentment for anyone receiving it.

Please note Hugh's appreciation for the efforts of Natalee Rosenstein, the editor who initially recognized the merit of *Liberated Spirits* and secured it for Penguin. After Natalee's departure from Penguin, Brent Howard took the reins of the project and, without any prior knowledge of the book, kept it alive. A change of position for Brent brought a third editor, Tracy Bernstein, to the project. Her thoughtful comments and suggestions have proven invaluable in improving the telling of the story. Andrea Ambrose and I are deeply appreciative of Penguin's desire to move forward with *Liberated Spirits* through a long period of uncertainty.

JOHN SCHUTTLER

Bibliography

ARCHIVAL SOURCES

AP Images (Associated Press Photo Archive)—Online

Archives of Canada, Ottawa, Canada
  Department of Marine and Fisheries

Chicago History Museum, Chicago, IL
  Chicago Daily News Photograph Negatives Collection
  Morton Family Papers
  Sterling Morton Papers

Columbia University, New York, NY
  Nicholas M. Butler Papers
  Herbert M. Parsons Papers
  "Reminiscences of James Wolcott Wadsworth." Transcript of oral interview.

Cornell University, Ithaca, NY
  Hyde Family Papers

Dwight D. Eisenhower Presidential Library, Abilene, KS
James H. Smith Papers

Federal Bureau of Investigation Headquarters, Washington, D.C.
William Whitney Case File

Hagley Museum and Library, Wilmington, DE
Mrs. (Alice) Pierre S. du Pont Papers
Papers of the Women's Organization for National Prohibition Repeal

Harvard University, Houghton Library, Cambridge, MA
Corinne Roosevelt Robinson Papers

Harvard University, Radcliffe Institute for Advanced Study, Cambridge, MA
Pauline Sabin Davis Papers
Mary Ware Dennett Papers
Elizabeth Tilton Papers
Emma Guffey Miller Papers
Maud Wood Park Papers
Mrs. (Elizabeth) William Lowell Putnam Papers

Herbert Hoover Presidential Library, West Branch, IA
Herbert Hoover Papers

Huntington Library, Pasadena, CA
Ralph Arnold Collection
Maynard L. Parker Collection

Indiana State Library, Indianapolis, IN
Will Hays Papers

Library of Congress, Washington, D.C.
Bain News Service Photograph Collection
Nannie Helen Burroughs Papers
Hanna-McCormick Family Papers
Harris & Ewing Photograph Collection
National Consumers' League
National Photography Company Photograph Collection

New York World Telegraph Photograph Collection
Helen Rogers Reid Papers
Theodore Roosevelt Jr. Papers
Harlan F. Stone Papers
James Wadsworth Family Papers
Mabel Walker Willebrandt Papers
Women's Organization for National Prohibition Repeal Papers

Maine Historical Society, Portland, ME
James Hopkins Smith Papers

National Archives and Records Administration, College Park, MD
Civil Service Commission
Department of Justice
Department of the Treasury
Federal Bureau of Investigation
Internal Revenue Service

National Archives and Records Administration, Pacific Northwest Region, Seattle, WA
Department of the Treasury
U.S. Coast Guard
U.S. Customs Service
U.S. District Court

National Archives and Records Administration, Pacific Sierra Region, San Bruno, CA
U.S. Court of Appeals

National Archives and Records Administration, Washington, D.C.
U.S. Coast Guard
U.S. Customs Service

New-York Historical Society, New York, NY
Jonathan M. Wainwright Papers

New York Public Library, New York, NY
Mary Garrett Hay Scrapbook
"Old" Catalog

New York State Library and Archives, Albany, NY
Central Subject and Correspondence Files
Journal of the Assembly of the State of New York
Legislative Bill and Veto Jackets
W. Kingsland Macy Papers
Republican Party Platforms, Speeches & Ephemera
Mrs. John S. Sheppard Papers

Ohio Historical Society, Columbus, OH
Harry M. Daugherty Papers

Stanford University, Palo Alto, CA
Lucille Lomen Collection

State University of New York–Geneseo
Wadsworth Family Papers

State University of New York–Potsdam
Bertrand Snell Papers

Syracuse University, Syracuse, NY
Nathan Lewis Miller Papers

United Press International Photo Archive (dba Corbis)

University of California, Berkeley, CA
Hiram W. Johnson Papers
Stephen Tyng Mather Papers
San Francisco News-Call Bulletin Newspaper Photograph Archive
St. Sure Family Papers
Hubert Work Papers

University of California, Davis, CA
Ruth Finney Papers

University of California, Los Angeles, CA
Edward A. Dickson Papers
Katherine Philips Edson Papers
John Randolph Haynes Papers
James H. Pope Papers

University of California, Film and Television Archives, Los Angeles, CA
"Mrs. Charles H. Sabin rallies anti-Prohibition forces at Princeton, NJ for drive on Congress." *Hearst Metrotone Newsreel.* 10 December 1932. Hearst Newsreels Collection.
"Women wets push war on dry law." *Hearst Metrotone Newsreel.* 5 December 1931. Hearst Newsreels Collection.

University of Washington, Gallagher Law Library, Seattle, WA
Briefs, *Olmstead v. U.S.*, 277 U.S. 438 (1928)

University of Washington, Suzzallo Library, Special Collections, Seattle, WA
Charles Moriarty Papers
Jeremiah Neterer Papers
Miles Poindexter Papers
Wesley Jones Papers

University of Wyoming, Laramie, WY
Papers of the Republican Party

Women's National Republican Club, New York, NY

Yale University, New Haven, CT
Charles D. Hilles Papers

NEWSPAPERS AND JOURNALS

Chicago Tribune
Kansas City Star
Kansas City Times
Los Angeles Times
New York Times
The Republican
Seattle Star
Seattle Times
Washington Post
The Woman Republican

GOVERNMENT PUBLICATIONS

Federal

Convention between the United States and Great Britain, Prevention of Smuggling of Intoxicating Liquors, U.S. Treaty Series No. 689, Washington, D.C.: Government Printing Office, 1924, 197–98.

U.S. Congress. *Congressional Record*. 1920–1932. Washington, D.C.

U.S. Congress. "How the National Prohibition Law Is Administered." *Congressional Digest*. October 1924.

U.S. Congress. House of Representatives. Committee on the Judiciary. *The Prohibition Amendment*, 71st Cong., 2nd sess., February 12–13, 19–20, 26–27 and March 4–6, 12–14, 19–20, 26 and April 2, 1930.

U.S. Congress. Senate. *Investigation of the Bureau of Internal Revenue*. 68th Cong., 2nd sess., March 1924–May 1925.

U.S. Congress. Senate. *Prohibition Enforcement: Letter from the Secretary of the Treasury Transmitting in Response to Senate Resolution No. 325, the Report of Lincoln C. Andrews, Assistant Secretary of the Treasury, and David H. Blair, Commissioner of Internal Revenue Relative to Undercover Work of the Prohibition Personnel*, 69th Cong., 2nd sess., 25 January 1927.

U.S. Congress. Senate. Committee on the Judiciary. *The National Prohibition Law*, 69th Cong., 1st sess., April 5–24, 1926.

U.S. Department of Justice. *Annual Reports of the Attorney General of the United States*. 1920–1932.

U.S. Department of Justice. Federal Bureau of Investigation. *The Identification Division of the Federal Bureau of Investigation*. Washington, D.C.: GPO, 1991.

U.S. Department of the Treasury. Bureau of Prohibition. *Digest of Supreme Court Decisions Interpreting the National Prohibition Act and Willis-Campbell Act*. Washington, D.C.: GPO, 1929.

State

California Assembly. *Final Calendar of Legislative Business, Forty-Third Session*. Sacramento: California State Printing Office, 1919.

California Assembly. *Journal of the Assembly during the Forty-Third Session of the Legislature of the State of California*. Sacramento: California State Printing Office, 1919.

California Senate. *Journal of the Senate during the Forty-Third Session of the Legislature of the State of California.* Sacramento: California State Printing Office, 1919.

New York State Reorganization Commission. *Report of the State Reorganization Commission, February 26, 1926.* Albany, NY: J.B. Lyon Company, 1926.

Local

King County, WA, Prosecuting Attorney. *Annual Report of Prosecuting Attorney.* 1920–1924, 1927–1933.

Seattle, WA, Police Department. *Annual Report.* 1920, 1922, 1926, 1930–1931.

BOOKS, ARTICLES, AND PUBLISHED MATERIALS

Adams, Samuel H., and Isabel Leighton. *The Aspirin Age, 1919–1941.* Mattituck, NY: Amereon House, 1949.

Allen, Frederick L. *Only Yesterday; An Informal History of the Nineteen-Twenties.* New York: Harper & Bros., 1931.

Andersen, Kristi. *After Suffrage: Women in Partisan and Electoral Politics Before the New Deal.* Chicago: University of Chicago Press, 1996.

Anderson, George J. "Making the Camps Safe for the Army." *Annals of the American Academy of Political and Social Science* 79 (September 1918): 143–51.

Andrews, Lincoln C. "Prohibition as a Phase of Federal Versus State Jurisdiction in American Life." *Annals of the American Academy of Political and Social Science* 129 (January 1927): 77–87.

Anti-Saloon League. *Proceedings of National Conventions.* 1913–21. Westerville, OH: the American Issue Publishing Co.

Anti-Saloon League. *Catalogue of Temperance Posters Issued by the American Issue Publishing Company.* Westerville, OH: American Issue Publishing Company, date unknown.

Bagby, Wesley M. *The Road to Normalcy: The Presidential Campaign and Election of 1920.* Baltimore, MD: Johns Hopkins University Press, 1962.

Baldwin, Fred D. "Smedley D. Butler and Prohibition Enforcement in Philadelphia, 1924–1925." *The Pennsylvania Magazine of History and Biography* 84, no. 3 (July 1960): 352–68.

Behr, Edward. *Prohibition: Thirteen Years That Changed America.* New York: Arcade Publishing, 1996.

Berner, Richard C. *Seattle, 1921–1940: From Boom to Bust.* Seattle: Charles Press, 1992.

Berry, John. "The History and Development of Fingerprinting," in Henry C. Lee and R. E. Gaensslen, eds. *Advances in Fingerprint Technology.* Boca Raton, FL: CRC Press, 1994: 1–38.

Black, Forrest R. *Ill-Starred Prohibition Cases.* Boston: R. G. Badger, 1931.

Blethen, C. B. "One Year Dry Does Prohibition Mean Less Business? Washington State's Answer." *Collier's* 39, no. 2 (March 24, 1917): 5–6, 31–34.

Bridges, B. C. *Practical Fingerprinting.* New York: Funk & Wagnalls Co., 1942.

Broderick, Henry. *Prohibition Seattle Style.* Seattle: Dogwood Press, 1968.

Brown, Dorothy M. *Mabel Walker Willebrandt: A Study of Power, Loyalty, and Law.* Knoxville: University of Tennessee Press, 1984.

Brown, Everett Somerville. *Ratification of the Twenty-First Amendment to the Constitution of the United States: State Convention Records and Laws.* New York: Da Capo Press, 1970. First published in 1938 by University of Michigan Press.

Burleigh, William G. *Mac Day, Crusader: A Study of the Fight for Americanism.* Self-published, 1925.

Burns, Eric. *The Spirits of America: A Social History of Alcohol.* Philadelphia, PA: Temple University Press, 2004.

Calder, J. William. *Booze and a Buck.* Antigonish, NS: FORMAC, 1977.

Cannadine, David. *Mellon: An American Life.* New York: Knopf, 2006.

Catt, Carrie Chapman, and Nettie Rogers Shuler. *Woman Suffrage and Politics: The Inner Story of the Suffrage Movement.* New York: C. Scribner's Sons, 1926.

Chafe, William H. *The American Woman: Her Changing Social, Political, and Economic Roles, 1920–1970.* New York: Oxford University Press, 1972.

Chase, Jefferson. "The Sabines Ravish the Senators." *Vanity Fair* 36 (August 1931): 42, 80.

Cherrington, Ernest H. *The Anti-Saloon League Yearbook.* 1909–1927. Westerville, OH: American Issue Publishing Co.

———. *History of the Anti-Saloon League.* Westerville, OH: American Issue Publishing Co., 1913.

Clark, Norman H. *Deliver Us from Evil: An Interpretation of American Prohibition.* New York: Norton, 1976.

————. *The Dry Years: Prohibition and Social Change in Washington*. Seattle: University of Washington Press, 1965.

————. "Roy Olmstead: A Rumrunning King on Puget Sound." *Pacific Northwest Quarterly* 54, no. 3 (July 1963): 89–103.

Cole, Simon A. *Suspect Identities: A History of Fingerprinting and Criminal Identification*. Cambridge, MA: Harvard University Press, 2001.

————. "Witnessing Identification: Latent Fingerprinting Evidence and Expert Knowledge." *Social Studies of Science* 28, 5–6 (October–December 1998): 687–712.

Comparative Criminal Law Project, New York University School of Law. *Prostitution: Regulation and Control*. Littleton, CO: Fred B. Rothman & Co., 1979.

Dash, Samuel, Richard F. Schwartz and Robert E. Knowlton. *The Eavesdroppers*. New Brunswick, NJ: Rutgers University Press, 1959.

Deverell, William, and Tom Sitton, eds. *California Progressivism Revisited*. Berkeley: University of California Press, 1994.

Dobyns, Fletcher. *The Amazing Story of Repeal: An Exposé of the Power of Propaganda*. New York: Willet, Clark & Company, 1940.

DuBois, Ellen C. *Feminism and Suffrage: The Emergence of an Independent Women's Movement in America, 1848–1869*. Ithaca, NY: Cornell University Press, 1978.

Ducas, Dorothy. "In Miniature: Mrs. Charles H. Sabin." *McCall's* 58 (September 1930): 4.

Dumenil, Lynn. "Women's Reform Organizations and Wartime Mobilization in World War I–Era Los Angeles." *Journal of the Gilded Age and Progressive Era* 10, no. 2 (April 2011): 213–45.

Einstein, Isidor. *Prohibition Agent No. 1*. New York: Frederick A. Stokes Co., 1932.

Fahey, Edmund. *Rum Road to Spokane*. Missoula: University of Montana Press, 1972.

Farley, James A. *Behind the Ballots: The Personal History of a Politician*. New York: Harcourt, Brace and Company, 1938.

"Faster Motor Boats." *Popular Mechanics* 48, no. 4 (October 1927): 537–39.

Fausold, Martin L. *James W. Wadsworth, Jr.: The Gentleman from New York*. Syracuse, NY: Syracuse University Press, 1975.

Finn, Jonathan. *Capturing the Criminal Image from Mug Shot to Surveillance Society*. Minneapolis: University of Minnesota Press, 2009.

"The First Legal Lady of the Land." *Literary Digest* 76 (May 1923): 39–41.

Fisk, Eugene Lyman. "Some Current Fallacies with Regard to Alcohol." *National Proceedings of Social Work at the Fifty-First Annual Session Held in Toronto, Ontario, June 25–July 2, 1924*: 48–54.

Flexner, Eleanor. *Century of Struggle: The Woman's Rights Movement in the United States*. Cambridge, MA: Belknap Press of Harvard University Press, 1959.

Fosdick, Raymond B. "The Commission on Training Camp Activities." *Proceedings of the Academy of Political Science* 7, no. 4 (February 1918): 819–26.

———. "The War and Navy Departments' Commission on Training Camp Activities." *Annals of the American Academy of Political and Social Science* 79 (September 1918): 130–42.

Freeman, Jo. *A Room at a Time: How Women Entered Party Politics*. Lanham, MD: Rowman & Littlefield, 2000.

Giglio, James N. *H. M. Daugherty and the Politics of Expediency*. Kent, OH: Kent State University, 1978.

Good, Josephine L. "The History of Women in Republican National Conventions and Women in the Republican National Committee." Prepared for the Republican National Committee, April 1963.

Greenberg, David. *Calvin Coolidge*. New York: Times Books, 2007.

Griffiths, Austin E. *Great Faith: An Autobiography of an English Immigrant Boy in America*. Seattle: unidentified publisher, 1950.

Gustafson, Melanie Susan. *Women and the Republican Party, 1854–1924*. Chicago: University of Illinois Press, 2001.

Gustavson, Todd. *Camera: A History of Photography from Daguerreotype to Digital*. New York: Sterling Innovation, 2009.

Guthrie, John T., Jr. "Hard Times, Hard Liquor, and Hard Luck: Selective Enforcement in North Florida, 1928–1933." *Florida Historical Quarterly* 72, no. 4 (April 1994): 435–52.

Haarsager, Sandra. *Bertha Knight Landes of Seattle, Big-City Mayor*. Norman: University of Oklahoma Press, 1994.

Hallwas, John E. *The Bootlegger: A Story of Small Town America*. Urbana: University of Illinois Press, 1998.

Harvey, Anna L. *Votes Without Leverage: Women in Electoral Politics Before the New Deal*. New York: University of Cambridge Press, 1998.

Hawes, Elizabeth. *New York, New York: How the Apartment House Transformed the Life of the City, 1869–1930*. New York: Knopf, 1993.

Hawley, Lowell S., and Ralph B. Potts. *Counsel for the Damned: A Biography of George F. Potts*. New York: J. B. Lippincott Co., 1953.

Haynes, Roy A. *Prohibition Inside Out*. Garden City, NY: Doubleday, Page & Company, 1923.

———. "The Prohibition Unit—Its Organization and Functions." *Congressional Digest* (October 1924): 7–8, 28.

Hearst Temperance Contest Committee. *Temperance—or Prohibition?* New York: J. J. Little and Ives Co., 1929.

Hennigar, Ted R. *The Rum Running Years*. Hantsport, NS: Lancelot Press, 1981.

Hiatt, Walter S. "Popularizing the Millionaire's Sport." *Technical World* 22, no. 2 (October 1914): 187–92.

Hicks, John D. *The Republican Ascendancy, 1921–1933*. New York: Harper, 1960.

Hirschfield, Al, and Gordon Kahn. *The Speakeasies of 1932*. Milwaukee, WI: Glenn Young Books, 2003. First published in 1932 by E. P. Dutton.

History of the Seattle Police Department, 1923. Seattle: Grettner-Diers Printing Co., 1923.

Hopkins, Ernest Jerome. *Our Lawless Police: A Study of the Unlawful Enforcement of the Law*. New York: Viking Press, 1931.

"Hundred Miles an Hour?" *Popular Mechanics* 44, no. 3 (September 1925): 361–64.

Irey, Elmer L., and William J. Slocum. *The Tax Dodgers: The Inside Story of the T-men's War with America's Political and Underworld Hoodlums*. New York. Garden City, 1948.

Jensen, Joan M. "Annette Abbott Adams, Politician." *Pacific Historical Review* 35, no. 2 (May 1966): 185–201.

Johnson, Donald Bruce, and Kirk H. Porter. *National Party Platforms, 1840–1972*. Urbana: University of Illinois Press, 1973.

Johnson, Robert E. *Guardians of the Sea: History of the United States Coast Guard, 1915 to the Present*. Annapolis, MD: Naval Institute Press, 1987.

Josephson, Matthew, Hannah Josephson, and Frances Perkins. *Al Smith: Hero of the Cities*. Boston: Houghton Mifflin, 1969.

Kerr, K. Austin. *Organized for Prohibition: A New History of the Anti-Saloon League*. New Haven, CT: Yale University Press, 1985.

Kessner, Thomas. *Fiorello H. La Guardia and the Making of Modern New York*. New York: McGraw-Hill, 1989.

Keve, Paul W. *The McNeil Century: The Life and Times of an Island Prison*. Chicago: Nelson-Hall, 1984.

Kidd, A. M. "The Proposed Community Property Bills." *California Law Review* 7, no. 3 (March 1919): 166–81.

Kobler, John. *Ardent Spirits: The Rise and Fall of Prohibition.* New York: Putnam, 1973.

Kyvig, David E. *Daily Life in the United States, 1920–1940: Decades of Promise and Pain.* Westport, CT: Greenwood Press, 2002.

———. *Repealing National Prohibition.* Kent, OH: Kent State University Press, 2000.

———. "Women Against Prohibition." *American Quarterly* 28, no. 4 (Autumn 1976): 465–82.

Langeluttig, Albert. *The Department of Justice of the United States.* Baltimore, MD: Johns Hopkins University Press, 1927.

———. "Federal Police." *Annals of the American Academy of Political and Social Science* 146: The Police and the Crime Problem (November 1929): 41–54.

La Rue, Lawrence. "The Pleasure Boat's Debt to the Racer." *Scientific American* 106, no. 1 (January 6, 1912): 14–15, 30.

Laubner, Ellie. *Fashions of the Roaring '20s.* Atglen, PA: Schiffer Publishing Ltd., 1996.

Lavine, Emanuel H. *Gimme: Or How Politicians Get Rich.* New York: Vanguard Press, 1931.

Lemann, Nicholas. *The Promised Land: The Great Black Migration and How It Changed America.* New York: Knopf, 1991.

Lemons, J. Stanley. *The Woman Citizen; Social Feminism in the 1920s.* Urbana: University of Illinois, 1973.

Lender, Mark E., and James K. Martin. *Drinking in America: A History.* New York: Free Press, 1982.

Lerner, Michael A. *Dry Manhattan: Prohibition in New York City.* Cambridge, MA: Harvard University Press, 2007.

Leuchtenburg, William E. *The Perils of Prosperity, 1914–1932.* Chicago: University of Chicago Press, 1993.

Lichtman, Allan J. *Prejudice and Old Politics: The Presidential Election of 1928.* Chapel Hill: University of North Carolina, 1979.

Longworth, Alice R. *The Crowded Hours: Reminiscences of Alice Roosevelt Longworth.* New York: Charles Scribner's Sons, 1933.

Lonsdale, L. A. "Rumrunners on Puget Sound." *American West* 9, no. 6 (November 1972): 28–33, 70.

Lynd, Robert S., and Helen Merrell Lynd. *Middletown: A Study in Modern American Culture.* New York: Harcourt, Brace and Co., 1929.

Martin, John S. "Mrs. Firebrand." Profiles. *New Yorker,* February 16, 1929.

Mayer, Martin. *Emory Buckner.* New York: Harper & Row, 1968.

McMahon, Stephanie H. "California Women: Trying to Use Federal Taxes to Put the 'Community' in Community Property." *Wisconsin Journal of Law, Gender & Society* 25, no. 1 (2010): 35–72.

McMillen, Neil R. "Perry W. Howard, Boss of Black-and-Tan Republicanism in Mississippi, 1924–1960." *Journal of Southern History* 48, no. 2 (May 1982): 205–24.

Metcalfe, Philip. *The Whispering Wires: The Tragic Tale of an American Bootlegger.* Portland, OR: Inkwater Press, 2007.

Miller, Nathan. *New World Coming: The 1920s and the Making of Modern America.* Cambridge, MA: Da Capo Press, 2003.

Morrison, Edwin M. *True Experiences of a Commercial and Rum Running Radio Operator.* NS: Adrienne Morrison, 1989.

Mowry, George E. *The California Progressives.* Chicago: Quadrangle Books, 1951.

Murchison, Kenneth M. *Federal Criminal Law Doctrine: The Forgotten Influence of National Prohibition.* Durham, NC: Duke University Press, 1994.

Murdock, Catherine G. *Domesticating Drink: Women, Men, and Alcohol in America, 1870–1940.* Baltimore, MD: Johns Hopkins University Press, 1998.

Murphy, Walter F. *Wiretapping on Trial: A Case Study in the Judicial Process.* New York: Random House, 1965.

Murray, Robert K. *The Harding Era: Warren G. Harding and His Administration.* Minneapolis: University of Minnesota Press, 1969.

———. *Red Scare: A Study in National Hysteria, 1919–1920.* Minneapolis: University of Minnesota Press, 1955.

Nelson, Gerald B. *Seattle: The Life and Times of an American City.* New York: Knopf, 1977.

Neumann, Caryn E. "The End of Gender Solidarity: The History of the Women's Organization for National Prohibition Reform in the United States, 1929–1933." *Journal of Women's History* 9 (Summer 1997): 31–51.

Newsome, Eric. *The Curious Case of the Beryl G.* Victoria, BC: Orca Publishers, 1989.

"A New Type of Displacement Speed Boat." *Scientific American* 124, no. 13 (March 26, 1921): 249.

New York Republican Committee. "Republican Organization of the State of New York, 1920–1921."

New York Republican Committee. "Republican Organization of the State of New York, 1924–1925."

O'Connor, Richard. *The First Hurrah: A Biography of Alfred E. Smith.* New York: G. Putnam's Sons, 1970.

O'Donnell, Jack. "Can This Woman Make America Dry?" *Collier's,* August 9, 1924, 16.

Odegard, Peter H. *Pressure Politics: The Story of the Anti-Saloon League.* New York: Columbia University Press, 1928.

Odem, Mary. "Single Mothers, Delinquent Daughters, and the Juvenile Court in Early 20th Century Los Angeles." *Journal of Social History* 25, no.1 (Autumn 1991): 27–43.

Okrent, Daniel. *Last Call: The Rise and Fall of Prohibition.* New York: Scribner, 2010.

Ostrander, Gilman M. "The Prohibition Movement in California, 1848–1933." *University of California Publications in History* 57 (1957).

Parker, Alison. *Purifying America: Women, Cultural Reform, and Pro-Censorship Activism, 1873–1933.* Urbana: University of Illinois Press, 1997.

Parker, Marion, and Robert Tyrrell. *Rumrunner: The Life and Times of Johnny Schnarr.* Seattle: Orca Book Publishers, 1988.

Peel, Roy V., and Thomas C. Donnelly. *The 1932 Campaign; An Analysis.* New York: Da Capo Press, 1973 (reprint of 1935 edition published by Farrar & Rinehart).

Pegram, Thomas R. *Battling Demon Rum: The Struggle for a Dry America, 1800–1933.* Chicago: Ivan R. Dee, 1998.

Perry, Lawrence. "What the War Is Doing for the Motor Boat." *New Country Life* 34, no. 2 (June 1918): 59–61.

Pieroth, Doris H. "Bertha Knight Landes: The Woman Who Was Mayor." Chapter 6 in *Women in Pacific Northwest History.* Seattle: University of Washington Press, 2001.

Reeves, Ira L. *Ol' Rum River: Revelations of a Prohibition Administrator.* Chicago: Thomas Rockwell Co., 1931.

Republican National Committee. *Book of the Republican National Convention, Cleveland, Ohio, June 10th, 1924.* 1924.

———. *Official Report of the Proceedings of the Republican National Convention.* 1924.

———. *Official Report of the Proceedings of the Republican National Convention.* 1928.

Richardson, David B. *Puget Sounds: A Nostalgic Review of the Radio and TV in the Great Northwest.* Seattle: Superior Publishing Co., 1981.

Ritchie, Donald A. *Electing FDR: The New Deal Campaign of 1932.* Lawrence, KS: University of Kansas Press, 2007.

Ritter, Gretchen. "Gender and Citizenship After the Nineteenth Amendment." *Polity* 32, no. 3 (Spring 2000): 345–75.

Robinson, Fred Miller. *The Man in the Bowler Hat: His History and Iconography.* Chapel Hill: University of North Carolina, 1993.

Rorabaugh, W. J. *The Alcoholic Republic: An American Tradition.* New York: Oxford University Press, 1979.

Rose, Kenneth D. *American Women and the Repeal of Prohibition.* New York: New York University Press, 1997.

Rymph, Catherine E. *Republican Women: Feminism and Conservatism from Suffrage Through the Rise of the New Right.* Chapel Hill: University of North Carolina Press, 2006.

"Running a Speakeasy." *New Freeman* 1 (1930): 297–99.

Sabin, Pauline Morton. "I Change My Mind on Prohibition." *Outlook,* June 13, 1928, 254, 277.

Sage, Elizabeth. *A Study of Costume.* New York: Charles Scribner's Sons, 1926.

Sargent, John G. "Law and Observance." An address before the New York State Bar Association, January 22, 1926.

Sawyer, Albert E. "The Enforcement of National Prohibition." *Annals of the American Academy of Political and Social Science* 164, Prohibition: A National Experiment (September 1932): 10–29.

Sawyer, Albert E. "Report on the Enforcement of the Prohibition Laws of the United States: Comment." *Michigan Law Review* 30, no. 1 (November 1931): 7–37.

Schmeckebier, Lawrence F. *The Bureau of Prohibition: Its History, Activities and Organization.* Washington, D.C.: Brookings Institution, 1929.

———, and Francis X. A. Eble. *The Bureau of Internal Revenue: Its History, Activities and Organization.* Baltimore, MD: Johns Hopkins Press, 1923.

Severyns, William. *Confessions of a Chief of Police.* Seattle: Seattle Union Record, 1926.

Sobel, Robert. *Coolidge: An American Enigma.* New York: Regnery Publishing, 1998.

Strakosch, Avery. "A Woman In Law." *Saturday Evening Post* 17 (September 24, 1927): 190–96.

Strauss, Samuel. "Things Are in the Saddle." *Atlantic Monthly* 134 (November 1924): 577–88.

Sweetman, Maude. *What Price Politics: The Inside Story of Washington State Politics.* Seattle: Whit & Hancock Corp., 1927.

Szymanksi, Ann-Marie. "Dry Compulsions: Prohibition and the Creation of State-Level Agencies." *Journal of Policy History* 11, no. 2 (1999): 115–46.

Tugwell, R. G. *The Brains Trust.* New York: Viking Press, 1968.

Van Voris, Jacqueline. *Carrie Chapman Catt: A Public Life.* New York: Feminist Press at the City University of New York, 1987.

Wadsworth, James W., Jr. "The Death Toll of Enforcement." *North American Review* 229, no. 3 (March 1930): 257–62.

Walkinshaw, R. *On Puget Sound.* New York: G. P. Putnam, 1927.

Waters, Harold. *Smuggler of Spirits: Prohibition and the Coast Guard.* New York: Hasting House Publishers, 1971.

White, William Allen. *A Puritan in Babylon: The Story of Calvin Coolidge.* New York: Macmillan Company, 1938.

Willebrandt, Mabel Walker. "Give Women a Fighting Chance." *Smart Set Magazine* 85, no. 12 (February 1930): 24–26, 106–7.

———. "Problems to Be Solved in Establishing 100% Enforcement." *Congressional Digest* (October 1924): 14–15.

———. "Prohibition—The Problem of Enforcement from the Federal Standpoint." *National Proceedings of Social Work at the Fifty-First Annual Session held in Toronto, Ontario, June 25–July 2, 1924,* 54–61.

———. "Smart Washington After Six O'Clock." *Ladies' Home Journal* 46 (July 1929): 10, 56.

———. "The U.S. Department of Justice—Its Work in Prosecuting Prohibition Cases." *Congressional Digest* (October 1924): 11.

Willoughby, Malcolm F. *Rum War at Sea.* Washington, D.C.: U.S. Government Printing Office, 1964.

Wilson, Jan Doolittle. *The Women's Joint Congressional Committee and the Politics of Maternalism, 1920–30.* Urbana: University of Illinois Press, 2007.

Wintz, Cary D. *Black Culture and Harlem Renaissance.* Houston: Rice University Press, 1988.

Women's Legislative Council of California. *Proposed Measure Amending the Present Community Property Law.* California: Women's Legislative Council of California, 1920.

Women's National Republican Club. *Report of the Proceedings of the Mock Convention of the Women's National Republican Club.* New York: Tenny Press, 1928.

"Workers for the Repeal at Mrs. Charles Sabin's." *Vogue* 78 (August 1932): 34–35.

Yellis, Kenneth A. "Prosperity's Child: Some Thoughts on the Flapper." *American Quarterly* 21, no. 1 (Spring 1969): 52–53.

Zeiger, Susan. "Finding a Cure for War: Women's Politics and the Peace Movement in the 1920s." *Journal of Social History* 24, no. 1 (Autumn 1990): 69–86.

Zeitz, Joshua. *Flapper: A Madcap Story of Sex, Style, Celebrity, and the Women Who Made America Modern.* New York: Crown Publishers, 2006.

DISSERTATIONS AND THESES

Auldino, Frank W. "The 'Noble Experiment' in Tampa: A Study of Prohibition in Urban America." Ph.D. dissertation, Florida State University, 1989.

Christman, Anastasia J. "The Best Laid Plans: Women's Clubs and City Planning in Los Angeles, 1890–1930." Ph.D. dissertation, University of California at Los Angeles, 2000.

Cole, Simon A. "Manufacturing Identity: A History of Criminal Identification Techniques from Photography Through Fingerprinting." Ph.D. dissertation, Cornell University, 1998.

Deacon, Florence Jean. "Why Wasn't Bertha Knight Landes Reelected?" Master of arts thesis, University of Washington, 1978.

Dohn, Norman Harding. "The History of the Anti-Saloon League." Ph.D. disssertation, Ohio State University, 1959.

Forth, William Stewart. "Wesley L. Jones, A Political Biography." Ph.D. dissertation, University of Washington, 1962.

Frazier, Paul. "Prohibition Philadelphia: Bootleg Liquor and the Failure of Enforcement." Ph.D. dissertation, State University of New York at Albany, 2001.

Fulton, S. A. "The Women's Organization for National Prohibition Reform, 1929–1933." Master of arts thesis, Western Ontario University, 1990.

Grantham, Caryl R. "A History of the Government of Suffolk County, 1683–1958." Ph.D. dissertation, New York University, 1963.

Heckman, Dayton E. "Prohibition Passes: The Story of the Association Against the Prohibition Amendment." Ph.D. dissertation, Ohio State University, 1939.

Kilkenny, Lucas Edward. "The Effect of Legislation upon the Wife's Interest in Community Property in California." JD thesis, University of California at Berkeley, 1923.

Kooistra, AnneMarie. "Angels for Sale: The History of Prostitution in Los Angeles, 1880–1940." Ph.D. dissertation, University of Southern California, 2003.

Kozakiewicz, Lauren. "Political Episodes, 1890–1960: Three Republican Women in Twentieth Century New York State Politics." Ph.D. dissertation, State University of New York at Albany, 2006.

Krause, Mary Lou. "Prohibition and the Reform Tradition in the Washington State Senatorial Election of 1922." Master of arts thesis, University of Washington, 1963.

Lamme, Margot Opdycke. "The Campaign Against the Second Edition of Hell: An Examination of the Messages and Methods of the Anti-Saloon League of America Through a Framework of Public Relations History, 1893–1933." Ph.D. dissertation, University of Alabama, 2002.

Lien, Jerry. "The Speechmaking of the Anti-Saloon League of America." Ph.D. dissertation, University of Southern California, 1968.

Mathews, Jane. "The Woman Suffrage Movement in Suffolk County, New York, 1911–1917: A Case Study of the Tactical Differences Between Two Prominent Long Island Suffragists, Mrs. Ida Bunce Sammis and Miss Rosalie Jones." Master of arts thesis, Adelphi University, 1987.

Moore, Timothy Stephen. "Bootleggers and the Borderlands: Canadians, Americans, and the Prohibition-era Northwest." Ph.D. dissertation, College of William and Mary, 2000.

Morrison, Glenda E. "Women's Participation in the 1928 Presidential Campaign." Ph.D. dissertation, University of Kansas, 1978.

Rouse, Timothy P. "The Media and Moral Reform: The *New York Times* and American Prohibition." Ph.D. dissertation, Colorado State University, 1992.

A Note on Sources

I [Hugh Ambrose] was fortunate to find a wealth of primary source materials, but am frustrated about those that I could not locate, especially three sets of documents that were intentionally destroyed or lost. First, Mabel Walker Willebrandt generated extensive correspondence during her tenure at the Department of Justice. Dorothy Brown cited many documents from that collection in her book *Mabel Walker Willebrandt: A Study of Power, Loyalty, and Law*, published in 1984. Brown reviewed those documents at the Washington National Records Center, a facility under the purview of the National Archives and Records Administration. In 1977, the Department of Justice placed the records that later would be reviewed by Brown on a schedule for destruction unless determined valuable by the Archives. Despite Brown's extensive use of the materials, no one at the Archives or the Justice Department saw any further value in the records and allowed their destruction. I understand that the National Archives cannot keep every scrap of paper the government generates, but these records had proven valuable to Brown's book and certainly would have proven useful to mine. When informed of the records' destruction, Ms. Brown was "appalled" at the loss of these "irreplaceable" materials. Second, Norman Clark conducted several interviews with Roy Olmstead in collecting materials for his book *The Dry Years: Prohibition and Social Change in Washington.* These are the only known personal reflections made by Olmstead on his activities during Prohibition and would have provided great insight into charges made against Olmstead's accuser, William Whitney. Unfortunately, Clark did not donate or otherwise preserve the interviews or any other materials associated with his book. Third, one of Pauline Sabin's sons, James Hopkins Smith Jr., undertook an effort before and after his mother's death to collect correspondence, diaries, photographs, and other memorabilia documenting his family's history. A few items, including one diary from 1923, found their way into archival collections, but the location of the vast majority of the materials assembled by Smith is unknown.

The loss of the DOJ records, Olmstead interviews, and Sabin diaries presented a significant obstacle in the early development of this book, but forced me to dig ever deeper into archival collections previously untapped for information on Prohibition or previously inaccessible due to their disorganization. In some instances, I was forced to cite Brown, Clark, or other secondary sources for lack of the primary source. I do not believe the use of secondary sources in any way diminished my analysis or interpretation, but my preference has always been, and will continue to be, to use original, primary documents in my work. I hope that the retelling of my experiences and disappointment may motivate records managers, archivists, authors, and family members to give greater consideration to the value, perhaps as yet unknown, of historical documents in their care.

Standardized abbreviations used in the endnotes:

BSP	Bertrand Snell Papers
CHC	Charles Hilles Collection
CSC	Civil Service Commission
DCW	District Courts Records for Washington
DOJ	Department of Justice
HHP	Herbert Hoover Papers
HJP	Hiram Johnson Papers
JHPP	James Harlan Pope Papers
JWFP	James Wadsworth Family Papers
KPEP	Katherine Philips Edson Papers
MJSSP	Mrs. J. S. Sheppard Papers
MWLPP	Mrs. William Lowell Putnam Papers
MWWP	Mabel Walker Willebrandt Papers
RWONPR	Records of the Women's Organization for National Prohibition Repeal
WFP	Wadsworth Family Papers
WJP	Wesley Jones Papers

Endnotes

Introduction

1. "Olmstead Home Is Up for Sale; He Still Selling Radios, Says His Wife," *Seattle Times*, February 22, 1926, 1.
2. Norman Clark, "Liquor Reform and Social Change: A History of the Prohibition Movement in the State of Washington," Ph.D. dissertation, University of Washington, 1964, 238–329.
3. Norman H. Clark, "Roy Olmstead, A Rumrunning King on Puget Sound," *Pacific Northwest Quarterly* 54, no. 3 (July 1963): 89–90.
4. "Two Policemen Held as Booze Smugglers," *Seattle Times*, March 22, 1920, 5.
5. "Statement Concerning Charles W. Kline," attachment to a letter from Roy Lyle to Senator Jones, dated February 23, 1929, Folder 13, Box 273, Wesley Jones Papers, Accession 0157-001, Special Collections, University of Washington, Seattle, WA (hereafter abbreviated as WJP).
6. "Charges Filed in Booze Ring Case," *Seattle Times*, March 23, 1920, 9.
7. "True Bills Returned by Grand Jury," *Seattle Times*, March 27, 1920, 1.
8. "Police Officers File Demurrers," *Seattle Times*, April 5, 1920, 8, 10.
9. "Liquor Smuggling Launch Captured," *Seattle Times*, April 8, 1920, 18.
10. "Booze Ring Hunt Shifts to Tacoma," *Seattle Times*, March 28, 1920, 2.
11. "Plead Not Guilty Booze Charge," *Seattle Times*, April 12, 1920, 3.

Chapter 1

1. "Republican Dinner Plans," *New York Times*, November 30, 1919, 12; "Republican Women Dine Hays," *New York Times*, December 4, 1919, 18.

2. "Republican Women Want Equal Status," *New York Times*, January 11, 1920, 16.

3. Mrs. Ogden M. Reid to William H. Hays, November 1, 1919, Part I: Box I, Reid Family Papers, Manuscript Division, Library of Congress, Washington, D.C.; William H. Hays to Mrs. Ogden M. Reid, November 6, 1919, Part I: Box I, Reid Family papers, Manuscript Division, Library of Congress, Washington, D.C.

4. Letter, Katherine Philips Edson to Meyer Lissner, July 12, 1921, Folder 1, Box 1, Katherine Philips Edson Papers (Collection 235), Department of Special Collections, Charles E. Young Research Library, UCLA, hereafter abbreviated as KPEP).

5. Anastasia Christman, "The Best Laid Plans: Women's Clubs and City Planning in Los Angeles, 1890–1930," Ph.D. dissertation, University of California at Los Angeles, 2000, pp. 180–89. See also *Prohibition in California, 1848–1933* by Gilman M. Ostrander, Berkeley and Los Angeles: University of California Press 1957, pp. 139, 145–47.

6. U.S. Bureau of the Census, *Women in Gainful Occupations, 1870 to 1920*, Census Monograph IX, Prepared by Joseph A. Hill (Washington, D.C.: U.S. Government Printing Office, 1929), 182, 164.

7. John S. Martin, "Profiles: Mrs. Firebrand," *New Yorker*, February 16, 1929, 23. See also, Babcock *Woman Lawyer*, 189–91; Avery Strakosch, "A Woman in Law," *Saturday Evening Post*, September 24, 1927, 194.

8. Barbara C. Babcock, *Woman Lawyer: The Trials of Clara Foltz* (Stanford, CA: Stanford University Press, 2011), 307–318. See also Walton J. Wood, "Unexpected Results from the Establishment of the Office of Public Defender," *Journal of American Institute of Criminal Law and Criminology* 7, no. 4 (November 1919), 598.

9. John S. Martin, "Profiles: Mrs. Firebrand," *New Yorker*, February 16, 1929, 23; see also Walton J. Wood, "Unexpected Results from the Establishment of the Office of Public Defender," *Journal of American Institute of Criminal Law and Criminology* 7, no. 4 (November 1919), 599.

10. Avery Strakosch, "A Woman in Law," *Saturday Evening Post*, September 24, 1927, 193.

11. John S. Martin, "Profiles: Mrs. Firebrand," *New Yorker*, February 16, 1929, 23.

12. Karen J. Blair, "General Federation of Women's Clubs," in Wilma Mankiller et al., eds., *The Readers Companion to U.S. Women's History* (1998), 242.

13. B. Edna Kinard, "Women and Men Battle Over Rights," *Oakland Tribune*, March 4, 1919, 11.

14. "Only Host of Signers Can Avert Dire Peril," *Los Angeles Times*, July 6, 1919, I11; "Referendum to Down Menace," *Los Angeles Times*, July 2, 1919; I11; "Many Sign to Kill Evil Property Law," *Los Angeles Times*, July 8, 1919, I11.

15. "Community Property Measure Is Opposed," *Los Angeles Times*, May 13, 1919, I8; "Governor Listens to Opposition Bills," *Los Angeles Times*, May 14, 1919, I6.

16. "Assembly Faces Strenuous Task," *Los Angeles Times*, April 20, 1919, I11; "Women Fear Property Act May Be Lost," *Oakland Tribune*, May 17, 1919, 8.

17. "Wife Can Will Her Interests," *Los Angeles Times*, May 28, 1919, I9.

18. "Only Host of Signers Can Avert Dire Peril," *Los Angeles Times*, July 6, 1919, I11; "Referendum to Down Menace," *Los Angeles Times*, July 2, 1919, I11; "Many Sign to Kill Evil Property Law," *Los Angeles Times*, July 8, 1919, I11.

19. "The Wife's Interest in Community Property," *Yale Law Journal*, 33, 5 (March 1924), 546. Edna Kinard, "Women and Men Battle Over Rights," *Oakland Tribune*, March 4, 1919, 11.

20. John S. Martin, "Profiles: Mrs. Firebrand," *New Yorker*, February 16, 1929, 23.

21. "Booms Mrs. Catt for Presidency," *New York Times*, February 15, 1920, 8; Jan Doolittle Wilson, *The Women's Joint Congressional Committee and the Politics of Materialism 1920–30* (Champaign, IL: University of Illinois Press, 2007), 9–27.

22. William H. Crawford. "A Big Woman Vote Seen by Mrs. Sabin," *New York Times*, October 27, 1924, 8.

23. "Charles H. Sabin, Banker, Dies at 65," *New York Times*, October 12, 1933, 25.

24. "Tales of Well Known Folk in Social and Official Life," *Washington Star*, October 16, 1921, 11.

25. "Newport's Glory Seems to Be Departing," *Philadelphia Inquirer*, September 11, 1921, 2.

26. "Wall Street Topics," *Baltimore Sun*, June 5, 1920, 10.

27. "Women Conference Back Socialists," *New York Times*, January 15, 1920, 4.

28. "Republican Women Criticize Miss Hay," *New York Times*, December 8, 1919, 2; "Senator Wadsworth," *New York Times*, July 26, 1920, 10.

29. "Republican Women Want Equal Status," *New York Times*, January 11, 1920, 16.

30. "Priming the Feminine Voter for the Primaries," *New York Times*, April 4, 1920, XXX2.

31. "Wadsworth Bowed to Women and Drys," *New York Times*, February 13, 1920, 17.

32. "Republicans Issue 'Model' Platform; Women Resentful," *New York Times*, February 21, 1920, 1; "Sees Socialist Plot in Socialist Trial," *New York Times*, February 7, 1920, 3.

33. "Republicans Issue 'Model' Platform; Women Resentful," *New York Times*, February 21, 1920, 1.

34. Proceedings of the State of New York Republican State Convention, February 19–20, 1920, Bertrand Snell Papers, Special Collections, State University of New York–Potsdam, Box C6.4 Politics-Republican State Committees, 112 (hereafter abbreviated as BSP); "Mrs. Livermore a 'Big 4' Alternate," *New York Times*, February 19, 1920, 1.

35. "255 N.Y. Delegates Cheered as They Leave for Chicago," *Evening Telegram*, June 5, 1920, page unknown; Box E-1, BSP.

36. "Legislature Ends 37-Hour Session," *New York Times*, April 25, 1920, 1.

37. Charles D. Hilles to Mrs. Charles H. Sabin, June 24, 1920, Folder 1324, Box 113, Charles Hilles Collection, Manuscripts and Archives, Yale University Library, New Haven, CT (hereafter abbreviated as CHC).

Chapter 2

1. Katherine Philips Edson letter to Meyer Lissner, July 12, 1921, Folder 1, Box 1, KPEP.

2. David Pietrusza, *1920: The Year of Six Presidents*, New York, NY: Basic Books, 2009.

3. Letter, Frank P. Doherty to Hiram Johnson, July 28, 1921, Hiram Johnson Papers, BANC MSS C-B 581, Part III, Box 33 (Doherty), Folder 1, Bancroft Library, University of California, Berkeley, CA (hereafter abbreviated as HJP); see also Letter, Katherine Philips Edson to Meyer Lissner, July 12, 1921, Folder 1, Box 1, KPEP.

4. Richard Coke Lower, *A Bloc of One: The Political Career of Hiram W. Johnson*, Stanford, CA: Stanford University Press, 1993, 29–30, 40, 140, 158, 266–68; Gilman M. Ostrander, "Prohibition in California, 1848–1933," *University Publications in History* 57, editors Paul Schaeffer, D. M. Brown, and J. D. Hicks, Berkeley and Los Angeles: University of California Press, 1957.

5. George E. Mowry, *The California Progressives*, Chicago: Quadrangle Books, 1951, 281–85.

6. "Women Plan Party Rally," *New York Times*, May 12, 1920, 2.

7. "Women and Campaign Fund," *New York Times*, June 4, 1920, 2.

8. "Wall Street Topics," *Baltimore Sun*, June 5, 1920, 10.

9. "255 N.Y. Delegates Cheered as They Leave for Chicago," *Evening Telegram*, June 5, 1920, page unknown; Box E-1, BSP.

10. Anna Steele Richardson, "Lessons Women Learned at Chicago," *New York Times*, June 20, 1920, XX2.

11. Charles D. Hilles to Dr. Nicholas Murray Butler, June 16, 1920, Box 113, Folder 1324, CHC.

12. Anna Steele Richardson, "Lessons Women Learned at Chicago," *New York Times*, June 20, 1920, XX2.

13. Kirk H. Porter and Donald B. Johnson, compilers, *National Party Platforms 1840–1968*, Urbana: University of Illinois Press, 229.

14. Anna Steele Richardson, "Lessons Women Learned at Chicago," *New York Times*, June 20, 1920, XX2.

15. Kirk H. Porter and Donald B. Johnson, compilers, *National Party Platforms 1840–1968*, Urbana: University of Illinois Press, 229.

16. Myra Nye, "Women's Work and Women's Clubs," *Los Angeles Times*, July 11, 1920, III3; see also James N. Giglio, *H. M. Daugherty and the Politics of Expediency*, Kent, OH: Kent State University Press, 1978, 108.

17. James N. Giglio, *H. M. Daugherty and the Politics of Expediency*, Kent, OH: Kent State University Press, 1978, 108.

18. Charles D. Hilles to Dr. Nicolas Murray Butler, June 16, 1920, Box 113, Folder 1324, CHC.

19. "New Yorkers May Swing to Sproul," *New York Times*, June 12, 1920, 1.

20. "Leaders Unable to Agree," *New York Times*, June 12, 1920, 1; James M. Giglio, *H. M. Daugherty and the Politics of Expediency*, 109–110; William Allen White, *A Puritan in Babylon, The Story of Calvin Coolidge*, New York: Macmillan Company, 1958, 208–9.

21. Anna Steele Richardson, "Lessons Women Learned at Chicago," *New York Times*, June 20, 1920, XX2.

Chapter 3

1. "No Compromise Says Uncle Sam in War on Booze," *Seattle Times*, May 2, 1920, 7.

2. "Two Hundred Cases Against Dry Law Violators Are Set," *Seattle Times*, May 2, 1920, 7.

3. "Heavy Fines for Smugglers Nabbed in Raid," *Seattle Times*, June 8, 1920, 1.

4. "Harding Great Candidate, Declares Mrs. C. H. Sabin," *New York Tribune*, June 15, 1920, 3.

5. Charles D. Hilles to Dr. Nicholas Murray Butler, June 16, 1920, Folder 1324, Box 113, CHC; "New York Group Divided on Ticket," *New York Times*, June 14, 1920, 1.

6. Charles D. Hilles to Mrs. Charles H. Sabin, June 24, 1920, Folder 1324, Box 113, CHC.

7. "Mrs. Charles H. Sabin Entertains 60 at Luncheon," *New York Tribune*, July 12, 1920, 9.

8. "Political Meeting Held in Mrs. Sabin's Ballroom," *New York Tribune*, July 16, 1920, 13.

9. William H. Crawford, "A Big Woman Vote Seen by Mrs. Sabin," *New York Times*, October 27, 1924, 8.

10. "Wadsworth Won't Debate or Retire," *New York Times*, July 21, 1920, 6.
11. "Leaders Decide Saratoga Slate Must Go Through," *New York Times*, July 27, 1920, 1.
12. "Wadsworth's Dilemmas," *New York Times*, July 25, 1920, 68.
13. "Saratoga Leaders Plan Last Rites of Direct Primary," *New York Times*, July 26, 1920, 1.
14. Charles D. Hilles to Dr. Nicholas M. Butler, August 2, 1920; June 29, 1920; Folder 1326, Box 113, CHC.
15. "Senator Wadsworth," *New York Times*, July 26, 1920, 10.
16. "Senator Wadsworth," *New York Times*, July 26, 1920, 10.
17. "Bids Women Aid Harding," *New York Times*, August 3, 1920, 3.
18. Elizabeth Kenney, "Denies Property Law Will Mean a Sex War," *Los Angeles Times*, July 13, 1920, II1; "Shows Evil in Property Law Plans," *Los Angeles Times*, September 30, 1920. II7.
19. Myra Nye, "Shall We Have a Sex War?" *Los Angeles Times*, June 2, 1920, I14.
20. L. H. Roseberry, "Hits Mooted Community Property Law as Peril," *Los Angeles Times*, June 20, 1920, II12.
21. "The Community Property Act," *Transactions of the Commonwealth Club*, vol. XV, March 1920 to February 1921, 256–62.
22. Edna Kinard, "Women and Men Battle Over Rights," *Oakland Tribune*, March 4, 1919, 11.
23. Mabel Walker Willebrandt and William J. Carr, "Proposed Measure Amending the Present Community Property Law," Community Property Committee (Southern Section) of the Women's Legislative Council of California, (undated, circa early 1920), John Randolph Haynes and Dora Haynes Foundation Collection, Special Collections, University of California at Los Angeles.
24. Carrie Chapman Catt and Nettie Rogers Shuler, *Woman Suffrage and Politics: The Inner Story of the Suffrage Movement*, New York: Charles Scribner's Sons, 1923, 439, 443–44, 452.
25. Frank P. Doherty to Hiram Johnson, July 28, 1921, Folder 1, Box 33 (Doherty), Part III, HJP.
26. "Miller Campaign Starts," *New York Times*, August 26, 1920, 3.
27. "Miller Denounces Article X. Here," *New York Times*, September 19, 1920, 18.
28. "Drop Fight on Wadsworth," *New York Times*, September 20, 1920, 16.
29. "Miller Lead, 64,014, 107 Dists. to Come," *New York Times*, November 5, 1920, 2.
30. Myra Nye, "Women's Work and Women's Clubs," *Los Angeles Times*, October 24, 1920, III18.
31. Edna Kinard, "Women and Men Battle Over Rights," *Oakland Tribune*, March 4, 1919, 11.

32. "Many Propositions Fail," *Los Angeles Times*, November 4, 1920, 15.

33. "The Community Property Act," *Transactions of the Commonwealth Club*, vol. XV, March 1920 to February 1921, 257.

34. Ostrander, *The Prohibition Movement in California, 1848–1933*, 140–47.

35. "Republican Women Meet," *New York Times*, November 5, 1920, 2.

36. "Women Organize Committee to Forward Bills in Congress," *New York Times*, November 23, 1920, 1.

37. "Film Interests Begin War on Crusaders," *New York Tribune*, December 12, 1920, 1.

38. "Republican Women Accord Honor to Mrs. A. L. Livermore," *New York Tribune*, December 16, 1920, 2.

39. Women's National Republican Club, http://www.wnrc.org/history.

40. Strakosch, Avery, "A Woman in Law," *Saturday Evening Post*, September 24, 1927, 194.

41. Senator Hiram Johnson to Major Frank P. Doherty, March 5, 1921, Folder 1, Box 3, Part II, HJP.

42. Hiram Johnson to Frank Doherty, June 24, 1921, Folder, 1, Box 3, Part II, HJP.

43. Babcock, *Woman Lawyer*, 267.

44. Frank P. Doherty to Senator Hiram Johnson, July 28, 1921, Folder: Shortridge, Samuel Morgan, Box 33, Part III, HJP.

45. Babcock, *Woman Lawyer*, 247.

46. "This Is the Opportunity of a Lifetime," Mrs. Foltz to "Direct to You," August 29, 1921, Folder: Foltz, Box 38, Part III, HJP.

47. Ostrander, *The Prohibition Movement in California*, 160, 175.

48. H. M. Daugherty, Attorney General, telegram to Mrs. Mabel Walker Willebrandt, August 13, 1921, Folder: Daugherty, Box 31, Part III, HJP.

49. "Federal Plum Is Awarded to Local Woman," *Los Angeles Times*, August 17, 1921, Section II, 11.

50. Dorothy M. Brown, *Mabel Walker Willebrandt: A Study in Power, Loyalty, and Law*, Knoxville: University of Tennessee Press, 1984, 47–48.

Chapter 4

1. *First Deficiency Appropriations*, House Bill 15848, 70th Cong., 2nd sess., *Congressional Record* 1905 (January 18, 1929).

2. "Receives Official Word," *Seattle Times*, July 28, 1921, 5.

3. "Haynes Bars Politics," *New York Times*, July 3, 1921, 12.

4. "Bootleggers Must Go," *Seattle Times*, August 20, 1921, 2.

5. "Liquor Worth $35,000 Stolen," *Seattle Times*, August 31, 1921, 1.

6. "Six Men Are Found With Big Cache," *Seattle Times*, September 11, 1921, 1.

7. "Dry Agents on Trial Tuesday," *Seattle Star,* April 4, 1921, 5; "Federal Prohibition Agents Go After Booze and Obtain Water," *Seattle Times,* September 21, 1921, 4.

8. "Counsel for Government Withdraws," *Seattle Times,* October 20, 1921, 1, 7.

9. Article, title unknown, *New York Times,* March 1, 1921, 12 and Article title unknown, *New York Evening Telegram,* March 2, 1921, as quoted in Jensen, *Annette Abbott Addams,* 197.

10. Giglio, James N., *H. M. Daugherty and the Politics of Expediency,* Kent, OH: Kent State University Press, 1978, 127.

11. "Woman Swayed by Logic," *Kansas City Star,* September 5, 1921, 13.

12. Avery Strakosch, "A Woman in Law," *Saturday Evening Post,* September 24, 1927, 17.

13. "Woman Here Is Appointed to Federal Place," *Los Angeles Times,* August 27, 1921, section II, 10.

14. Frank P. Doherty to Senator Hiram Johnson, August 29, 1921; Folder 1, Box 33, Part III, HJP.

15. "Mrs. Mabel Willebrandt Wants No Publicity," *Berkeley Daily Gazette,* August 31, 1921, 8.

16. A friend to Mabel Walker Willebrandt, September 1, 1921, Folder: General Correspondence, Box 4, Mabel Walker Willebrandt Papers, Manuscript Division, Library of Congress, Washington, D.C. (hereafter abbreviated as MWWP).

17. "Urges Prison For Bootleggers Revelle Wants Laws Enforced," *Seattle Times,* October 23, 1921, 1.

18. William Whitney to Wesley Jones, November 23, 1928, Folder 13, Box 272, WJP.

19. "Lyle Starts Campaign," *Seattle Times,* October 27, 1921, 24.

20. William Whitney to Senator Wesley Jones, May 31, 1927, Folder 3, Box 278, WJP; William Whitney to Wesley Jones, May 4, 1930, Folder 26, Box 13, WJP.

21. H. A. Chadwick (editor and publisher of *Argus*) to Wesley Jones, July 23, 1930, Folder 31, Box 275, WJP.

22. William Whitney to Senator Wesley Jones, May 6, 1926, Folder 31, Box 271, WJP.

23. Exhibit A, Roy Lyle to Commissioner Haynes, September 5, 1925, included in a letter from William Whitney to James Yaden, dated November 27, 1927, forwarded by Whitney to Senator Jones on December 16, 1927, Folder 1, Box 272, WJP.

24. "B.C. Rules Aid Liquor Smuggler," *Seattle Times,* November 11, 1921, 1.

25. "Americans and Canadians Make Booze Restrictions," *Seattle Times,* November 8, 1921, 9.

26. "Housebreakers Find Profit in Booze Running," *Seattle Times*, December 10, 1921, 3; "Canada to Stop Liquor Leak," *Seattle Times*, December 21, 1921, 1.

27. "US State Department May Take Hand in Booze Fight," *Seattle Times*, January 4, 1922, 4.

28. William Whitney to James Yaden, "Supplemental Answers: Exhibit C," dated December 16, 1927, and attached to a cover note from William Whitney to Senator Wesley Jones, December 16, 1927, Folder 1, Box 272, WJP.

29. "Building Owners to Get Rid of Bootleggers," *Seattle Times*, January 25, 1922, 1.

30. Nomination of Mabel Walker Willebrandt, 67th Cong., 2nd sess., *Congressional Record* 61 (September 22, 1921): 5737; Nomination of Mabel Walker Willebrandt, 67th Cong., 2nd sess., *Congressional Record* 61 (September 27, 1921): 5831.

31. "Woman Swayed by Logic," *Kansas City Star*, September 5, 1921, 13.

32. Lower, *A Bloc of One*, 19.

33. Liva Baker, *The Justice from Beacon Hill: The Life and Times of Oliver Wendell Holmes*, New York: HarperCollins, 1991, 465.

34. "Mrs. C. H. Sabin Joins Lobbyists," *New York Times*, February 1, 1922, 4.

35. "Assembly Votes for Committeewomen," *New York Times*, February 16, 1922, 2.

36. Mabel Walker Willebrandt to David and Myrtle Walker, March 22, 1922, Folder: General Correspondence, Box 4, MWWP.

37. *Justus S. Wardell, as Collector of Internal Revenue v. James A. Blum et al.*, 258 U.S. 617 (1922)

38. Alma Whitaker, "The Last Word," *Los Angeles Times*, April 4, 1922, I18.

39. Mabel Walker Willebrandt to David and Myrtle Walker, March 22, 1922, Folder: General Correspondence, Box 4, MWWP.

40. Norman H. Clark, "Roy Olmstead: A Rumrunning King on Puget Sound," *Pacific Northwest Quarterly* 54, no. 3 (July 1963), 91–92.

41. "Transfers of Liquor Made from Ships at Sea," *Seattle Times*, January 21, 1926, 1.

42. "Finest Kind of Whiskey Brought in from Sound," *Seattle Times*, May 19, 1922, 1.

43. "Booze Ring Suspect in Jail Here," *Seattle Times*, May 24, 1922, 1.

44. "Discovery of Caches Described by Whitney," *Seattle Times*, January 23, 1926, 1.

45. "Little Giant Got $600 A Month, Says Testimony," *Seattle Times*, January 28, 1926, 8.

46. "Ex-Policeman Accused as Booze Gang Chief," *Seattle Times*, June 8, 1922, 1.

47. "To Fight Booze Wars," *Seattle Times*, June 9, 1922, 5.

Chapter 5

1. "10,000 Cheer Pleas for Beer and Wine," *New York Times*, May 4, 1922, 1.
2. "Runners Sought Here," *Seattle Times*, June 23, 1922, 4.
3. "Federal Grand Jury Called," *Seattle Times*, June 25, 1922, 2.
4. "Liquor Expose Coming," *Seattle Times*, July 6, 1922, 2.
5. "Olmsted Free of Charges by Dry Officers," *Seattle Times*, July 7, 1922, 1.
6. "Olmsted Named Plot Chief; Revelle Outlines His Case," *Seattle Times*, January 21, 1926, 1.
7. "Women Will Not Debate," *New York Times*, February 24, 1922.
8. "Bans Radio Broadcast for Women's Speeches," *New York Times*, May 21, 1922, 18.
9. Theodore Roosevelt Jr. to Pauline Sabin, May 24, 1922, Folder: 1922 S-Z 002, Container 12, Theodore Roosevelt (1887–1944) Papers, Manuscript Division, Library of Congress, Washington, D.C.
10. "Consumers' League Meets," *New York Tribune*, July 11, 1922, 11.
11. "Consumers to Attack Blanket Equality Bill," *Washington Star*, November 1, 1922, 1.
12. "Platform Pleases Republican Women," *New York Times*, September 29, 1922.
13. "Republican Leaders Admit a Real Fight," *New York Times*, October 11, 1922, 4.
14. "Praises Miller's Work for Welfare," *New York Times*, October 22, 1922.
15. "Miller Women Confident," *New York Times*, November 6, 1922, 3.
16. "Miller Is Relying on Votes of Women," *New York Times*, November 7, 1922, 2.
17. "The Result in New York," *New York Times*, November 8, 1922, 11; "Republican Chiefs Admit Defeat Early," *New York Times*, November 8, 1922, 5.
18. Frank Doherty to Hiram Johnson, May 6, 1922, Part III, Box 33 (Doherty), Folder 3, HJP.
19. Frank Doherty to Hiram Johnson, May 10, 1922, Part III, Box 33 (Doherty), Folder 3, HJP.
20. Frank Doherty to Hiram Johnson, June 30, 1922, Part III, Box 33 (Doherty), Folder 4, HJP.
21. Hiram Johnson to Mabel Walker Willebrandt, July 20, 1922, Part III, Box 3, HJP.
22. James H. Pope to Mabel Walker Willebrandt, September 20, 1922, Folder: Correspondence between Pope and Mabel Walker Willebrandt, Box 3, James Harlan Pope Papers (Collection 752), Department of Special Collections, Charles E. Young Research Library, UCLA (hereafter abbreviated as JHPP).
23. Press Release, October 31, 1922, Folder: Sam Robinson, Box 4, MWWP.
24. Margaret Smith, Secretary to Mabel Willebrandt, to Myrtle Walker, October 11, 1922, Folder: Family Papers, Box 2, MWWP.

25. Diary, Mabel Walker Willebrandt, October 2, 1922, Folder: Diary, Box 3, MWWP.
26. Diary, Mabel Walker Willebrandt, December 7, 1922, Folder: Diary, Box 3, MWWP.
27. Mabel Walker Willebrandt to David and Myrtle Walker, December 25, 1922, Folder: General Correspondence, Box 4, MWWP.
28. Hiram Johnson to Frank Doherty, January 2, 1923, Part III, Box 5, HJP.
29. Frank Doherty to Hiram Johnson, January 8, 1923, Part III, Box 33 (Doherty), Folder 4, HJP.
30. Mabel Walker Willebrandt to David and Myrtle Walker, March 20, 1923, Folder: Correspondence, Box 2, MWWP.
31. James H. Pope to Mabel Walker Willebrandt, March 20, 1923, Folder: Correspondence between Pope and Mabel Walker Willebrandt, Box 3, JHPP.
32. Diary, Mabel Walker Willebrandt, June 18, 1923, Folder: Diary, Box 3, MWWP.
33. "Anderson Rebuked by Women's Club," New York Times, December 21, 1922.
34. Charles Hilles to George Morris, January 2, 1923, Folder 1357, Box 115, CHC.
35. "Paper for Women Voters Planned by Two Leaders," New York Times, November 28, 1922, 3.
36. Pauline Sabin to Charles Hilles, April 3, 1923, Folder 1360, Box 115, CHC.
37. Charles Hilles to Mrs. Charles Sabin, April 3, 1923, Folder 1369, Box 115, CHC.
38. Charles Hilles to George Morris, May 31, 1923, Folder 1361, Box 115, CHC.
39. "Republican Committeewomen," New York Times, June 29, 1923.
40. "Mrs. Sabin Advises Women to Stick to Old Parties," New York Times, July 15, 1923.
41. "Mrs. Sabin Advises Women to Stick to Old Parties," New York Times, July 15, 1923.
42. "Stand by Film Censorship," New York Times, February 29, 1924, 19.
43. Frank Buckley, Department of Justice, to Mabel Walker Willebrandt, January 29, 1923, Case 5-647, Folder: Special Section 3, Box 2471, Class 5 (Tax-Income and Inheritance) Litigation Case Files, Record Group 60, Department of Justice, National Archives and Records Administration, College Park, MD (hereafter abbreviated as DOJ).
44. David Blair, Commissioner, Internal Revenue Bureau, to Mabel Walker Willebrandt, April 28, 1923, Folder 2, Box 2470, Case 5-647, Class 5 (Tax-Income and Inheritance) Case Files, DOJ.
45. David Blair, Commissioner, Internal Revenue Bureau, to Mabel Walker Willebrandt, date unknown (but sometime after the 28th because Blair made

reference to that letter), Folder: Special Section 3, Box 2471, Case 5-647, Class 5 (Tax-Income and Inheritance) Case Files, DOJ.

46. White B. Miller, Special Assistant to the Attorney General, to Mabel Walker Willebrandt, May 12, 1923, Folder 2, Box 2470, Case 5-647, Class 5 (Tax-Income and Inheritance) Case Files, DOJ.

47. Mabel Walker Willebrandt to David and Myrtle Walker, June 19, 1923, Folder: Correspondence, Box 2, MWWP.

48. Mabel Walker Willebrandt to David and Myrtle Walker, August 11, 1923, Folder: Correspondence, Box 2, MWWP.

49. Mabel Walker Willebrandt to David and Myrtle Walker, June 19, 1923, Folder: Correspondence, Box 2, MWWP.

50. Mabel Walker Willebrandt to David and Myrtle Walker, June 4, 1924, Folder: General Correspondence, Box 4, MWWP.

51. Harry Daugherty to Mabel Walker Willebrandt, April 12, 1922, Folder 23-1907-1, Box 1807, Class 23 materials, DOJ.

52. Mabel Walker Willebrandt to Thomas Morrow, U.S. Attorney, May 2, 1922, Folder 23-1907-1, Box 1807, Class 23 materials, DOJ.

53. Roy Haynes to Mabel Walker Willebrandt, May 27, 1922, Folder 23-1907-1, Box 1807, Class 23 materials, DOJ.

54. Mabel Walker Willebrandt to Thomas Morrow and R. T. Dickerson, July 3, 1923, Folder 23-1907-2, Box 1807, Class 23 materials, DOJ.

55. Thomas Morrow, U.S. Attorney, to Mabel Walker Willebrandt, May 24, 1922, Folder 23-1907-1, Box 1807, Class 23 materials, DOJ.

56. Mabel Walker Willebrandt to Granby Millyer, U.S. Attorney, May 16, 1923, Folder 23-10-1, Box 141, Class 23 (Liquor Violations) Litigation Case Files, DOJ.

57. Norman H. Clark, "Roy Olmstead, A Rumrunning King on Puget Sound," *Pacific Northwest Quarterly* 54, no. 3 (July 1963), 92.

58. "Dry Chiefs to Make Capital of Repeal," *New York Times*, June 3, 1923, 1.

59. "United States Will Stay Dry, Harding Tells Denver, *Rocky Mountain News*, June 26, 1923, 2.

60. Library of Congress, Washington, D.C.

61. Diary, Mabel Walker Willebrandt, April 13, 1923, Folder: Diary, Box 3, MWWP.

62. Myrtle Walker to Mabel Walker Willebrandt, November 28, 1923, Folder: Poems, Box 2, MWWP.

63. Mabel Walker Willebrandt to Myrtle Walker, December 31, 1923, Folder: Poems, Box 2, MWWP.

64. "U.S. Dry Agents in Seattle Said to Receive Fees," *Seattle Times*, October 28, 1923, 1.

65. "U.S. Agents Here to Unify Liquor Law Enforcers," *Seattle Times*, September 12, 1923, 1, 6.

66. "Jones Urges Aid for Dry Chief; Senator Praises Work of Lyle," *Seattle Times*, September 17, 1923, 5.

67. "Lyle Report Finished," *Seattle Times*, November 23, 1923, 14.

68. "Friends Rally to Lyle Support," *Seattle Times*, December 18, 1923, 1; "Ministers of Olympia Indorse Director Lyle," *Seattle Times*, December 5, 1923, 20.

69. "Drys Denounce Attack on Director Roy Lyle," *Seattle Times*, December 16, 1923, 9.

Chapter 6

1. Pauline Sabin to James Wadsworth, October 23, 1923, Folder: World Court, Box J112E, Wadsworth Family Papers, Special Collections, Milne Library, State University of New York–Geneseo (hereafter abbreviated as WFP).

2. Pauline Sabin to James Wadsworth, November 5, 1923, Folder: Child Labor, Box J112E, WFP.

3. James Wadsworth to Pauline Sabin, November 10, 1923, Folder: Child Labor, Box J112E, WFP.

4. Pauline Sabin to James Wadsworth, May 19, 1924, Folder: Child Labor, Box J112E, WFP.

5. Senate Subcommittee of the Committee on the Judiciary, *Proposal and Ratification of Amendments to the Constitution of the United States: Hearings on S.J. Res. 40*, 67th Cong., 4th sess., 1923, 1.

6. "Plan Gains for Direct Vote on Constitutional Changes," *New York Times*, February 11, 1923, X15.

7. House Committee on the Judiciary, Proposal and Ratification of Amendments to the Constitution of the United States: Hearings on H.J. Res. 68, 6th Cong., 1st sess., 1924, 2–3.

8. James Wadsworth to Pauline Sabin, December 15, 1924, Folder: Child Labor, Box J112E, WFP.

9. "Fears for State Rights," *New York Times*, May 30, 1924, 30.

10. "'First Lady' Buys First Bond for Women's Club," *New York Tribune*, circa May 19, 1923, Scrapbook, Archives, Women's National Republican Club, New York City.

11. "Women Sell Club Bonds," *New York Times*, June 20, 1923, 10.

12. "'First Lady' Buys First Bond for Women's Club," *New York Tribune*, circa May 19, 1923, and "A Big and Active Club for Women," *National Republican*, May 19, 1923, Scrapbook, Archives, Women's National Republican Club, New York City.

13. "Number Six and Eight East Thirty-Seventh," *Woman Republican*, February 1924, page unknown, Scrapbook, Archives, Women's National Republican Club, New York City.

14. "Coolidge to Speak in City Tomorrow," *New York Times*, February 11, 1924, 17; "Republican Women Receive Coolidges," *New York Times*, February 13, 1924, 3.

15. "Republican Women Receive Coolidges," *New York Times*, February 13, 1924, 3.

16. Mabel Walker Willebrandt to David and Myrtle Walker, February 19, 1924, Folder: General Correspondence, Box 4, MWWP.

17. Mabel Walker Willebrandt to David and Myrtle Walker, April 13, 1924, Folder: General Correspondence, Box 4, MWWP.

18. Margaret Smith to Myrtle Walker, March 18, 1924, Folder: General Correspondence, Box 4, MWWP; Mabel Walker Willebrandt to Myrtle Walker, April 4, 1924, Folder: General Correspondence, Box 4, MWWP; Margaret Smith to David and Myrtle Walker, April 10, 1924, Folder: General Correspondence, Box 4, MWWP.

19. Mabel Walker Willebrandt to David and Myrtle Walker, April 20, 1924, Folder: General Correspondence, Box 4, MWWP.

20. "Women Alone Can Rid Cities of Vice, Says Women Asst. Atty. Gen.," *Buffalo Enquirer*, April 24, 1924, 1.

21. Charles Hilles to George Morris, November 8, 1923, Folder 1370, Box 116, CHC.

22. Charles Hilles to George Morris, February 19, 1924, Folder 1378, Box 116, CHC.

23. Charles Hilles to Mrs. Charles Sabin, April 4, 1924, Folder 1381, Box 116, CHC.

24. Charles Hilles to George Morris, September 6, 1924, Folder 1386, Box 116, CHC; and Nicholas Murray Butler to Mrs. Charles Sabin, September 12, 1924, Folder 1386, Box 116, CHC.

25. "Seize Rum from Garage of Wife of Banker Sabin," *Chicago Tribune*, April 5, 1924, 5.

26. "Setting a Bad Example," *Long Islander*, May 2, 1924, 1.

27. "Cherish the Mother," *New York Times*, May 9, 1924, 1.

28. "Federal Jurors Hear Evidence of Booze Trust," *Seattle Times*, December 23, 1923, 1.

29. "Roy Olmstead Is Sued for Divorce and Alimony," *Seattle Times*, January 16, 1924, 3.

30. "The Wife's Interest in Community Property," *Yale Law Journal* 33, no. 5 (March 1924), 543.

31. Jerry Finch, Testimony, *U.S. v. Olmstead et al.*, 5 F.2d 712 (W.D. Wash. 1925), 244; trial transcript held in File 3, Box 37, Record Group 21, Records of the

U.S. District Court for Washington, Pacific Northwest Region, National Archives, Seattle, WA (hereafter abbreviated as DCW).

32. "Who's Who in Indictments," *Seattle Times*, January 20, 1925, 4.

33. "Wife's Property Rights Are Held to Be Absolute," *Oakland Tribune*, November 9, 1923, 22.

34. "$50,000,000 Tax Refund Sought by Shortridge," *Oakland Tribune*, December 3, 1923, 6.

35. Community Property Law to Be Recognized," *Bakersfield Californian*, March 27, 1924, 8.

36. Mabel Walker Willebrandt to Myrtle Walker, May 1924 (circa), Folder: General Correspondence, Box 4, MWWP.

37. Mabel Walker Willebrandt to Hiram Johnson, November 28, 1923, Part III, Box 80, Folder: Willebrandt, HJP.

38. Stephen Timothy Moore, "Bootlegging and the Borderlands: Canadians, Americans, and the Prohibition-Era Northwest," Ph.D. dissertation, William & Mary College, 2000, 124.

39. "Removal of Butler Urged by W.C.T.U.," *New York Times*, May 10, 1924, 3.

40. Dayton E. Heckman, "Prohibition Passes: The Story of the Association Against the Prohibition Amendment," PhD. dissertation, Ohio State University, 1939, 59–61.

41. "Republican Women Aid the Democrats," *New York Times*, May 22, 1924, 19.

42. "F. Trubee Davison Attacks Vanderlip," *New York Times*, March 30, 1924, 2.

43. Hortense Saunders, "Fall Elections Will Show Women Really Wanted Vote, Leaders Say," *Bay City (MI) Times-Tribune*, March 21, 1924, Scrapbook, Archives, Women's National Republican Club, New York City.

44. "Wadsworth Out of Chairmanship at G.O.P. Convention," *New York Times*, May 28, 1924, 1.

45. "Women Will Take Active Part in G.O.P. Convention," *Monroe [WI] Times*, June 2, 1924, Scrapbook, Archives, Women's National Republican Club, New York City.

46. "Women Certain of Party Equality Celebrate 'Victory' with Tea," *New York Evening World*, June 10, 1924, Scrapbook, Archives, Women's National Republican Club, New York City.

47. "New Yorkers Back Anti-Klan Plank," *New York Times*, June 10, 1924, 1.

48. "Mrs. Sabin Replies to Mrs. Blair's Charge," *New York Times*, June 22, 1924, 24; "Story of Morning Session," *New York Times*, June 12, 1924, 2.

49. "Five Women to Help Policies Committee," *New York Evening Post*, June 10, 1924, Scrapbook, Archives, Women's National Republican Club, New York City.

50. Richard Oulahan, "Choose Butler Head of G.O.P. Committee; Resentment Hidden," *New York Times*, June 14, 1924, 1.

51. "Women of Both Parties Take Political Stock," *New York Times*, July 13, 1924, XX10.

52. "Olmsted Mere Link in Chain," *Seattle Times*, November 25, 1924, 1.

53. Richard Fryant, Testimony, *U.S. v. Olmstead et al.*, 5 F.2d 712 (W.D. Wash. 1925), 155; trial transcript held in File 3, Box 37, DCW.

54. Richard Fryant, Testimony, *U.S. v. Olmstead et al.*, 5 F.2d 712 (W.D. Wash. 1925), 260; trial transcript held in File 3, Box 37, DCW.

55. Richard Fryant, Testimony, *U.S. v. Olmstead et al.*, 5 F.2d 712 (W.D. Wash. 1925), 256–57; trial transcript held in File 3, Box 37, DCW.

56. "Olmsted Named Plot Chief; Revelle Outlines His Case," *Seattle Times*, January 21, 1926, 1.

57. Richard Fryant, Testimony, *U.S. v. Olmstead et al.*, 5 F.2d 712 (W.D. Wash. 1925), 256–57; trial transcript held in File 3, Box 37, DCW.

58. Unknown newspaper, dated August 10, 1930, "Two 'Roys' Disrupt Northwest . . . ," Whitney News Clipping File, 8C. 2011F, Civil Service Commission Records, Record Group 146, National Archives, College Park, MD (hereafter abbreviated as CSC).

59. John McLean, Testimony, *U.S. v. Olmstead et al.*, 5 F.2d 712 (W.D. Wash. 1925), 130–32; trial transcript held in File 3, Box 37, DCW.

60. John McLean, Testimony, *U.S. v. Olmstead et al.*, 5 F.2d 712 (W.D. Wash. 1925), 36 and 206; trial transcript held in File 3, Box 37, DCW.

61. William Whitney and Harry Behneman offered conflicting accounts of this. Richard Fryant, Testimony, *U.S. v. Olmstead et al.*, 5 F.2d 712 (W.D. Wash. 1925); trial transcript held in File 3, Box 37, DCW.

Chapter 7

1. Mabel Walker Willebrandt, "Prohibition—The Problem of Enforcement from the Federal Standpoint," Proceedings of the National Conference of Social Work, June 25–July 2, 1924, 55–56 and 60–61; quotation is found on p. 61.

2. Jack O'Donnell, "Can This Woman Make America Dry?" *Collier's*, August 9, 1924, 16–17.

3. James H. Pope to Mabel Walker Willebrandt, August 11, 1924, Folder: Correspondence between Pope and Mabel Walker Willebrandt, Box 3, JHPP.

4. Mabel Walker Willebrandt to David and Myrtle Walker, Winnie, and Fred Horowitz, September 23, 1924, Folder: General Correspondence, Box 4, MWWP.

5. Mabel Walker Willebrandt to David and Myrtle Walker, October 1, 1924, Folder: General Correspondence, Box 4, MWWP.

6. Mabel Walker Willebrandt to Fred Horowitz, October 13, 1924, Folder: General Correspondence, Box 4, MWWP.

7. Mabel Walker Willebrandt to David and Myrtle Walker, November 11, 1924, Folder: General Correspondence, Box 1, MWWP.

8. "G.O.P. Plans Hard Campaign in Maine," *New York Times*, August 21, 1926, 2.

9. "Butler and Mellon Confer for Hours," *New York Times*, September 4, 1924, 4.

10. William H. Crawford, "A Big Woman Vote Seen by Mrs. Sabin," *New York Times*, October 27, 1924, 8.

11. "Coolidge Dictated Campaign Policies," *New York Times*, November 9, 1924.

12. Richard Fryant, Testimony, *U.S. v. Olmstead et al.*, 5 F.2d 712 (W.D. Wash. 1925), 151; trial transcript held in File 3, Box 37, Record Group 21, Records of the U.S. District Court for Washington, Pacific Northwest Region, National Archives, Seattle, WA.

13. William Whitney, Testimony, *U.S. v. Olmstead et al.*, 5 F.2d 712 (W.D. Wash. 1925), 43–44; trial transcript held in File 3, Box 37, Record Group 21, Records of the U.S. District Court for Washington, Pacific Northwest Region, National Archives, Seattle, WA.

14. "Olmsted Named Plot Chief; Revelle Outlines His Case," *Seattle Times*, January 21, 1926, 1.

15. The last notes by agents of the phone taps are made in November. Richard Fryant, Testimony, *U.S. v. Olmstead et al.*, 5 F.2d 712 (W.D. Wash. 1925), 121; trial transcript held in File 3, Box 37, DCW.

16. Elise "Elsie" Olmstead's testimony is at odds with the version told by Whitney, particularly on this point. He denied threatening her. However, Whitney's propensity toward violence against men and women was well-known.

17. William Whitney, Testimony, *U.S. v. Olmstead et al.*, 5 F.2d 712 (W.D. Wash. 1925), 45; trial transcript held in File 3, Box 37, DCW.

18. "Court Forbids Dismantling of Radio Station," *Seattle Times*, November 28, 1924, 1.

19. "$10,500 in Cash Bail Releases Suspects," *Seattle Times*, November 18, 1924, 1.

20. "U.S. Raid on Olmsted Attorney's Office," *Seattle Times*, November 23, 1924, 4.

21. "Court Forbids Dismantling of Radio Station," *Seattle Times*, November 28, 1924, 1.

22. "Asks Action on Dry Law," *New York Times*, January 19, 1925, 6.

23. "Asks 4,000 Pastors to Aid New Dry Act," *New York Times*, February 28, 1925, 14.

24. "Wadsworth Wants to Stay in Senate," *New York Times*, April 7, 1925, 1.

25. "Drys Declare War on J. W. Wadsworth," *New York Times*, April 15, 1925, 12.

26. "Mrs. O'Day Assails Wadsworth's Rule," *New York Times*, July 15, 1925, 3.

27. "Mills and Scudder to Handle Patronage," *Long Islander*, May 29, 1925, 15.

28. "Harmony Not Discord," *Long Islander*, May 29, 1925, 1.
29. "Regular Commuting by Airplane Fire Island Beach to Manhattan," *Suffolk County News*, August 28, 1925, 9.
30. "Burton G. Howe Wins. McDonald Forces Retain Control of County Committee," *Port Jefferson Echo*, September 17, 1925, 1.
31. "McDonald Wins G.O.P. Chairmanship," *Suffolk County News*, October 2, 1925, 1, 8.
32. Katherine Philips Edson to Hiram Johnson, February 14, 1925, Folder 15, Box 1, KPEP.
33. Mabel Walker Willebrandt to David and Myrtle Walker, January 29, 1925, Folder: Parents, Box 3, MWWP.
34. Mabel Walker Willebrandt to the Walkers, February 19, 1925, Folder: Parents, Box 3, MWWP.
35. Mabel Walker Willebrandt to the Walkers, February 27, 1925, Folder: Parents, Box 3, MWWP.
36. Thomas Revelle to the Attorney General, January 2, 1925, Folder 23-82-79-1, Box 1627, Class 23 materials, DOJ.
37. Mabel Walker Willebrandt to Rush Holland, Assistant Attorney General, January 16, 1925, Folder 23-82-79-1, Box 1627, Class 23 materials, DOJ.
38. Mabel Walker Willebrandt to the Attorney General, March 25, 1925, Folder 23-82-79-1, Box 1627, Class 23 materials, DOJ.
39. "'Whispering Wires' Tell Tales; Grand Jury May Hear Names," *Seattle Times*, January 4, 1925, 1.
40. "U.S. Grand Jury to Get Olmsted Expose Monday," *Seattle Times*, January 11, 1925, 1.
41. Senate Select Committee on Investigation of Internal Revenue Bureau, Investigation of the Internal Revenue Bureau: Hearings Before the Committee, 68th Cong., 2nd sess., 1925, Part 14, 2625–30.
42. Mabel Walker Willebrandt to J. J. Britt, April 8, 1924, appearing in Senate Select Committee on Investigation of Internal Revenue Bureau, Investigation of the Internal Revenue Bureau: Hearings Before the Committee, 68th Cong., 2nd sess., 1925, Part 14, 2636–38.
43. Senate Select Committee on Investigation of Internal Revenue Bureau, Investigation of the Internal Revenue Bureau: Hearings Before the Committee, 68th Cong., 2nd sess., 1925, Part 14, 2636–38, 2642.
44. Mabel Walker Willebrandt to the Walkers, April 1, 1925, Folder: Parents, Box 3, Manuscript Division, Library of Congress, Washington, D.C.
45. Senate Select Committee on Investigation of Internal Revenue Bureau, Investigation of the Internal Revenue Bureau: Hearings before the Committee, 68th Cong., 2nd sess., 1925, Part 14, 2737.

46. Brown, *Mabel Walker Willebrandt*, 122. (Actual source is an interview of Grace Knoeller by Dorothy Brown, October 1979.)
47. Myrtle Walker to Mabel Walker Willebrandt, October 3, 1924, Folder: Parents, Box 3, MWWP.
48. Mabel Walker Willebrandt to David and Myrtle Walker, August 2, 1925, Folder: Parents, Box 3, MWWP.
49. Brown, *Mabel Walker Willebrandt*, 124. (Actual sources are interviews with Dorothy Van Dyke by Dorothy Brown, October 20, 1978, and in November 1981.)
50. State Reorganization Commission, *Report of the State Reorganization Commission, February 26, 1926*, Albany, NY: J. B. Lyon Press, 1926, 59–66.
51. "Four Crime Bills Passed by Senate," *New York Times*, April 2, 1926, 2; "$15,000,000 Pay Rise for Teachers Out," *New York Times*, April 16, 1926, 10; "Legislature Ends; Teachers' Pay Rise Voted Amid Clash," *New York Times*, April 24, 1926, 1.
52. "Organize to Get Citizens to Poll," *New York Times*, December 14, 1925, 16.
53. "U.S. to Rush Olmsted Trials," *Seattle Times*, January 23, 1925, 1.
54. "Hubbard Called Him Honest, Says Corwin," *Seattle Post Intelligencer*, September 13, 1930, Folder: Whitney News Clippings, Container 2912, CSC.
55. Exhibit A, September 5, 1925, Roy Lyle to Roy A. Haynes, Federal Prohibition Commissioner "Personal and Confidential," in a letter from William Whitney to James Yaden, dated November 26, 1927, forwarded by William Whitney to Senator Jones in a letter dated December 16, 1927, Box 272, Folder 1, WJP.
56. "Jones Admits Part in Hiring Hubbard," *Seattle Post Intelligencer*, September 18, 1930, Folder Whitney News Clippings, Container 2912, CSC.
57. Exhibit A, Roy Lyle to Commissioner Haynes, September 5, 1925, "Personal and Confidential," Exhibit A in a letter from William Whitney to James Yaden, dated November 27, 1927, forwarded by Whitney to Senator Jones on December 16, 1927, Box 272, Folder 1, WJP.
58. "Roy Olmsted Jailed; Deputy Sheriff Also Trapped in Rum Raid!" *Seattle Times*, November 26, 1925, 1.
59. "Dry Agent Hits Broker and Sheriff in Evidence," *Seattle Times*, October 20, 1927, 1.

Chapter 8

1. Mabel Walker Willebrandt to Fred Horowitz, December 2, 1925, Folder: General Correspondence, Box 4, MWWP.
2. Mabel Walker Willebrandt to David and Myrtle Walker, February 13, 1926, Folder: Parents, Box 3, MWWP; Mabel Walker Willebrandt to David and

Myrtle Walker, April 21, 1926, Folder: Parents, Box 3, MWWP; Mabel Walker Willebrandt to David and Myrtle Walker, circa May 1926, Folder: Parents, Box 3, MWWP.

3. Mabel Walker Willebrandt to David and Myrtle Walker, April 21, 1926, Folder: Parents, Box 3, MWWP.

4. "Alice Chittenden Heads Republican Women; Long Foe of Suffrage, Said Men Would Rue It," *New York Times*, January 15, 1926, 1.

5. "State Republicans Will Confer Today," *New York Times*, January 16, 1926, 3.

6. "Dry Law in Peril, Mrs. Catt Warns," *New York Times*, January 17, 1926, 20.

7. "Longworth Wants Radicals Deported," *New York Times*, January 17, 1926, 2.

8. "Poland Answers Critics of Dry Law," *New York Times*, January 12, 1926, 8.

9. "New State Dry Bill Roils Republicans," *New York Times*, January 31, 1926, 21.

10. "Dry Bill Defeated in State Senate," *New York Times*, March 23, 1926, 1.

11. "Assembly Wets Gain; Expect to Prevent Vote on the Dry Bill," *New York Times*, March 26, 1926, 1.

12. "Referendum Bill Passed," *New York Times*, April 14, 1926, 1.

13. "Wets Win in Assembly," *New York Times*, April 20, 1926, 1.

14. Some discrepancies exist between the newspaper coverage and the existing trial transcript, one created for Jerry Finch in preparation for future appeals.

15. This passage is a summary of days of testimony, comprising dozens of pages in the trial transcripts, primarily congregated in File #3.

16. "Jury Asks What Charge Is No Change, Judge Tells Him," *Seattle Times*, January 26, 1926, 7.

17. William Whitney, Testimony, *U.S. v. Olmstead et al.*, 5 F.2d 712 (W.D. Wash. 1925), 37–39; trial transcript held in File 3, Box 37, DCW.

18. "Discovery of Caches Described by Whitney," *Seattle Times*, January 23, 1926, 1.

19. William Whitney, Testimony, *U.S. v. Olmstead et al.*, 5 F.2d 712 (W.D. Wash. 1925), 48; trial transcript held in File 3, Box 37, DCW.

20. "More Names Are Revealed in Dry Agent's Records," *Seattle Times*, January 27, 1926, 12.

21. William Whitney, Testimony, *U.S. v. Olmstead et al.*, 5 F.2d 712 (W.D. Wash. 1925), 56, 99; trial transcript held in File 3, Box 37, DCW.

22. Richard Fryant, Testimony, *U.S. v. Olmstead et al.*, 5 F.2d 712 (W.D. Wash. 1925), 115–123; trial transcript held in File 3, Box 37, DCW.

23. "New Booze Trial Sensations Due," *Seattle Times*, January 31, 1926, 4.

24. "Atty. Looie in Coats Guard [*sic*]," *Seattle Times*, February 4, 1926, 9.

25. "Tapped Wire Testimony Attacked by Counsel," *Seattle Times*, February 10, 1926, 1.

26. "Mrs. Willebrandt to Arrive Here Monday," *Seattle Times*, February 13, 1926, 3.

27. "More Liquor Trials Planned; Revelle Keeps His Evidence," *Seattle Times*, February 14, 1926, 12.

28. "Revelle Greets Superior Officer," *Seattle Times*, February 15, 1926, 5.

29. Mabel Walker Willebrandt to David and Myrtle Walker, February 15, 1926, Folder: Parents, Box 3, MWWP.

30. "Attack on Fryant Is Launched," *Seattle Times*, February 15, 1926, 1, 5. The reporter wrote "thirty pages," then a few sentences later "twenty-seven pages," but the clerk marked them as evidence B 1–27.

31. Jeremiah Neterer, Jury Instructions, *U.S. v. Olmstead et al.*, 5 F.2d 712 (W.D. Wash. 1925), 286; trial transcript held in File 3, Box 37, DCW.

32. "Judge Chuckles; Strain Over; Sidelights on Trial's End," *Seattle Times*, February 21, 1926, 5.

33. "Olmsted, 20 Others Guilty!" *Seattle Times*, February 21, 1926, 1.

34. Pauline Sabin to James Wadsworth, March 1, 1926, Folder 3, Box J112K, WFP.

35. "Women Leaders Back Wadsworth," *New York Times*, April 14, 1926, 2.

36. Pauline Sabin to James Wadsworth, June 17, 1926, Folder: Pauline Sabin Correspondence, Box J112E, WFP.

37. "State West Form Committee of 1,000," *New York Times*, May 8, 1926.

38. Senate Subcommittee of the Committee on the Judiciary, The National Prohibition Law: Hearings on S. 33, S. 34, S. 591, S. 592, S. 3118, S.J. Res. 34, S.J. Res. 81, S.J. Res. 85, S. 3823, S. 3411, and S. 3891 to Amend the National Prohibition Act, 69th Cong., 1st sess., 1926, vol. 1, 42.

39. Senate Subcommittee of the Committee on the Judiciary, The National Prohibition Law: Hearings on S. 33, S. 34, S. 591, S. 592, S. 3118, S.J. Res. 34, S.J. Res. 81, S.J. Res. 85, S. 3823, S. 3411, and S. 3891 to Amend the National Prohibition Act, 69th Cong., 1st sess., 1926, vol. 1, 1129.

40. "Attorney Jerry L. Finch and Nineteen Others to Serve Prison Sentences," *Seattle Times*, March 8, 1926, 1; "20 Liquor Conspiracy Defendants File Writs," *Seattle Times*, March 9, 1926, 1.

41. "Only Echoes Left in Mansion; Olmstead Furniture Is Bid On," *Seattle Times*, March 19, 1926, 1, 18.

42. "Olmstead Tells How 'Frame-ups' Convicted Men," *Seattle Times*, August 23, 1930, 3; "Hubbard's Role Jolted Olmsted, Whitney States," *Seattle Times*, September 6, 1930, 3.

43. "Comstock Is Included in Hundred Defendants," *Seattle Times*, May 13, 1926, 1.

44. "Olmsted Indicted Again on Two Charges," *Seattle Times*, May 14, 1926, 1.

45. "Hubbard Is Revealed as Secret Aide of Whitney," May 15, 1926, 1. See also unknown newspaper, "Two 'Roys' Disrupt Northwest . . . ," August 10, 1930, Folder: Whitney News Clippings, Container 2011, CSC.

46. "Hubbard Is Revealed as Secret Aide of Whitney," *Seattle Times*, May 16, 1926, 1.

Chapter 9

1. "Pick Ogden Mills as Keynote Orator," *New York Times*, July 23, 1926, 3.
2. "O.S. Poland Hits Smith," *New York Times*, August 2, 1926, 6.
3. James Wadsworth to Pauline Sabin, August 30, 1926, Folder: August 27–September 1, 1926, JWFP.
4. "Cropsey Boom Fades as Wadsworth Hits Jurist's Dry Plank," *New York Times*, August 31, 1926, 1.
5. "Cropsey Quits Race, Yielding to Attacks, Friend Announces," *New York Times*, September 1, 1926, 1.
6. "Fish Denounces Wadsworth as Wet," *New York Times*, September 10, 1926.
7. "Mrs. Sabin Favors Wets Poll," *New York Times*, September 13, 1926, 4.
8. "Drys Take Fight on Wadsworth to National Committee," *New York Times*, August 20, 1926, 1.
9. "Cropsey or Hilles May Head Ticket," *New York Times*, August 22, 1926, 1.
10. "Wadsworth States His Dry Law Views," *New York Times*, September 25, 1926, 19.
11. "Garden Stage Set for Republicans," *New York Times*, September 26, 1926, 1.
12. "Chiefs at Harmony Dinner," *New York Times*, September 27, 1926, 1.
13. "Call Party's Future Dark," *New York Times*, September 27, 1926, 1.
14. "Drys in Convention Assail Wadsworth," *New York Times*, September 29, 1926, 2.
15. "58 Balk at Senator," *New York Times*, September 29, 1926, 1.
16. "Text of the Republican Platform with Its Prohibition Plank," *New York Times*, September 28, 1926, 1.
17. "To Nominate Mills Today," *New York Times*, September 28, 1926, 1.
18. "Wadsworth States His Dry Law Views," *New York Times*, September 25, 1926, 19.
19. "Mrs. Sabin Warns Republican Drys," *New York Times*, October 5, 1926, 2.
20. "Cristman Manager Warns Republicans," *New York Times*, October 16, 1926, 3.
21. Hiram Johnson to Alex McCabe, May 21, 1926, Part III, Box 8, HJP.
22. "Nation's Portia and Hiram at Outs," *Nevada State Journal*, June 15, 1924, 6.
23. Hiram Johnson to Harold Ickes, May 22, 1926, Part III, Box 8, HJP.
24. Frank Doherty to Hiram Johnson, July 24, 1926, Part III, Box 34, Folder 2, HJP.
25. Hiram Johnson to Frank Doherty, July 31, 1926, Part III, Box 8, HJP.
26. Mabel Walker Willebrandt to David and Myrtle Walker, late December 1926, Folder: Parents, Box 3, MWWP.

27. "Wadsworth Lauds Tariff in Suffolk," *New York Times*, October 24, 1926, 3; "Wadsworth to Ask Business Support," *New York Times*, October 25, 1926, 3.

28. "1,193,183 Voted Here to Elect Governor," *New York Times*, November 4, 1926, 18.

29. "Where Were the Drys?" *New York Times*, November 4, 1926, 26.

30. "See Dry Law Reaction," *New York Times*, November 4, 1926, 9.

31. "Six States Vote Wet," *New York Times*, November 4, 1926, 9.

32. "Coolidge Again, Says Wadsworth," *New York Times*, December 12, 1926, 27.

33. Mabel Walker Willebrandt to David and Myrtle Walker, December 25, 1926, Folder: Parents, Box 3, MWWP.

34. Vylla Poe Wilson, Article 6—No title, *Washington Post*, January 16, 1927, F6.

35. James Wadsworth to Charles Sabin, January 6, 1927, Folder: Pauline Sabin Correspondence, Box J112E, WFP.

36. "Dignity and Stateliness Mark Judicial Reception," *Washington Post*, January 14, 1927, 2.

37. James Wadsworth to Pauline Sabin, January 17, 1927, Folder: Pauline Sabin Correspondence," Box J112E, WFP.

38. "President Gives Women Praise for G.O.P. Work," *Lexington (KY) Leader*, January 16, 1927, 10.

39. No title—editorial, *New York Evening Post*, January 14, 1927. (A clipping of this article was attached to the following correspondence: James Wadsworth to Pauline Sabin, January 17, 1927, Folder: Pauline Sabin Correspondence, Box J112E, WFP.)

40. "Opposes Feminine Blocs," *New York Times*, May 11, 1927, 27.

41. "Qualities for Successful Leadership," *Long Islander*, January 14, 1927, 1.

42. "Prohibition Enforcement," Letter from the Secretary of the Treasury, January 29, 1927, Washington, U.S. Government Printing Office, 24; "Prohibition Enforcement," Letter from the Secretary of the Treasury, January 29, 1927, Washington: U.S. Government Printing Office, 2–3, 24.

43. William Whitney to Wesley Jones, September 4, 1929, Box 277, Folder 20, WJP.

44. Thomas Revelle to Wesley Jones, May 5, 1927, Box 271, Folder 35, WJP; September 4, 1929; William Whitney to Wesley Jones, September 4, 1929, Box 277, Folder 20, WJP.

45. William Whitney to Wesley Jones, September 4, 1929, Box 277, Folder 20, WJP.

46. Thomas Revelle to Wesley Jones, March 26, 1927, Box 271, Folder 31, WJP.

47. "Dry Reorganization Effective as More Opposition Is Bared," *Washington Post*, April 2, 1927, 5.

48. Letter sent to Coast Guard Commanders, Prohibition Administrators, and Collectors of Customs on the Pacific Coast, May 7, 1926; an attachment to a

letter from the Assistant to the Assistant Secretary of the Treasury, June 3, 1926, Box 271, Folder 32, WJP.

49. Thomas Revelle to Wesley Jones, June 2, 1926, Box 271, Folder 31, WJP.

50. Thomas Revelle to Wesley Jones, May 5, 1927, Box 271, Folder 31, WJP.

51. "*Zev* Case Will Be Highlight of Testimony," *Seattle Times*, August 14, 1930, Container 2011, Folder: Whitney News Clippings, CSC.

52. "Here's Pal Letter Sent by Hubbard to Whitney," *Seattle Post-Intelligencer*, August 19, 1930.

53. Thomas Revelle to Wesley Jones, May 5, 1927, Box 271, Folder 35, WJP.

54. "Debunking the Myth That All Women Are Dry," *New York Evening World*, May 6, 1927, Scrapbook, Archives, Women's National Republican Club, New York City.

55. Untitled editorial, *New York Evening Post*, May 4, 1927, Scrapbook, Archives, Women's National Republican Club, New York City.

56. "Will the Women Bolt?" *Boston Transcript* (reprinted from the *Philadelphia Ledger*), June 15, 1927, Scrapbook, Archives, Women's National Republican Club, New York City.

57. Emma Bugbee, "Women Assail Republican Poll on Volstead Act," *New York Herald Tribune*, May 12, 1927, Scrapbook, Archives, Women's National Republican Club, New York City.

58. Thomas Revelle to Wesley Jones, May 14, 1927, Box 271, Folder 35, WJP.

59. Wesley Jones to Thomas Revelle, May 13, 1927, Box 271, Folder 35, WJP.

60. "Hubbard Outlay on $155 Salary Arouses Defense," *Seattle Times*, September 9, 1930, 4.

Chapter 10

1. "President Acted Alone," *New York Times*, August 3, 1927, 1.

2. Thomas Revelle to Wesley Jones, August 19, 1927, Box 272, Folder 6, WJP.

3. "Telegrams Reveal How Revelle Tried to Block Dry Query," *Seattle Post-Intelligencer*, September 11, 1930.

4. Roy Lyle to Wesley Jones, September 8, 1927, Box 272, Folder 4, WJP.

5. "Mrs. Sabin Gives Up Republican Committee Job," *Patchogue Advance*, September 9, 1927, 14.

6. "Political Debate by Women Radioed," *New York Times*, November 3, 1927, 29.

7. "Mrs. Sabin Still Leading," *New York Times*, November 5, 1927, 38; "Democrats Now to Press Smith 4-Year Term Plan; Republicans to Fight It," *New York Times*, November 10, 1927, 1.

8. "Warrant Is Issued for 'Rum King' By Bourquin," *Seattle Times*, October 18, 1927, 1.

9. Thomas Revelle to Wesley Jones, October 25, 1927, Box 271, Folder 33, WJP.

10. "Witness Accuses Revelle; Says Job Was Threatened," *Seattle Times*, October 21, 1927, 5.

11. "Bribers Hard to Catch," *Seattle Post-Intelligencer*, September 11, 1930.

12. Thomas Revelle to Wesley Jones, October 25, 1927, Box 271, Folder 33, WJP.

13. "Roy Olmsted in U.S. Court to Face Trial," *Seattle Times*, November 8, 1927, 1, 9.

14. "Olmsted Waits in County Jail for Next Trial," *Seattle Times*, November 9, 1927, 11.

15. "'Rum King,' 20 Others Must Serve Sentences," *Seattle Times*, November 21, 1927, 1.

16. "Olmsted Goes to Prison Tonight; Loses Appeal After Brief Stay," *Seattle Times*, November 29, 1927, 1.

17. "Debonair 'Rum King' Fades into 'No. 6538,'" *Seattle Times*, November 30, 1927, 1.

18. Exhibit A, Roy Lyle to Commissioner Haynes, September 5, 1925, "Personal and Confidential," in a letter from William Whitney to James Yaden, dated November 27, 1927, forwarded by William Whitney to Wesley Jones on December 16, 1927, Box 272, Folder 1, WJP.

19. Exhibit A, Roy Lyle to Commissioner Haynes, September 5, 1925, "Personal and Confidential," Exhibit A in a letter from William Whitney to James Yaden, dated November 27, 1927, forwarded by Whitney to Wesley Jones on December 16, 1927, Box 272, Folder 1; and Roy Lyle to Roy Haynes, Federal Prohibition Commissioner, September 5, 1925, Box 272, Folder, WJP.

20. William Whitney to Wesley Jones, December 16, 1927, Box 272, Folder 1, WJP.

21. Exhibit C of a letter from William Whitney to James Yaden, December 16, 1927, included in a letter from Whitney to Wesley Jones of the same date; Box 272, Folder 1, WJP.

22. William Whitney to Wesley Jones, April 25, 1928, Box 272, File 23, WJP.

23. "Republican Women Want 3 Delegates," unknown newspaper, January 14, 1928, Scrapbook, Archives, Women's National Republican Club, New York City.

24. "Women Pick Delegates," *New York Times*, January 16, 1928, 10.

25. "Republican Wets Give Peace Pledge," *New York Times*, May 19, 1928, 3.

26. "Woman Delegate Backs Hoover Here," *New York Times*, May 29, 1928, 3.

27. "Women, for Hoover, Threaten to Bolt," *New York Times*, May 30, 1928, 21.

28. WNRC, Report of the Proceedings of the Mock Convention of the Women's National Republican Club held at the Waldorf-Astoria Hotel, New York City, Tuesday, April 24, 1928 (New York: The Tenney Press, 1928), 9.

29. WNRC, Report of the Proceedings of the Mock Convention of the Women's National Republican Club held at the Waldorf-Astoria Hotel, New York City, Tuesday, April 24, 1928 (New York: The Tenney Press, 1928).

30. Carlisle Bargeron, "Mrs. Willebrandt's Hoover Statement Stirs Up Democrats," *Washington Post*, April 13, 1928, 4.
31. "Declares Women Jurors Insure Honest Trials," *Washington Post*, April 29, 1928, SM2.
32. "Tapping of Wires by Dry Agents to Be Aired," *Seattle Times*, January 9, 1928, 1.
33. Wesley Jones to Mabel Walker Willebrandt, January 27, 1928, File: 23-82-79 (*U.S. v. Dow* case file), Entry 23, Class 23 (Liquor Violations) Litigation Case Files and Formerly Classified Subject Correspondence, DOJ.
34. Mabel Walker Willebrandt to Wesley Jones, January 31, 1928, File: 23-82-79 (*U.S. v. Dow* case file), Entry 23, Class 23 (Liquor Violations) Litigation Case Files and Formerly Classified Subject Correspondence, DOJ.
35. "Roy Olmsted at Liberty Again as Bail Is Arranged," *Seattle Times*, February 5, 1928, 10.
36. William Whitney to Wesley Jones, March 12, 1928, Box 272, File 22, WJP.
37. William Whitney to Wesley Jones, May 4, 1930, Box 13, Folder 26, WJP.
38. Thomas Revelle to Wesley Jones, March 24, 1928, Box 272, Folder 17, WJP.
39. William Whitney to Wesley Jones, September 4, 1929, Box 277, Folder 20, WJP.
40. "Women Pile Up Planks," *Kansas City Star*, June 3, 1928, 1B.
41. *Olmstead v. U.S.* 277 U.S. 438.
42. "Olmsted, Eight Others Return to Prison Today," *Seattle Times*, June 21, 1928, 12.
43. "Revelle Plans to Retire from Official Work," *Seattle Times*, May 20, 1928, 4.
44. "The 'Show' on Outside," *Kansas City Star*, June 3, 1928, 3A.
45. "Women's Power Is Felt," *Kansas City Star*, June 10, 1928, 6A.
46. "No Lead-Pipe Blow, This," *Kansas City Star*, June 6, 1928, 3.
47. "And How Press-Wise," *Kansas City Star*, June 6, 1928, 16.
48. "Both Parties to Be Dry," *Kansas City Star*, June 11, 1928, 4.
49. "In Politics Like a Man," *Kansas City Star*, June 5, 1928, 3.
50. "'Play the Game Like Men' Is Women's Cry in Politics Now," *Charleston (SC) Gazette*, June 7, 1928, 5.
51. "An O.K. on Hilles Slate," *Kansas City Times*, June 12, 1928, 10; Albert Warner, "Hilles Men Swamp Hoover Supporters," *New York Times*, June 12, 1928, 1.
52. W. A. Warn, "Allies Centre on South," *New York Times*, June 9, 1928, 1.
53. Winifred Mallon, "Women Are Active Among the Boomers," *New York Times*, June 11, 1928, 2.
54. "A 'Lesson' on Hoover," *Kansas City Times*, June 9, 1928, 17.
55. Republican National Committee, Hearing on Contests, June 6, 1928, Papers of the Republican Party.
56. "They Shriek for Hoover," *Kansas City Star*, June 10, 1928, 12A.

57. "Anti-Hoover Efforts Stopped in Credentials Committee," *Washington Post*, June 13, 1928, 4; Republican National Committee, *Official Report of the Proceedings of the Nineteenth Republican National Convention*, June 12–15, 1928, 50.

58. James Williams, "Nomination Plans Are Being Held Up; Hoover Still Gains," *Washington Post*, June 14, 1928, 1.

59. Republican National Committee, *Official Report of the Proceedings of the Nineteenth Republican National Convention*, June 12–15, 1928, 52–69.

60. Albert Warner, "New York to Vote Solidly for Hoover," *New York Times*, June 14, 1928, 1.

61. Republican National Committee, *Official Report of the Proceedings of the Nineteenth Republican National Convention*, June 12–15, 1928, 127.

62. "No Fee Mention," *Kansas City Times*, June 14, 1928, 1; Republican National Committee, *Official Report of the Proceedings of the Nineteenth Republican National Convention*, June 12–15, 1928, 171–73.

63. Republican National Committee, *Official Report of the Proceedings of the Nineteenth Republican National Convention*, June 12–15, 1928, 172–73.

64. Republican National Committee, *Official Report of the Proceedings of the Nineteenth Republican National Convention*, June 12–15, 1928, 139, 253.

65. Maxine Davis, "For Woman in Cabinet," *Kansas City Star*, June 14, 1928, 13.

66. Herbert Corey, "A Woman as the Mate," *Kansas City Star*, June 14, 1928, 15.

67. "Crown to Parent Pride," *Kansas City Star*, June 15, 1928, 6.

68. "So the Women Go Home," *Kansas City Star*, June 16, 1928, 4.

69. "Women to Earn Place," *Kansas City Times*, June 6, 1928, 6.

Chapter 11

1. Pauline Morton Sabin, "I Change My Mind on Prohibition," *Outlook*, June 13, 1928, 254, 277.

2. Pauline Morton Sabin, "I Change My Mind on Prohibition," *Outlook*, June 13, 1928, 277.

3. "Mrs. Sabin's Address," *Suffolk County News*, August 31, 1928, 12.

4. "Broadway Raiding to Go On, Is Word; 100 Arrests Made," *Washington Post*, June 30, 1928, 5.

5. "Dry Raids Result in 113 New York Indictments," *Washington Post*, July 31, 1928, 5; "31 More Indicted in New York as Dry Law Conspirators," *Washington Post*, August 1, 1928, 4.

6. "U.S. Attorney Abruptly Halts New York Night Club Quiz," *Washington Post*, August 21, 1928, 1.

7. "Jurors Quiz Police About Night Clubs," *Washington Post*, August 23, 1928, 1.

8. Carlisle Bargeron, "New York Dry Row Is Placed Before Hoover," *Washington Post*, August 31, 1928, 1.

9. William Whitney to Wesley Jones, July 4, 1928, Box 272, Folder 15, and William Whitney to Wesley Jones, July 7, 1928, Box 272, File 14, WJP.

10. William Whitney to Wesley Jones, July 7, 1928, Box 272, File 14, WJP.

11. Roy Lyle to Wesley Jones, August 6, 1928, Box 272, Folder 20, WJP.

12. William Whitney to Wesley Jones, August 8, 1928, Box 272, File 14, WJP.

13. "Lyle, Whitney Transfers Seen as Possibility," *Seattle Times*, August 2, 1928, 9.

14. "Women Plan Fight to Elect Hoover," *New York Times*, July 25, 1928, 2.

15. "Women Organize New Hoover Drive," *New York Times*, July 26, 1928, 3.

16. Eunice Fuller Barnard, "The Woman Voter Gains Power," *New York Times*, August 12, 1928, SM1.

17. Richard V. Oulahan, "New Hoover Group Seeks Kitchen Vote," *New York Times*, August 17, 1928, 2.

18. "Women to Aid Hoover in Parlor and Street," *New York Times*, September 5, 1928, 3; "Mrs. Robinson Head of Women Orators," *New York Times*, September 23, 1928, 7.

19. Republican National Committee, Press Release, October 3, 1928, Folder: Women's National Republican Club, Box 73, General Correspondence, Herbert Hoover Papers, Herbert Hoover Presidential Library, West Branch, IA (hereafter abbreviated as HHP).

20. New York Republican State Committee, Miscellaneous Press Releases, September 8, 1928, to October 3, 1928, Folder: Women's National Republican Club, Box 73, General Correspondence, HHP.

21. No title, *New York Times*, September 3, 1928, 28.

22. "100 Women Leaders Plan to Beat Smith," *New York Times*, September 6, 1928, 5.

23. "Trend to Hoover by Women Is Seen," *New York Times*, September 16, 1928, 10.

24. Mabel Walker Willebrandt to Hubert Work, September 6, 1928, Box 72, Folder: Willebrandt, Mabel Walker, General Correspondence Series, Campaign & Transition Papers, HHP.

25. Carlisle Bargeron, "Roles of G.O.P. Leaders Shifted," *Washington Post*, September 9, 1928, 4.

26. Carlisle Bargeron, "Work Denounces Whisper Campaign," *Washington Post*, September 10, 1928, 1.

27. "Mrs. Willebrandt Assails Gov. Smith," *Washington Post*, September 24, 1928, 1.

28. "Mrs. Willebrandt Hits Smith Again," *Washington Post*, September 25, 1928, 1.

29. Mabel Walker Willebrandt to George Akerson, September 24, 1928, Box 72, Folder: Willebrandt, Mabel Walker, General Correspondence, Campaign & Transition Papers, HHP.

30. Untitled article, dateline Chicago, *Washington Post*, September 25, 1928, 2.

31. Harriet Taylor Upton to Herbert Hoover, September 26, 1928, Box 69, Folder: Upton, Harriet Taylor, General Correspondence, Campaign & Transition Papers, HHP.

32. "Hilles Repudiates Support by Bigots; Stresses Dry Issue," *New York Times,* September 25, 1928, 1.

33. "Mrs. Willebrandt Confers in Chicago on Future Speeches," *New York Times,* September 26, 1928, 1.

34. "Attacks on Mrs. Willebrandt Not to End Speeches," *Sandusky Star-Journal,* September 27, 1928, 2.

35. Mabel Walker Willebrandt to Hubert Work, September 27, 1928, Box 72, Folder: Willebrandt, Mabel Walker, General Correspondence, Campaign & Transition Papers, HHP.

36. "Mrs. Willebrandt Denies Church Slur," *Washington Post,* October 9, 1928, 10.

37. "Willebrandt Name Hissed by Women," *Washington Post,* October 3, 1928, 2; "Mrs. Willebrandt Denies Church Slur," *Washington Post,* October 9, 1928, 10; "Davis Would Hush Mrs. Willebrandt," *Washington Post,* October 12, 1928, 3.

38. "Mrs. Willebrandt Denies She Is a Bigot," *Washington Post,* November 4, 1928, M3.

39. "Fisher Analyzes Hoover's Victory," *New York Times,* November 25, 1928, N1.

40. "Figures 39,000,000 Voted on Tuesday," *New York Times,* November 11, 1928, 11.

41. The quotation is cited from the original report in Anna L. Harvey, *Votes Without Leverage: Women in American Electoral Politics, 1920–1970* (Cambridge, UK: Cambridge University Press, 1998), 146.

42. "Republicans Here Exult at Victory," *New York Times,* November 7, 1928, 22.

43. "Mrs. Sabin Resigns Republican Post," *New York Times,* March 9, 1929, 3.

44. Various persons to Herbert Hoover, January 1929, Box 90, Folder: Cabinet Appointments—Willebrandt, Mabel Walker, Subject Series, Campaign & Transition Papers, HHP.

45. Mabel Walker Willebrandt to Lawrence Richey, January 9, 1929, Box 72, Folder: Willebrandt, Mabel Walker, General Correspondence, Campaign & Transition Papers, HHP; Mabel Walker Willebrandt to David and Myrtle Walker, February 3, 1929, Folder: Correspondence, Box 2, MWWP.

46. Mabel Walker Willebrandt to David and Myrtle Walker, February 3, 1929, Folder: Correspondence, Box 2, MWWP.

47. J. M. Doran, Commissioner, to Roy C. Lyle, December 6, 1928, Box 272, Folder 21, WJP.

48. Roy Lyle to J. M Doran, December 20, 1928, Box 272, Folder 21, WJP.

49. Roy Lyle to Wesley Jones, December 20, 1928, Box 272, Folder 21, WJP.

50. Mabel Walker Willebrandt to Herbert Hoover, February 8, 1929, Box 90, Folder: Cabinet Appointments—Miscellaneous, Inquiries—Willebrandt, Mabel W., Subject Series, Campaign & Transition Papers, HHP.

51. Mabel Walker Willebrandt to David and Myrtle Walker, February 12, 1929, Folder: Correspondence, Box 2, MWWP.

52. John S. Martin, "Mrs. Firebrand," *New Yorker*, February 16, 1929, 13–14, 25–26

53. Mabel Walker Willebrandt to David and Myrtle Walker, February 22, 1929, Folder: Correspondence, Box 2, MWWP.

54. Mabel Walker Willebrandt to David and Myrtle Walker, March 29, 1929, Folder: Correspondence, Box 2, MWWP.

55. Wesley Jones to William Whitney, February 11, 1929, Box 272, Folder 36, WJP.

56. Alf Oftedal to William Whitney, February 16, 1929, attached to William Whitney to Wesley Jones, February 22, 1929, Box 273, Folder 13, WJP.

57. William Whitney to Wesley Jones, February 22, 1929, Box 273, Folder 13, WJP.

58. "Plot Is Laid to Hubbard and Whitney," *Seattle Post-Intelligencer*, September 9, 1930.

59. J. Edgar Hoover to Mabel Walker Willebrandt, May 16, 1929, File 1183412-000 62-Hq-21578, Case File 62-625 re U.S. v. William M. Whitney et al., Record/Information Dissemination Section, Federal Bureau of Investigation, Winchester, VA.

60. Mabel Walker Willebrandt to Attorney General, April 4, 1929, Box 54E, Folder: Treasury, Prohibition Commissioner, Correspondence, 1929, March–May, Cabinet Office Series, HHP.

61. Mabel Walker Willebrandt to David and Myrtle Walker, April 21, 1929, Folder: Correspondence, Box 2, MWWP.

62. "Juries Will Not Convict," *Washington Post*, April 21, 1929, S1.

63. An Act to Amend the National Prohibition Act, Public Law 899, 70th Cong., 2nd sess. (March 2, 1929), 1446.

64. "Juries Will Not Convict," *Washington Post*, April 21, 1929, S1.

65. Mabel Walker Willebrandt to Herbert Hoover, May 26, 1929, Box 21, Folder: Willebrandt, Mabel W., March–June 1929, Cabinet Office Series, HHP.

66. Herbert Hoover to Mabel Walker Willebrandt, May 28, 1929, Box 21, Folder: Willebrandt, Mabel W., March–June 1929, Cabinet Office Series, HHP.

Chapter 12

1. Mrs. Courtlandt Nicoll, "Statement made by Mrs. Courtlandt Nicoll at the Meeting of the New York County Advisory Council at the Plaza Hotel, June twelfth," 1929, Folder 443, Box 25, Mrs. William Lowell Putnam Papers, Radcliffe Institute, Harvard University, Cambridge, MA.

2. Mrs. Courtlandt Nicoll, "Statement made by Mrs. Courtlandt Nicoll at Southampton, L.I., July 26," 1929, Folder 443, Box 25, Mrs. William Lowell Putnam Papers, Radcliffe Institute, Harvard University, Cambridge, MA (hereafter abbreviated as MWLPP).

3. Mrs. Courtlandt Nicoll, "Statement made by Mrs. Courtlandt Nicoll at the Meeting of the New York County Advisory Council at the Plaza Hotel, June twelfth," 1929, Folder 443, Box 25, MWLPP.

4. Pauline Sabin to Florence Hyde, June 13, 1929, Folder 1921–1929, Box 1, Hyde Family Papers, #1670, Division of Rare Books and Manuscript Collections, Cornell University Library.

5. Mrs. Charles H. Sabin, "Address made by Mrs. Charles H. Sabin at a Meeting of the Massachusetts Branch of the National Civic Federation," November 18, 1929, Box 3, Mrs. J. S. Sheppard Papers, New York State Library, Albany, NY (hereafter abbreviated as MJSSP).

6. Dayton E. Heckman, "Prohibition Passes: The Story of the Association Against the Prohibition Amendment," Ph.D. dissertation, Ohio State University, 1939, 214.

7. J. S. Cullinan to Pauline Sabin, December 31, 1929; and J. S. Cullinan to Pauline Sabin, January 2, 1930, both letters from Folder: (AAPA) Women's Committee 1930 (Reel 11), Records of the Women's Organization for National Prohibition Repeal, Manuscripts Division, Library of Congress, Washington, D.C. (hereafter abbreviated as RWONPR).

8. Senate Committee on the Judiciary, Lobby Investigation, 71st Cong., 2nd sess., 1930, 4060–61, 4121, 4170–72.

9. Dayton E. Heckman, "Prohibition Passes: The Story of the Association Against the Prohibition Amendment," Ph.D. dissertation, Ohio State University, 1939, 379 (see footnote 38).

10. Mabel Walker Willebrandt, "Smart Washington After Six O'Clock," Ladies' Home Journal, July 1929, 11.

11. Mabel Walker Willebrandt, "The Inside of Prohibition," New York Times, August 5, 1929, 23.

12. Mabel Walker Willebrandt, "The Inside of Prohibition," New York Times, August 8, 1929, 19.

13. Ibid.

14. Mabel Walker Willebrandt, "The Inside of Prohibition," New York Times, August 9, 1929, 13.

15. Mabel Walker Willebrandt, "The Inside of Prohibition," New York Times, August 11, 1929, N1.

16. Mabel Walker Willebrandt, "The Inside of Prohibition," New York Times, August 14, 1929, 17.

17. Mabel Walker Willebrandt, "The Inside of Prohibition," *New York Times*, August 20, 1929, 23.
18. Mabel Walker Willebrandt, "The Inside of Prohibition," *New York Times*, August 21, 1929, 29.
19. Mabel Walker Willebrandt, "The Inside of Prohibition," *New York Times*, August 24, 1929, 15.
20. Ibid.
21. "Attempt to Hush Olmstead Told," *Seattle Post-Intelligencer*, September 11, 1930.
22. "Mysterious Investigation of Seattle Prohibition Office," *Seattle Post-Intelligencer*, October 4, 1929, 1, a clipping attached to letter, Roy Lyle to Wesley Jones, October 11, 1929, Box 277, Folder 24, WJP.
23. Roy Lyle to Wesley Jones, October 11, 1929, Box 277, Folder 24, WJP.
24. William Whitney to Wesley Jones, November 24, 1929, Box 274, Folder 4, WJP.
25. William Whitney to Wesley Jones, December 10, 1929, Box 274, Folder 5, WJP.
26. "Dry Personally, He Says," *New York Times*, November 2, 1929, 1.
27. "Dyer Carries Plea for Beer to Hoover," *New York Times*, January 1, 1930, 1.
28. "Ignore Sex in Jobs, Women Are Told," *New York Times*, September 30, 1929, 2.
29. Mabel Walker Willebrandt, "Give Women a Fighting Chance!" *Smart Set Magazine*, February 1930, 23–24, 27.
30. House Committee on the Judiciary, *The Prohibition Amendment: Hearings on H.J. Res. 11, 38, 99, 114, 219, and 246*, 71st Cong., 2nd sess., 1930, 1481–83.
31. House Committee on the Judiciary, *The Prohibition Amendment: Hearings on H.J. Res. 11, 38, 99, 114, 219, and 246*, 71st Cong., 2nd sess., 1930, 41–44.
32. House Committee on the Judiciary, *The Prohibition Amendment: Hearings on H.J. Res. 11, 38, 99, 114, 219, and 246*, 71st Cong., 2nd sess., 1930, 1223–30.
33. "Women Wets Here Heckle Mrs. Boole," *New York Times*, April 9, 1930, 19.
34. Women's Organization for National Prohibition Reform, "Declaration of Principles," 1930, Folder 443, Box 25, MWLPP.
35. Mrs. B. G. du Pont, "Report of Cleveland Meeting given at meeting at Mrs. Wm. C. Spruance's," May 8, 1930, Folder: Appointments for Cleveland meeting (Reel 13), RWONPR.
36. "The Wet Label," *New York World*, May 27, 1930 (as reprinted by the Women's Organization for National Prohibition Reform), Elizabeth Tilton Papers, 1914–1949, Folder 343, Box 12, Schlesinger Library, Radcliffe Institute, Harvard University, Cambridge, MA.
37. "Questions asked by Mr. Henry W. Farnham," July 8, 1930, Box 3, MJSSP.

38. Unknown author, "Copy of a Response to a Letter Stating that Prohibition Has Not Been Given a Fair Trial in New York," circa 1930, Box 3, MJSSP.
39. Wesley Jones to Roy Lyle, May 14, 1930, Box 276, Folder 26, WJP.
40. Wesley Jones to William Whitney, May 19, 1930, Box 13, Folder 26, WJP.
41. Wesley Jones to Roy Lyle, May 27, 1930, Box 276, Folder 25, WJP.
42. William Whitney to Wesley Jones, May 30, 1930, Box 277, Folder 7, WJP.
43. "Jones Wants Modification, if State Does," *Seattle Times*, May 27, 1930, 1.
44. William Whitney to Wesley Jones, May 30, 1930, Box 277, Folder 7, WJP.
45. William Whitney to Wesley Jones, June 11, 1930, Box 276, Folder 24, WJP.
46. Wesley Jones to William Whitney, June 16, 1930, Box 276, Folder 24, WJP.
47. William Whitney to Wesley Jones, June 23, 1930, Box 272, Folder 22, WJP.
48. "Attack on Lyle Begins," *Seattle Times*, August 14, 1930, 1.
49. "Where Did All of the Millions of Dollars Supposed to Have Been Handled by Olmstead and Other Liquor Rings Go?" *Seattle Times*, August 14, 1930.
50. "Booze Brought in by Rail, Sail, Freight, Court Told," *Seattle Post-Intelligencer*, August 19, 1930.
51. "Yes! Times Do Change!" *Seattle Post-Intelligencer*, August 19, 1930.
52. "$95,000 in Graft Paid to Drys, Says Hubbard," *Seattle Post-Intelligencer*, August 19, 1930.
53. "Defense Gets Hubbard," *Seattle Post-Intelligencer*, August 19, 1930.
54. "Whitney Denies Hubbard's Story of Graft Ring 'Greasing,'" *Seattle Post-Intelligencer*, September 9, 1930.
55. "Attempt to Huth Olmstead Told," *Seattle Post-Intelligencer*, September 11, 1930.
56. "Wire Messages Between U.S. Attorney and Mrs. Willebrandt Introduced at Trial of Four Officials Accused as Conspirators," *Seattle Post-Intelligencer*, September 11, 1930.
57. "Bribers Hard to Catch," *Seattle Post-Intelligencer*, September 11, 1930.
58. "Wire Messages Between U.S. Attorney and Mrs. Willebrandt Introduced at Trial of Four Officials Accused as Conspirators," *Seattle Post-Intelligencer*, September 11, 1930.
59. "Jones Admits Part in Hiring Hubbard," *Seattle Post-Intelligencer*, September 18, 1930.
60. "Jury Gets Lyle Case Today," *Seattle Post-Intelligencer*, September 20, 1930.
61. "Lyle-Whitney Victims of Wet Trend—Moriarty," *Seattle Times*, September 21, 1930, 14.
62. "Jury Gets Lyle Case Today," *Seattle Post-Intelligencer*, September 20, 1930; "Lyle-Whitney Victims of Wet Trend—Moriarty," *Seattle Times*, September 21, 1930, 14.
63. "Lyle-Whitney Victims of Wet Trend—Moriarty," *Seattle Times*, September 21, 1930, 14.

64. "Jury Instructed by Norcross to 'Use Great Care,'" *Seattle Times*, September 21, 1930, 14.
65. William Whitney to J. M. Doran, January 17, 1931; and William Whitney to Wesley Jones, January 19, 1931 (the second of two dated January 19) Box 277, Folder 3, WJP.
66. "Lyle Named as Alcohol Permit Director Here," *Seattle Times*, January 1, 1931, 21.
67. William Whitney to Wesley Jones, January 19, 1931, Box 277, Folder 3, WJP.

Chapter 13

1. "Some Punch Recipes for the Law-Abiding," *New York Times*, September 14, 1930, 117.
2. "Mrs. Willebrandt in Denial," *New York Times*, August 19, 1930, 14.
3. "Wine Juice Makers Ask Gangster Curb," *New York Times*, November 20, 1930, 1.
4. "Willebrandt Gets Ovation at Dry Rally," *Washington Post*, January 7, 1931, 1.
5. Women's National Republican Club, Minutes of the Executive Committee, November 10, 1930, Archives, Women's National Republican Club, New York City.
6. Women's National Republican Club, Minutes of the Executive Committee, January 31, 1933, Archives, Women's National Republican Club, New York City.
7. Women's Organization for National Prohibition Reform, "Mrs. Sabin's Report," Report of Second Annual Conference of Women's Organization for National Prohibition Reform, April 14–15, 1931, 11–12, Box 3, MJSSP.
8. Women's Organization for National Prohibition Reform, "Resolution to the President," Report of Second Annual Conference of Women's Organization for National Prohibition Reform, April 14–15, 1931, p. 56, Box 3, MJSSP.
9. "Olmsted Free; Wife Welcomes Him at Landing," *Seattle Times*, May 12, 1931, 2.
10. Jefferson Chase, "The Sabines Ravish the Senators," *Vanity Fair*, 36 (August 1931): 80.
11. WONPR, Copy of letter sent to each of Congress, September 15, 1931, Folder: 73rd Congress 1928–1933 (Reel 12), RWONPR.
12. WONPR, Press Release, December 1, 1931, Folder: 73rd Congress 1928–1933, Archives, Women's National Republican Club, New York City.
13. WONPR, Report of WONPR on the Results of the Poll of the 73rd Congress on Resubmission of the Eighteenth Amendment," December 15, 1931, Folder: 73rd Congress 1928–1933, Archives, Women's National Republican Club, New York City.

14. Vera Quinn to Mrs. Rowland Paynter (Quinn quoting Pauline Sabin), September 22, 1931, Folder correspondence September 1930–December 1931 (Reel 13), RWONPR.

15. Women's Organization for National Prohibition Reform, "What, Why, How and Who," 1931, Box 3, MJSSP.

16. "Wine Brick Firm Drops Home Sales," New York Times, November 6, 1931, 23.

17. WONPR, Announcement, November 1, 1931, Folder: (AAPA) Women's committee 1931 (Reel 11), RWONPR.

18. WONPR, News Letter, March 1932, Folder: Publicity-General 1930–1932 (Reel 14), RWONPR.

19. "Women Will Battle for Dry Law Repeal," Atlanta Constitution, March 1, 1932, 13.

20. "Impromptu Talks Mark Luncheon for Prohibition Reform Leaders," Atlanta Constitution, March 4, 1932, 17; R. E. Powell, "Dry Propaganda, Prohibition Evils Scored by Women," Atlanta Constitution, March 4, 1932, 1.

21. Women's Organization for National Prohibition Reform, "What, Why, How and Who," 1931, Box 3, MJSSP; and Beck-Linthicum Resolution, Journal of the House of Representatives: 247, January 15, 1932.

22. WONPR, News Letter, March 1932, Folder: Publicity-General 1930–1932 (Reel 14), RWONPR.

23. "Wet Bloc Polls 187, but Loses in Test of Dry Law in House," New York Times, March 15, 1932, 1.

24. Mrs. Charles H. Sabin, "Forces of Both Sides of Prohibition Taking Shape for Final Battle," Baton Rouge Advocate, June 2, 1932, 20

25. Theodore Roosevelt Jr. to Charles Hilles, July 21, 1932, Folder 1454, Box 119, CHC.

26. "Roosevelt Favors State Handling Sale of Liquor," Dallas Morning News, 21 February 1932.

27. R. G. Tugwell, The Brains Trust (New York: Viking Press, 1968), 216–21.

28. W. E. Norvell, Jr., to Mrs. Pierre du Pont, April 24, 1932, Folder: (AAPA) Women's Committee 1932 (Reel 11), RWONPR; and Matthew Woll to Mrs. Pierre du Pont, May 11, 1932, Folder: (AAPA) Women's Committee 1932 (Reel 11), RWONPR.

29. Charlotte Farrar to Mrs. Pierre du Pont, April 25, 1932, Folder: General Correspondence January–June 1932 (Reel 13), RWONPR.

30. "Dry Law Foes Seek 1,000,000 Recruits," New York Times, May 16, 1932, 10.

31. WONPR—Delaware Division, untitled statement or press release, July 1932, Folder: Diogenes (Reel 12), RWONPR.

32. WONPR, News Letter, August 18, 1932, Folder: Publicity 1932–1933 (Reel 14), RWONPR.

33. Milton Lusk (for WONPR), WONPR song, circa 1932, Folder: Miscellaneous Material (Reel 11), RWONPR.

34. Hearst Metrotone, December 5, 1931 and December 10, 1932; Fox Movietone, May 1932; June 7, 1932; June 13, 1932; and October 9, 1929.

35. Mrs. Charles H. Sabin, "Why American Mothers Demand Repeal," unknown publication, 1932, Folder: Special Pamphlets and Articles 1931–1933 (Reel 16), RWONPR.

36. "Mrs. Willebrandt Opposes Dry Poll," *New York Times*, June 12, 1932, 23.

37. "Wet Plank Certain, Willebrandt Holds," *New York Times*, June 15, 1932, 13.

38. "The Prohibition Plank Which Was Adopted," *New York Times*, June 16, 1932, 1.

39. Pauline Sabin to Mrs. Pierre du Pont, circa June 1, 1932, Folder: General Correspondence January–June 1932; WONPR, News Letter, March 1932, Folder: Publicity-General 1930–1932 (Reel 13), RWONPR.

40. Associated Press, Photograph of Pauline Sabin, Al Smith, and John Raskob, June 30, 1932, AP Photo Archive.

41. James A. Farley, *Behind the Ballots: The Personal History of a Politician* (New York: Harcourt, Brace & Co., 1938) 113.

42. Arthur Krock, "Big Majority for Repeal," *New York Times*, June 30, 1932, 1.

43. WONPR, "Action by the National Executive Committee of the Women's Organization for National Prohibition Reform," July 7, 1932, Folder: National Executive Committee Meeting; Local Committee Work, Memos & Reports 1932 (Reel 13), RWONPR.

44. WONPR, News Letter, August 18, 1932, Folder: Publicity 1932–1933 (Reel 14), RWONPR.

45. "Ladies at Roslyn," *Time*, July 18, 1932. (Page numbers not provided in electronic download of this article.)

46. Pauline Sabin to Pierre du Pont, August 17, 1932, Folder: (AAPA) Women's Committee 1932 (Reel 11), RWONPR.

47. James C. Bell, "Wet Bodies Agree upon Nonpartisan Drive for Repeal," *Springfield Republican*, 31 August 1932, 1.

48. WONPR, copy of essential part of instructions from the National office of the WONPR to State Chairmen regarding the poll of candidates for Congress, circa September 1, 1932, Folder: General Correspondence July–December 1932 (Reel 14), RWONPR.

49. Dayton E. Heckman, "Prohibition Passes: The Story of the Association Against the Prohibition Amendment," Ph.D. dissertation, Ohio State University, 1939, 310.

50. Pauline Sabin, "Address of Mrs. Charles H. Sabin, National Chairman of the Women's Organization for National Prohibition Reform at Mass Meeting in

Auditorium, St. Paul, Minnesota," September 28, 1932, Folder: Publicity 1932–1933 (Reel 14), RWONPR.

51. "Mrs. Willebrandt Replies," *New York Times*, October 30, 1932, 31.

52. Pauline Sabin to Charles Hilles, November 21, 1932, Folder 1458, Box 119, CHC.

53. Pauline Sabin, Press Release, November 14, 1932, Folder: Publicity Delaware Releases (Reel 14), RWONPR.

54. WONPR, Press Release, November 21, 1932, RWONPR.

55. Pauline Sabin to Mrs. Pierre du Pont, December 30, 1932, Folder: Executive Committee Minutes; Delegates to National Political Conventions, Politics 1931–1933 (Reel 13), RWONPR.

56. Pauline Sabin to Mrs. Pierre du Pont, January 14, 1933, Folder: Procedure for Conventions; Membership Work (Reel 13), RWONPR.

57. WONPR, Press Release, January 16, 1933, Folder: Study Course 1933 (Reel 12), RWONPR.

58. Pauline Sabin to Miss Eckman, February 3, 1933, Folder: General Correspondence January–June 1933 (Reel 14), RWONPR.

59. Pauline Sabin to Mrs. Pierre du Pont, January 9, 1933, Folder: General Correspondence January–June 1933 (Reel 14), RWONPR.

60. Unknown author to Mrs. Pierre du Pont, January 19, 1933, Folder: General Correspondence January–June 1933 (Reel 14), RWONPR.

61. "Shouse Hits Blaine Plan," *New York Times*, February 7, 1933, 8.

62. "Repeal in Danger, Mrs. Sabin Warns," *New York Times*, February 14, 1933, 2.

63. "Repeal Vote Today Set in the Senate; Filibuster Broken," *New York Times*, February 16, 1933, 1; "Text of Repeal Resolution," *New York Times*, February 17, 1933, 1.

64. "Leaders Here Hail Move for Repeal," *New York Times*, February 17, 1933, C13.

65. "Roosevelt Gets First Cases of Capital's 3.2 Beer," *New York Times*, April 7, 1933, 1.

66. WONPR, "Plan for Bringing Out Large Vote in Each State for Election of Delegates to Ratification Convention," April 1933, Folder: Procedure for Conventions; Membership Work (Reel 13), RWONPR.

67. WONPR, Press Release, May 9, 1933, Folder: Ratification Work Delaware & Other States 1933 (Reel 16), RWONPR.

68. Pauline Sabin to Mrs. Pierre du Pont, August 29, 1933, Folder: New York Correspondence 1933 (Reel 12), RWONPR.

69. Pauline Sabin to Mrs. Pierre du Pont, August 16, 1933, Folder: New York Correspondence 1933 (Reel 12), RWONPR.

70. Pauline Sabin to John Raskob, October 26, 1932, File 2017, John J. Raskob papers (Accession 0473), Hagley Museum and Library, Wilmington, DE.
71. Mrs. Christian Holmes to Mrs. Pierre du Pont, November 20, 1933, Folder: Special Publicity 1933 (Reel 12), RWONPR.
72. WONPR, "Program of Victory Dinner Women's Organization for National Prohibition Reform," December 7, 1933, Folder: Special Publicity 1933 (Reel 12), RWONPR.

Index